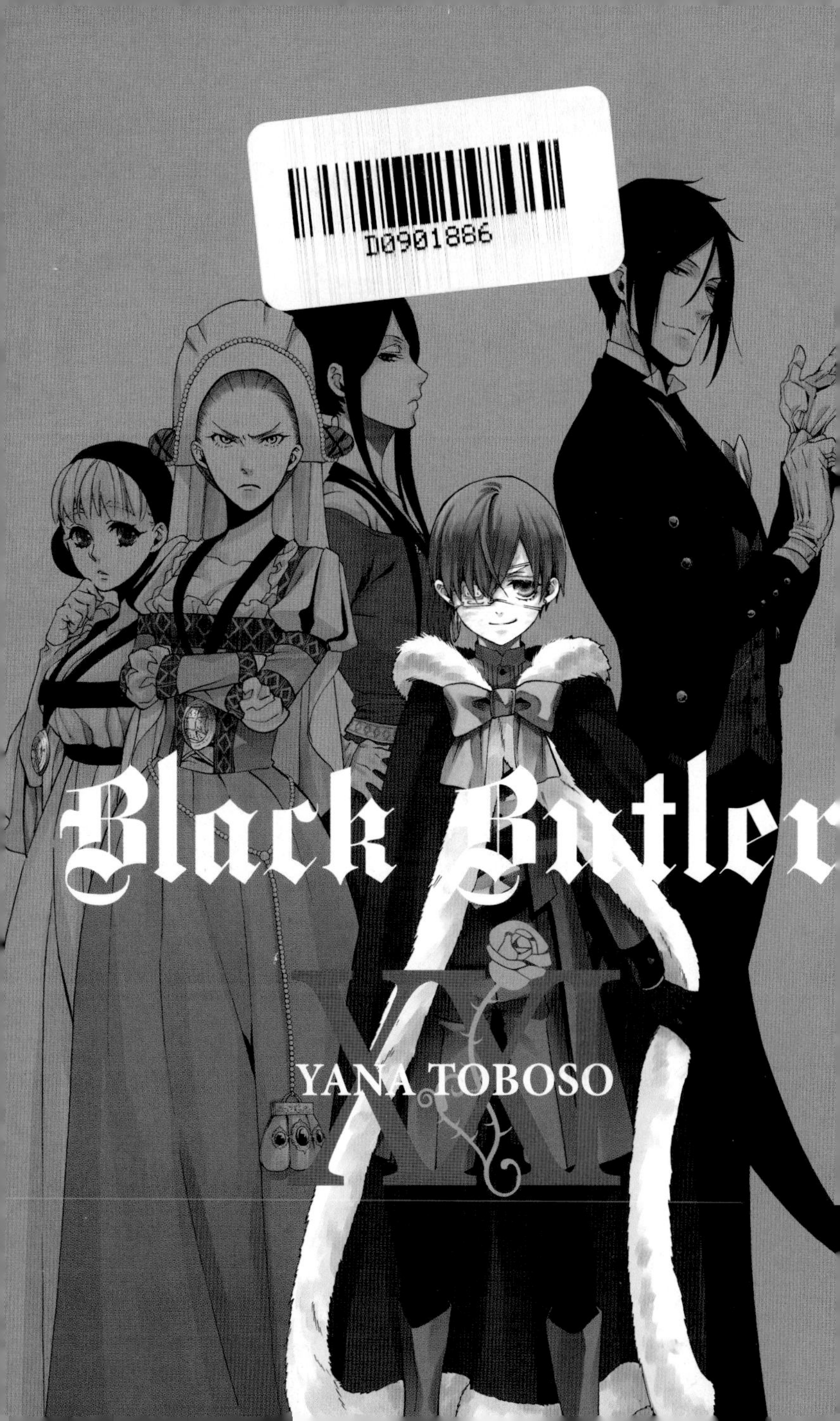
Black Butler
YANA TOBOSO

Contents

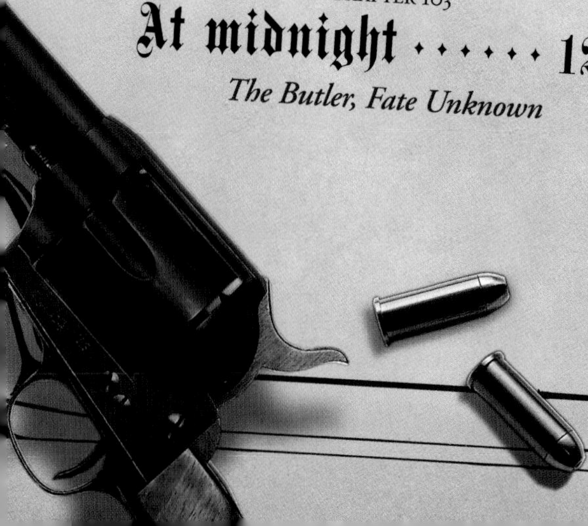

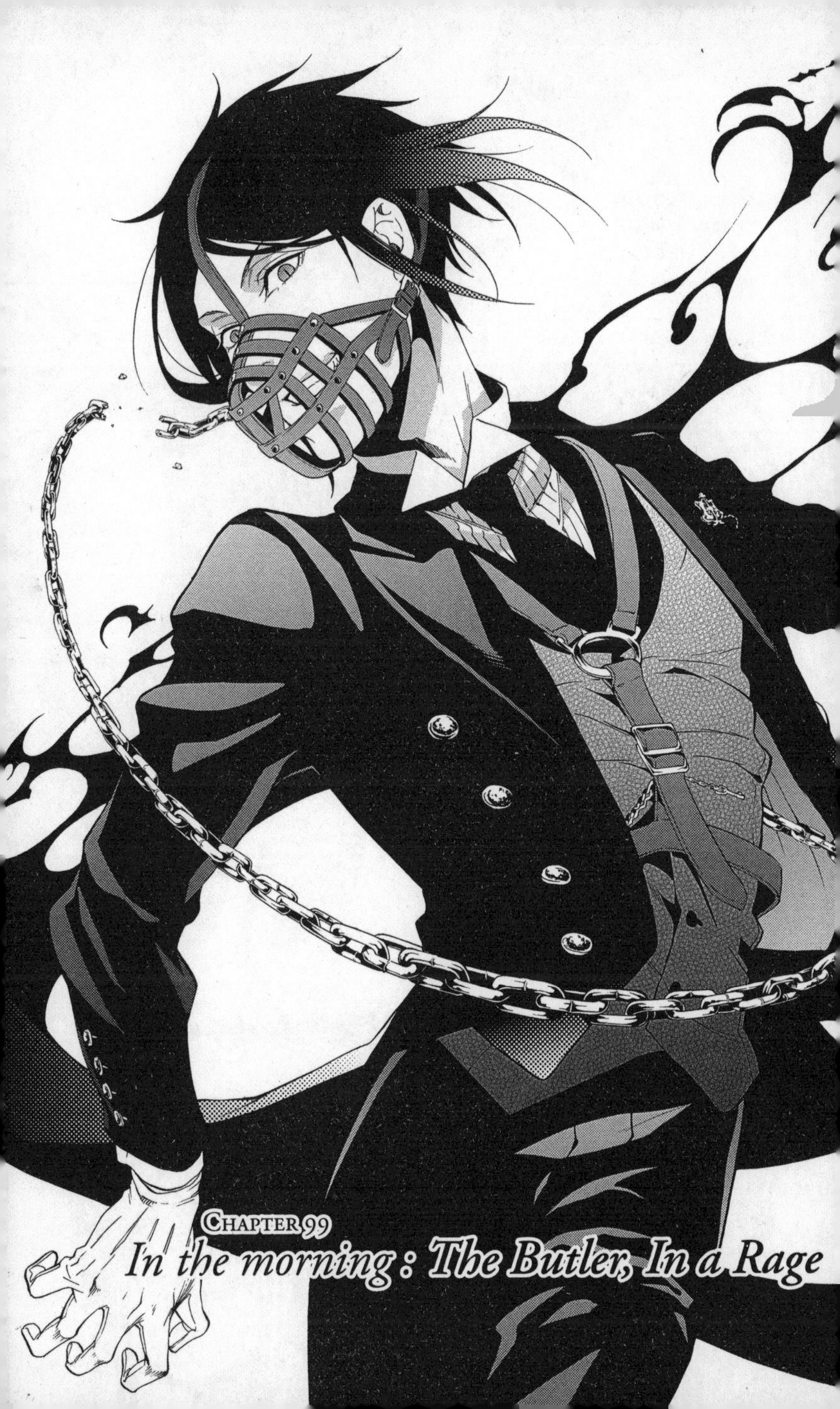
Chapter 99
In the morning : The Butler, In a Rage

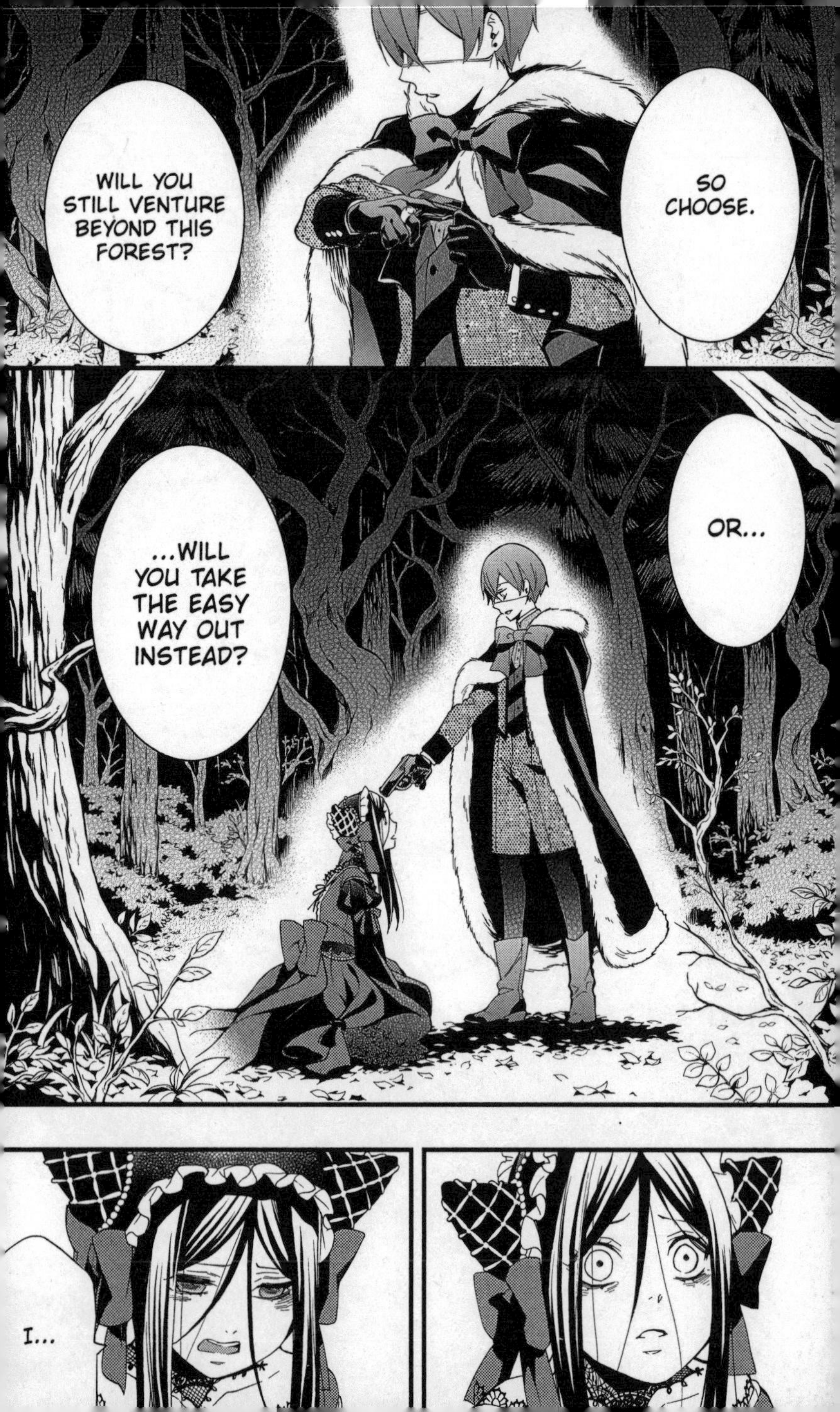
SO CHOOSE.
WILL YOU STILL VENTURE BEYOND THIS FOREST?
OR...
...WILL YOU TAKE THE EASY WAY OUT INSTEAD?
I...

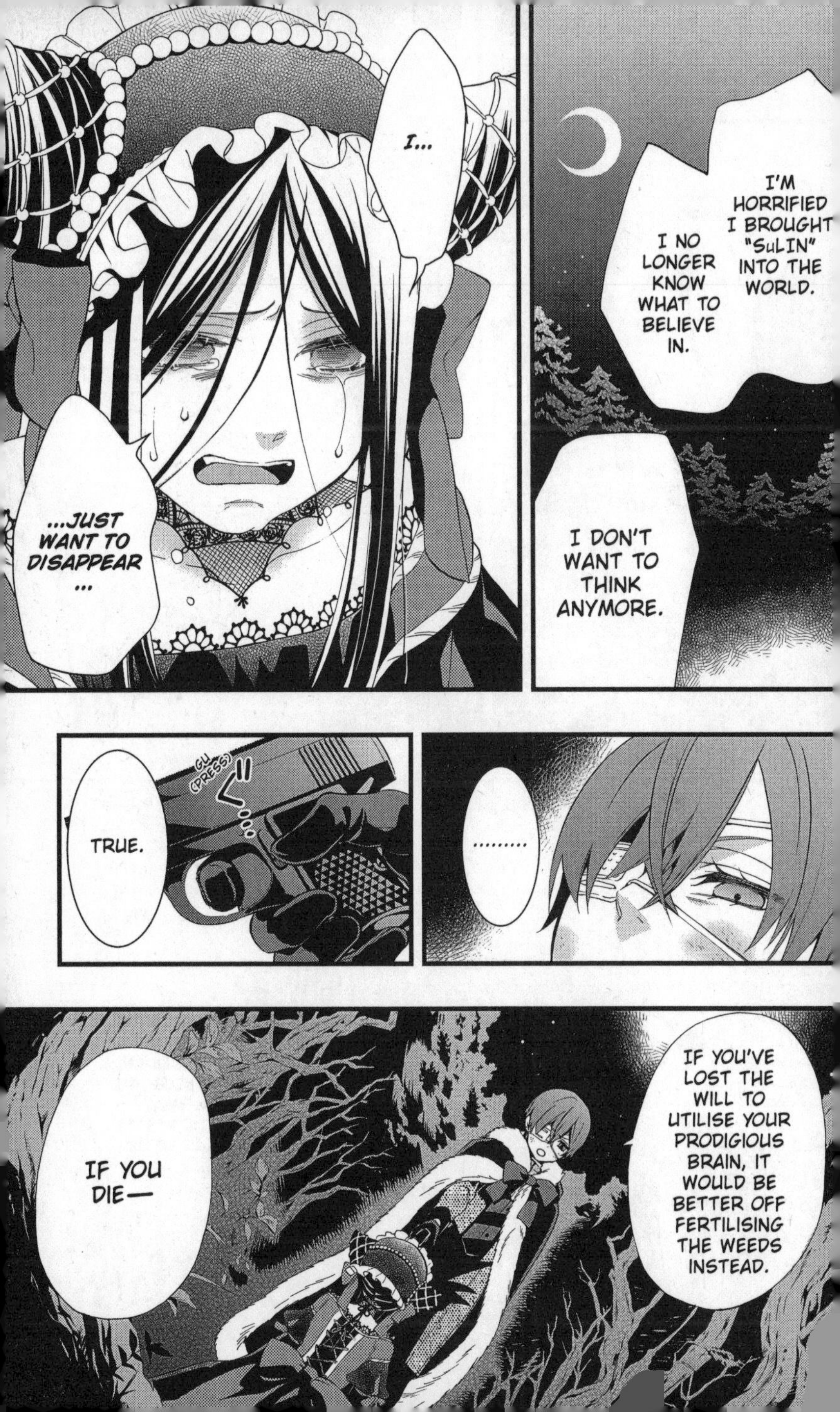
I'M HORRIFIED I BROUGHT "SuLIN" INTO THE WORLD.
I NO LONGER KNOW WHAT TO BELIEVE IN.
I DON'T WANT TO THINK ANYMORE.
I...
...JUST WANT TO DISAPPEAR ...
....
GU (PRESS)
TRUE.
IF YOU'VE LOST THE WILL TO UTILISE YOUR PRODIGIOUS BRAIN, IT WOULD BE BETTER OFF FERTILISING THE WEEDS INSTEAD.
IF YOU DIE—

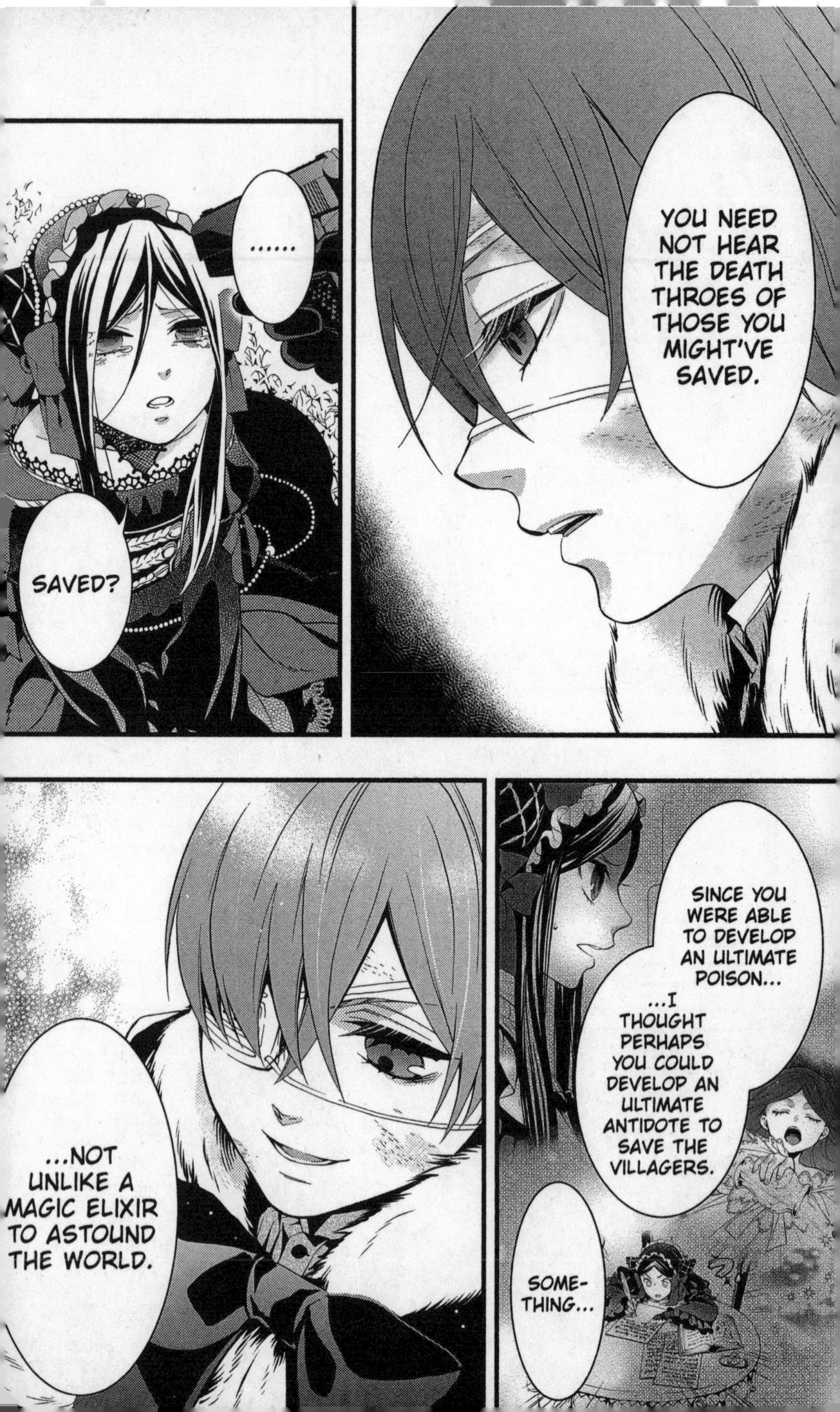
YOU NEED NOT HEAR THE DEATH THROES OF THOSE YOU MIGHT'VE SAVED.
......
SAVED?
SINCE YOU WERE ABLE TO DEVELOP AN ULTIMATE POISON...
...I THOUGHT PERHAPS YOU COULD DEVELOP AN ULTIMATE ANTIDOTE TO SAVE THE VILLAGERS.
SOME-THING...
...NOT UNLIKE A MAGIC ELIXIR TO ASTOUND THE WORLD.

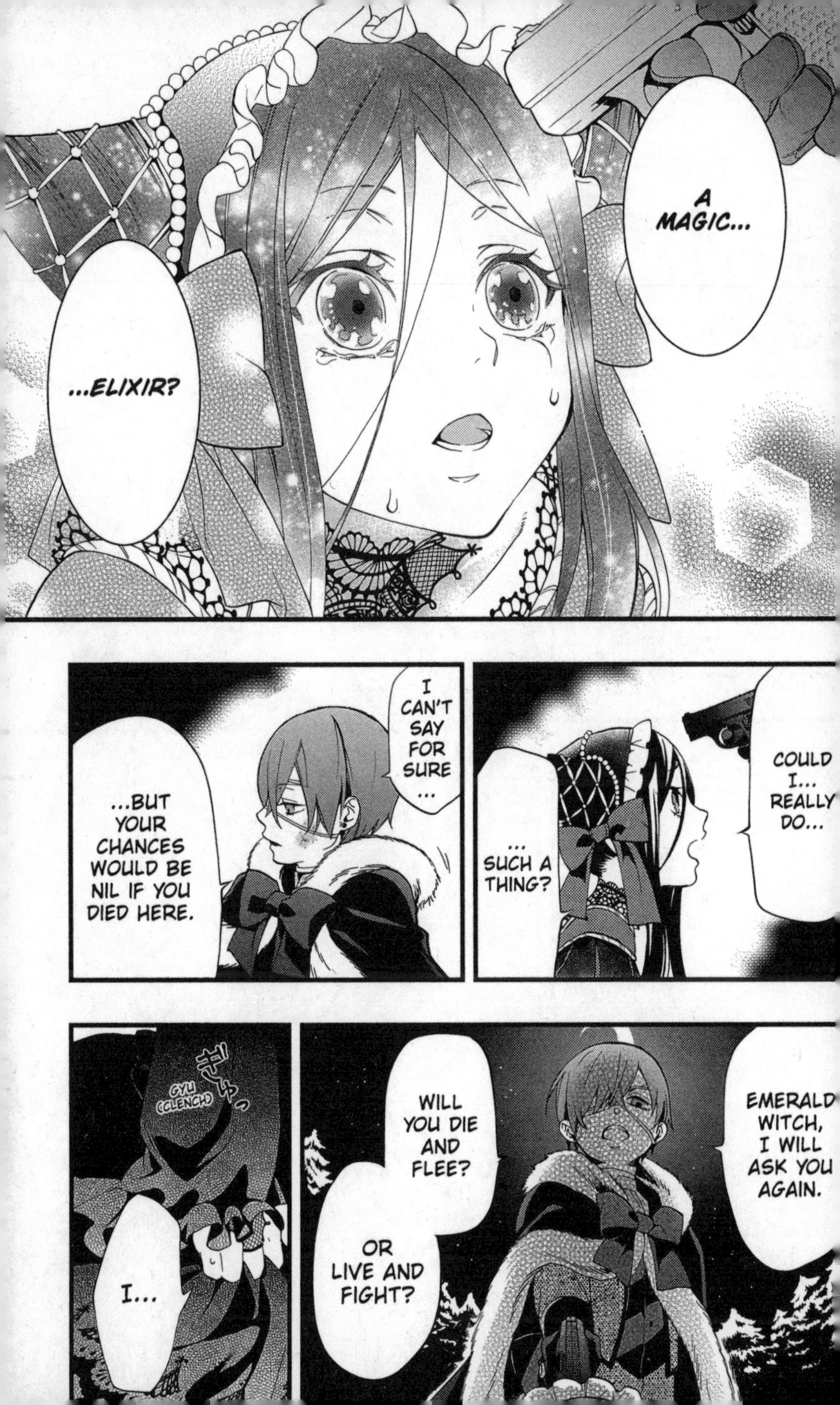
A MAGIC...
...ELIXIR?
COULD I... REALLY DO...
...SUCH A THING?
I CAN'T SAY FOR SURE...
...BUT YOUR CHANCES WOULD BE NIL IF YOU DIED HERE.
EMERALD WITCH, I WILL ASK YOU AGAIN.
WILL YOU DIE AND FLEE?
OR LIVE AND FIGHT?
GYU (CLENCH)
I...

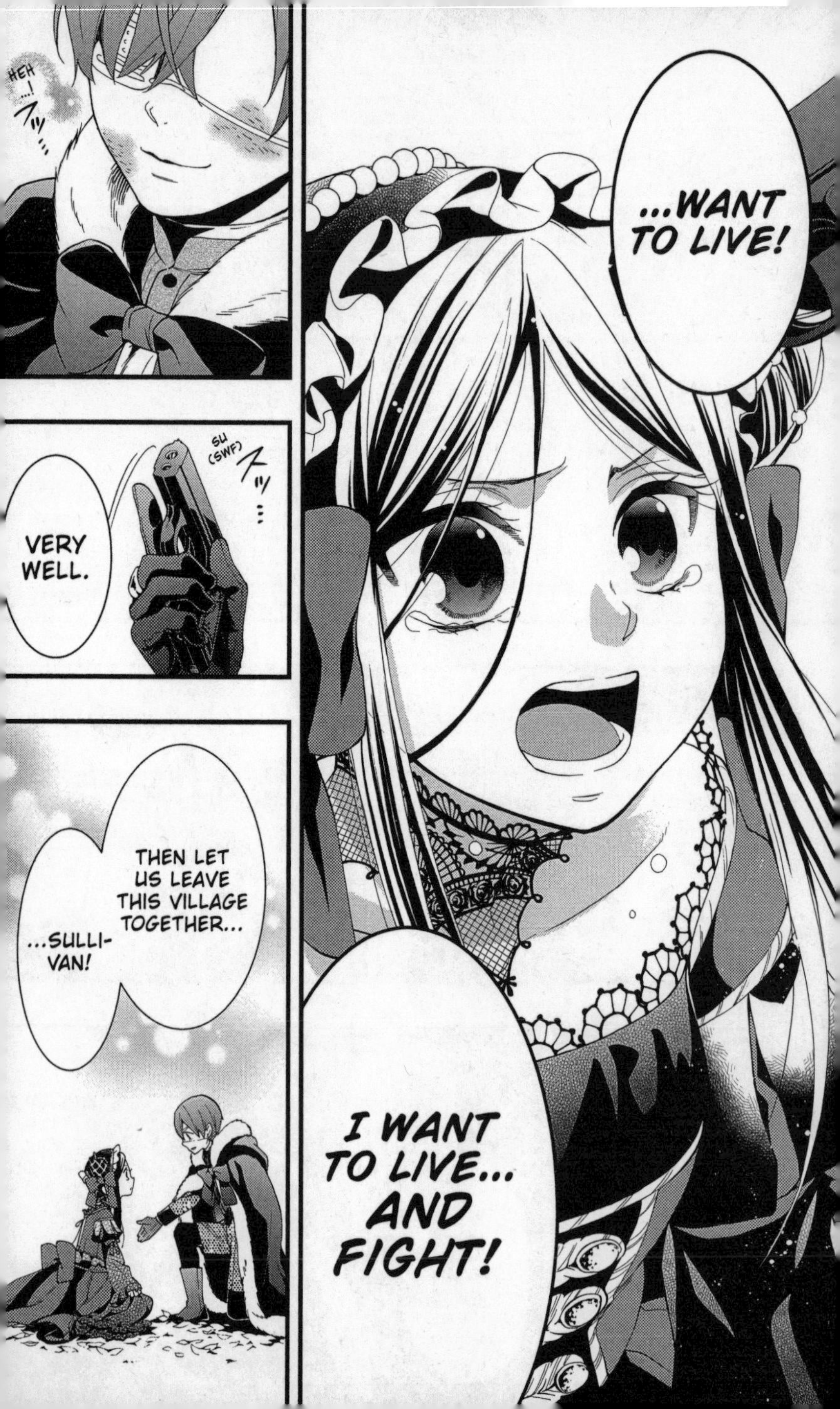

...WANT TO LIVE!
I WANT TO LIVE... AND FIGHT!
HEH ...!
フッ...
SU (SWF)
スッ...
VERY WELL.
THEN LET US LEAVE THIS VILLAGE TOGETHER...
...SULLI-VAN!

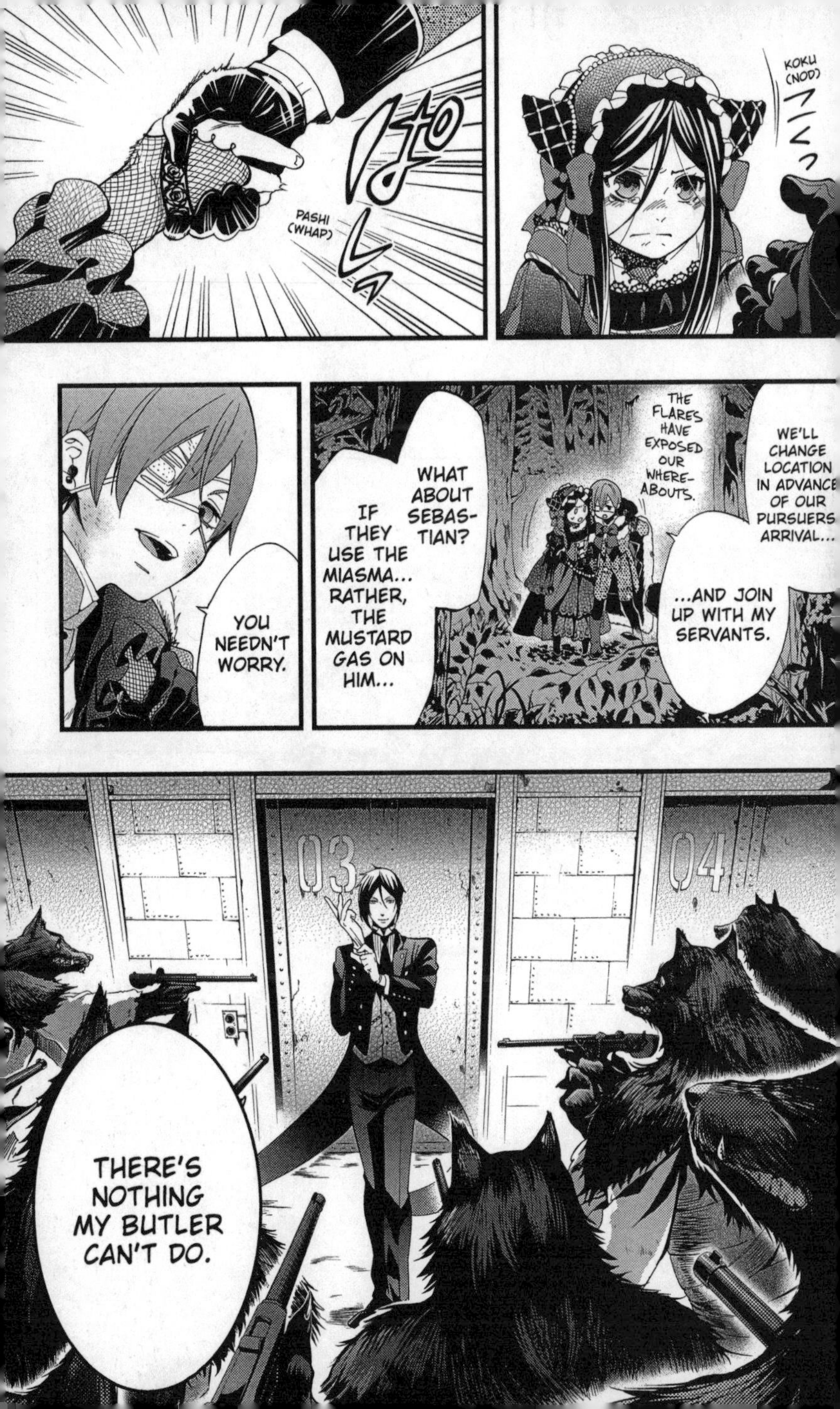
KOKU (NOD)
PASHI (WHAP)
THE FLARES HAVE EXPOSED OUR WHERE-ABOUTS.
WE'LL CHANGE LOCATION IN ADVANCE OF OUR PURSUERS ARRIVAL...
...AND JOIN UP WITH MY SERVANTS.
WHAT ABOUT SEBAS-TIAN?
IF THEY USE THE MIASMA... RATHER, THE MUSTARD GAS ON HIM...
YOU NEEDN'T WORRY.
03
04
THERE'S NOTHING MY BUTLER CAN'T DO.

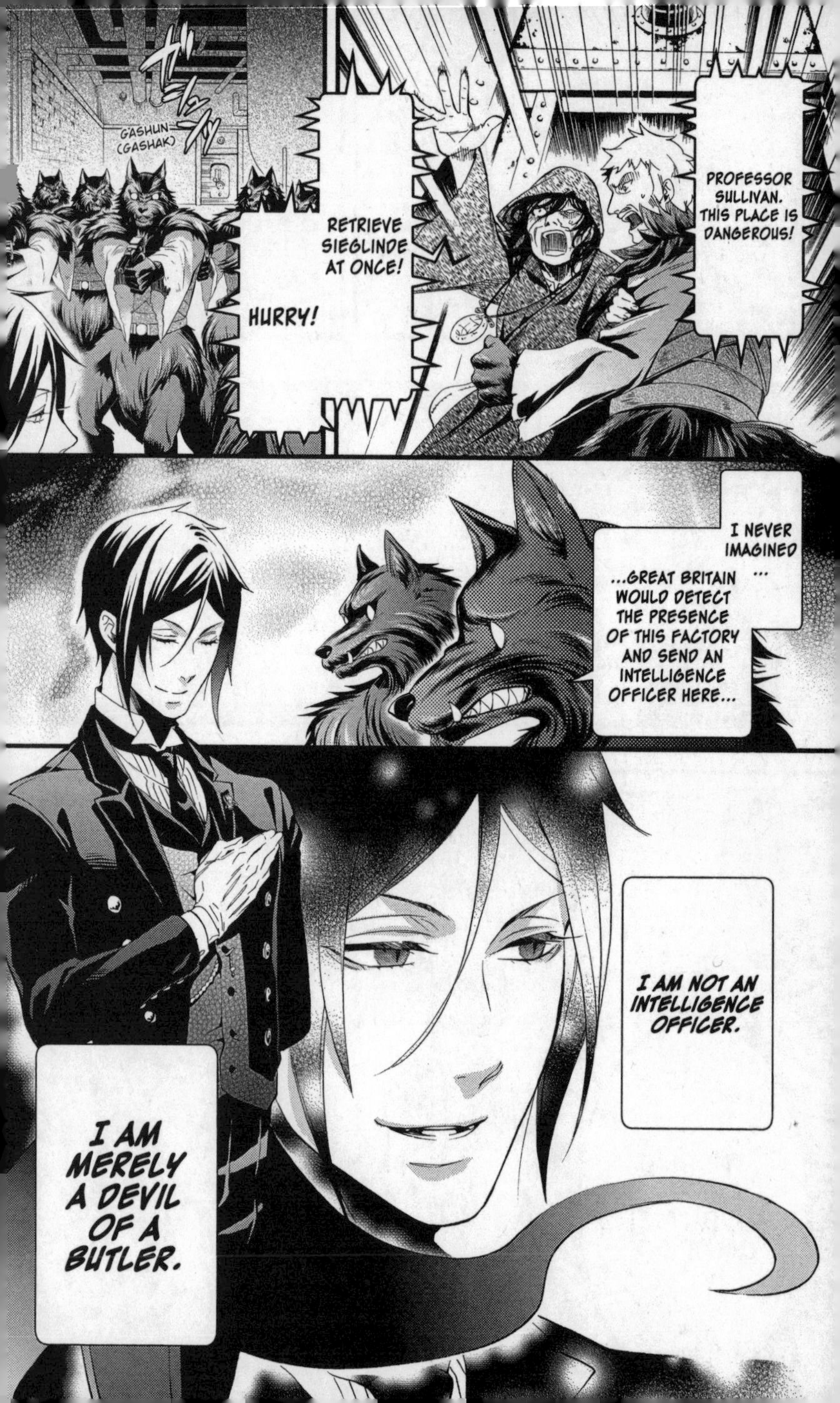
PROFESSOR SULLIVAN. THIS PLACE IS DANGEROUS!
RETRIEVE SIEGLINDE AT ONCE!
HURRY!
GASHUN (GASHAK)
I NEVER IMAGINED ...
...GREAT BRITAIN WOULD DETECT THE PRESENCE OF THIS FACTORY AND SEND AN INTELLIGENCE OFFICER HERE...
I AM NOT AN INTELLIGENCE OFFICER.
I AM MERELY A DEVIL OF A BUTLER.

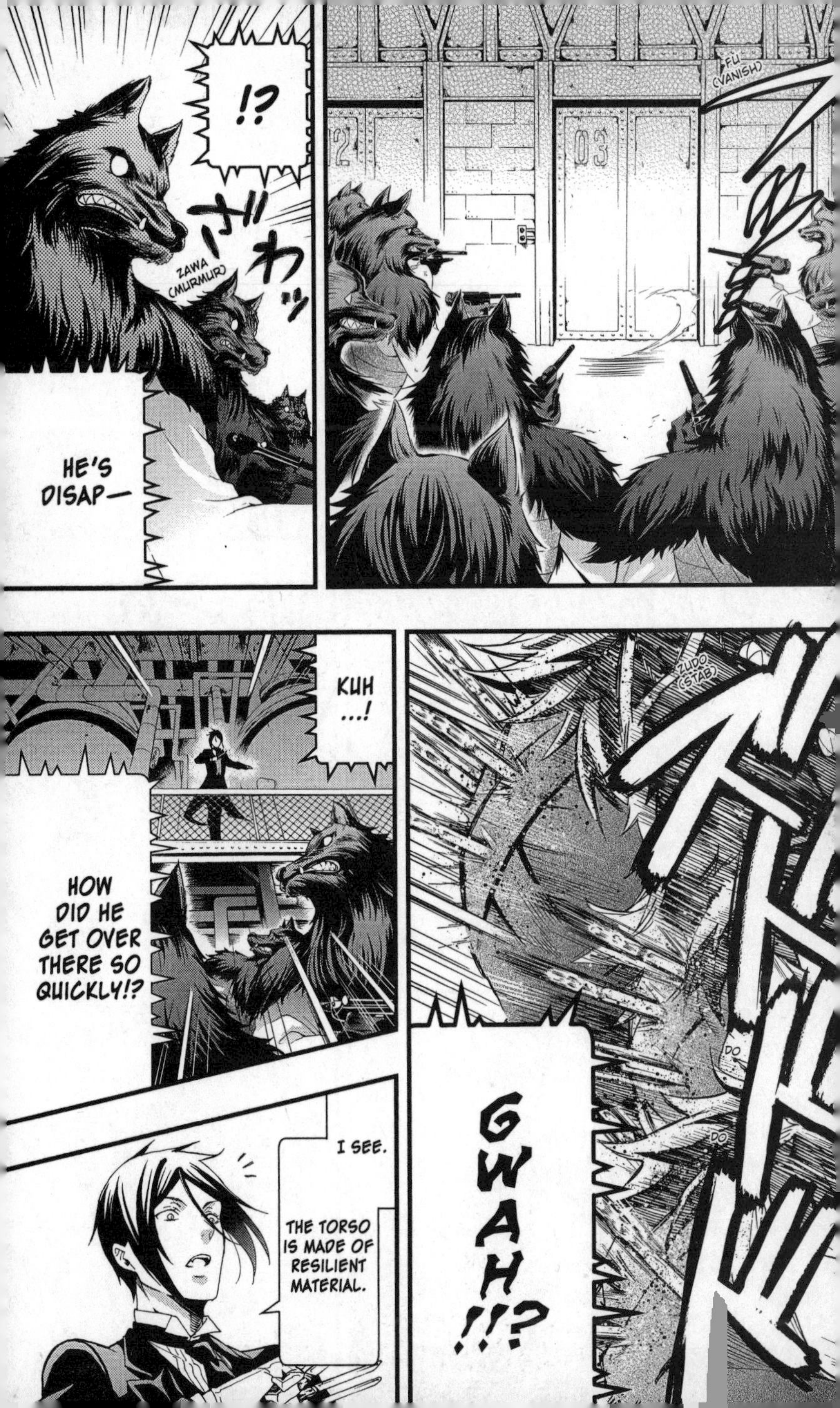
FU (VANISH)
!?
ZAWA (MURMUR)
HE'S DISAP—
ZUDO (STAB)
DO
DO
GWAH!!?
KUH ...!
HOW DID HE GET OVER THERE SO QUICKLY!?
I SEE.
THE TORSO IS MADE OF RESILIENT MATERIAL.

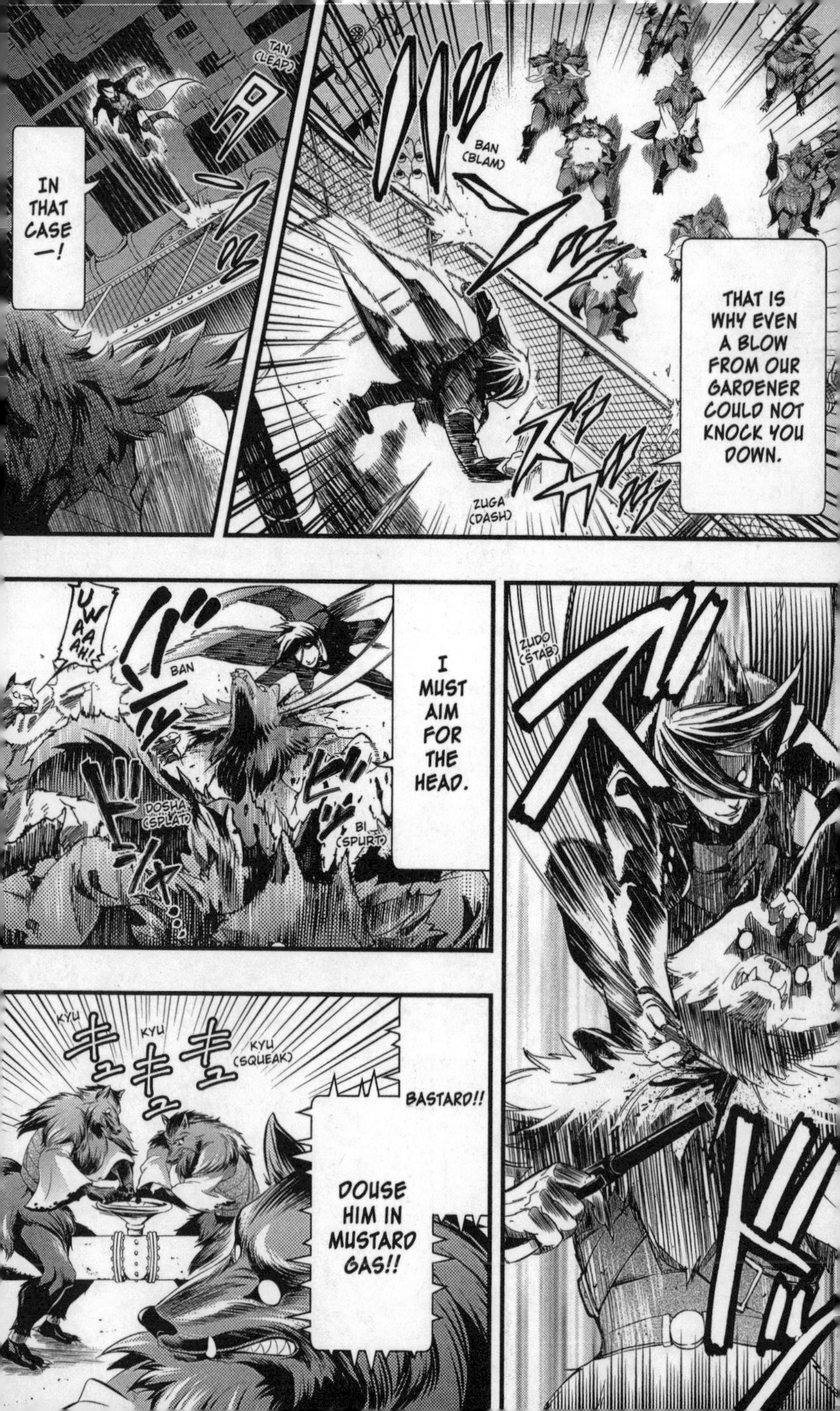
THAT IS WHY EVEN A BLOW FROM OUR GARDENER COULD NOT KNOCK YOU DOWN.
BAN (BLAM)
ZUGA (DASH)
TAN (LEAP)
IN THAT CASE—!
ZUDO (STAB)
I MUST AIM FOR THE HEAD.
BAN
UWAAAH!
BI (SPURT)
DOSHA (SPLAT)
BASTARD!!
DOUSE HIM IN MUSTARD GAS!!
KYU
KYU
KYU (SQUEAK)

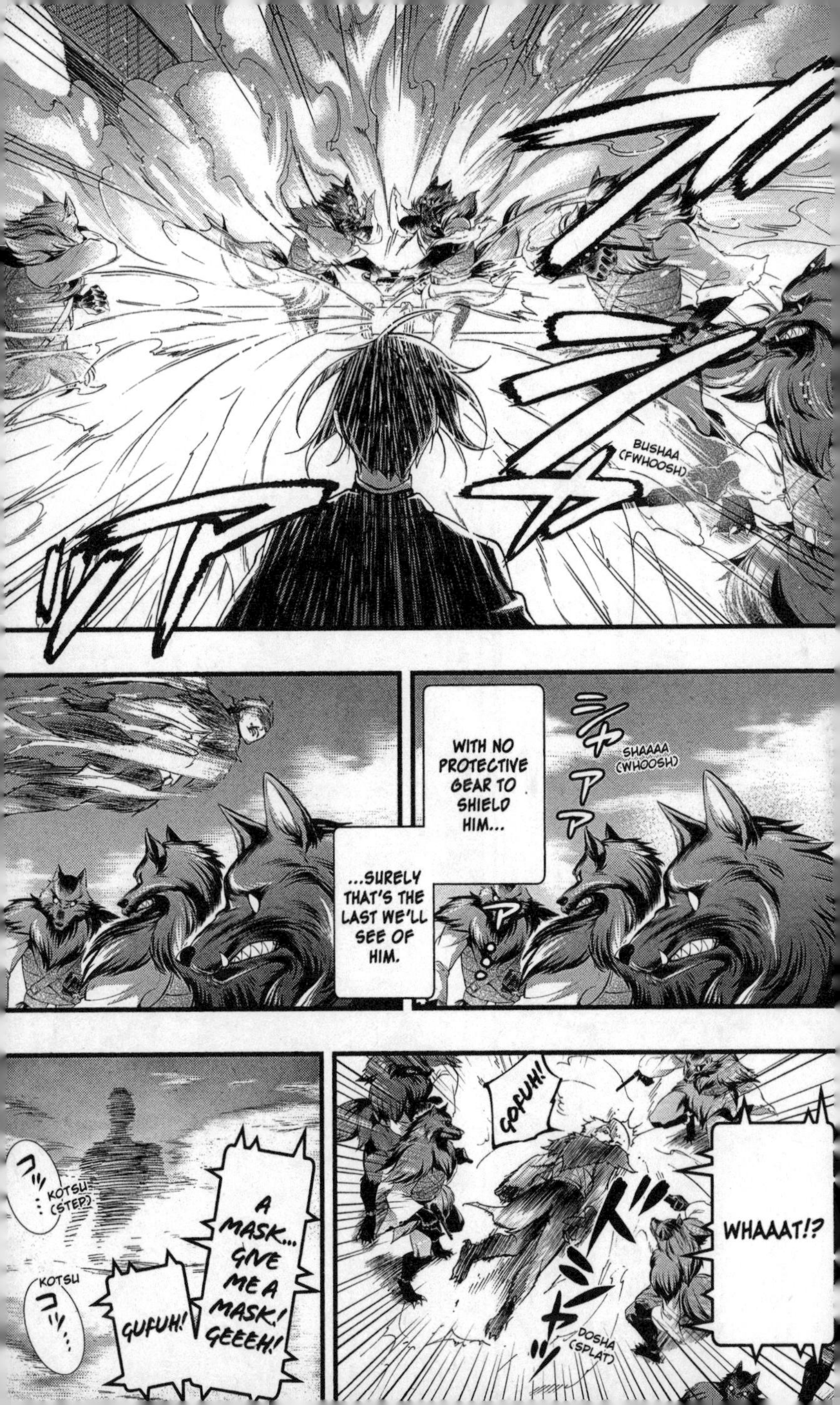
BUSHAA (FWHOOSH)
WITH NO PROTECTIVE GEAR TO SHIELD HIM...
...SURELY THAT'S THE LAST WE'LL SEE OF HIM.
SHAAAA (WHOOSH)
GOFUH!
WHAAAT!?
DOSHA (SPLAT)
KOTSU (STEP)
A MASK... GIVE ME A MASK! GEEEH!
GUFUH!
KOTSU

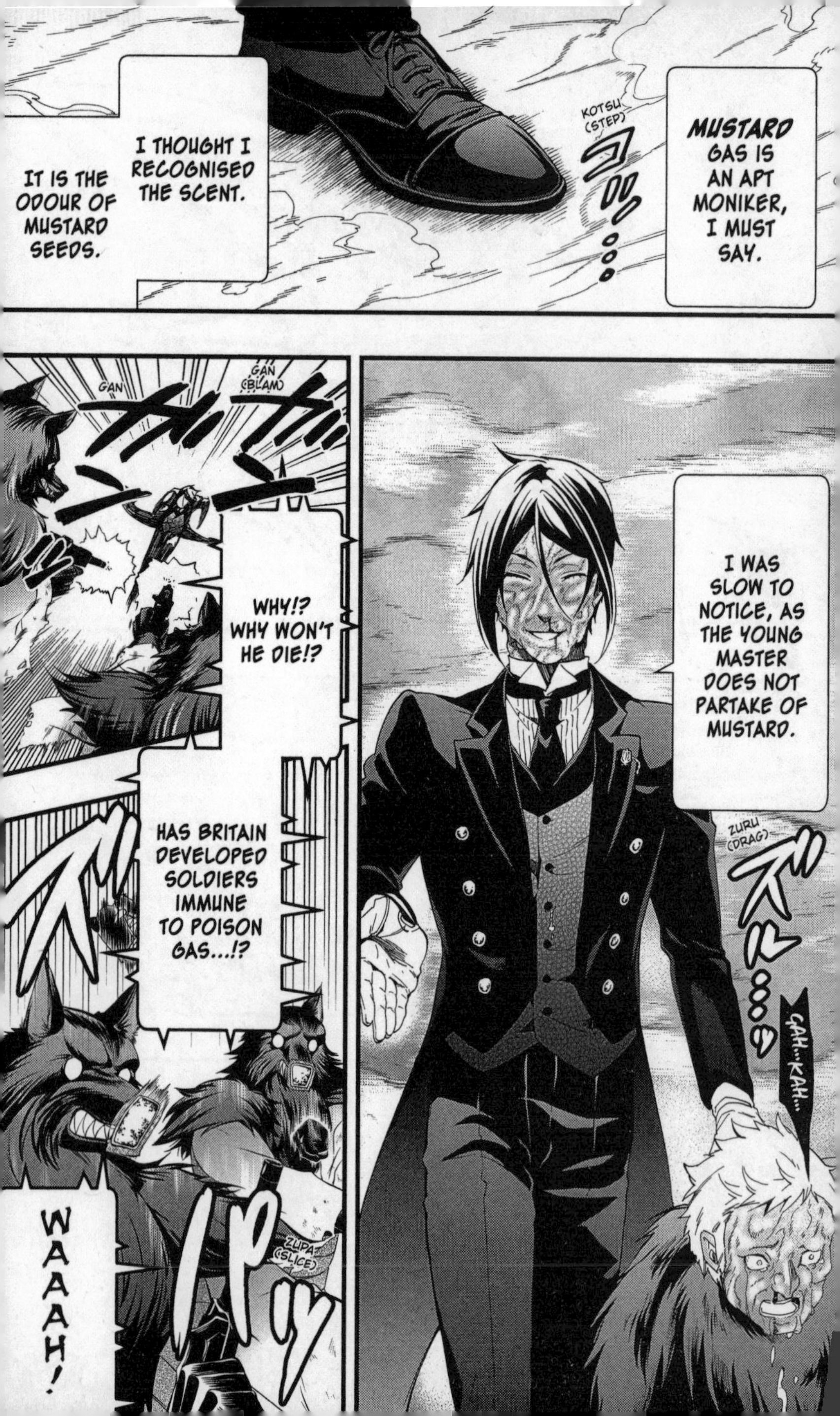
MUSTARD GAS IS AN APT MONIKER, I MUST SAY.
KOTSU (STEP)
I THOUGHT I RECOGNISED THE SCENT.
IT IS THE ODOUR OF MUSTARD SEEDS.
I WAS SLOW TO NOTICE, AS THE YOUNG MASTER DOES NOT PARTAKE OF MUSTARD.
ZURU (DRAG)
GAH...KAH...
GAN (BLAM)
GAN
WHY!? WHY WON'T HE DIE!?
HAS BRITAIN DEVELOPED SOLDIERS IMMUNE TO POISON GAS...!?
ZUPA (SLICE)
WAAAH!

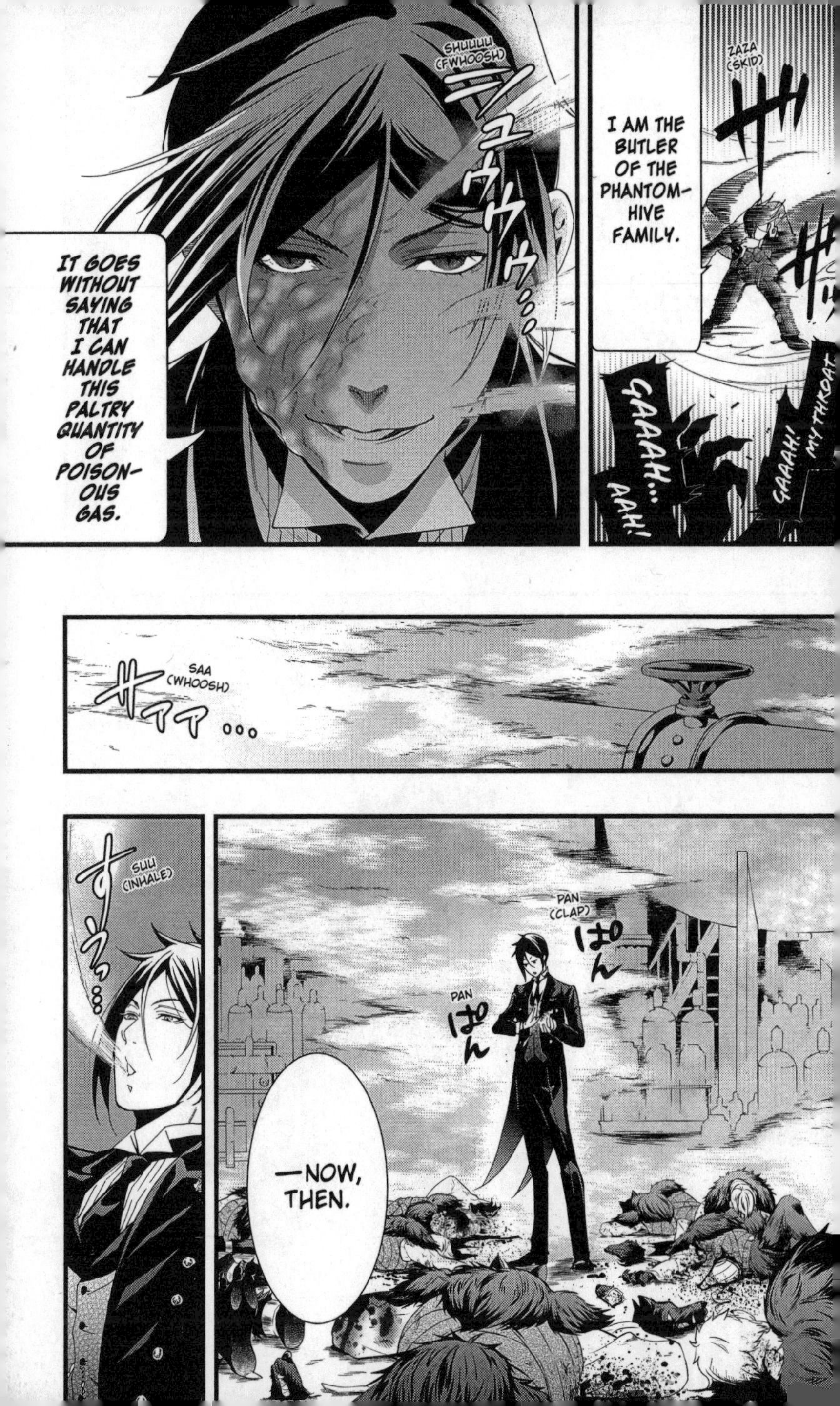
ZAZA (SKID)
I AM THE BUTLER OF THE PHANTOM-HIVE FAMILY.
MY THROAT
GAAAH!
GAAAH... AAH!
SHUUUU (FWHOOSH)
IT GOES WITHOUT SAYING THAT I CAN HANDLE THIS PALTRY QUANTITY OF POISON-OUS GAS.
SAA (WHOOSH)
PAN (CLAP)
PAN
—NOW, THEN.
SUU (INHALE)

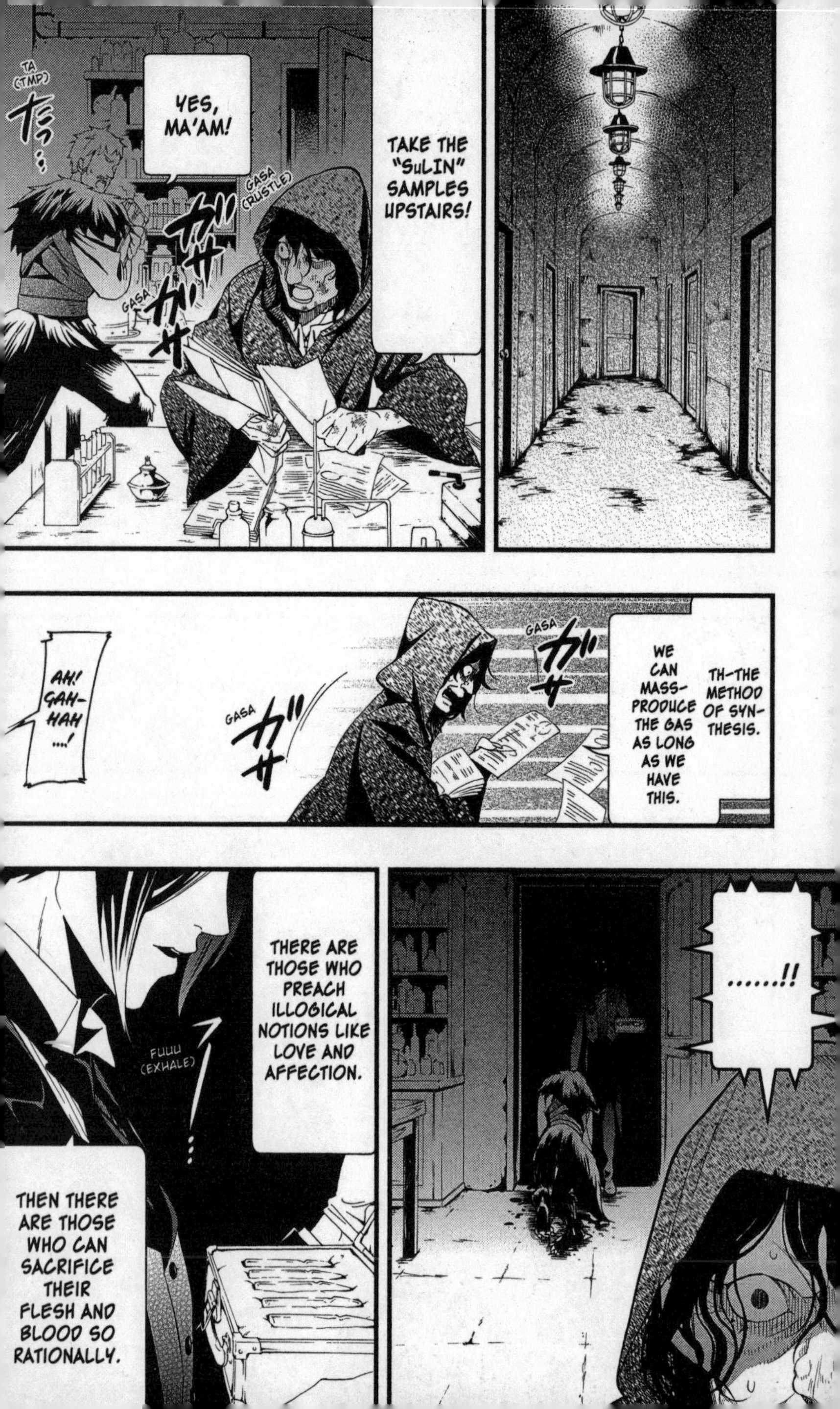
TAKE THE "SuLIN" SAMPLES UPSTAIRS!
GASA (RUSTLE)
YES, MA'AM!
TA (TMP)
GASA
TH-THE METHOD OF SYN-THESIS.
WE CAN MASS-PRODUCE THE GAS AS LONG AS WE HAVE THIS.
GASA
GASA
AH! GAH-HAH ....!
......!!
THERE ARE THOSE WHO PREACH ILLOGICAL NOTIONS LIKE LOVE AND AFFECTION.
FUUU (EXHALE)
THEN THERE ARE THOSE WHO CAN SACRIFICE THEIR FLESH AND BLOOD SO RATIONALLY.

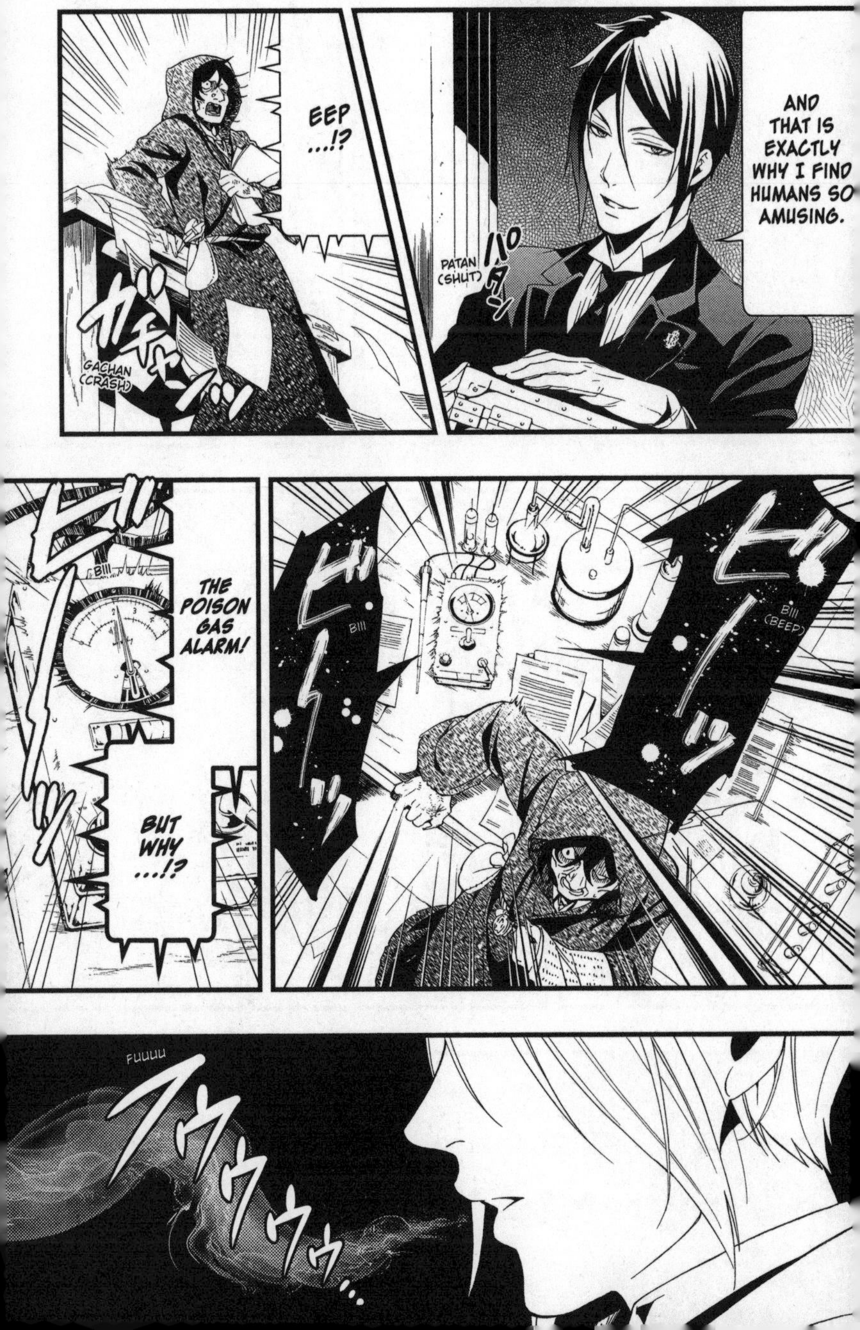
AND THAT IS EXACTLY WHY I FIND HUMANS SO AMUSING.
PATAN (SHUT)
EEP ...!?
GACHAN (CRASH)
BIII (BEEP)
BIII
BIII
THE POISON GAS ALARM!
BUT WHY ...!?
FUUUU

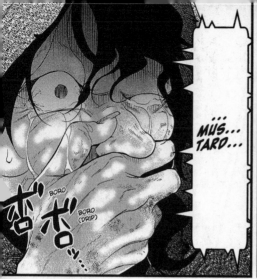

MÜS...
TARD...

BIII
(BEEP)

FUUUU
(EXHALE)

TH—

THIS
IS THE
SMELL
OF...

BORO

BORO
(DRIP)

ZURURU
(SLIDE)

GASHAN
(CRASH)

URGH
...

GUH...

BASASA
(FLAP)

YOU
LOVE THIS
POISON GAS
SO DEARLY...

...THAT YOU
SACRIFICED
YOUR
BELOVED
DAUGHTER'S
LIFE.

BIII

BIII

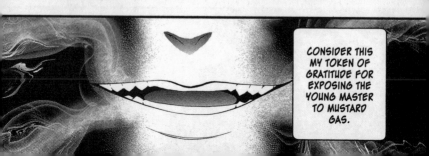

CONSIDER THIS
MY TOKEN OF
GRATITUDE FOR
EXPOSING THE
YOUNG MASTER
TO MUSTARD
GAS.

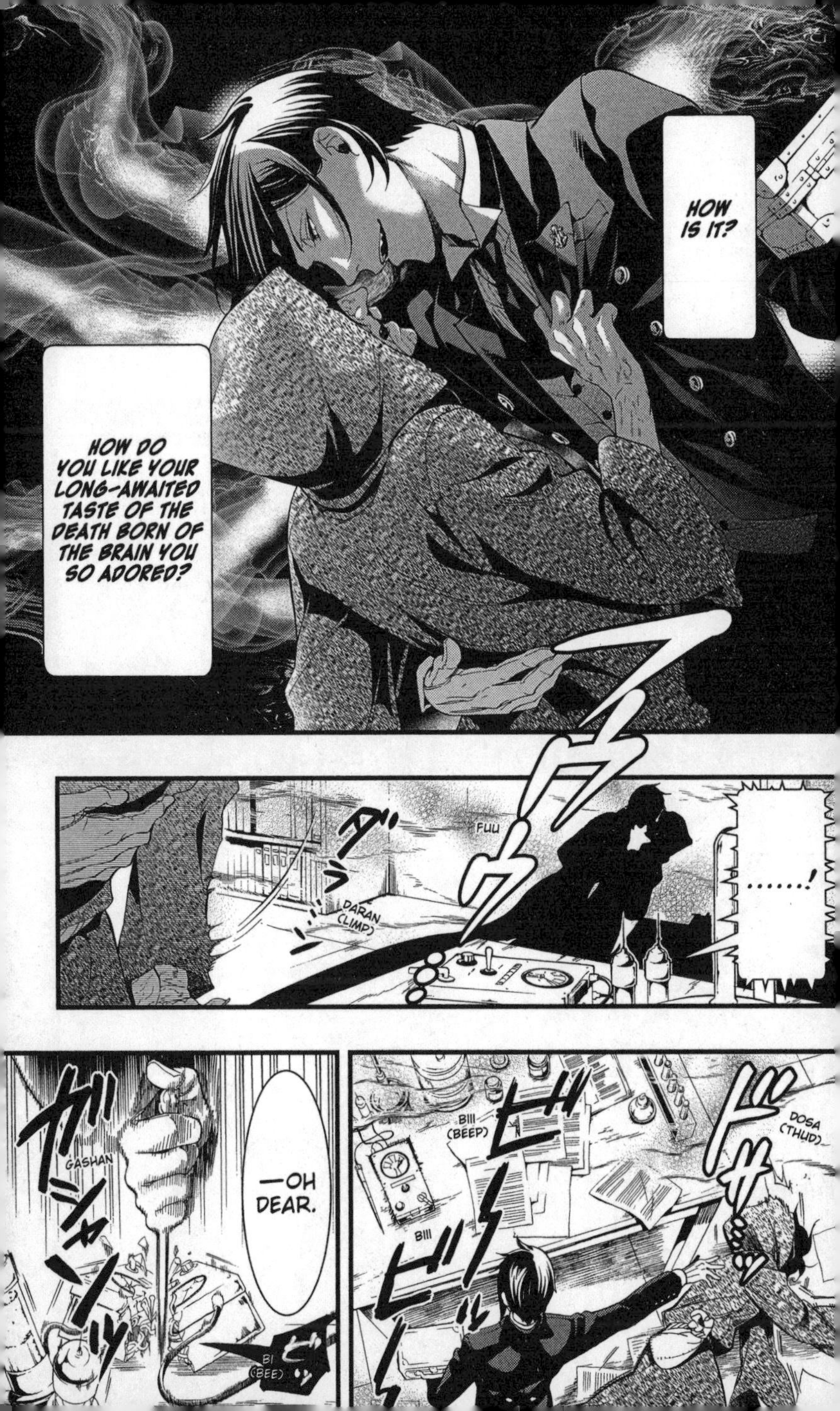
HOW IS IT?
HOW DO YOU LIKE YOUR LONG-AWAITED TASTE OF THE DEATH BORN OF THE BRAIN YOU SO ADORED?
......!
FUU
DARAN (LIMP)
DOSA (THUD)
BIII (BEEP)
BIII
—OH DEAR.
GASHAN
BI (BEE)

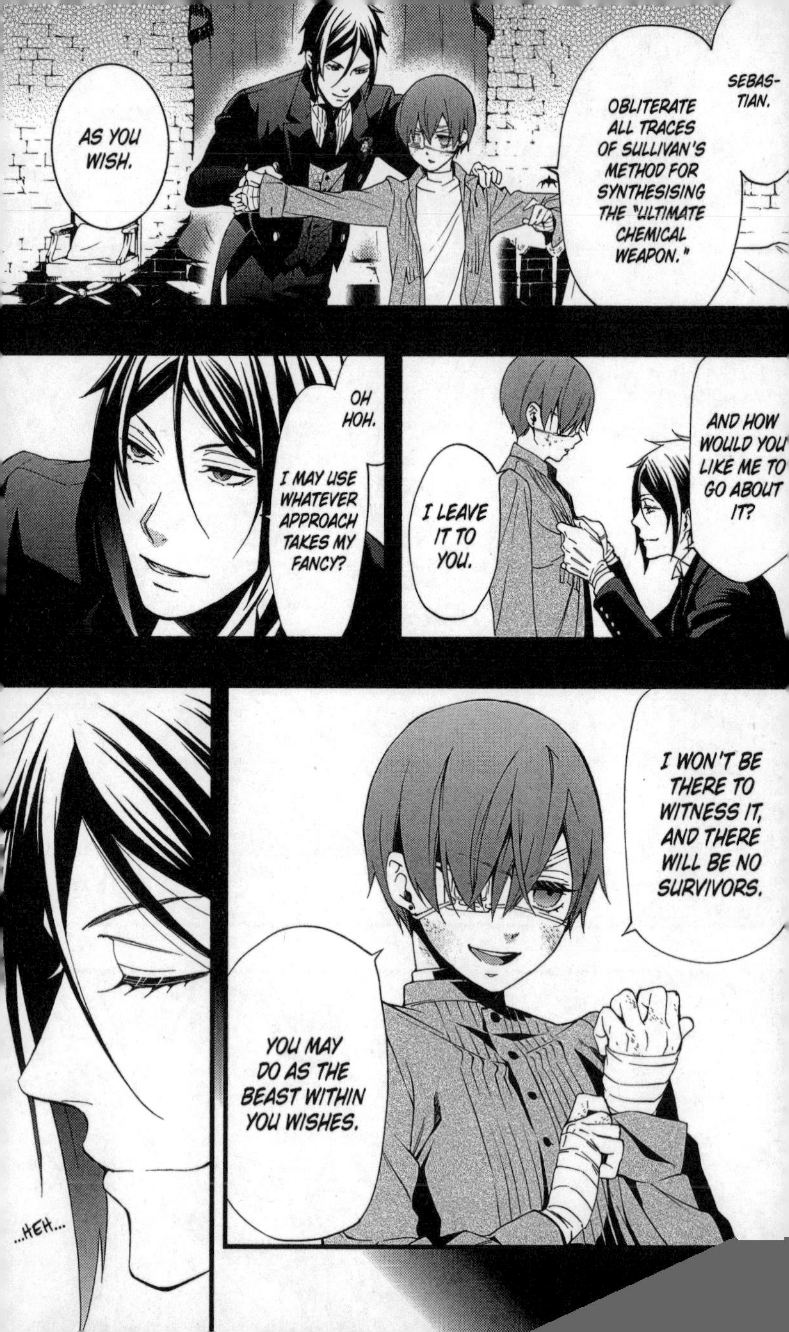
SEBASTIAN.
OBLITERATE ALL TRACES OF SULLIVAN'S METHOD FOR SYNTHESISING THE "ULTIMATE CHEMICAL WEAPON."
AS YOU WISH.
AND HOW WOULD YOU LIKE ME TO GO ABOUT IT?
I LEAVE IT TO YOU.
OH HOH.
I MAY USE WHATEVER APPROACH TAKES MY FANCY?
I WON'T BE THERE TO WITNESS IT, AND THERE WILL BE NO SURVIVORS.
YOU MAY DO AS THE BEAST WITHIN YOU WISHES.
...HEH...

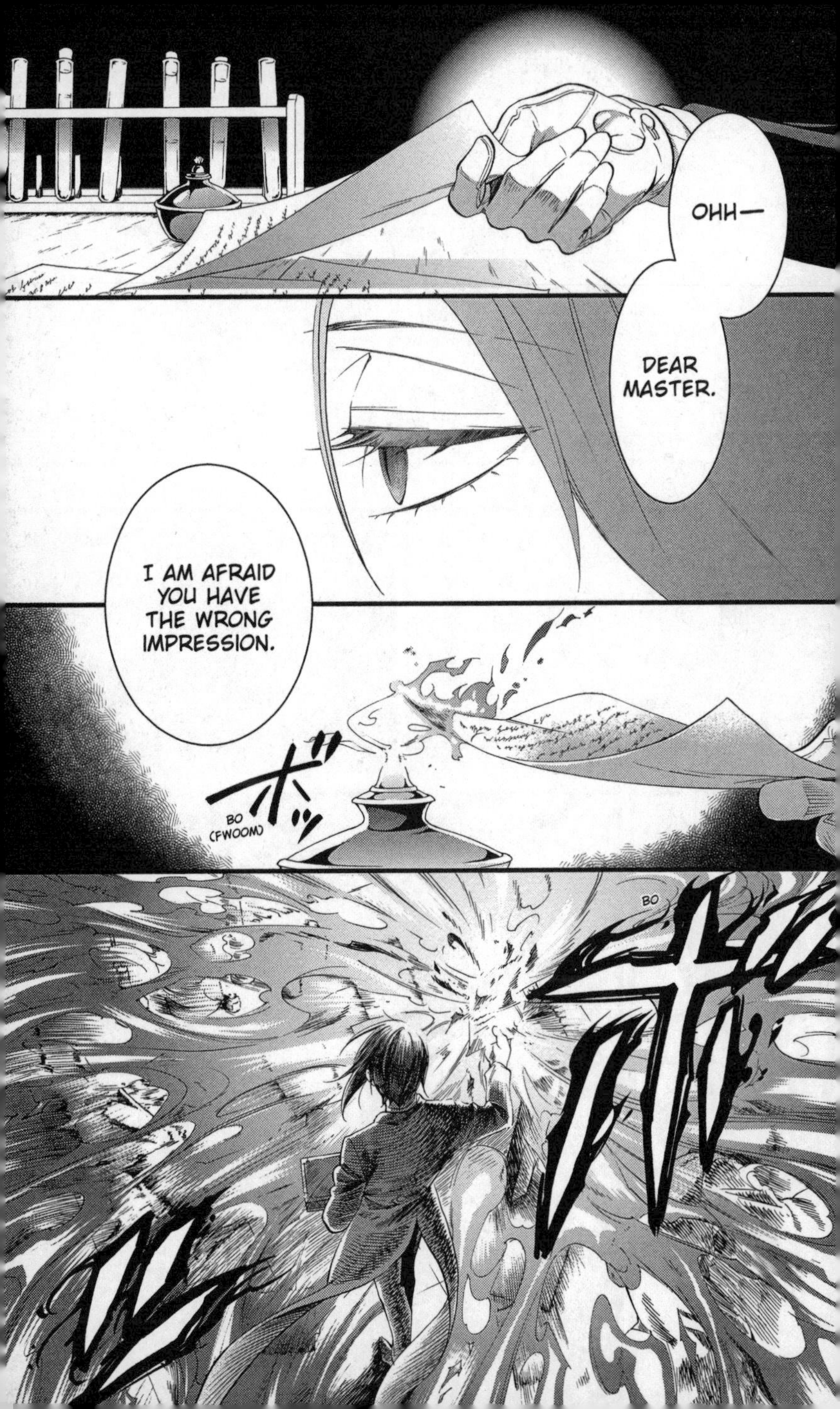
OHH—
DEAR MASTER.
I AM AFRAID YOU HAVE THE WRONG IMPRESSION.
BO (FWOOM)
BO

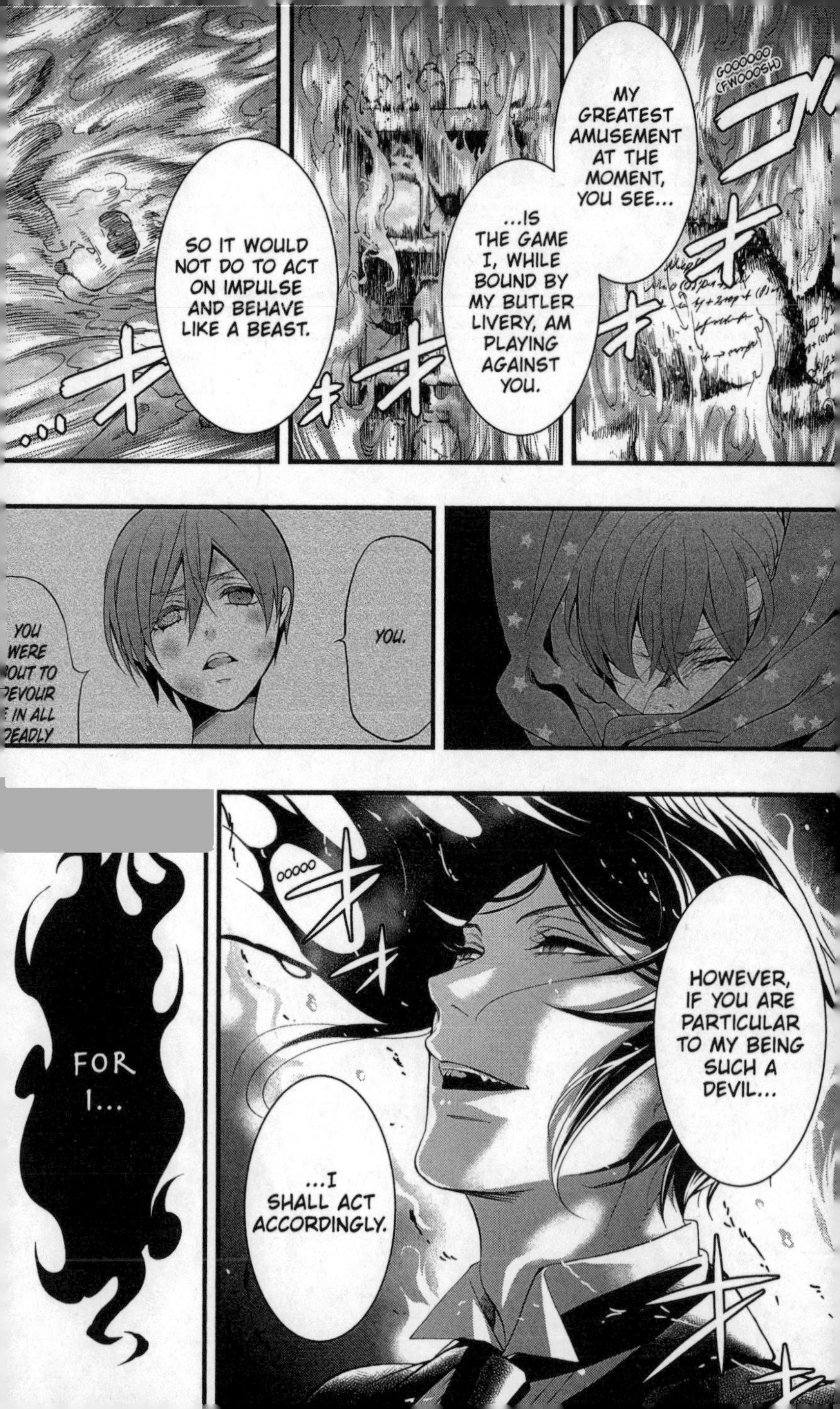
GOOOOOO (FWOOOSH)
MY GREATEST AMUSEMENT AT THE MOMENT, YOU SEE...
...IS THE GAME I, WHILE BOUND BY MY BUTLER LIVERY, AM PLAYING AGAINST YOU.
SO IT WOULD NOT DO TO ACT ON IMPULSE AND BEHAVE LIKE A BEAST.
...OOO
YOU.
YOU WERE OUT TO EVOUR IN ALL EADLY
HOWEVER, IF YOU ARE PARTICULAR TO MY BEING SUCH A DEVIL...
OOOOO
...I SHALL ACT ACCORDINGLY.
FOR I...

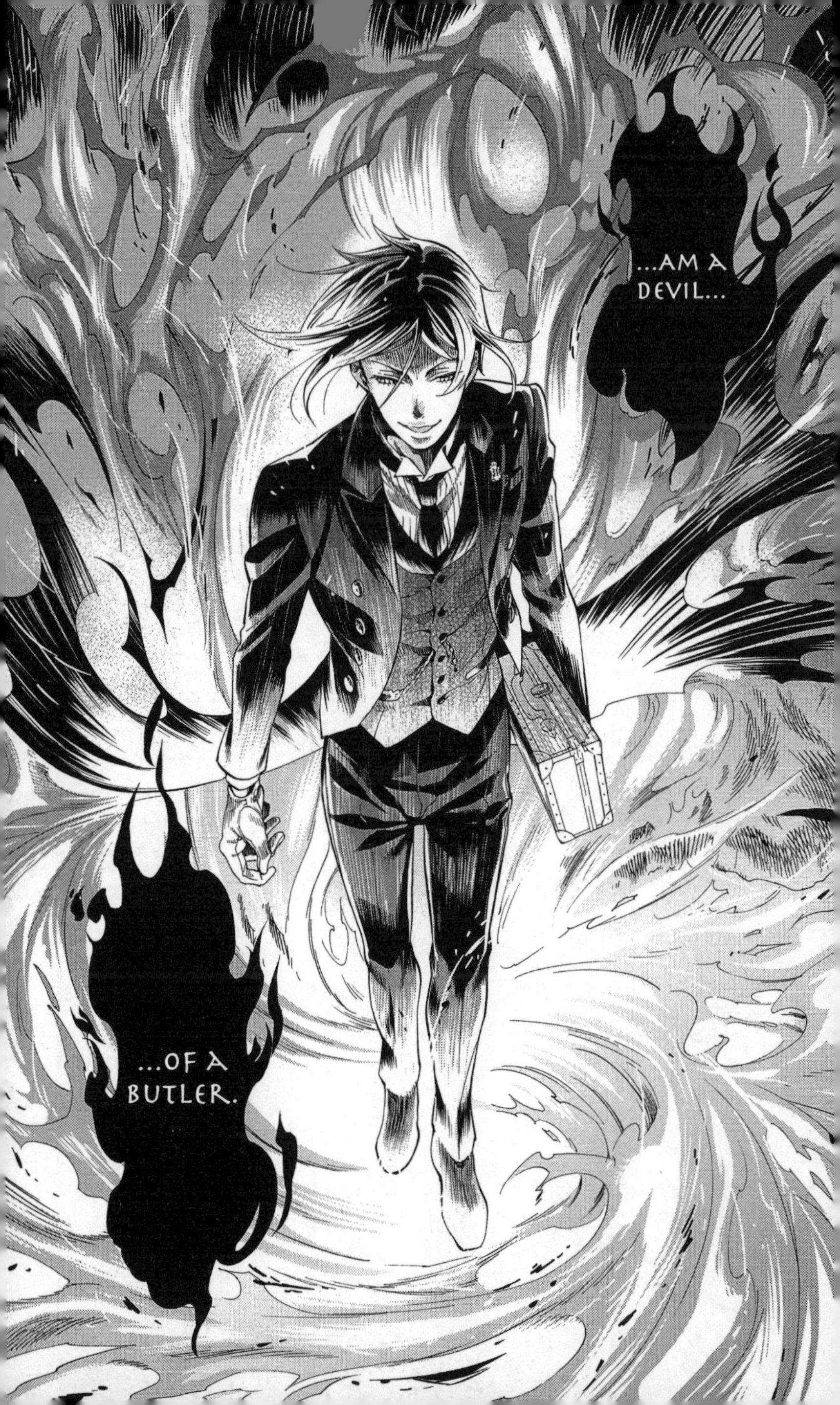
...AM A DEVIL...
...OF A BUTLER.

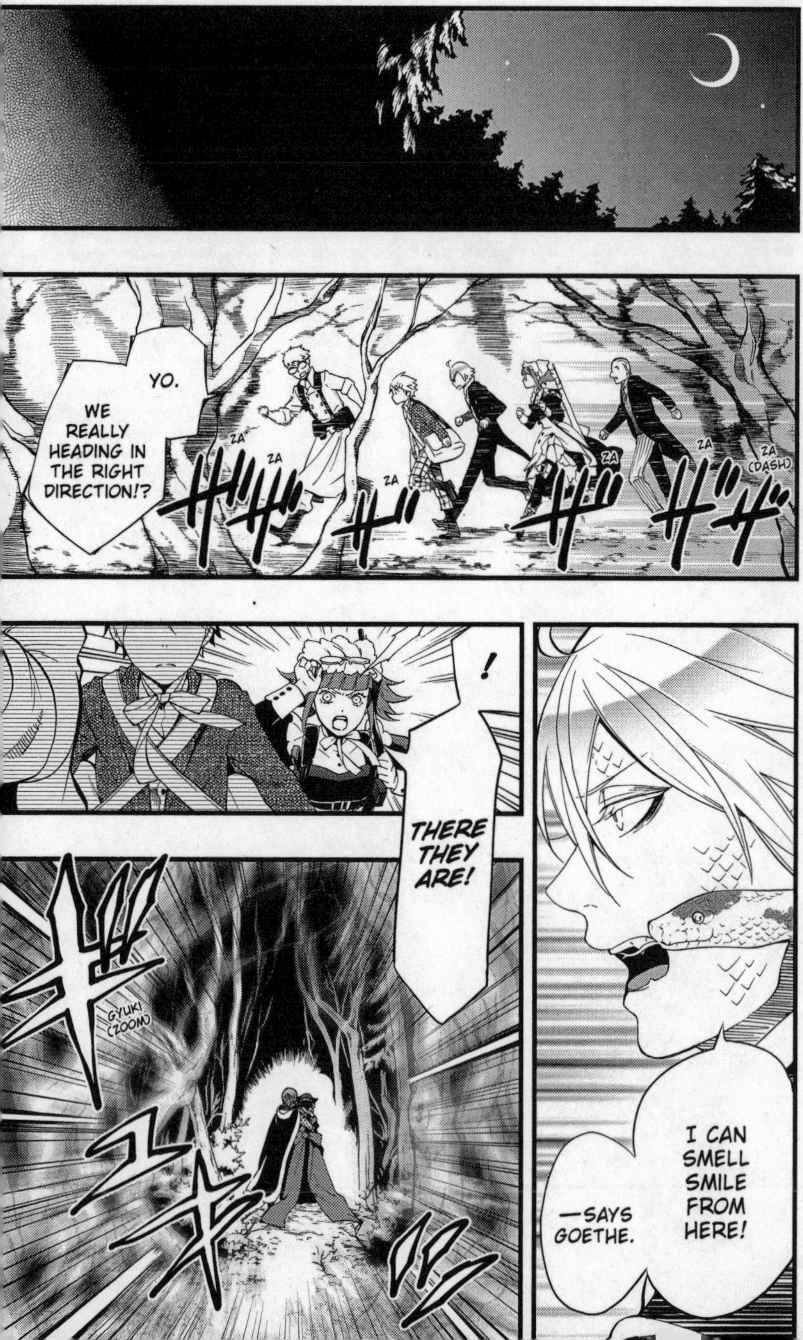
ZA (DASH)
ZA
ZA
ZA
ZA
ZA
YO.
WE REALLY HEADING IN THE RIGHT DIRECTION!?
I CAN SMELL SMILE FROM HERE!
—SAYS GOETHE.
!
THERE THEY ARE!
GYUKI (ZOOM)

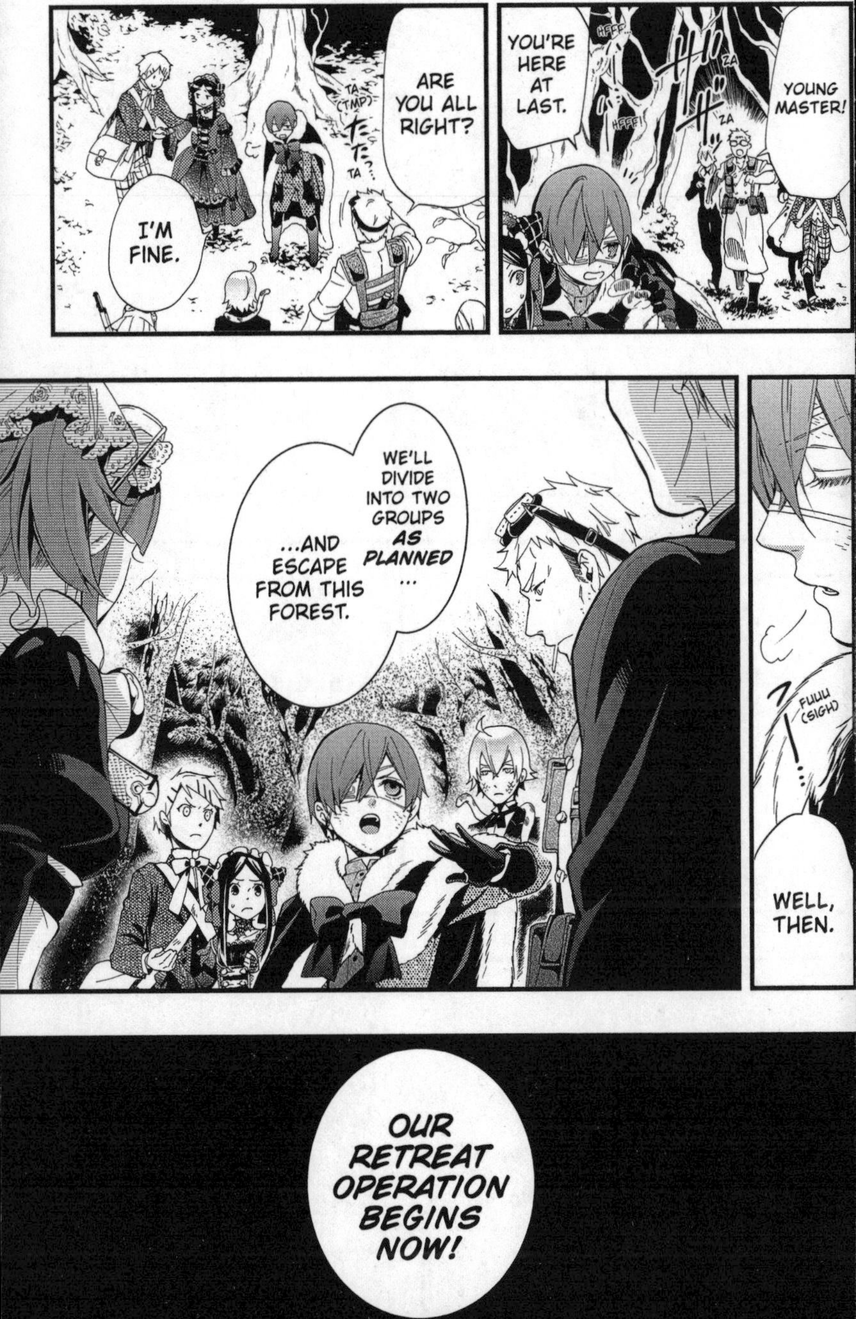
YOUNG MASTER!
HFFF...
ZA
ZA
HFFF
YOU'RE HERE AT LAST.
ARE YOU ALL RIGHT?
TA (TMP)
TA
I'M FINE.
FUUU (SIGH)
WELL, THEN.
WE'LL DIVIDE INTO TWO GROUPS AS PLANNED...
...AND ESCAPE FROM THIS FOREST.
OUR RETREAT OPERATION BEGINS NOW!

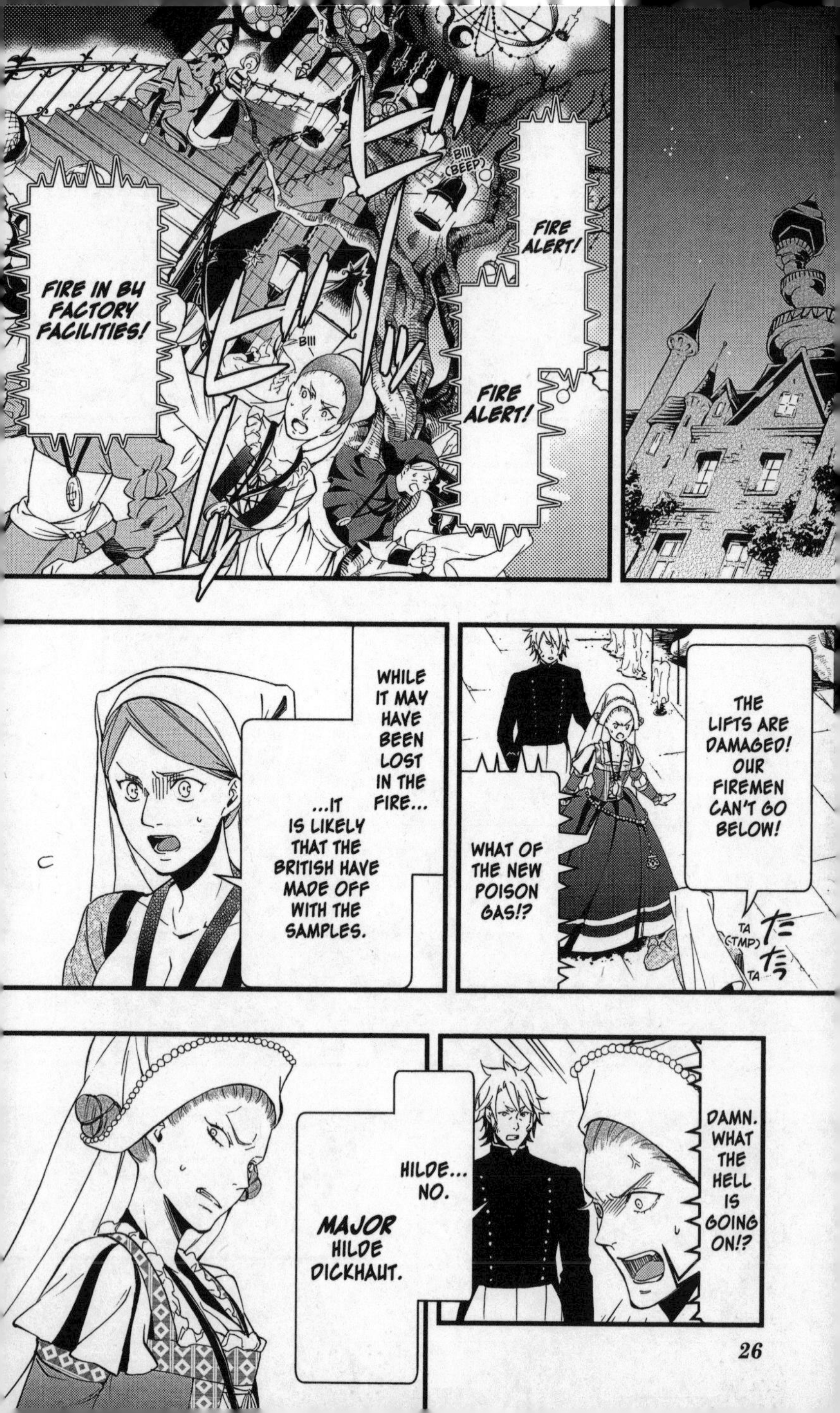
BIII (BEEP)
FIRE ALERT!
FIRE ALERT!
FIRE IN B4 FACTORY FACILITIES!
BIII
THE LIFTS ARE DAMAGED! OUR FIREMEN CAN'T GO BELOW!
TA (TMP) TA
WHAT OF THE NEW POISON GAS!?
WHILE IT MAY HAVE BEEN LOST IN THE FIRE...
...IT IS LIKELY THAT THE BRITISH HAVE MADE OFF WITH THE SAMPLES.
DAMN. WHAT THE HELL IS GOING ON!?
HILDE... NO.
MAJOR HILDE DICKHAUT.

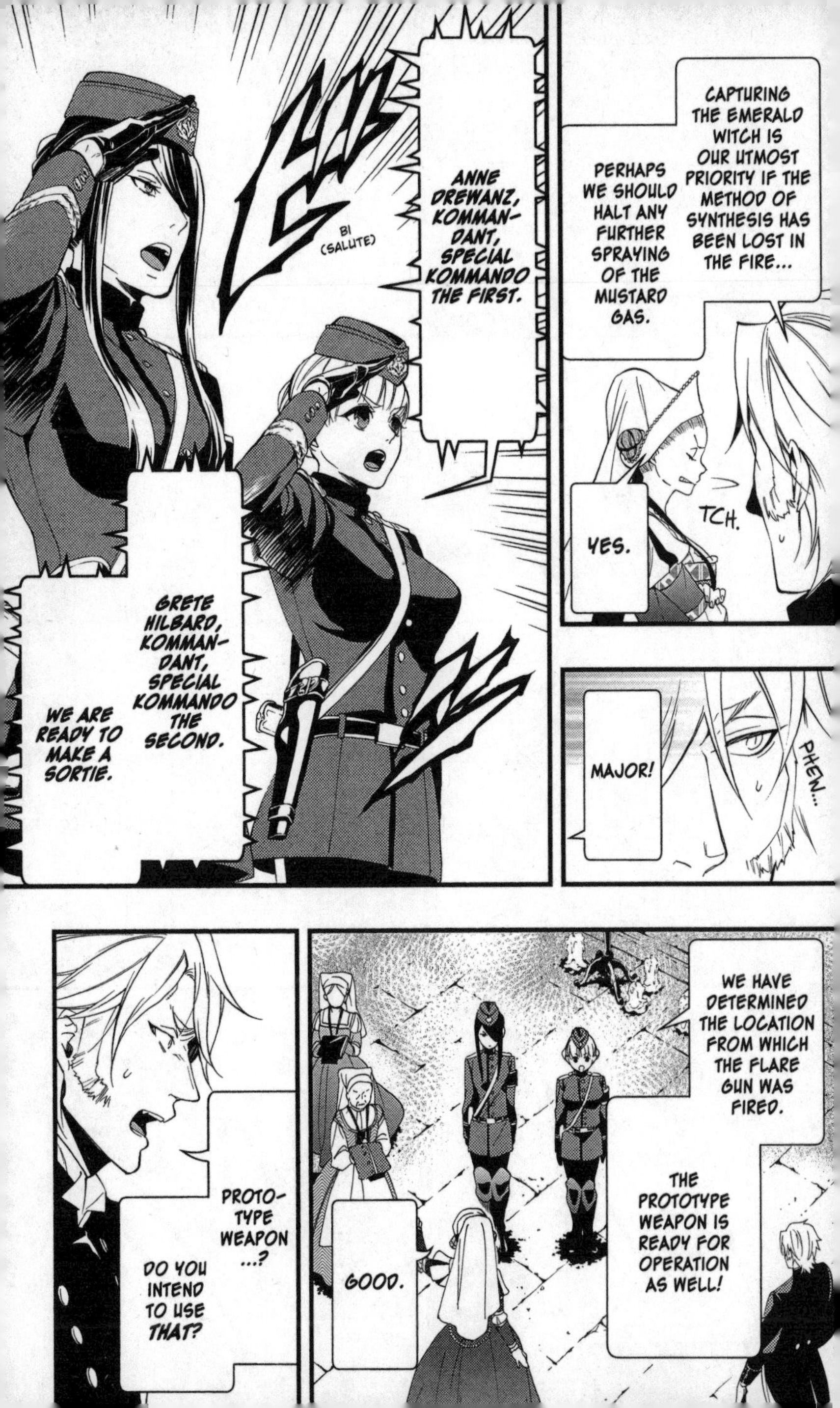
CAPTURING THE EMERALD WITCH IS OUR UTMOST PRIORITY IF THE METHOD OF SYNTHESIS HAS BEEN LOST IN THE FIRE...
PERHAPS WE SHOULD HALT ANY FURTHER SPRAYING OF THE MUSTARD GAS.
TCH.
YES.
MAJOR!
PHEW...
ANNE DREWANZ, KOMMANDANT, SPECIAL KOMMANDO THE FIRST.
BI (SALUTE)
GRETE HILBARD, KOMMANDANT, SPECIAL KOMMANDO THE SECOND.
WE ARE READY TO MAKE A SORTIE.
WE HAVE DETERMINED THE LOCATION FROM WHICH THE FLARE GUN WAS FIRED.
THE PROTOTYPE WEAPON IS READY FOR OPERATION AS WELL!
GOOD.
PROTOTYPE WEAPON ...?
DO YOU INTEND TO USE THAT?

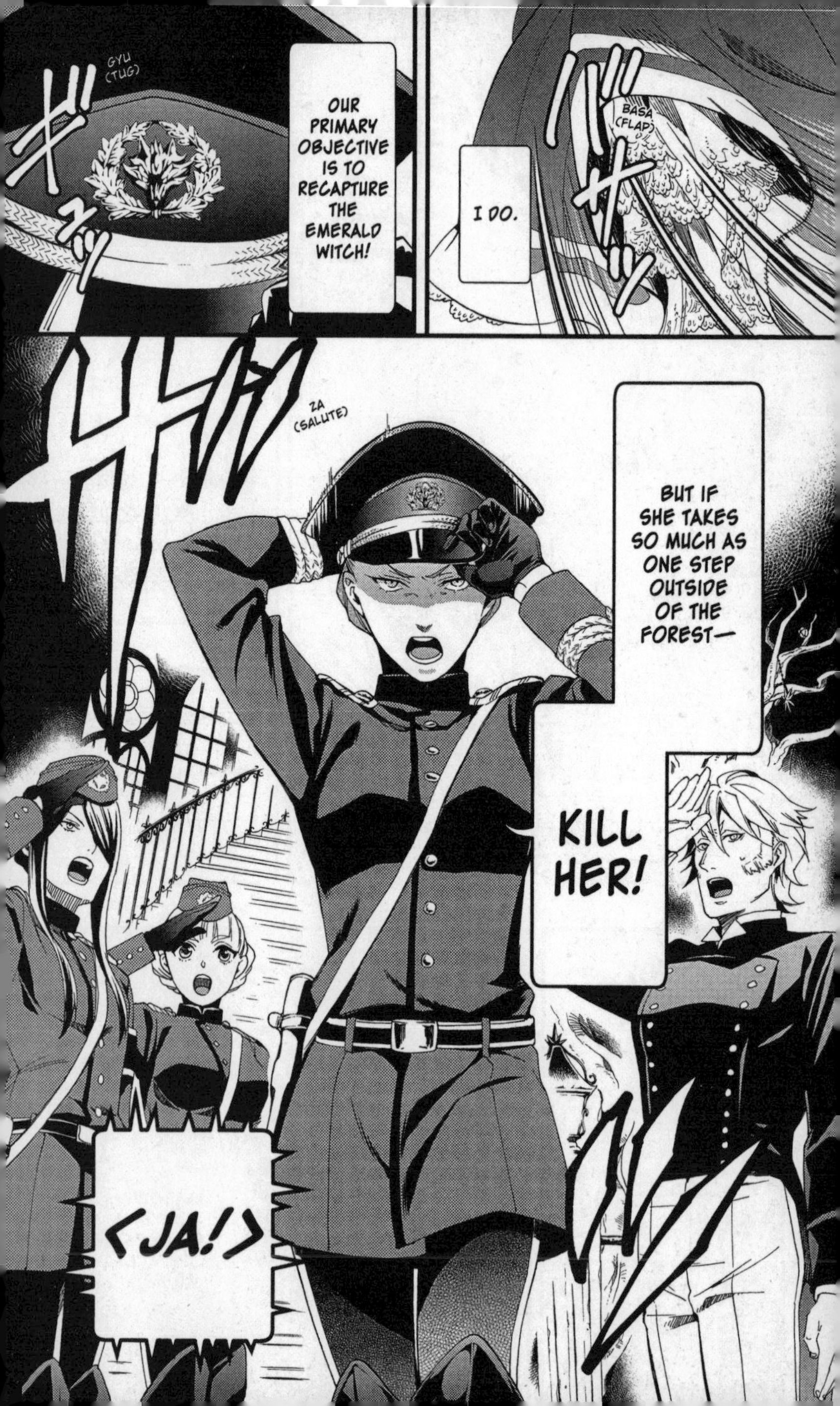
BASA (FLAP)
I DO.
GYU (TUG)
OUR PRIMARY OBJECTIVE IS TO RECAPTURE THE EMERALD WITCH!
BUT IF SHE TAKES SO MUCH AS ONE STEP OUTSIDE OF THE FOREST—
ZA (SALUTE)
KILL HER!
<JA!>

Black Butler

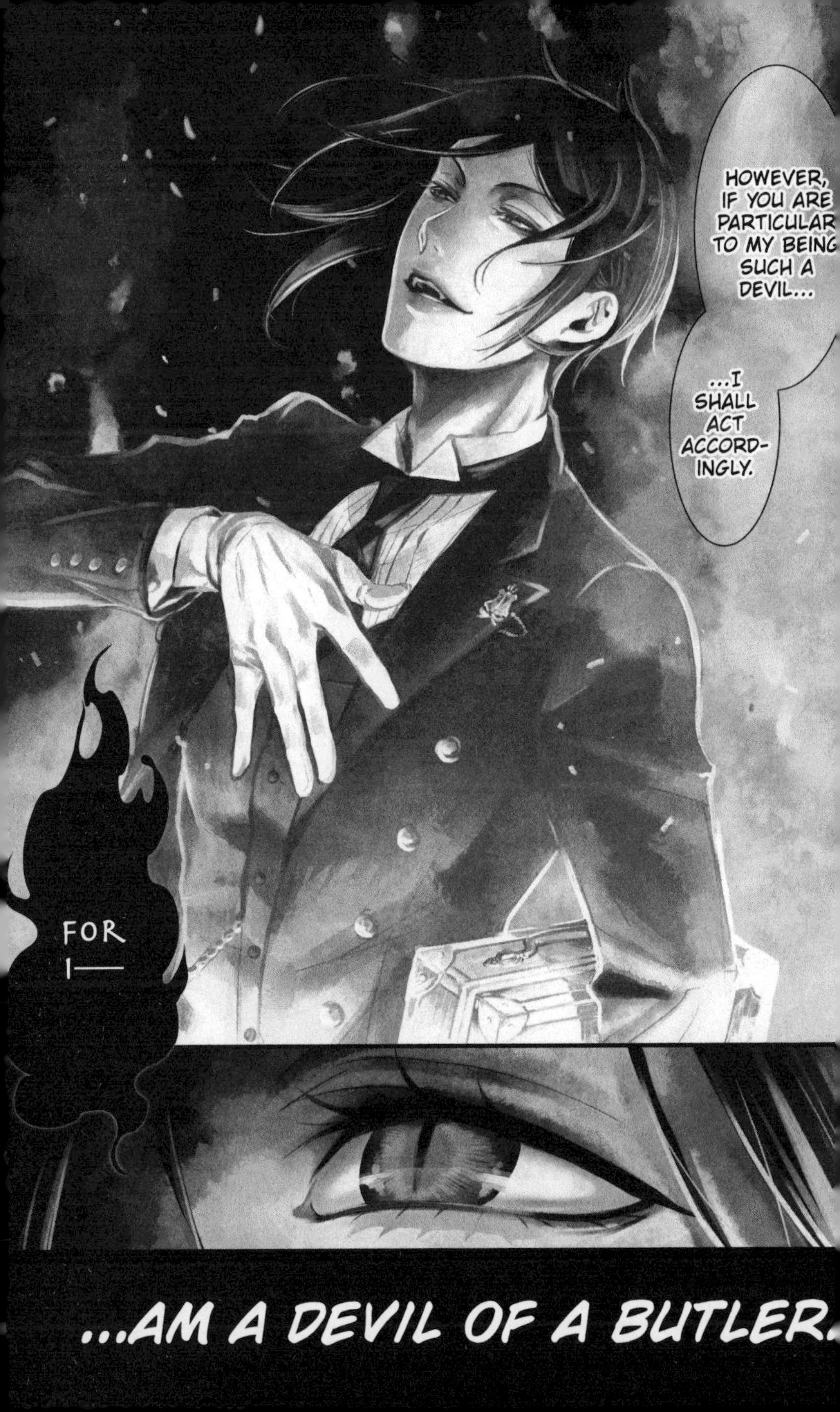
HOWEVER, IF YOU ARE PARTICULAR TO MY BEING SUCH A DEVIL...
...I SHALL ACT ACCORD-INGLY.
FOR I—
...AM A DEVIL OF A BUTLER.

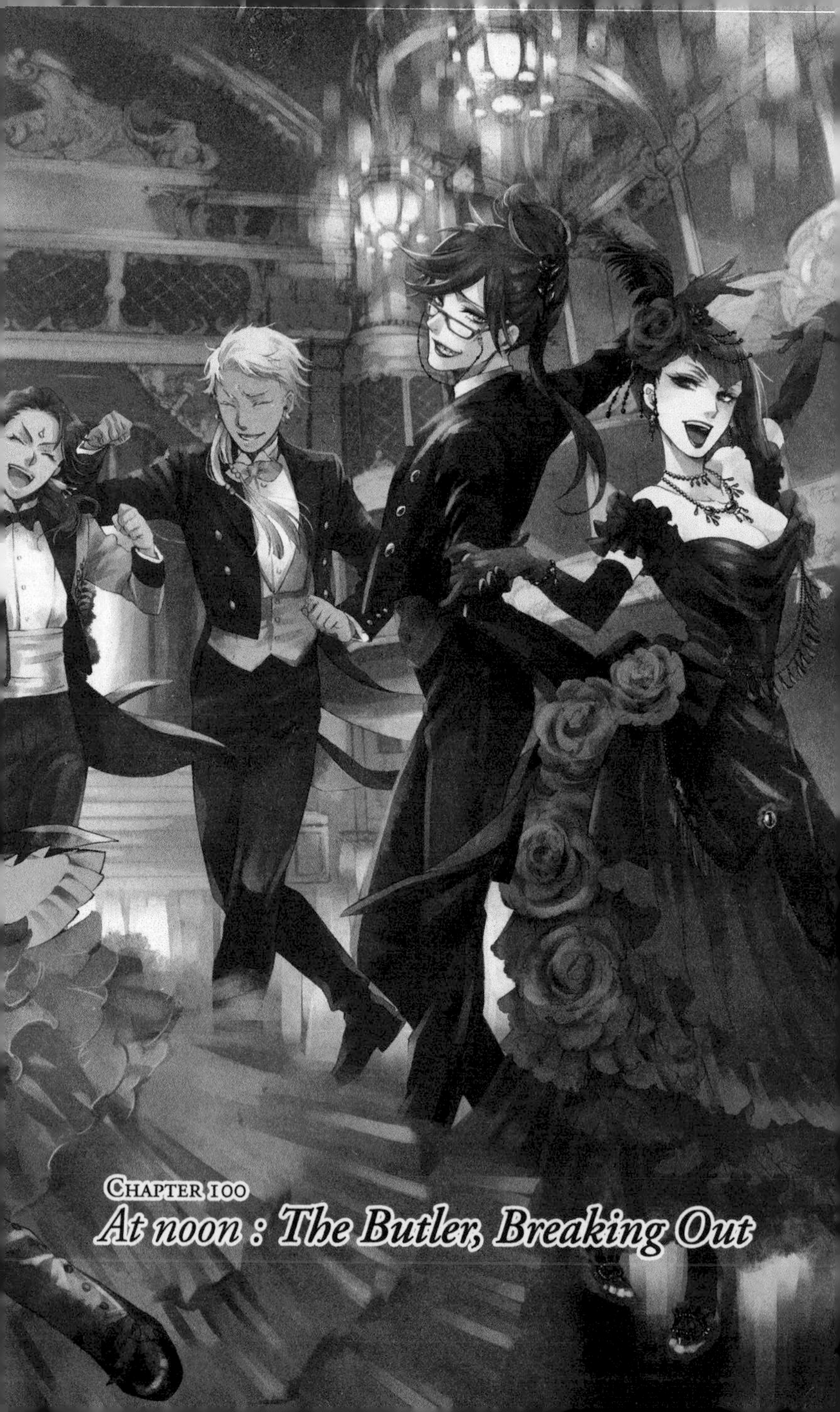

Chapter 100

At noon : The Butler, Breaking Out

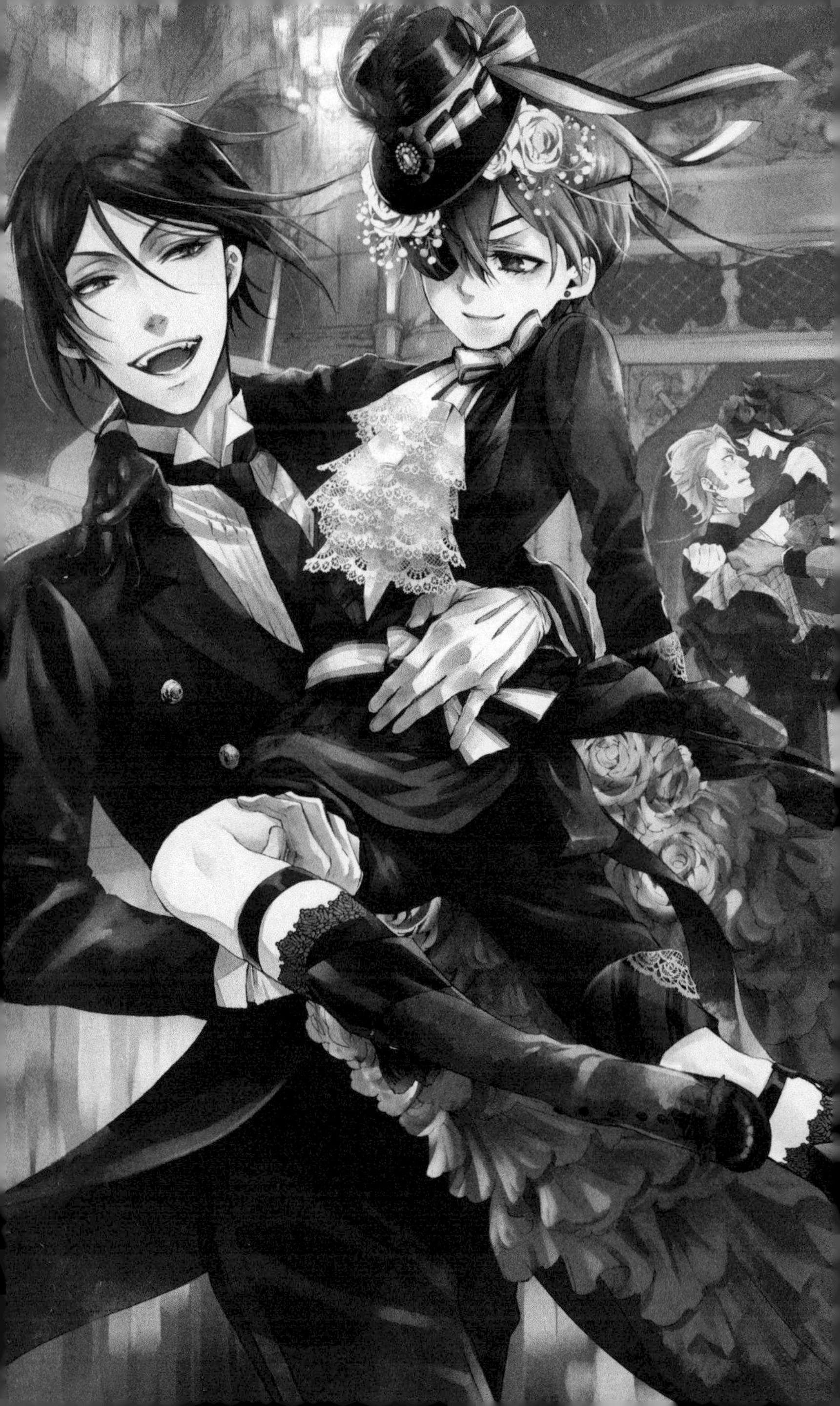

Black Butler

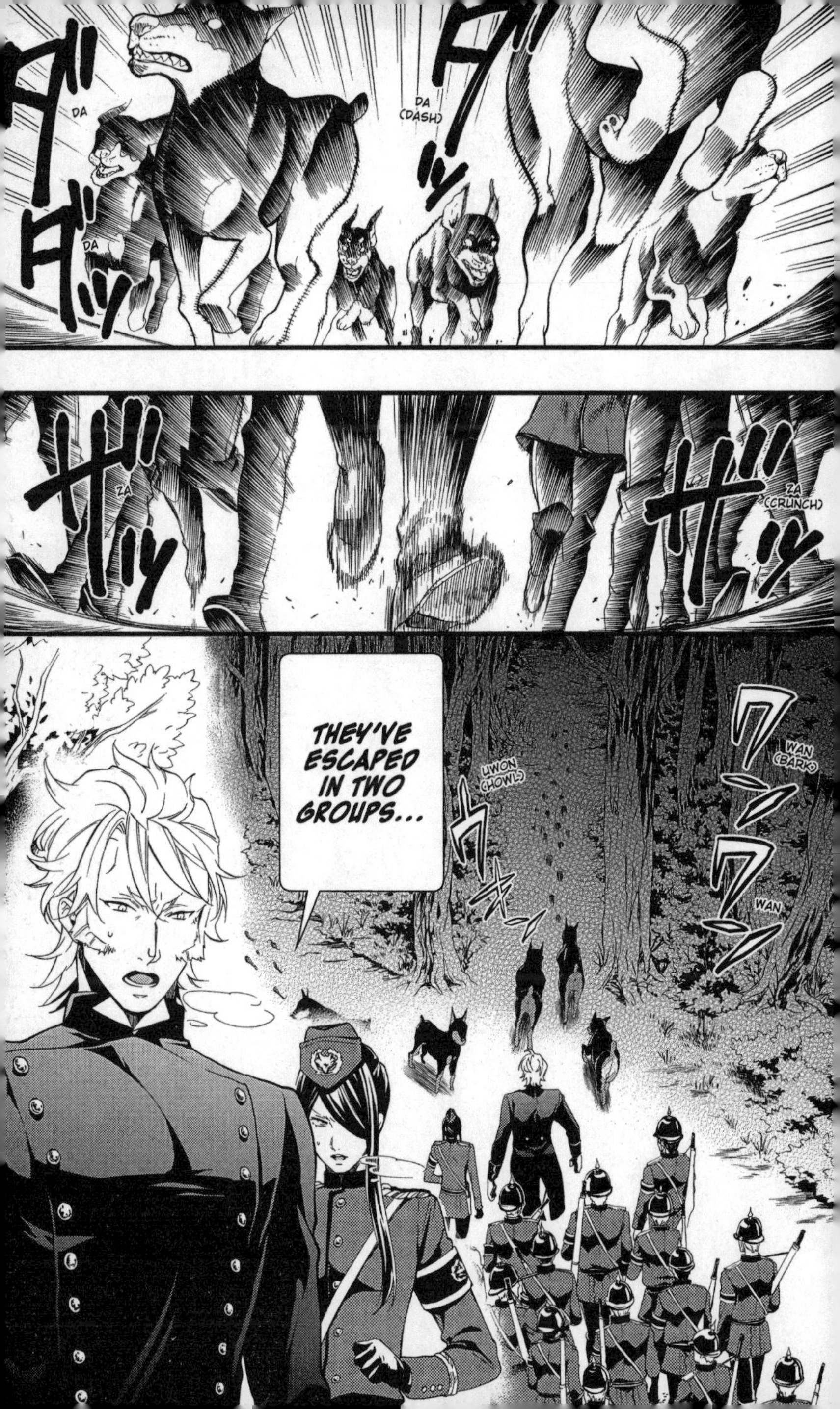
DA (DASH)
DA
DA
ZA (CRUNCH)
ZA
WAN (BARK)
WAN
UWON (HOWL)
THEY'VE ESCAPED IN TWO GROUPS...

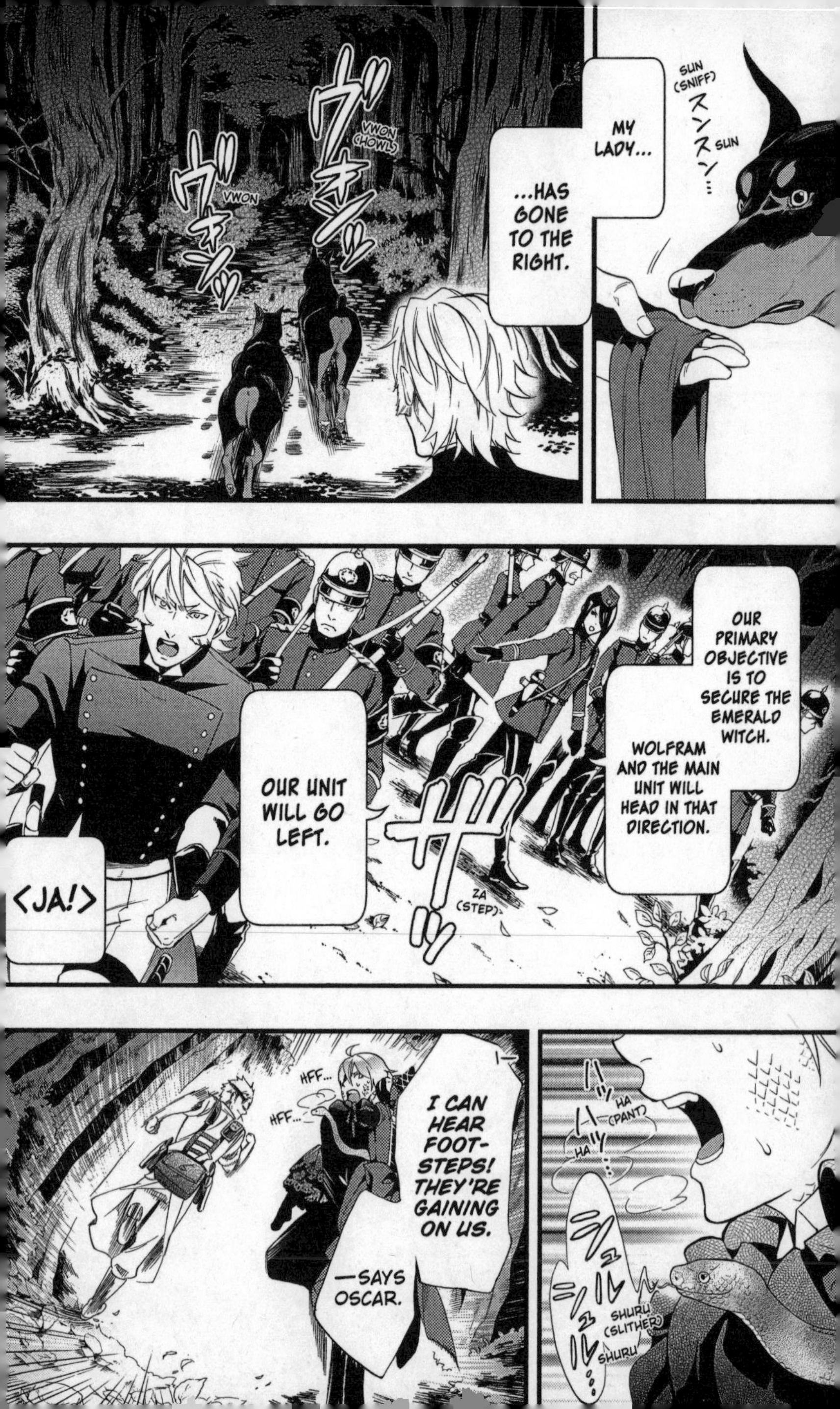
SUN (SNIFF)
スンスン…
SUN
MY LADY...
...HAS GONE TO THE RIGHT.
VWON (HOWLS)
VWON
OUR PRIMARY OBJECTIVE IS TO SECURE THE EMERALD WITCH.
WOLFRAM AND THE MAIN UNIT WILL HEAD IN THAT DIRECTION.
ZA (STEP)
OUR UNIT WILL GO LEFT.
<JA!>
HA (PANT)
HA
SHURU (SLITHER)
SHURU
I CAN HEAR FOOT-STEPS! THEY'RE GAINING ON US.
—SAYS OSCAR.
HFF...
HFF...

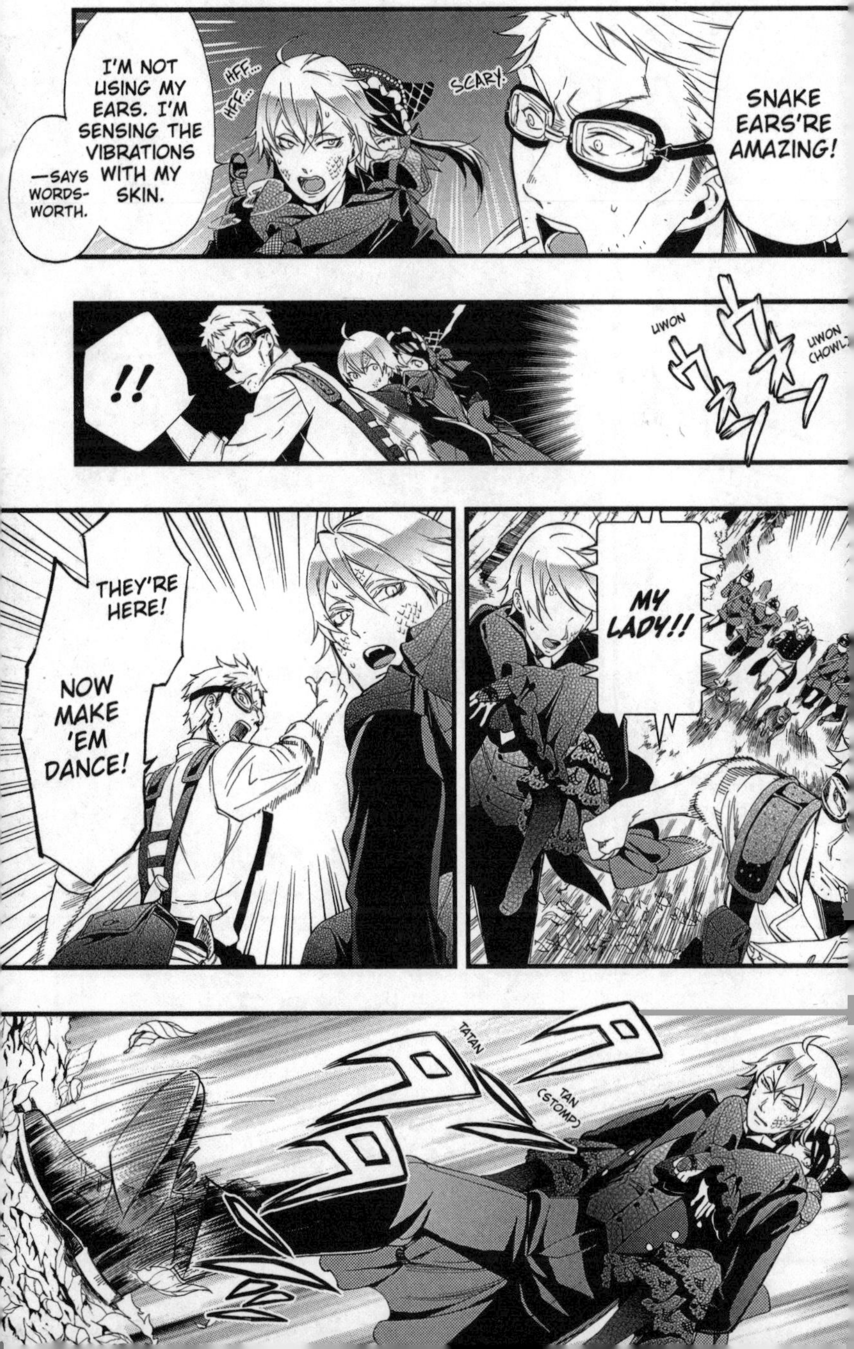
SNAKE EARS'RE AMAZING!
SCARY.
HFF... HFF...
I'M NOT USING MY EARS. I'M SENSING THE VIBRATIONS WITH MY SKIN.
—SAYS WORDS-WORTH.
UWON UWON (HOWL)
UWON
!!
MY LADY!!
THEY'RE HERE!
NOW MAKE 'EM DANCE!
TATAN
TAN (STOMP)

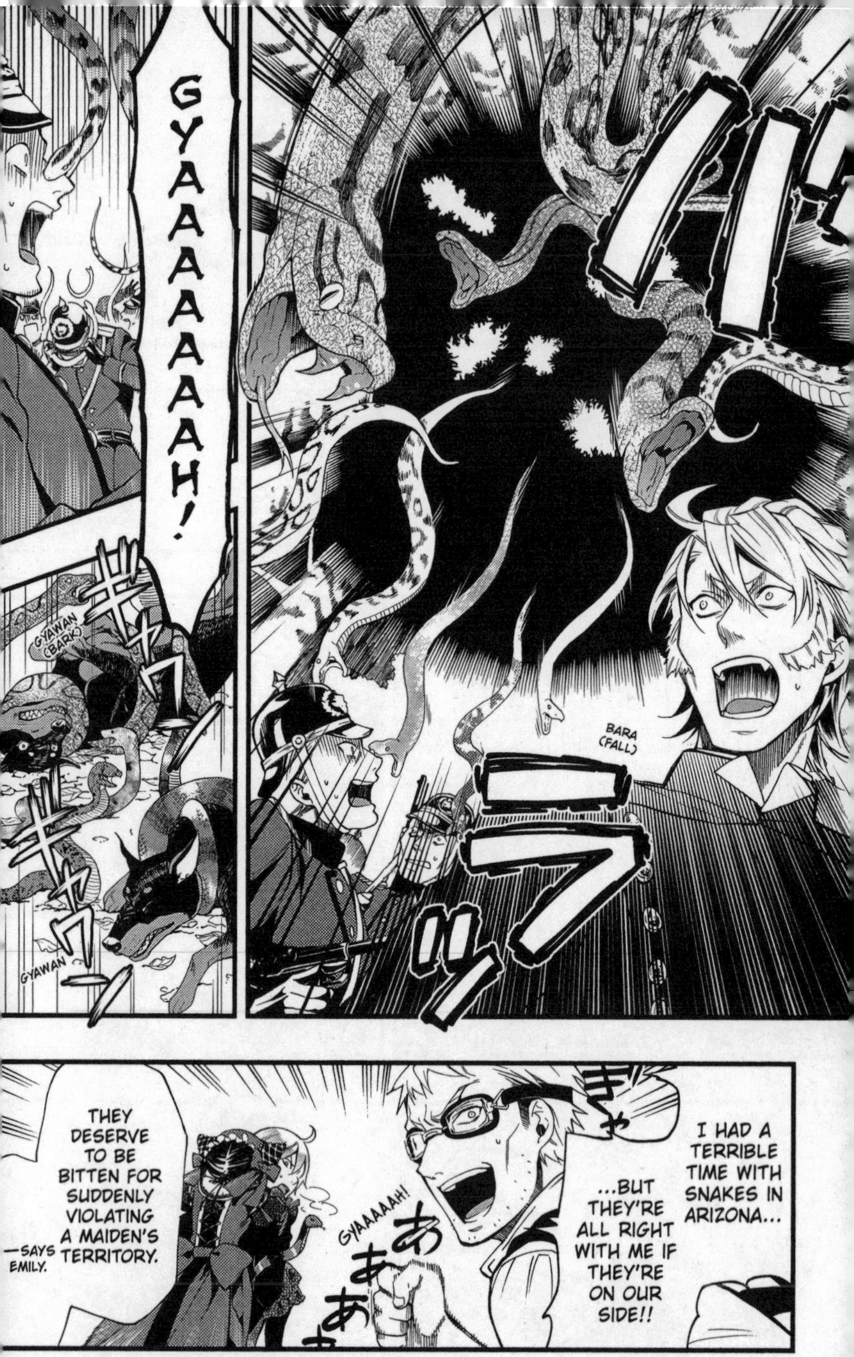

BARA (FALL)
GYAAAAAAAH!
GYAWAN (BARK)
GYAWAN
I HAD A TERRIBLE TIME WITH SNAKES IN ARIZONA...
...BUT THEY'RE ALL RIGHT WITH ME IF THEY'RE ON OUR SIDE!!
GYAAAAAH!
THEY DESERVE TO BE BITTEN FOR SUDDENLY VIOLATING A MAIDEN'S TERRITORY.
—SAYS EMILY.

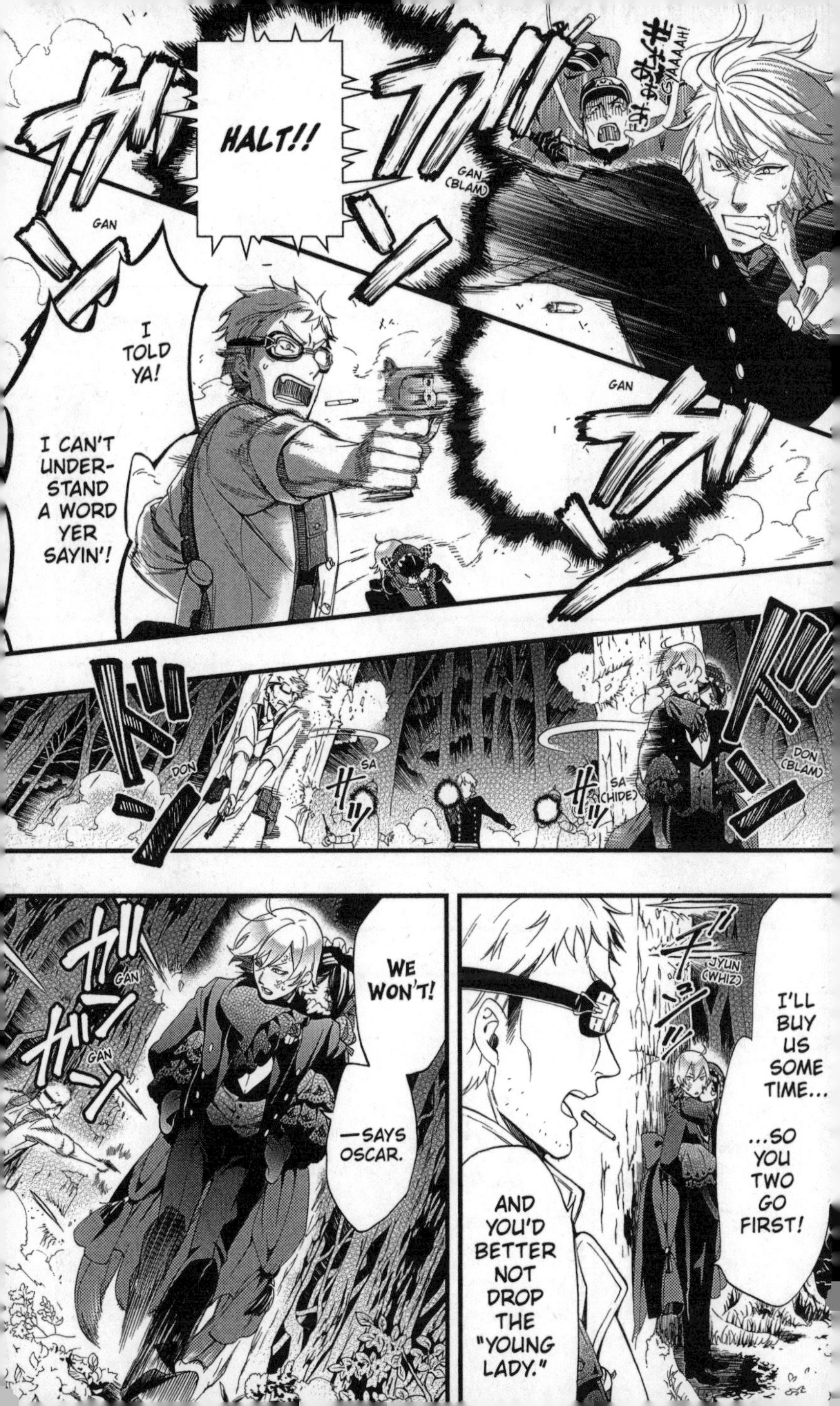
GYAAAAAH!
GAN (BLAM)
HALT!!
GAN
GAN
I TOLD YA!
I CAN'T UNDER-STAND A WORD YER SAYIN'!
DON (BLAM)
SA (CHIDE)
SA
DON
JYUN (WHIZ)
I'LL BUY US SOME TIME...
...SO YOU TWO GO FIRST!
AND YOU'D BETTER NOT DROP THE "YOUNG LADY."
WE WON'T!
—SAYS OSCAR.
GAN
GAN

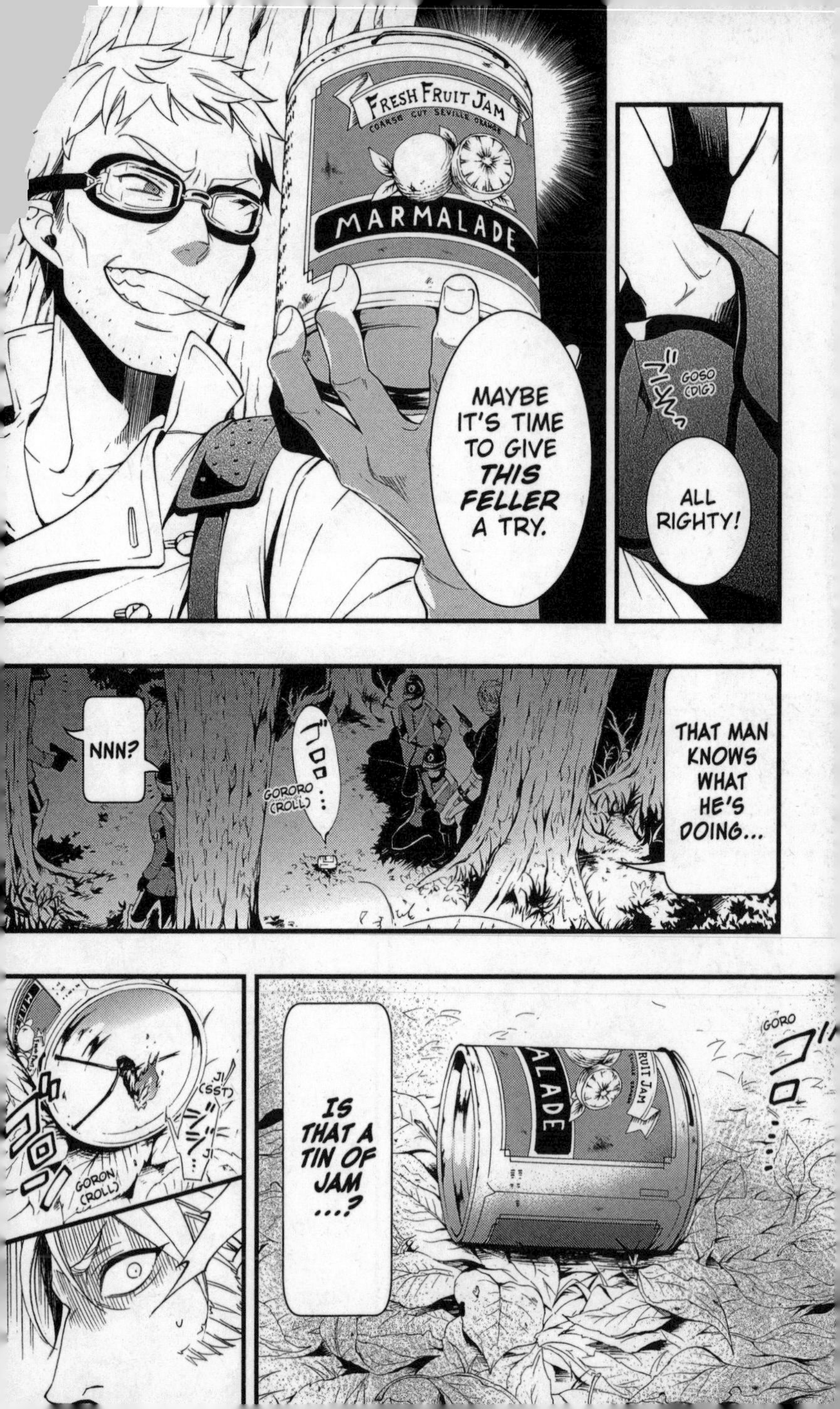
GOSO (DIG)
ALL RIGHTY!
FRESH FRUIT JAM
COARSE CUT SEVILLE ORANGE
MARMALADE
MAYBE IT'S TIME TO GIVE THIS FELLER A TRY.
THAT MAN KNOWS WHAT HE'S DOING...
GORORO (ROLL)
NNN?
GORO
IS THAT A TIN OF JAM ...?
MALADE
FRUIT JAM
JI (SST)
GORON (ROLL)

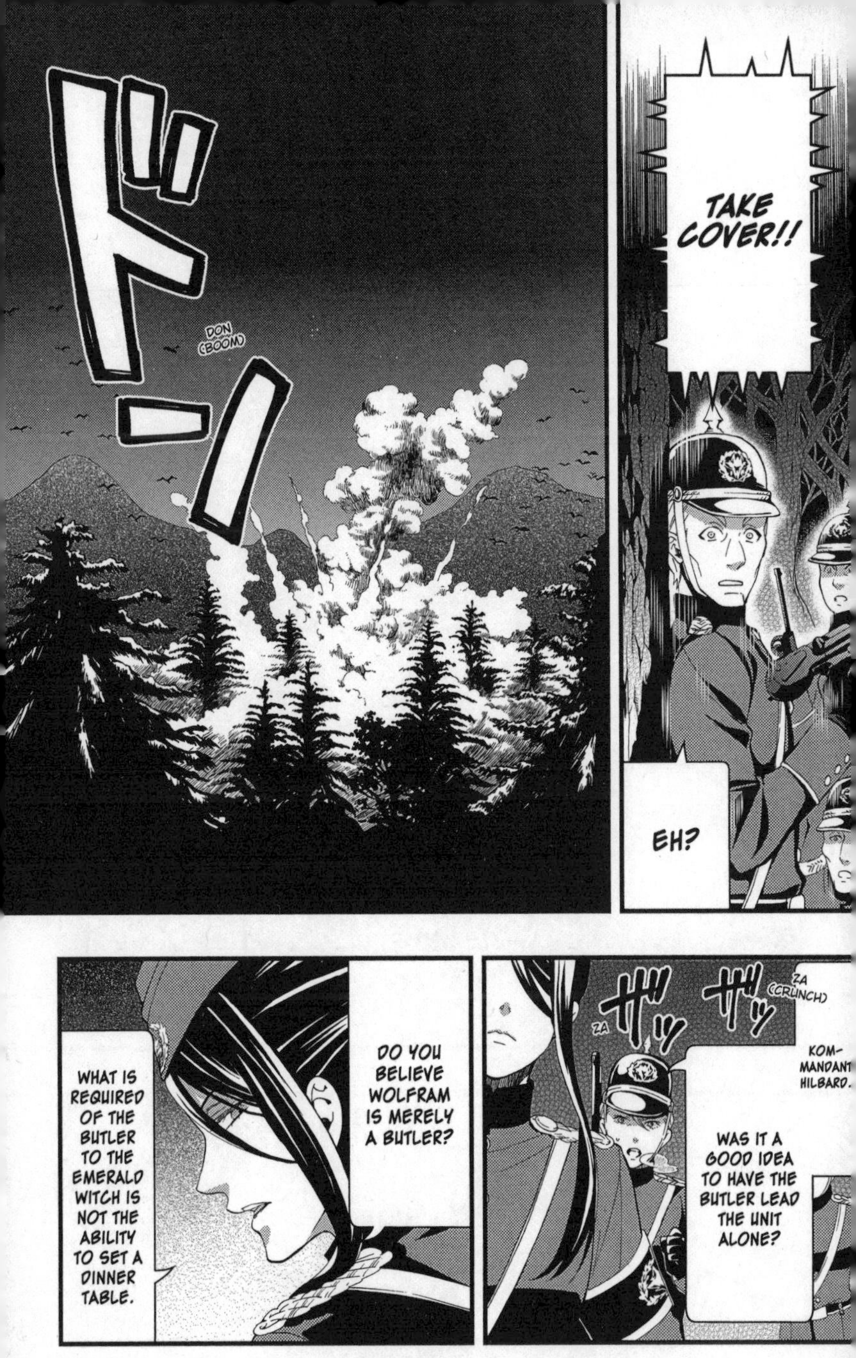
TAKE COVER!!
EH?
DON (BOOM)
ZA
ZA (CRUNCH)
KOM-MANDANT HILBARD.
WAS IT A GOOD IDEA TO HAVE THE BUTLER LEAD THE UNIT ALONE?
DO YOU BELIEVE WOLFRAM IS MERELY A BUTLER?
WHAT IS REQUIRED OF THE BUTLER TO THE EMERALD WITCH IS NOT THE ABILITY TO SET A DINNER TABLE.

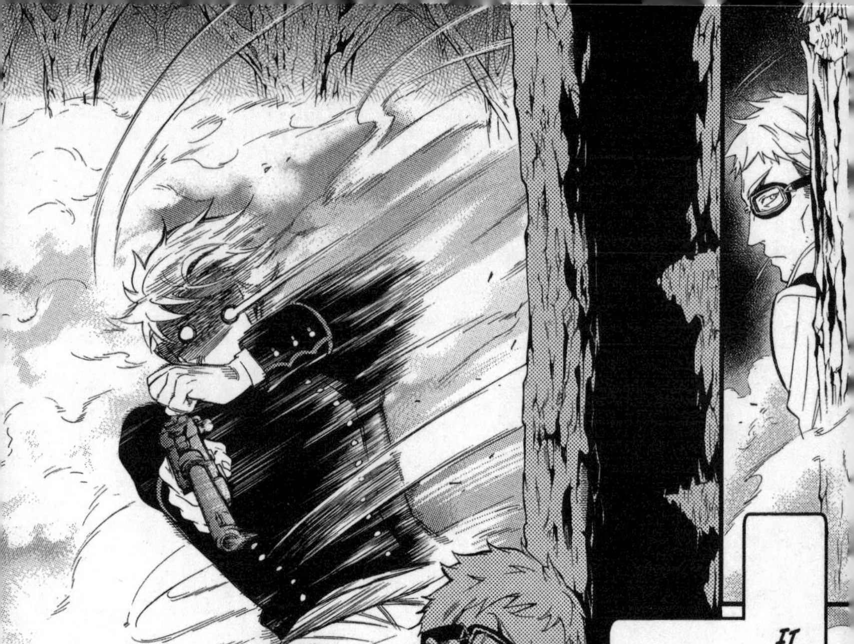
IT IS...
...THE ABILITY TO FIGHT SECOND TO NONE!!

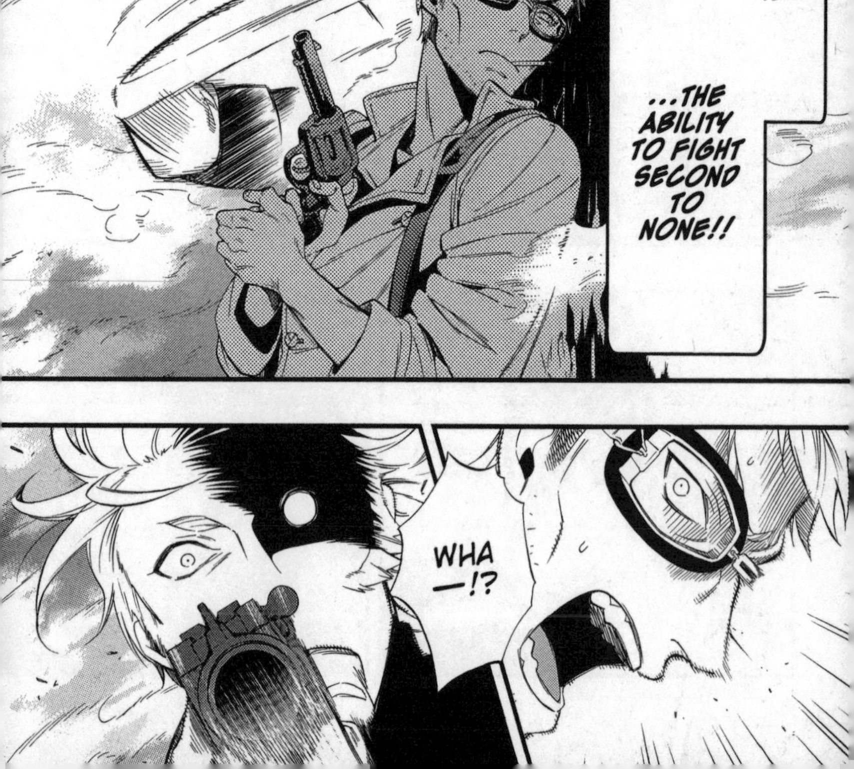
WHA—!?

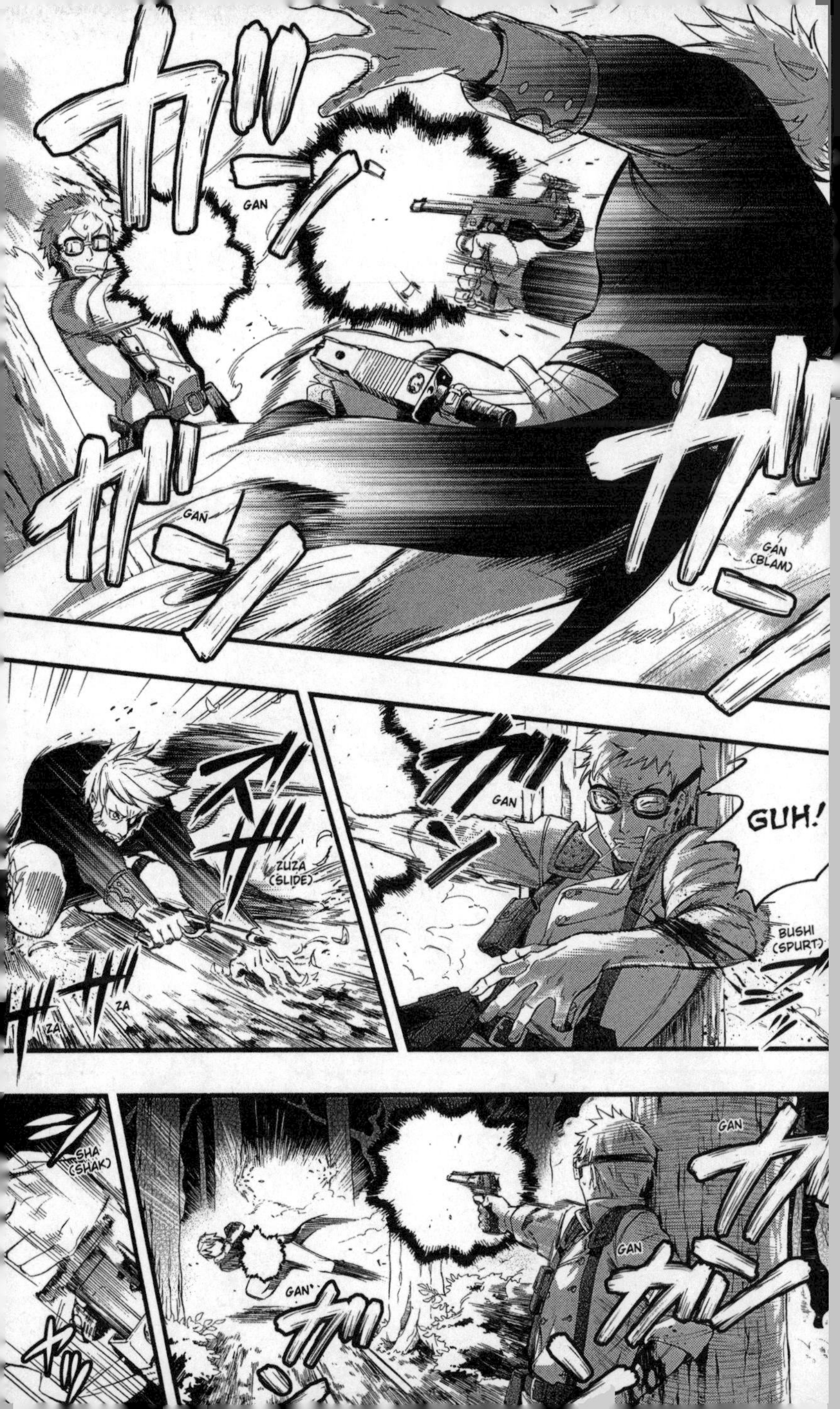
GAN
GAN (BLAM)
GAN
GAN
GUH!
BUSHI (SPURT)
ZUZA (SLIDE)
ZA
ZA
GAN
GAN
GAN
SHA (SHAK)

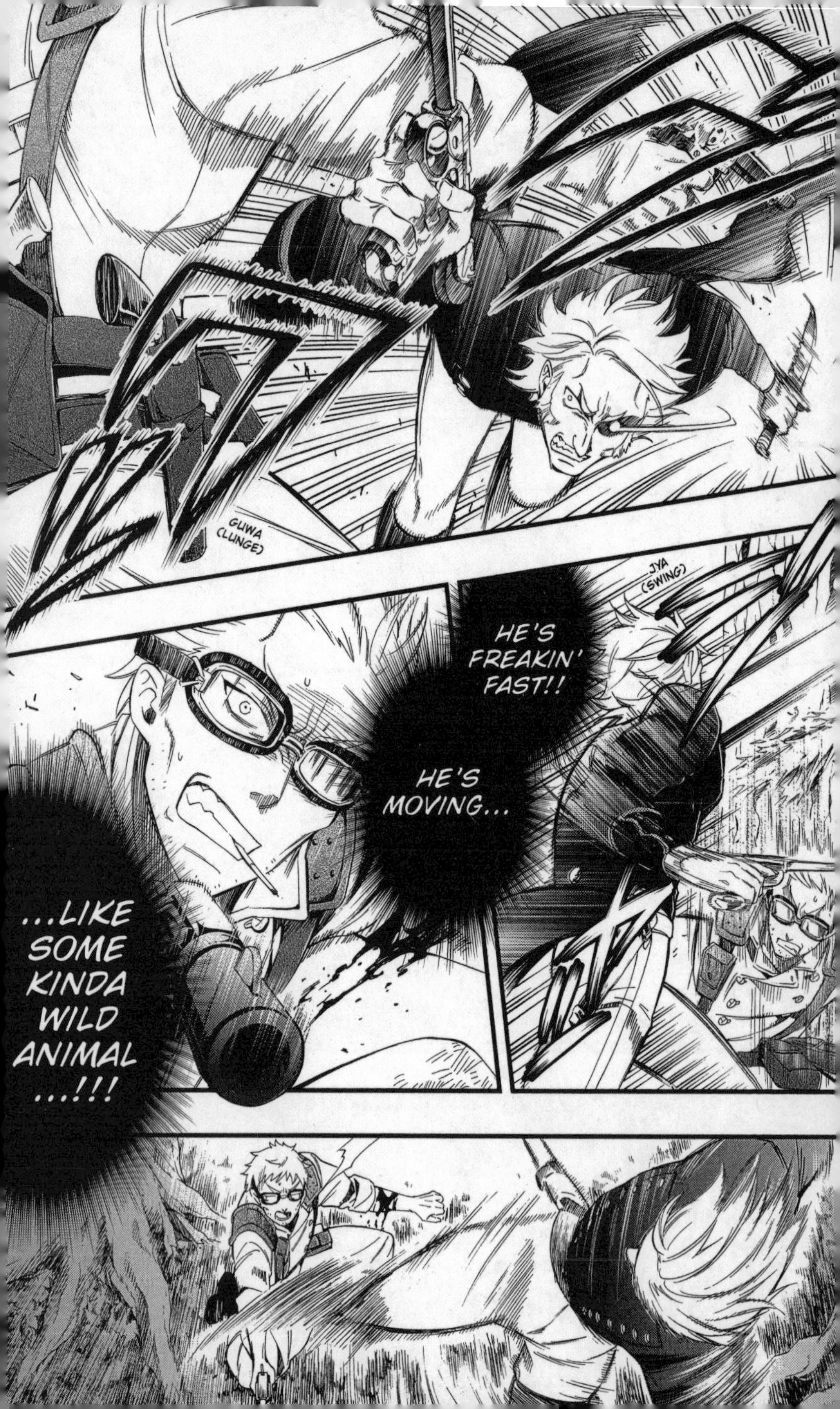
GUWA
(LUNGE)
JYA
(SWING)
HE'S FREAKIN' FAST!!
HE'S MOVING...
...LIKE SOME KINDA WILD ANIMAL ...!!!

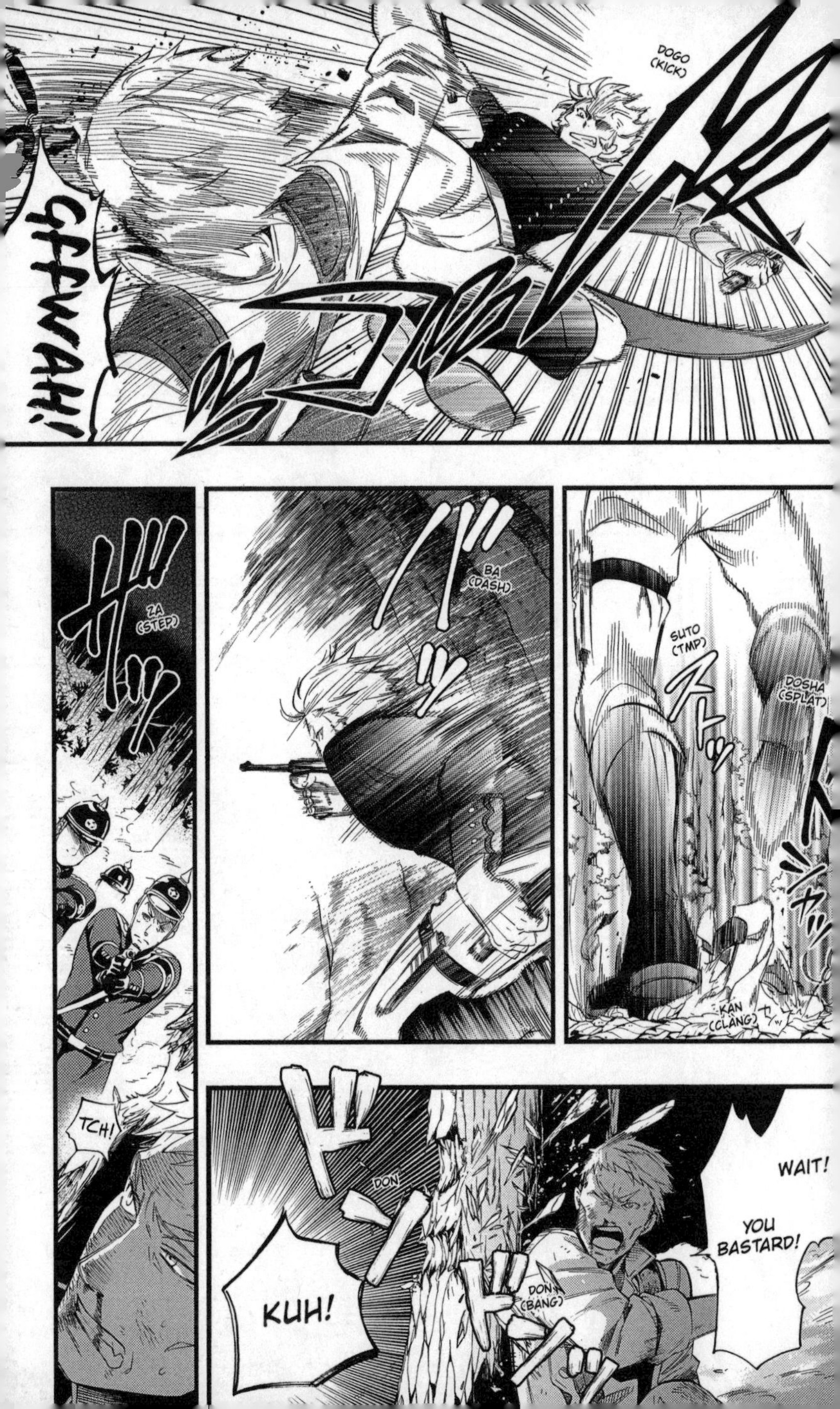
DOGO
(KICK)
GFFWAH!
SUTO
(TMP)
DOSHA
(SPLAT)
KAN
(CLANG)
BA
(DASH)
WAIT!
YOU
BASTARD!
DON
(BANG)
DON
KUH!
ZA
(STEP)
TCH!

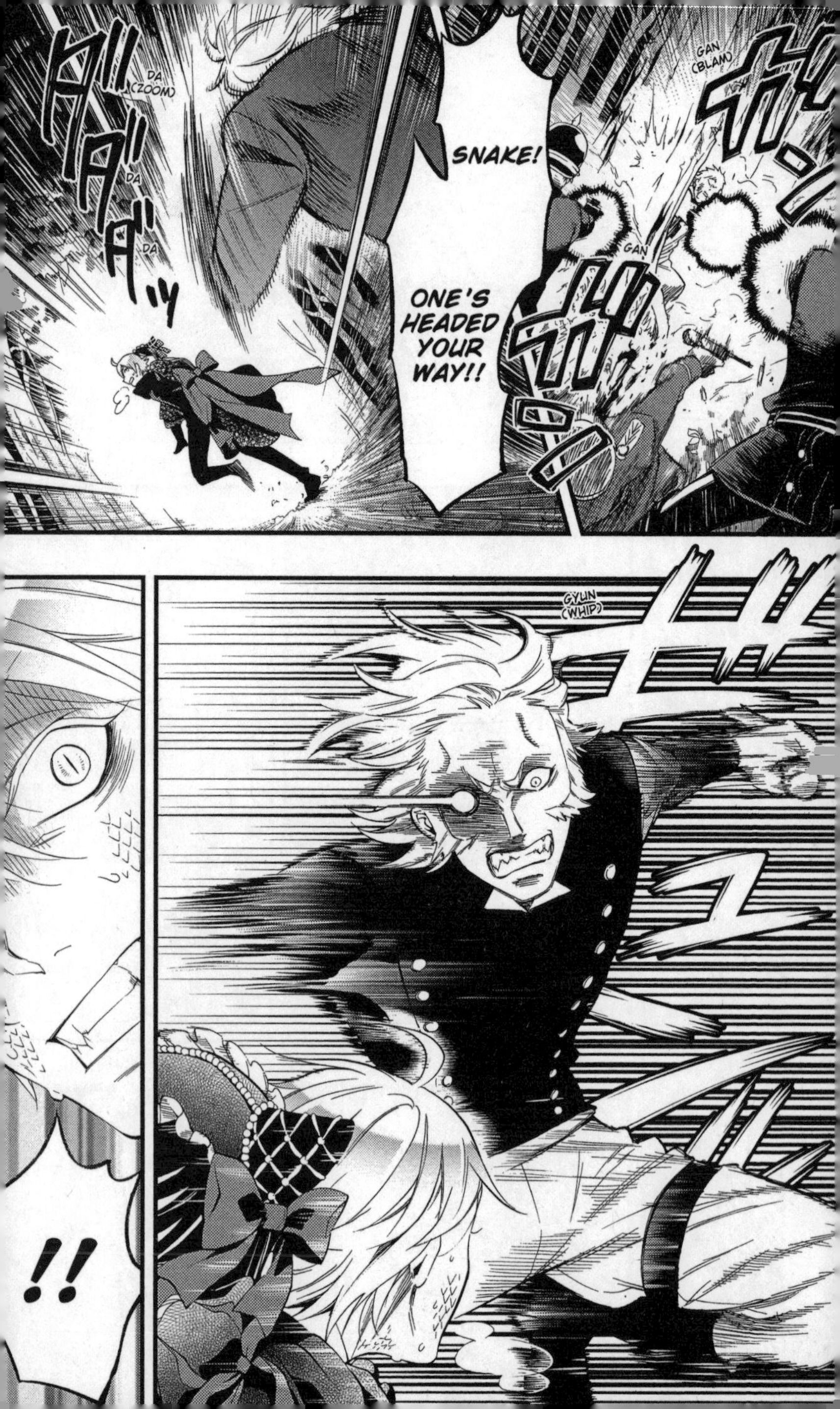
GAN
(BLAM)
GAN
SNAKE!
ONE'S HEADED YOUR WAY!!
DA
(ZOOM)
DA
DA
GYUN
(WHIP)
!!

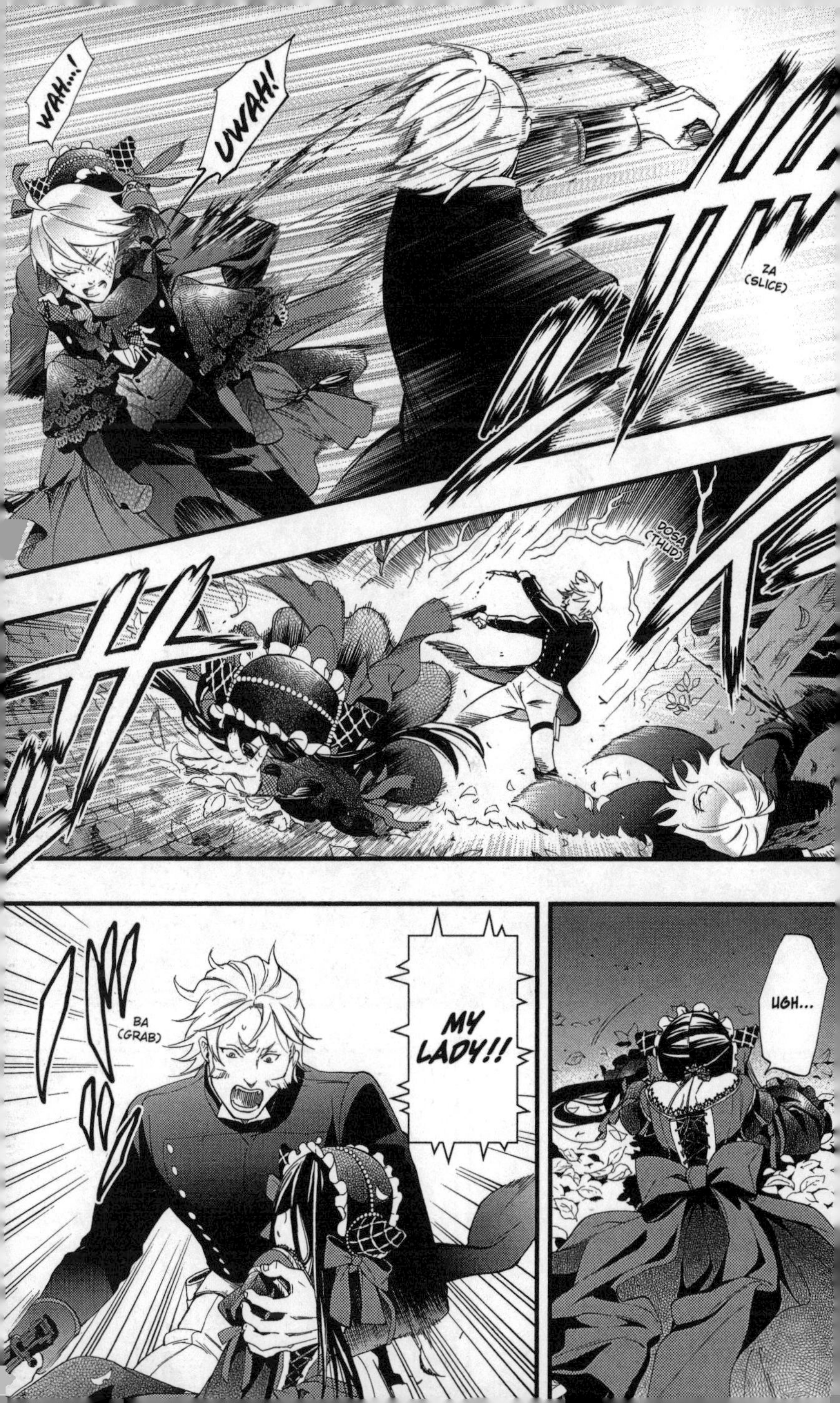
ZA
(SLICE)
UWAH!
WAH...!
DOSA
(THUD)
UGH...
MY LADY!!
BA
(GRAB)

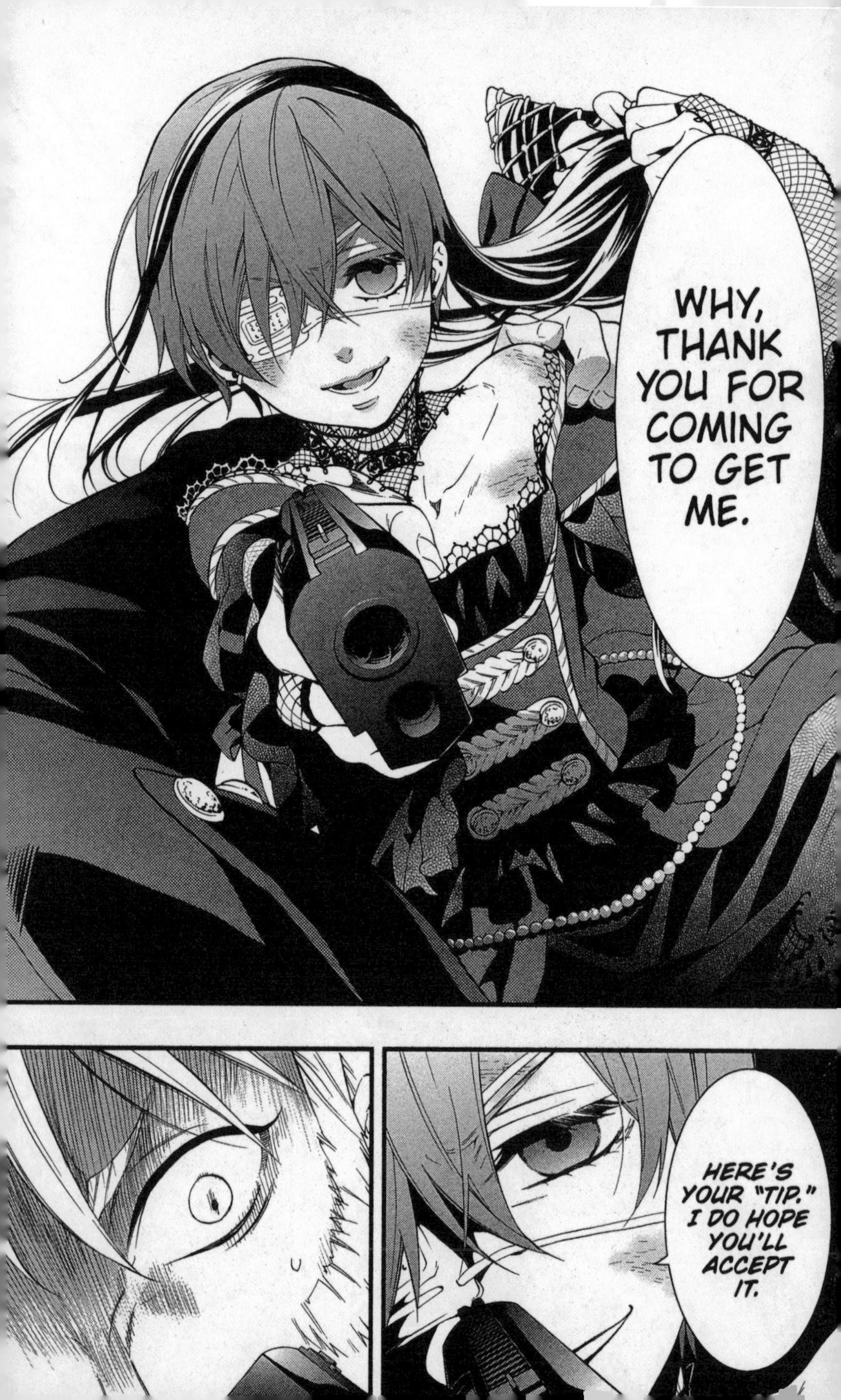
WHY, THANK YOU FOR COMING TO GET ME.
HERE'S YOUR "TIP." I DO HOPE YOU'LL ACCEPT IT.

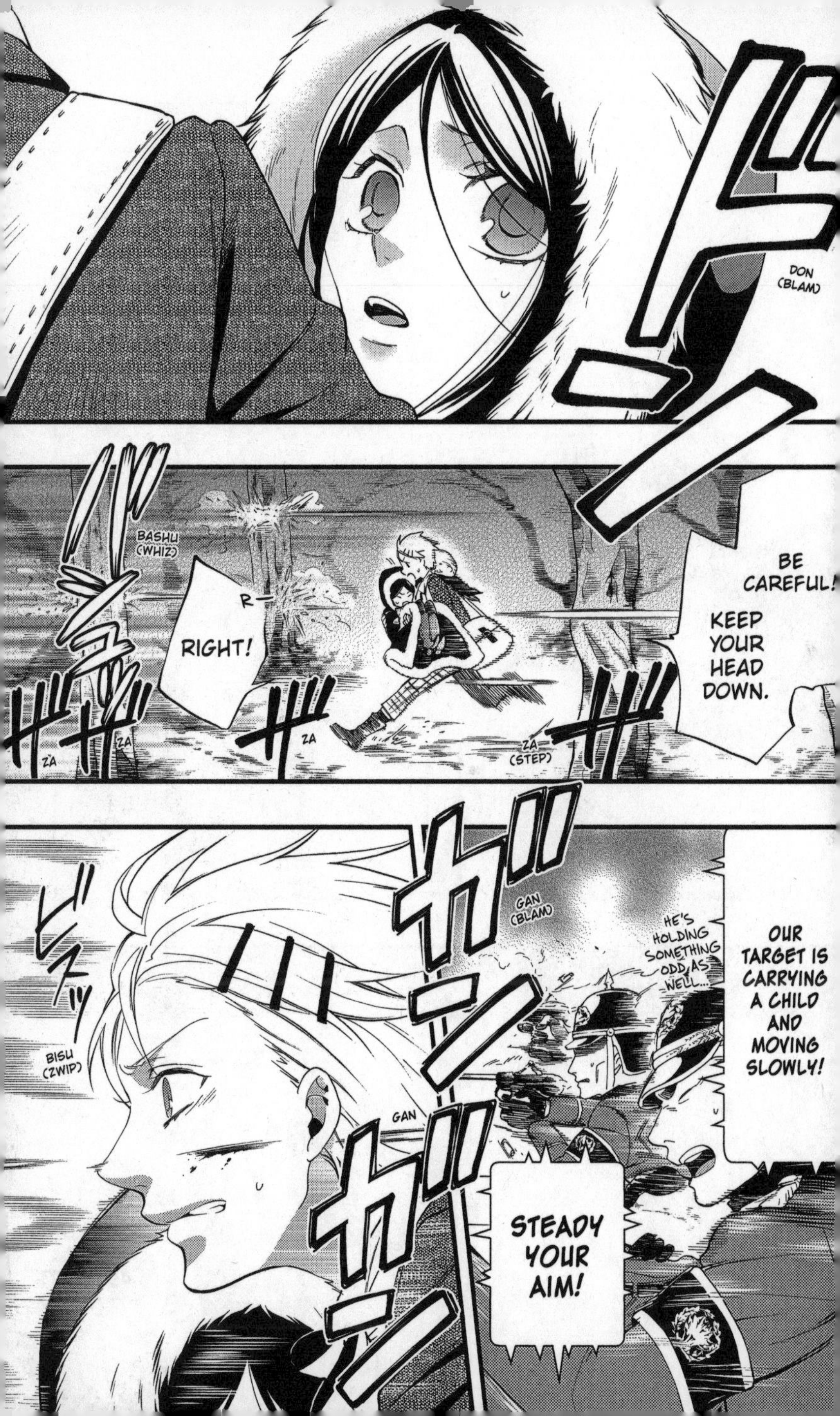
DON (BLAM)
BE CAREFUL!
KEEP YOUR HEAD DOWN.
BASHU (WHIZ)
R—
RIGHT!
ZA (STEP)
ZA
ZA
ZA
OUR TARGET IS CARRYING A CHILD AND MOVING SLOWLY!
HE'S HOLDING SOMETHING ODD AS WELL...
GAN (BLAM)
STEADY YOUR AIM!
GAN
BISU (ZWIP)

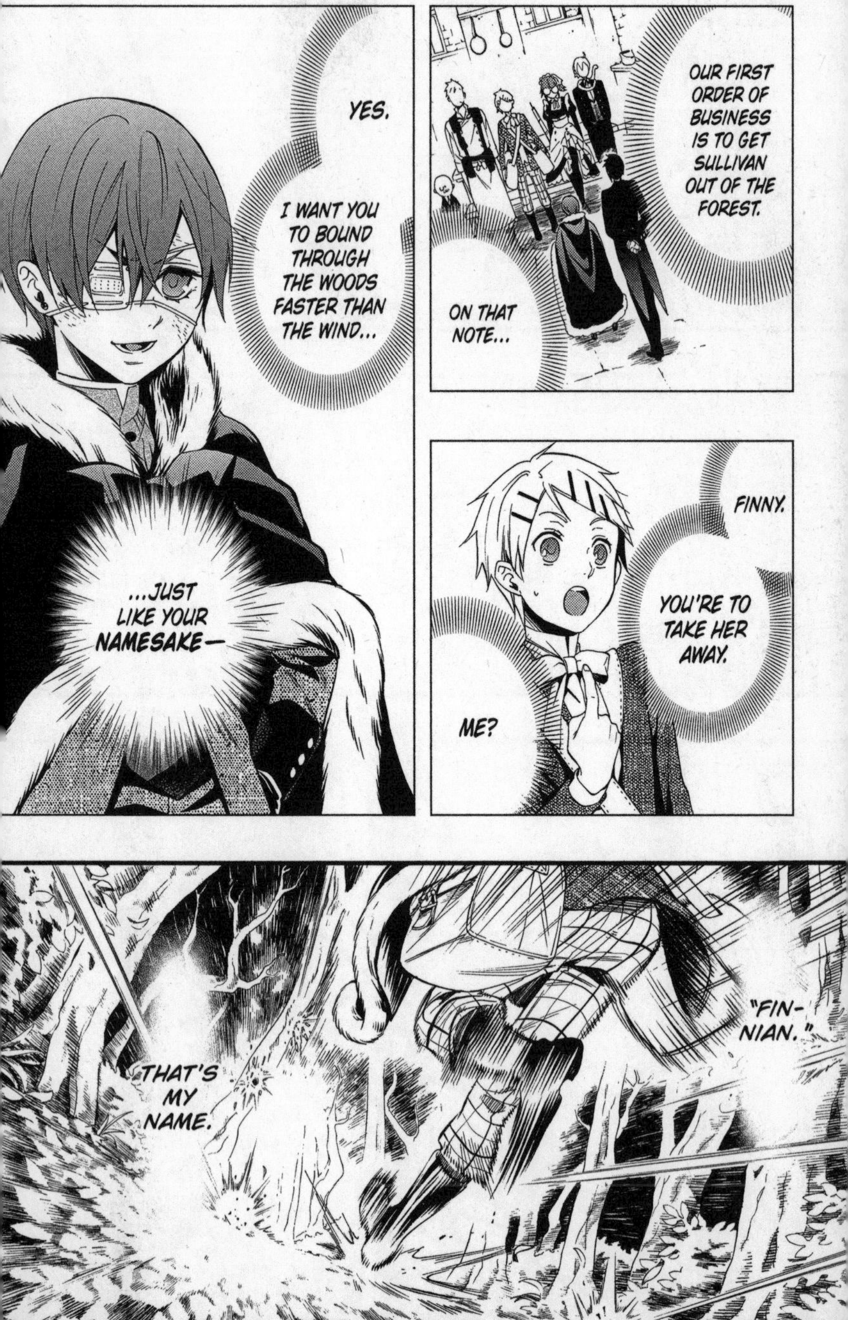
OUR FIRST ORDER OF BUSINESS IS TO GET SULLIVAN OUT OF THE FOREST.
ON THAT NOTE...
FINNY.
YOU'RE TO TAKE HER AWAY.
ME?
YES.
I WANT YOU TO BOUND THROUGH THE WOODS FASTER THAN THE WIND...
...JUST LIKE YOUR NAMESAKE—
"FIN-NIAN."
THAT'S MY NAME.

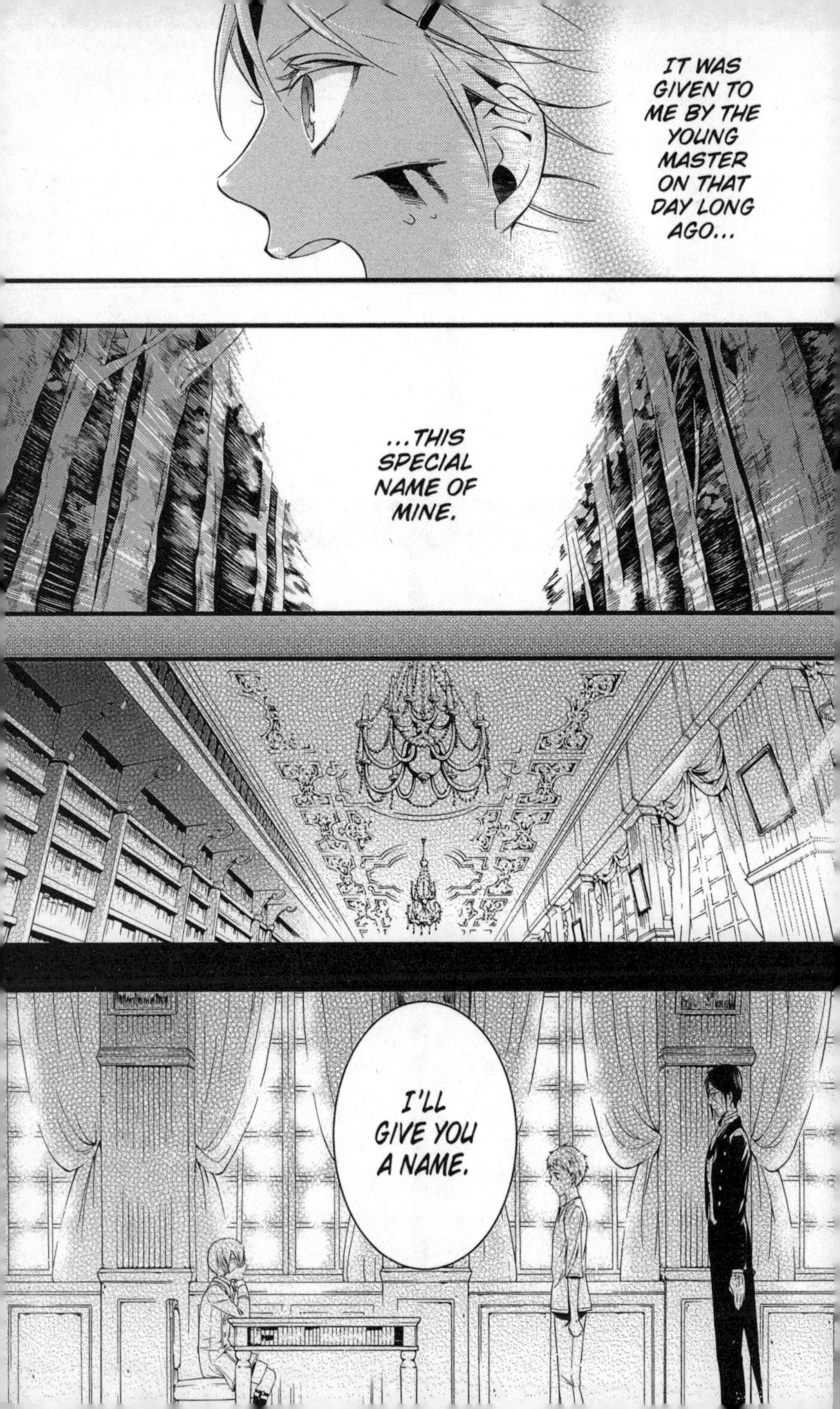
IT WAS GIVEN TO ME BY THE YOUNG MASTER ON THAT DAY LONG AGO...
...THIS SPECIAL NAME OF MINE.
I'LL GIVE YOU A NAME.

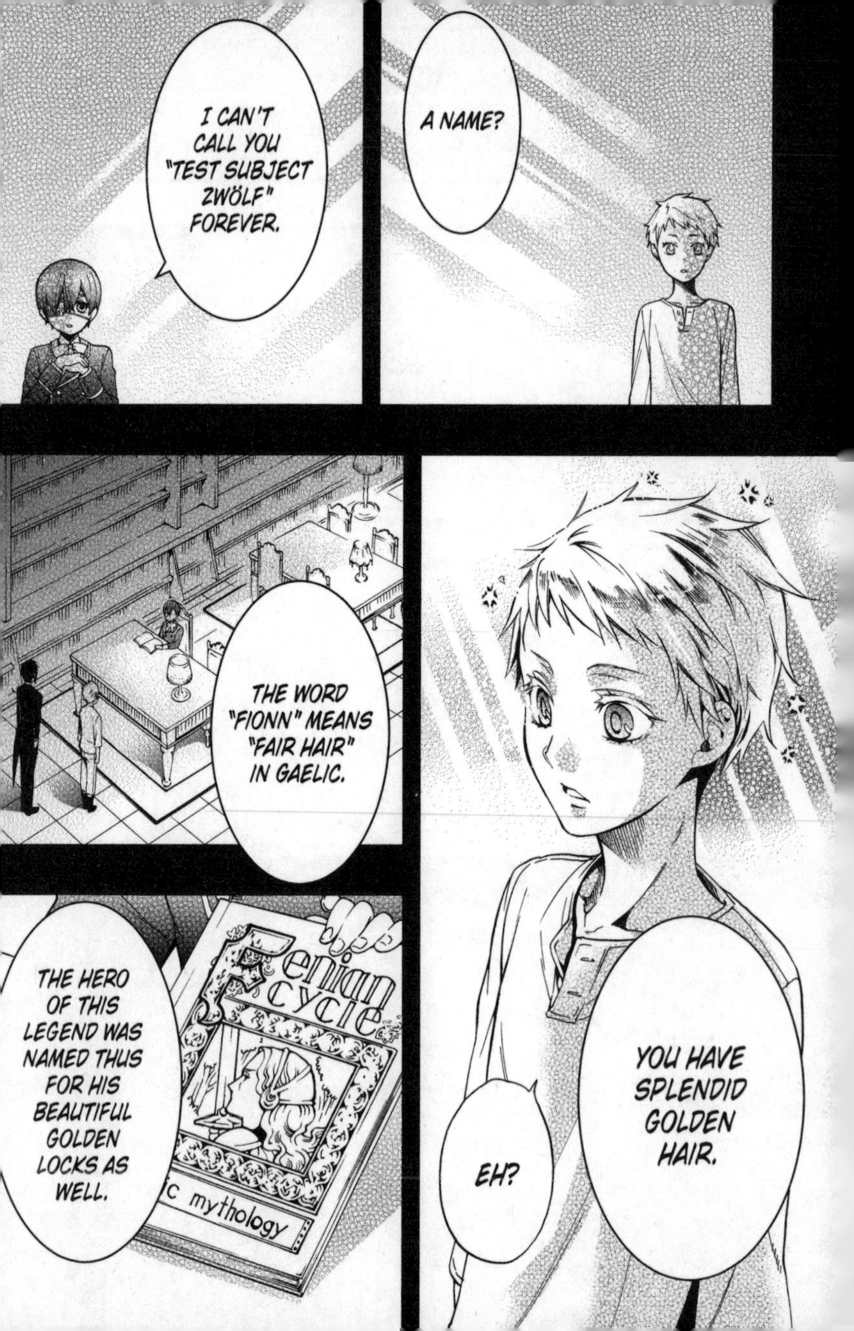
A NAME?
I CAN'T CALL YOU "TEST SUBJECT ZWÖLF" FOREVER.
YOU HAVE SPLENDID GOLDEN HAIR.
EH?
THE WORD "FIONN" MEANS "FAIR HAIR" IN GAELIC.
THE HERO OF THIS LEGEND WAS NAMED THUS FOR HIS BEAUTIFUL GOLDEN LOCKS AS WELL.
Fenian cycle

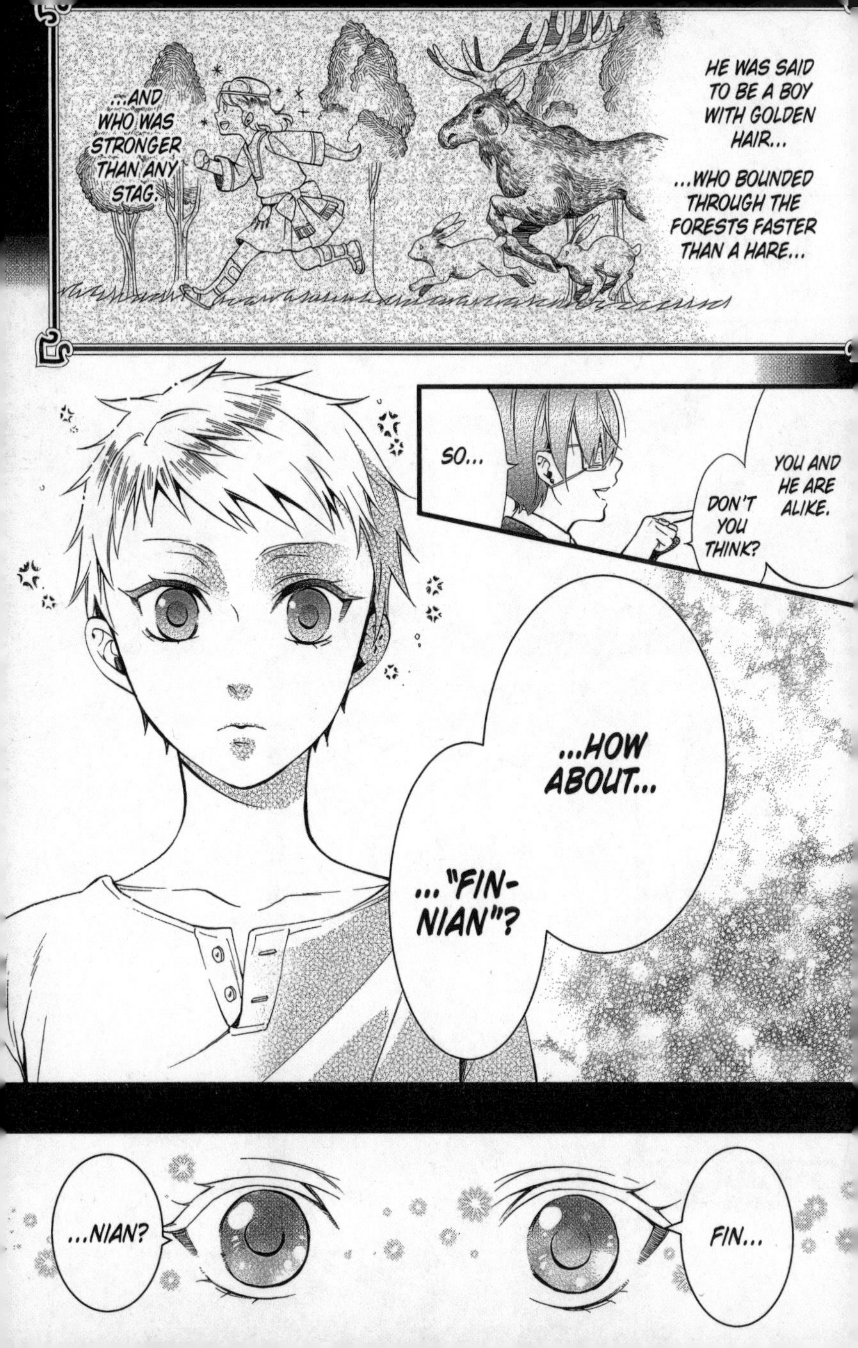
HE WAS SAID TO BE A BOY WITH GOLDEN HAIR...
...WHO BOUNDED THROUGH THE FORESTS FASTER THAN A HARE...
...AND WHO WAS STRONGER THAN ANY STAG.
YOU AND HE ARE ALIKE.
DON'T YOU THINK?
SO...
...HOW ABOUT...
..."FIN-NIAN"?
FIN...
...NIAN?

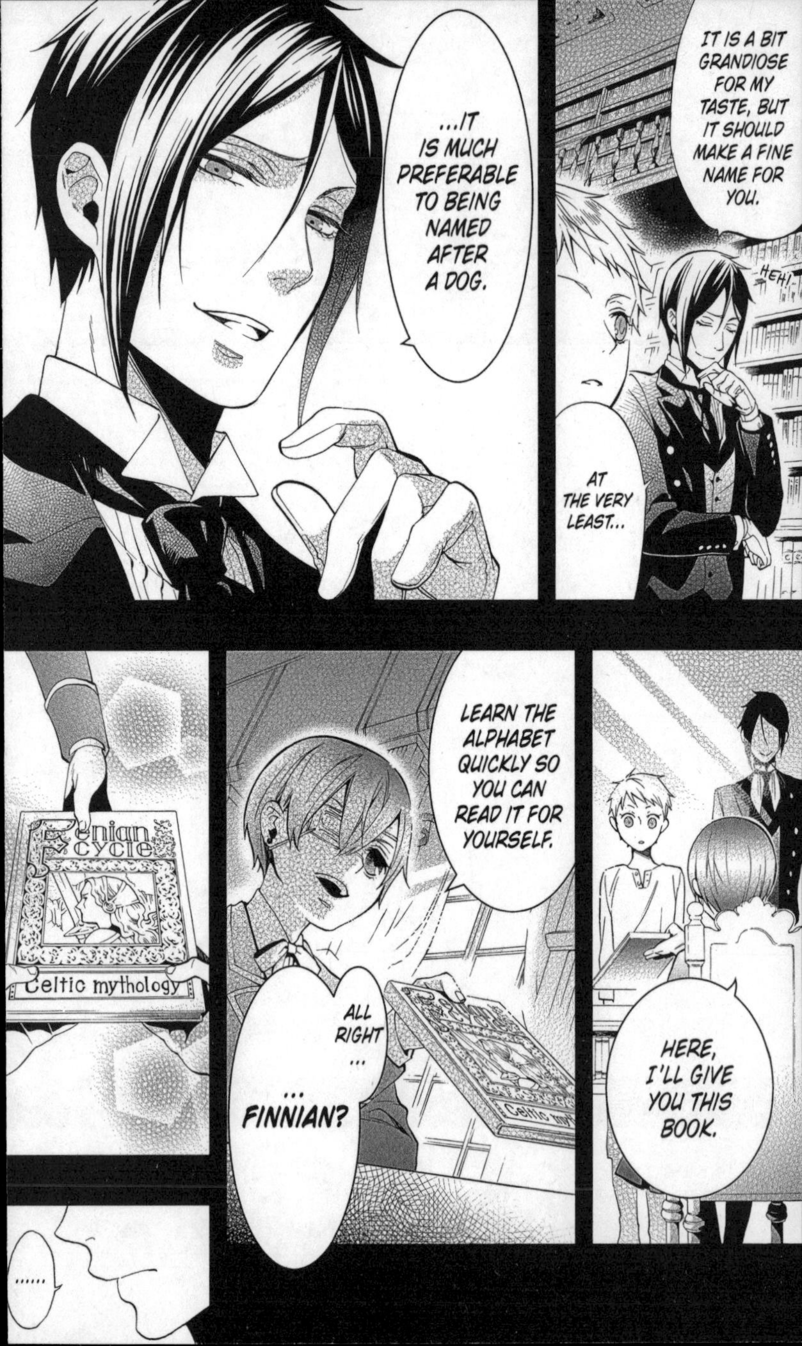
IT IS A BIT GRANDIOSE FOR MY TASTE, BUT IT SHOULD MAKE A FINE NAME FOR YOU.
HEH!
AT THE VERY LEAST...
...IT IS MUCH PREFERABLE TO BEING NAMED AFTER A DOG.
HERE, I'LL GIVE YOU THIS BOOK.
LEARN THE ALPHABET QUICKLY SO YOU CAN READ IT FOR YOURSELF.
ALL RIGHT ...
... FINNIAN?
Fenian cycle
Celtic mythology
......

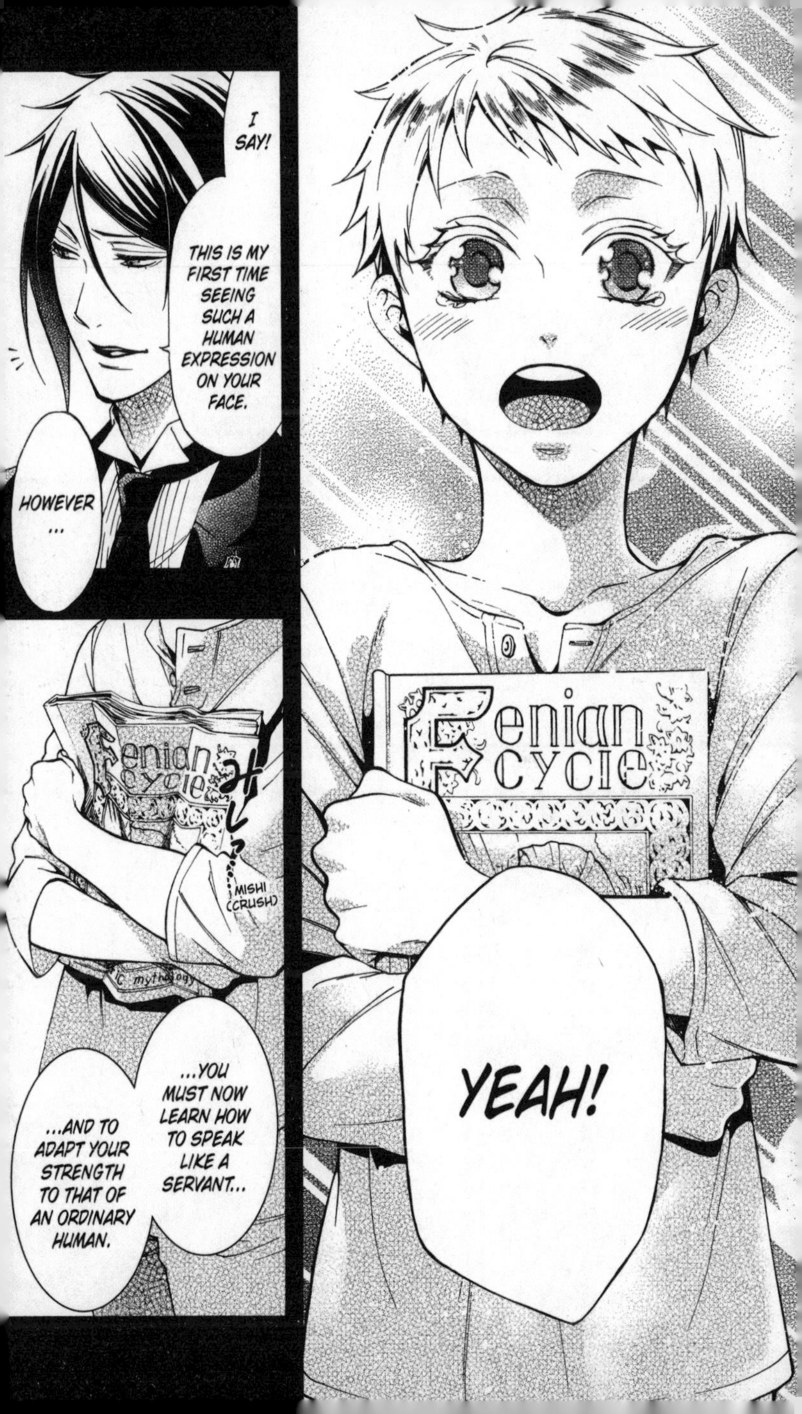
Fenian cycle
YEAH!
I SAY!
THIS IS MY FIRST TIME SEEING SUCH A HUMAN EXPRESSION ON YOUR FACE.
HOWEVER...
Fenian cycle
MISHI (CRUSH)
...YOU MUST NOW LEARN HOW TO SPEAK LIKE A SERVANT...
...AND TO ADAPT YOUR STRENGTH TO THAT OF AN ORDINARY HUMAN.

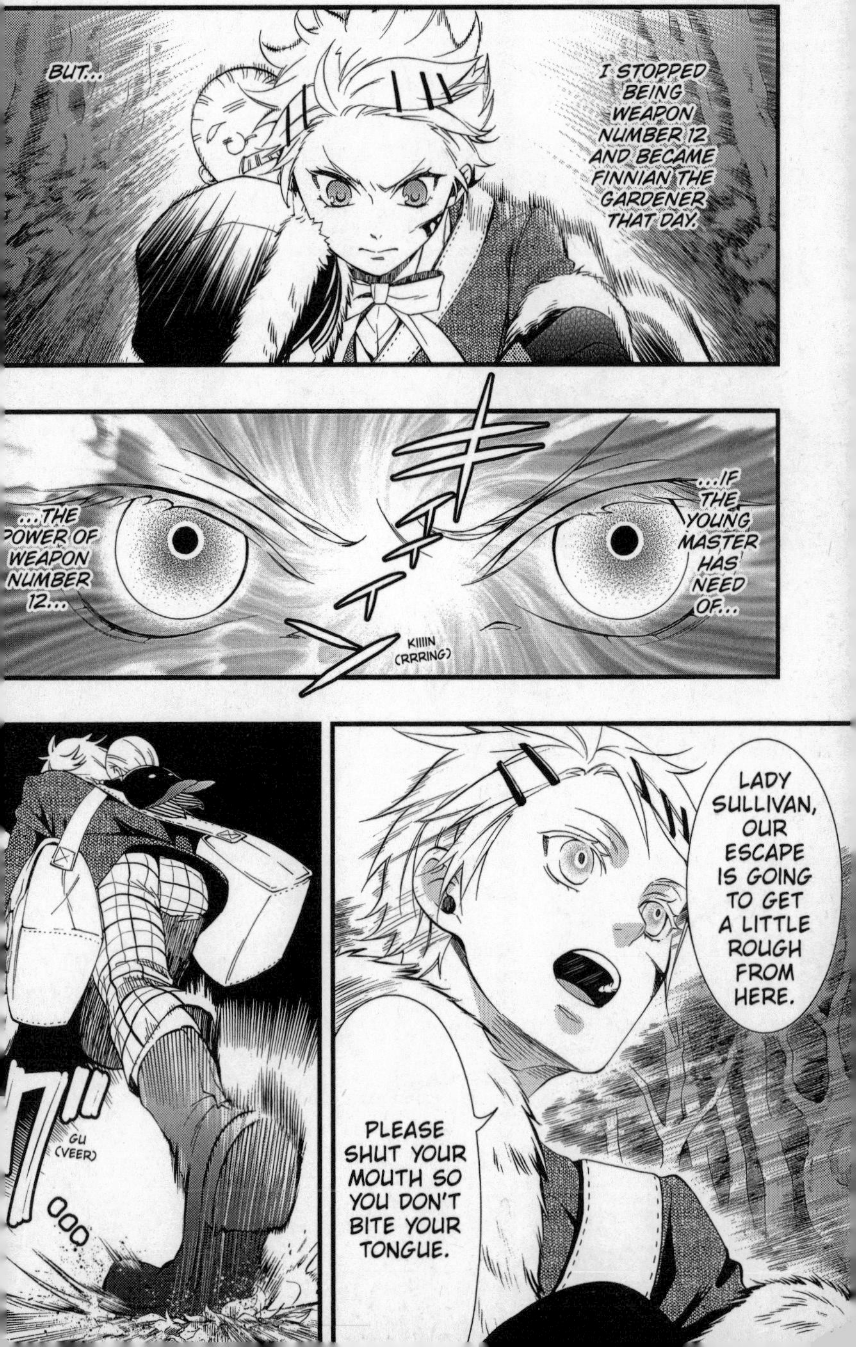
I STOPPED BEING WEAPON NUMBER 12 AND BECAME FINNIAN THE GARDENER THAT DAY.
BUT...
...IF THE YOUNG MASTER HAS NEED OF...
KIIIN (RRRING)
...THE POWER OF WEAPON NUMBER 12...
LADY SULLIVAN, OUR ESCAPE IS GOING TO GET A LITTLE ROUGH FROM HERE.
PLEASE SHUT YOUR MOUTH SO YOU DON'T BITE YOUR TONGUE.
GU (VEER)

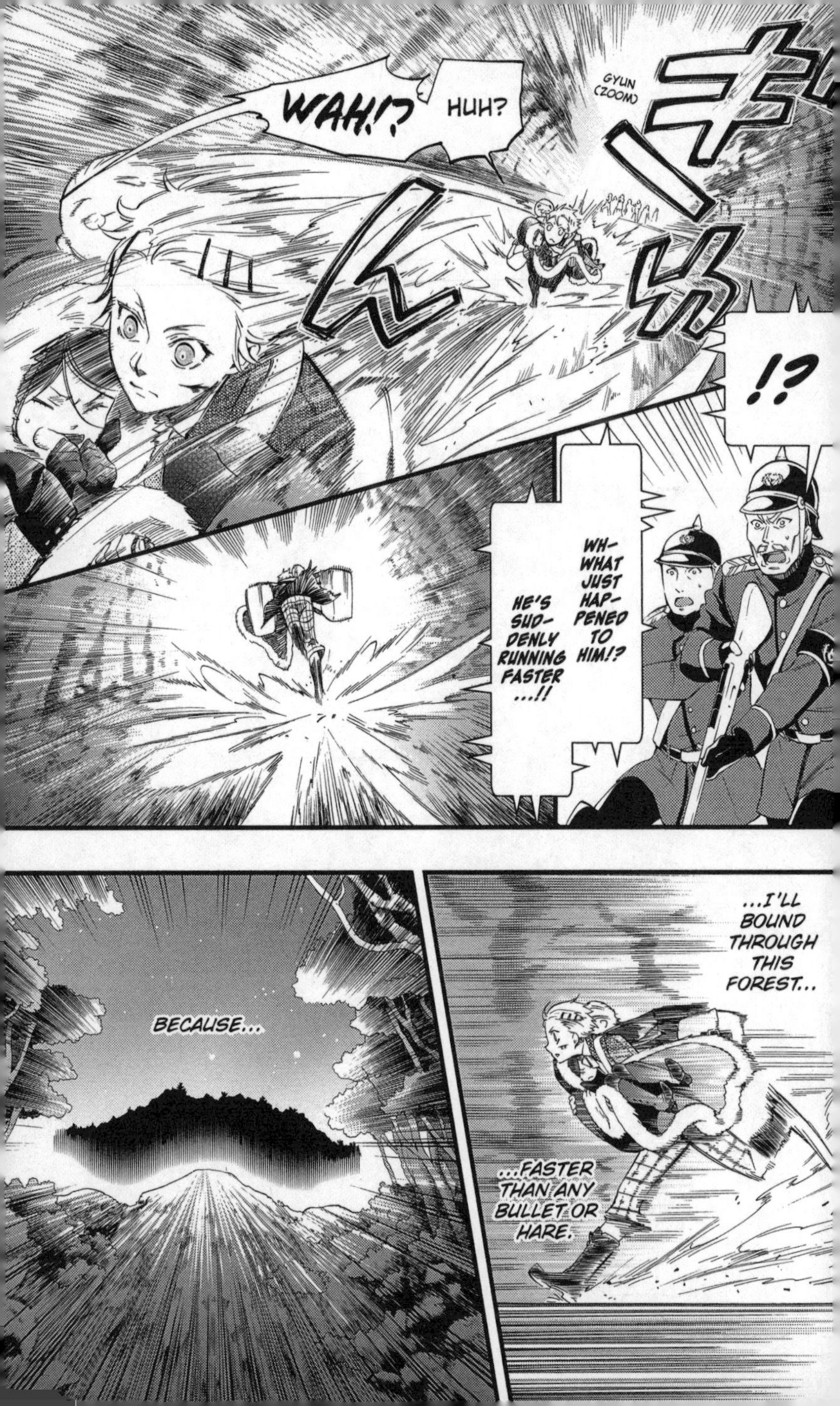
GYUN (ZOOM)
HUH?
WAH!?
!?
WH-WHAT JUST HAPPENED TO HIM!?
HE'S SUDDENLY RUNNING FASTER...!!
...I'LL BOUND THROUGH THIS FOREST...
...FASTER THAN ANY BULLET OR HARE.
BECAUSE...

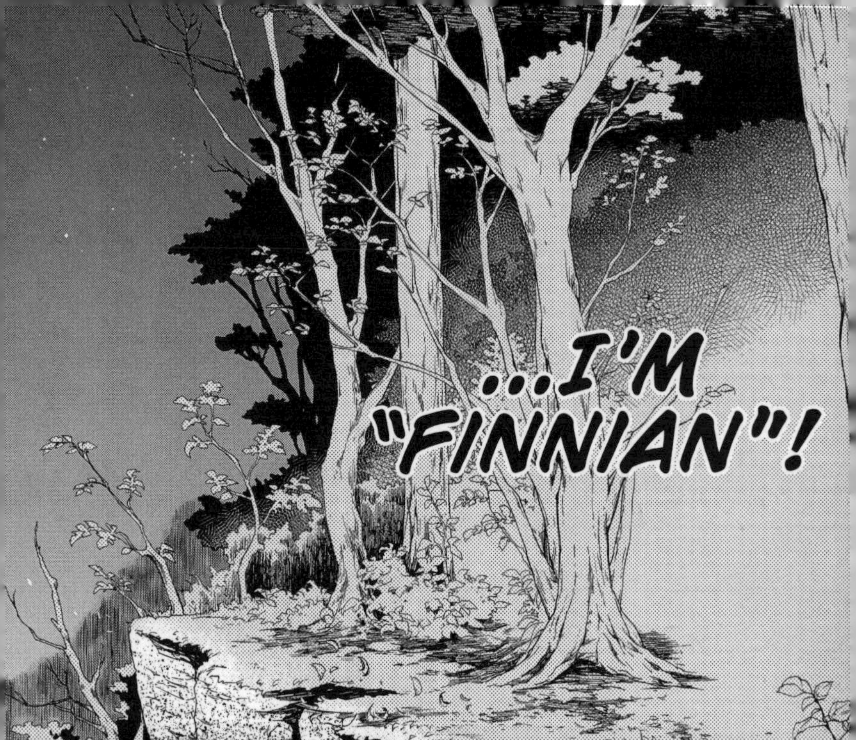
..."I'M "FINNIAN"!
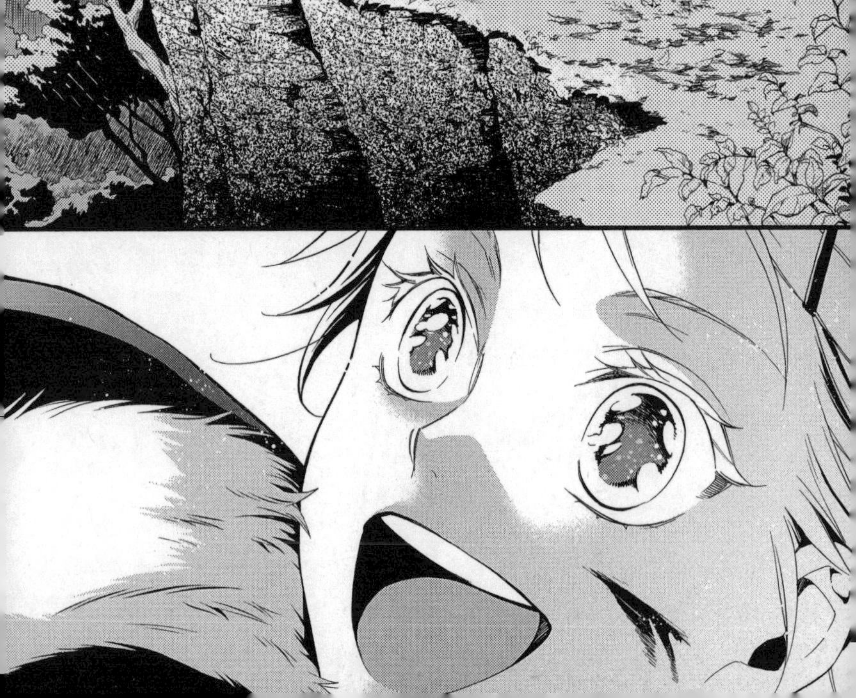

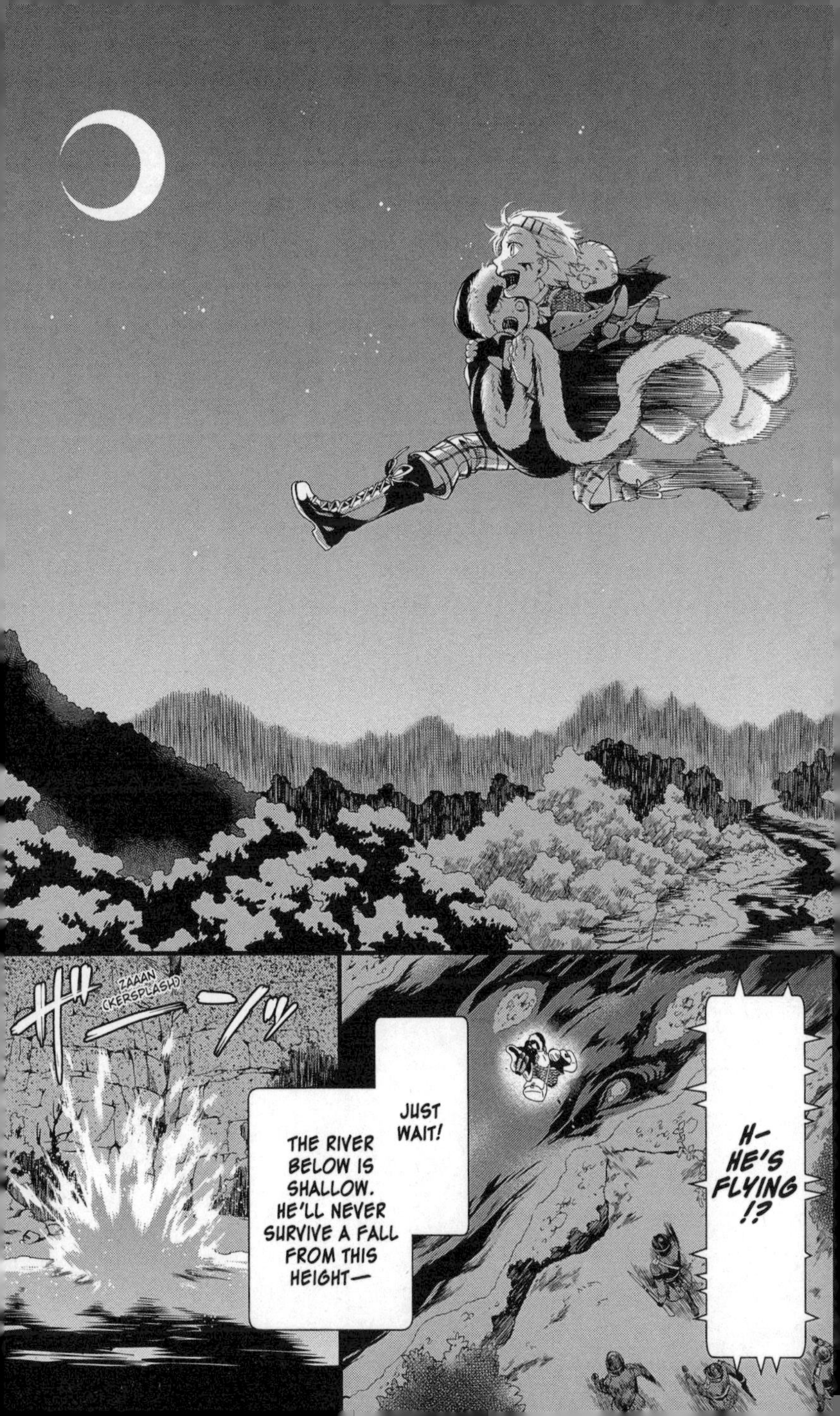
H-HE'S FLYING!?
JUST WAIT!
THE RIVER BELOW IS SHALLOW. HE'LL NEVER SURVIVE A FALL FROM THIS HEIGHT—
ZAAAN (KERSPLASH)

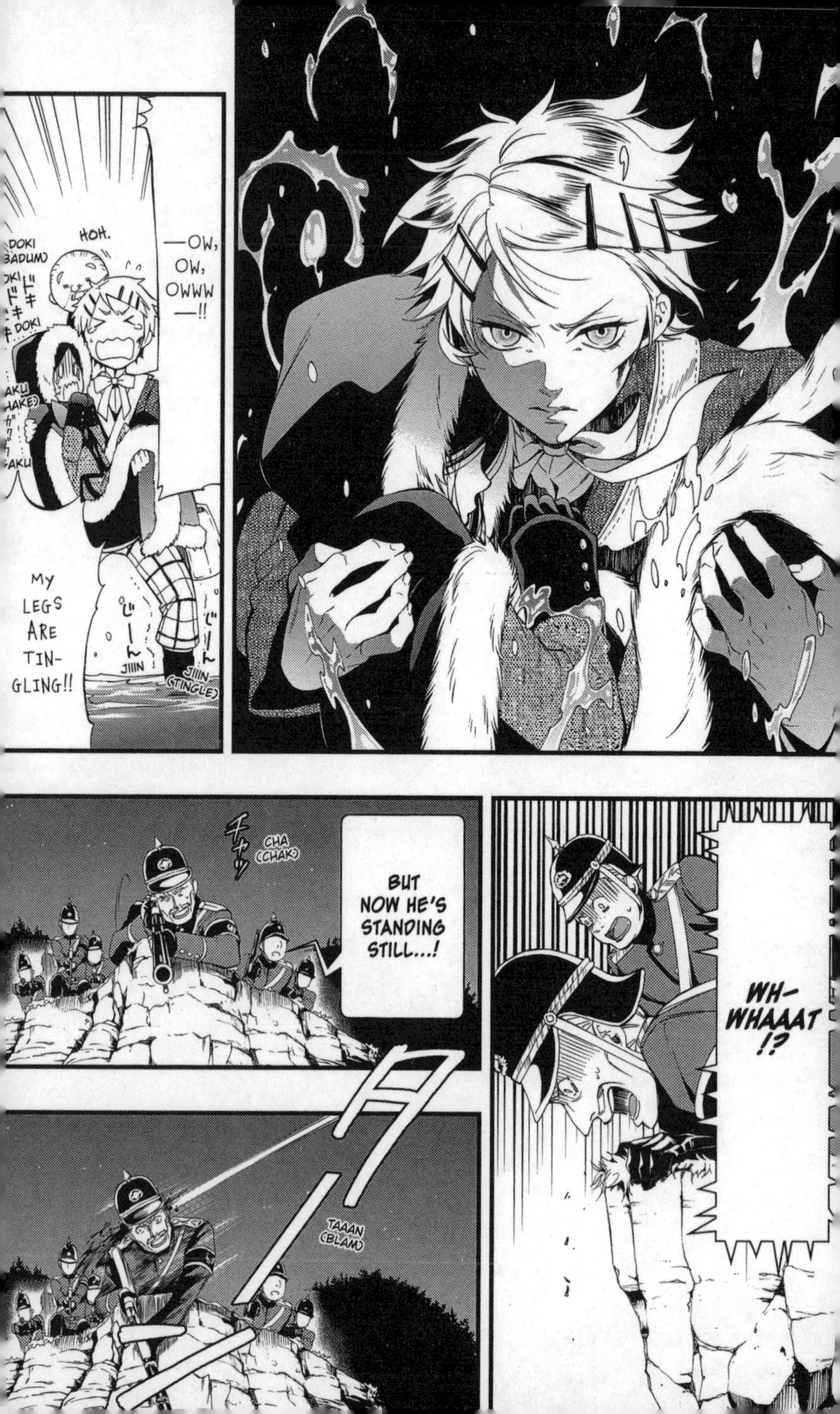
—OW, OW, OWWW—!!
HOH.
DOKI
DOKI
MY LEGS ARE TIN-GLING!!
JIIIN
JIIIN (TINGLE)
WH-WHAAAT!?
CHA (CHAK)
BUT NOW HE'S STANDING STILL...!
TAAAN (BLAM)

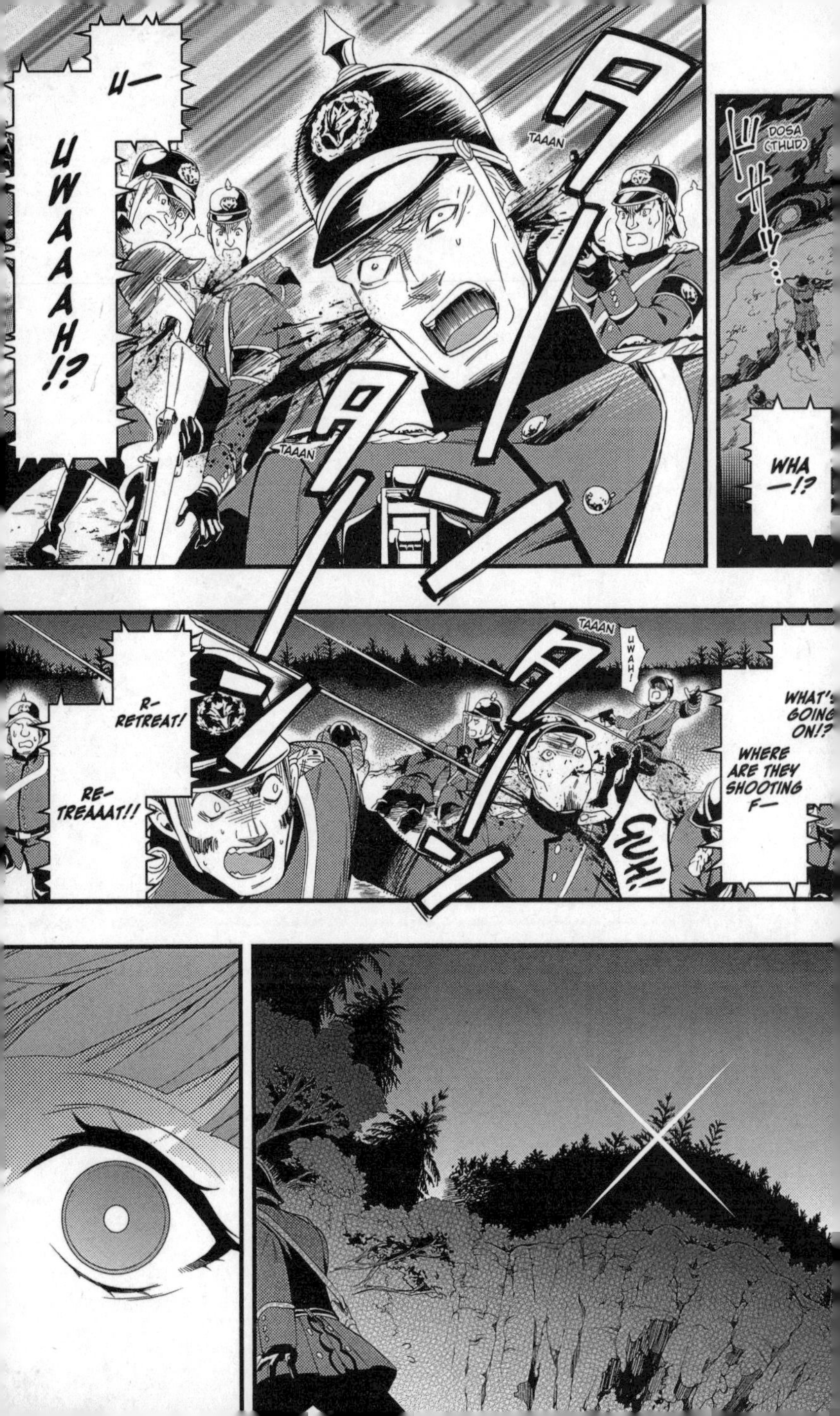
DOSA (THUD)
WHA—!?
TAAAN
U—
UWAAAAAH!?
TAAAN
WHAT'S GOING ON!?
WHERE ARE THEY SHOOTING F—
TAAAN
UWAH!
GUH!
R-RETREAT!
RE-TREAAAT!!

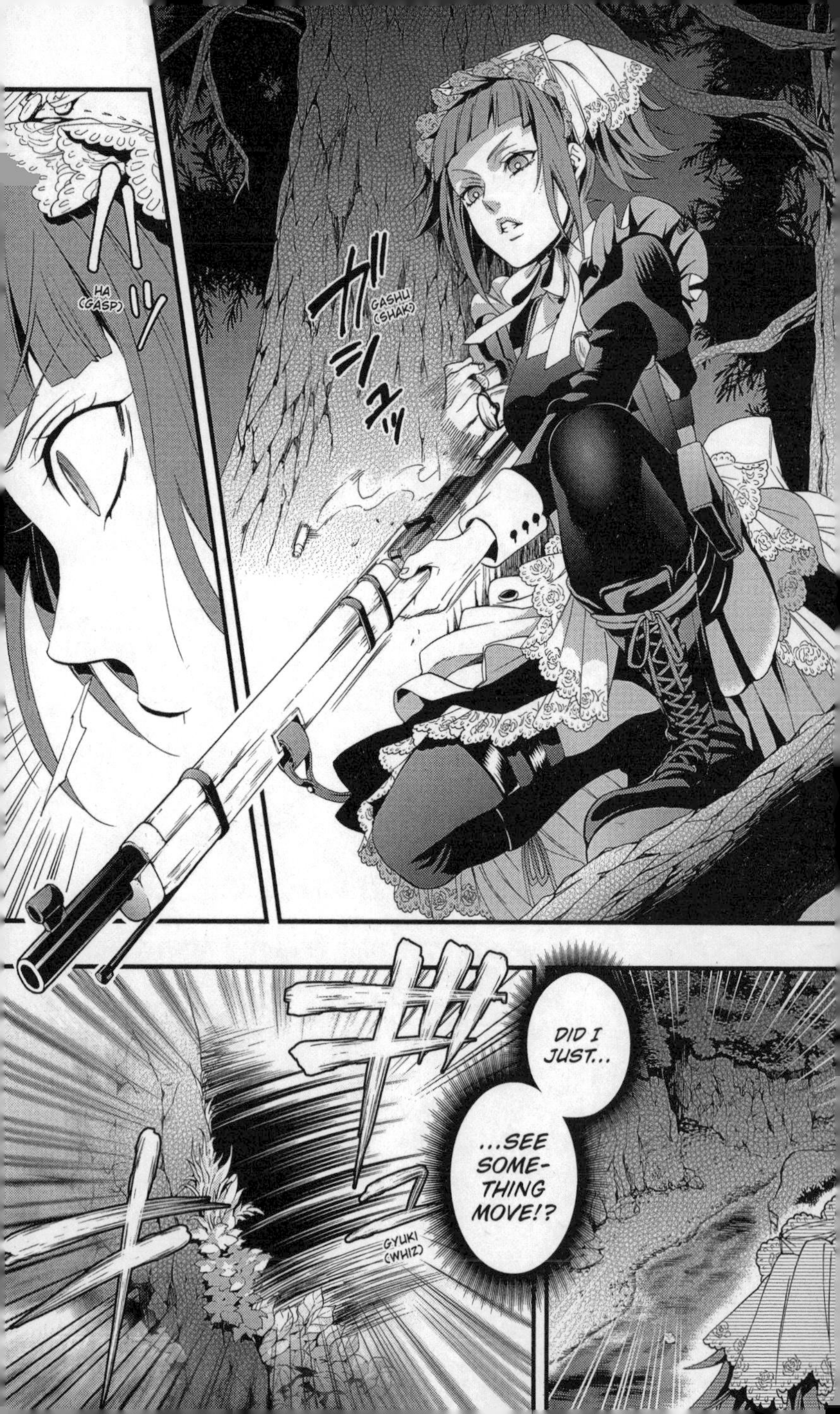
GASHU (SHAK)
HA (GASP)
DID I JUST...
...SEE SOME-THING MOVE!?
GYUKI (WHIZ)

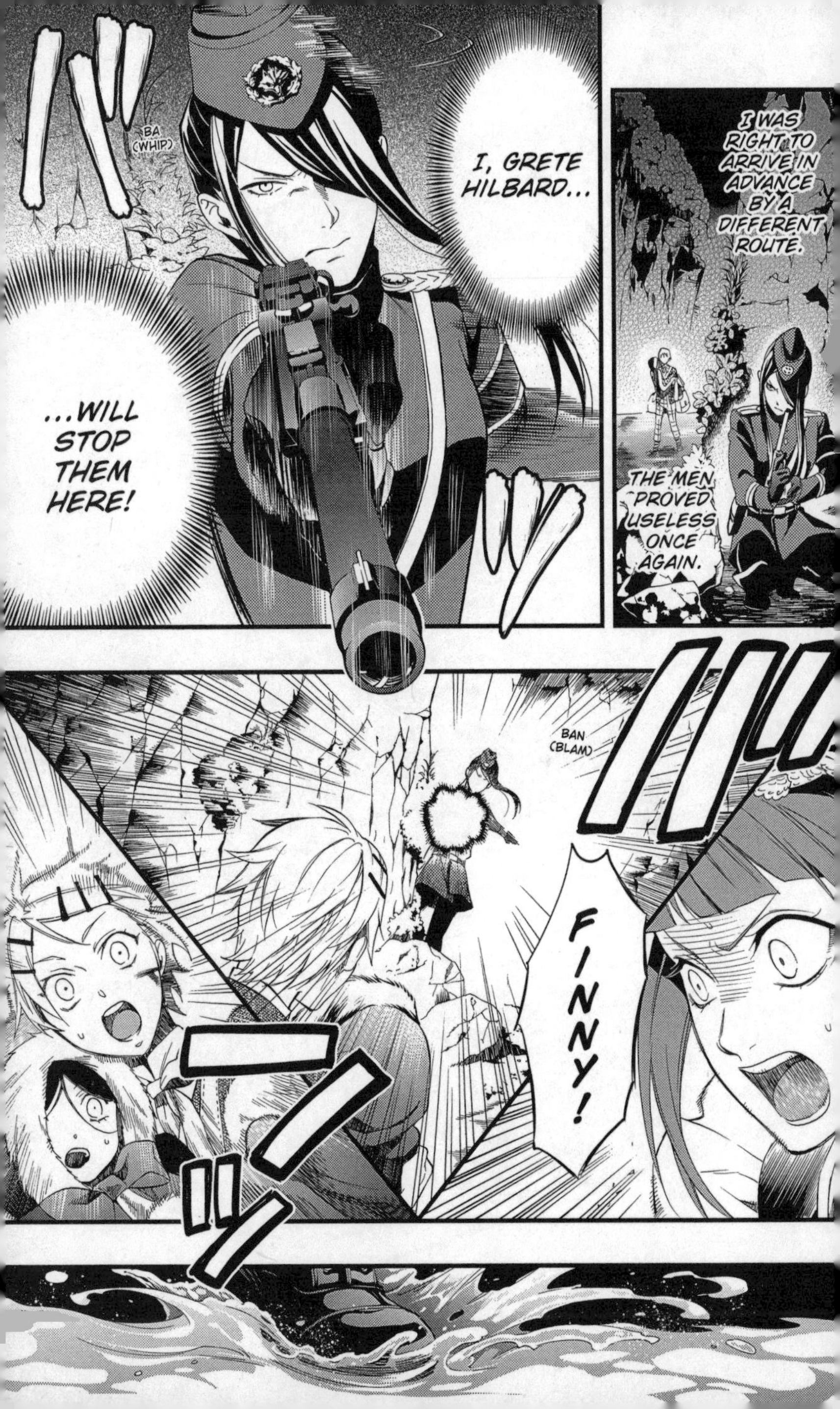
I WAS RIGHT TO ARRIVE IN ADVANCE BY A DIFFERENT ROUTE.
THE MEN PROVED USELESS ONCE AGAIN.
I, GRETE HILBARD...
BA (WHIP)
...WILL STOP THEM HERE!
BAN (BLAM)
FINNY!

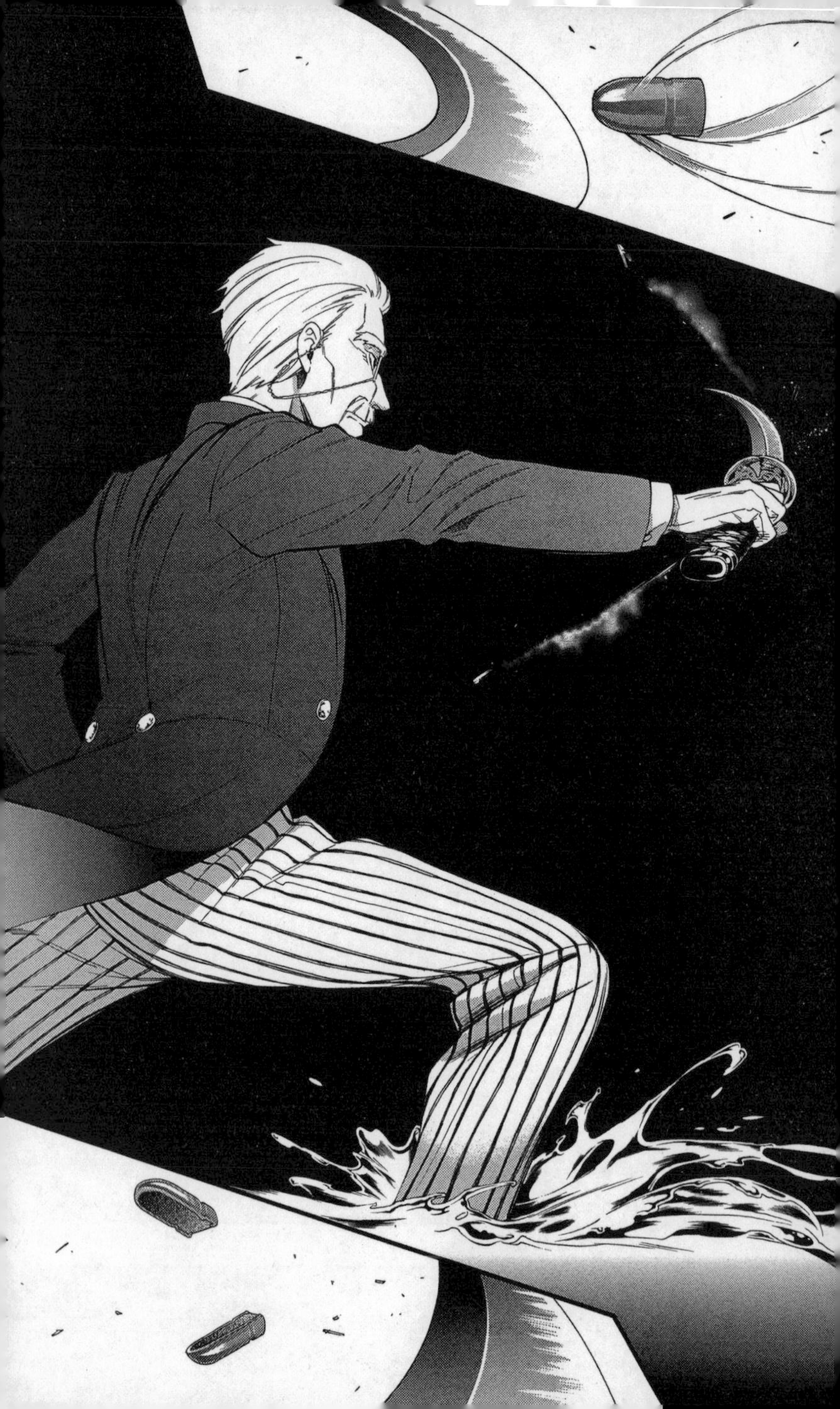

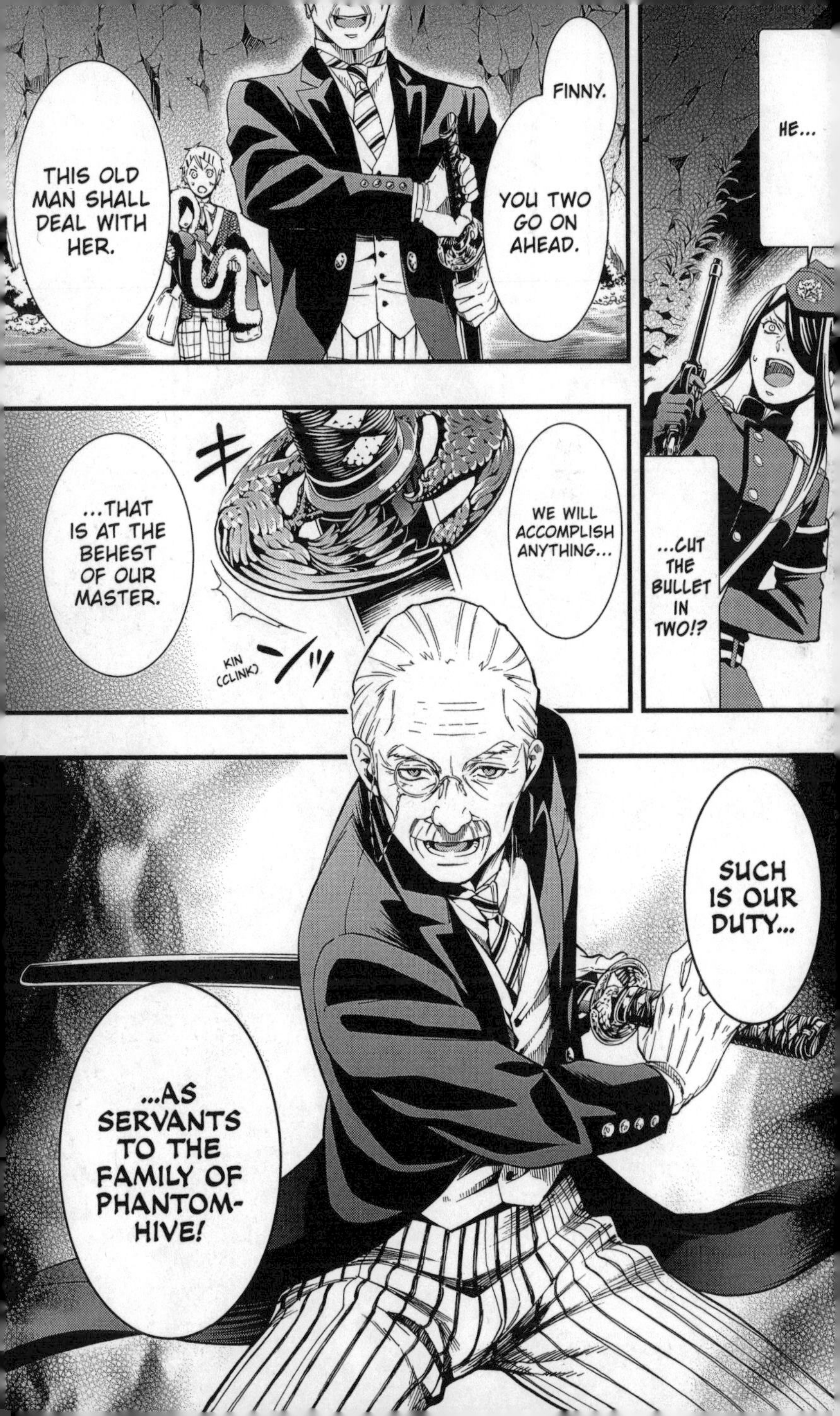
HE...
...CUT THE BULLET IN TWO!?
FINNY.
YOU TWO GO ON AHEAD.
THIS OLD MAN SHALL DEAL WITH HER.
WE WILL ACCOMPLISH ANYTHING...
...THAT IS AT THE BEHEST OF OUR MASTER.
KIN (CLINK)
SUCH IS OUR DUTY...
...AS SERVANTS TO THE FAMILY OF PHANTOM-HIVE!

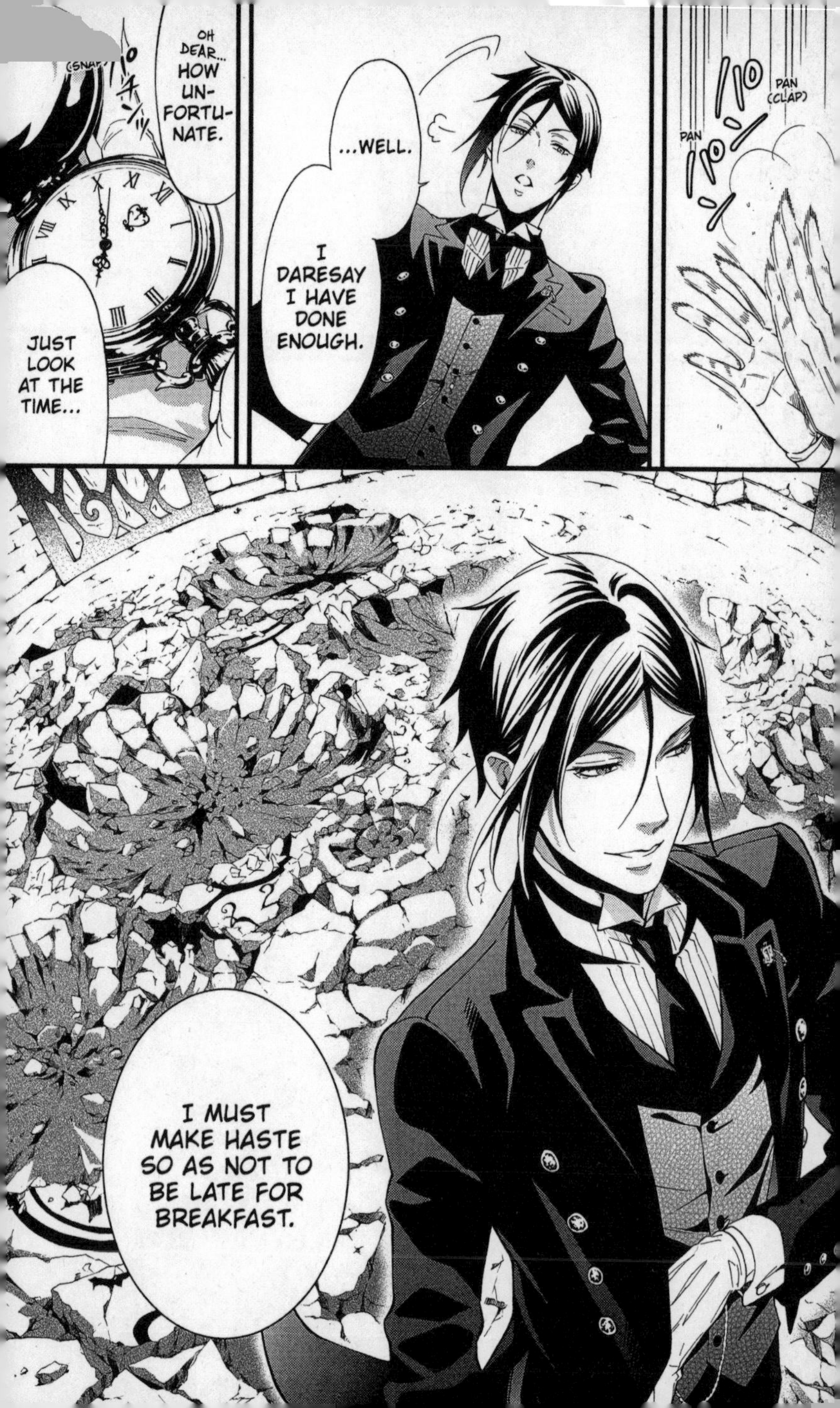

PAN (CLAP)
PAN
...WELL.
I DARESAY I HAVE DONE ENOUGH.
(SNAP
OH DEAR... HOW UN-FORTUNATE.
JUST LOOK AT THE TIME...
I MUST MAKE HASTE SO AS NOT TO BE LATE FOR BREAKFAST.

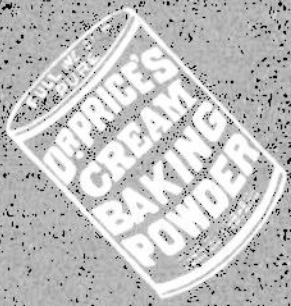
DR PRICE'S
CREAM
BAKING
POWDER

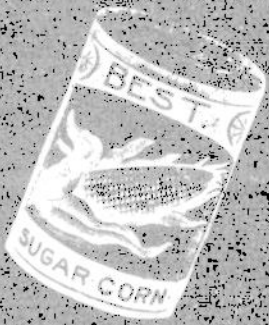
BEST
SUGAR CORN

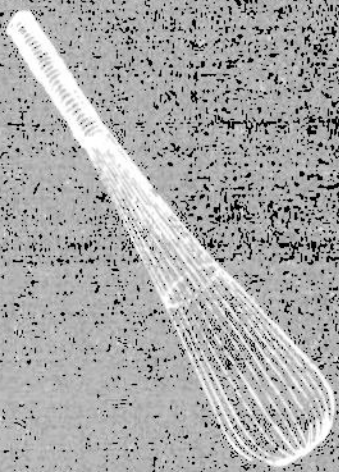

Black Butler

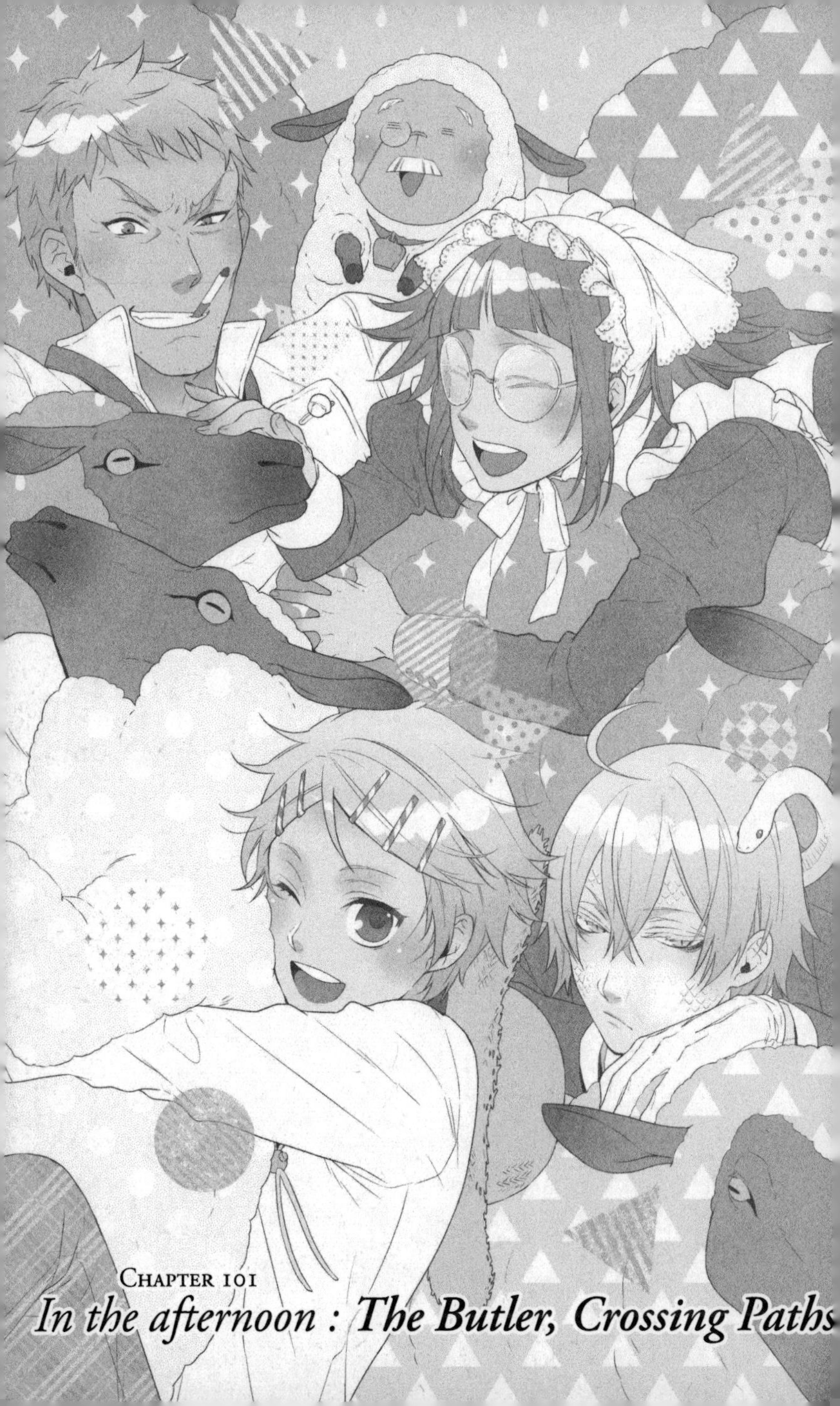

CHAPTER 101

In the afternoon : The Butler, Crossing Paths

Black Butler

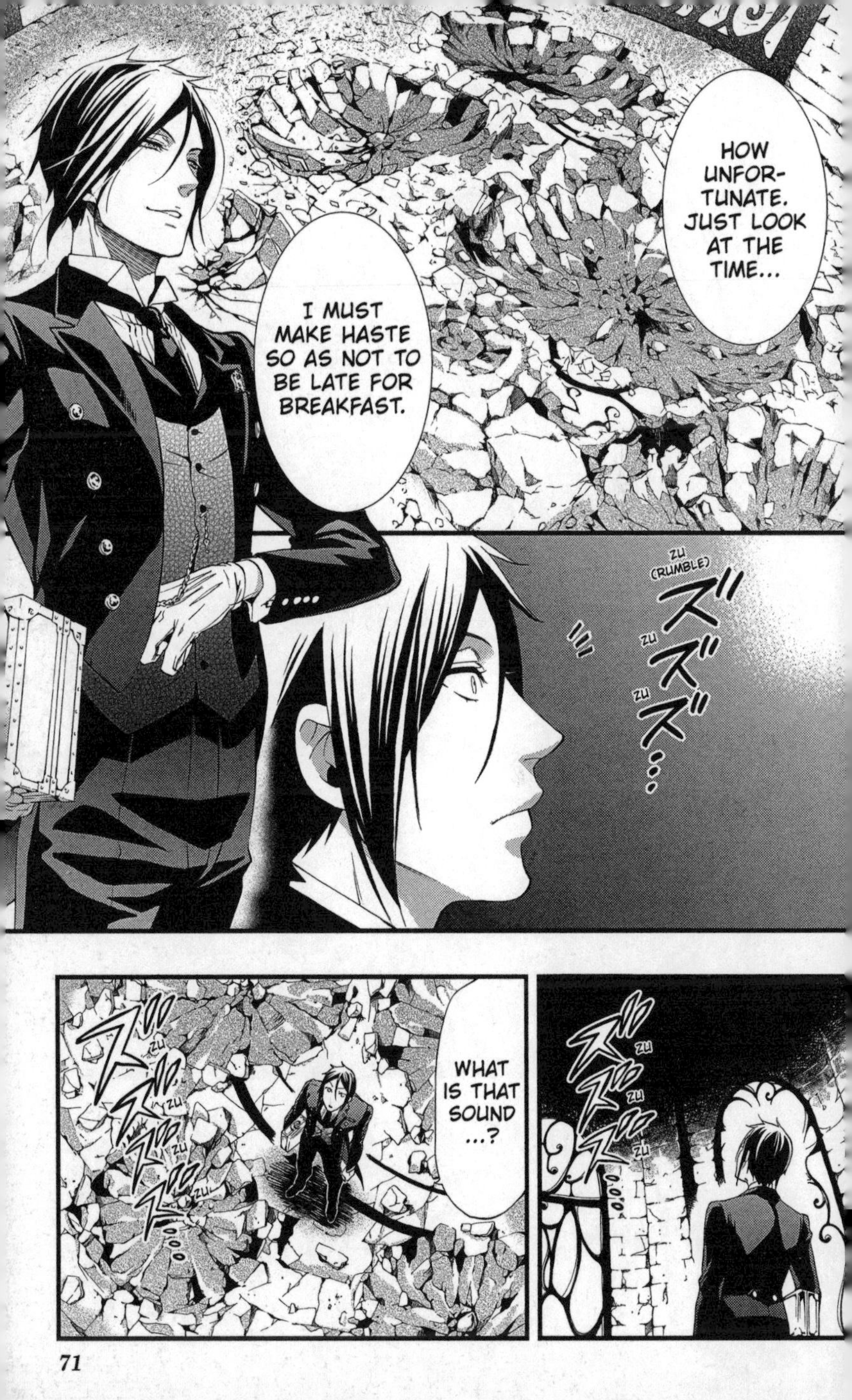
HOW UNFORTUNATE. JUST LOOK AT THE TIME...
I MUST MAKE HASTE SO AS NOT TO BE LATE FOR BREAKFAST.
ZU (RUMBLE)
ズズズ…
ZU
ZU
ZU
ZU
ZU
WHAT IS THAT SOUND ...?
ZU
ZU
ZU
ZU

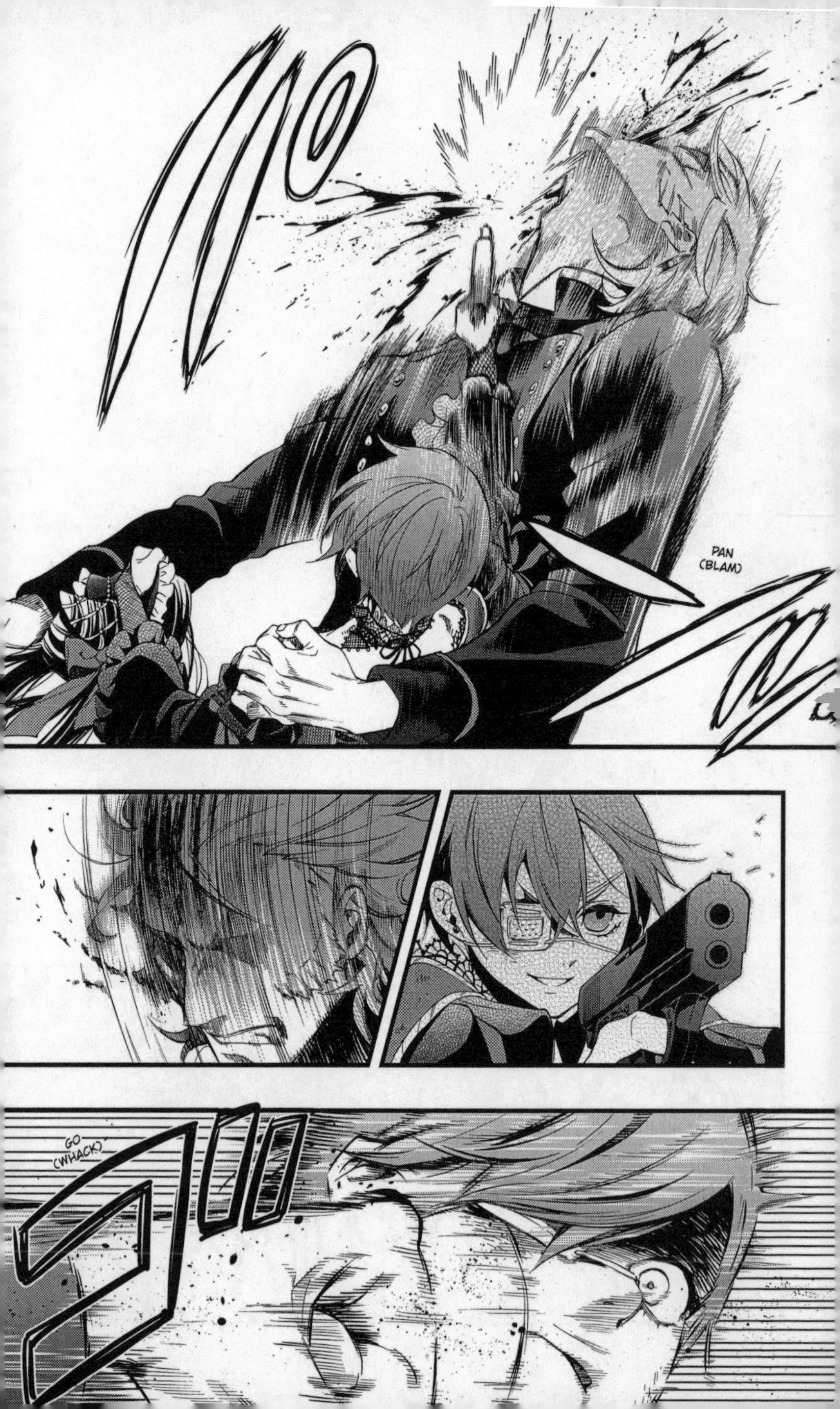
PAN
(BLAM)
GO
(WHACK)

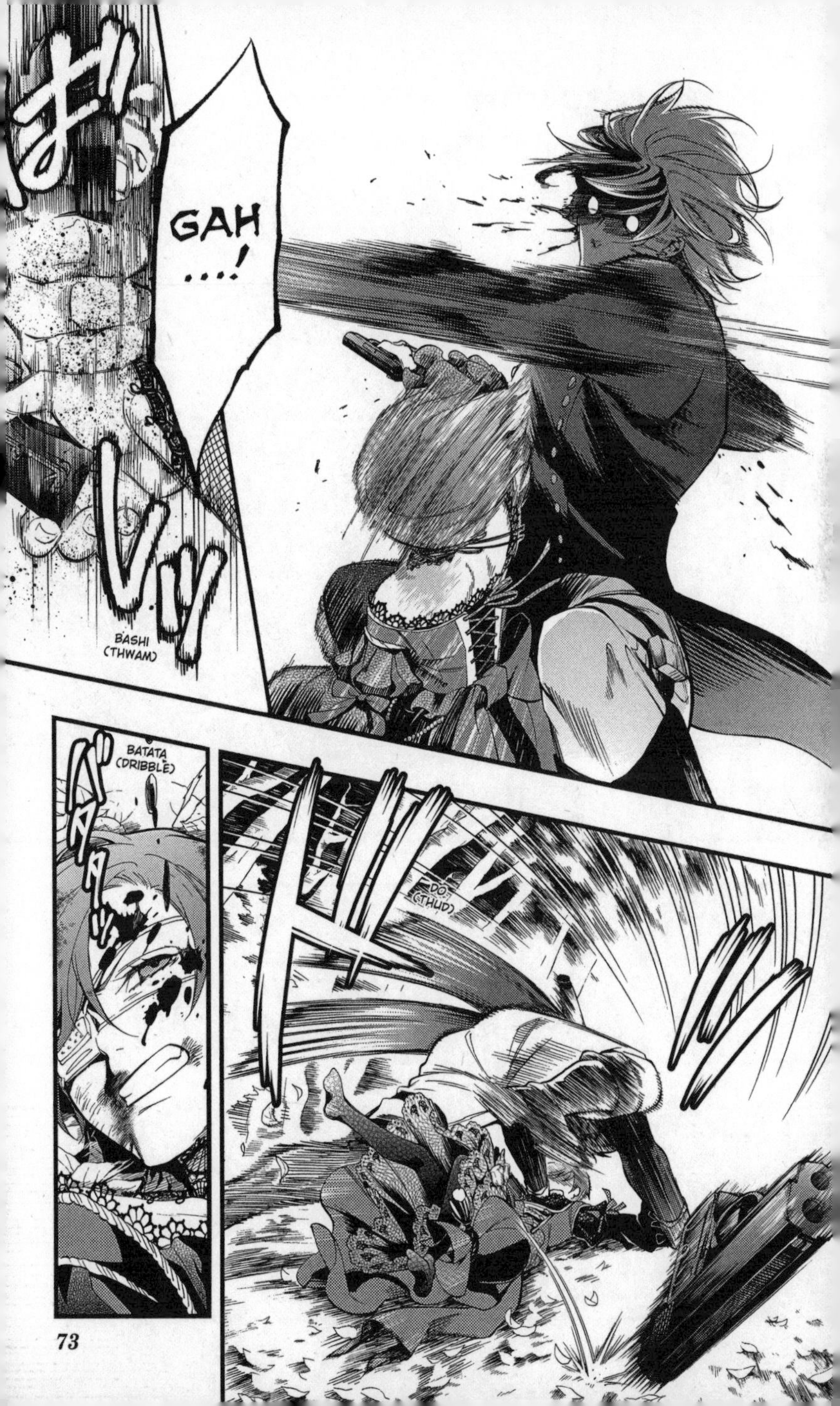
GAH ...!
BASHI (THWAM)
DO (THUD)
BATATA (DRIBBLE)

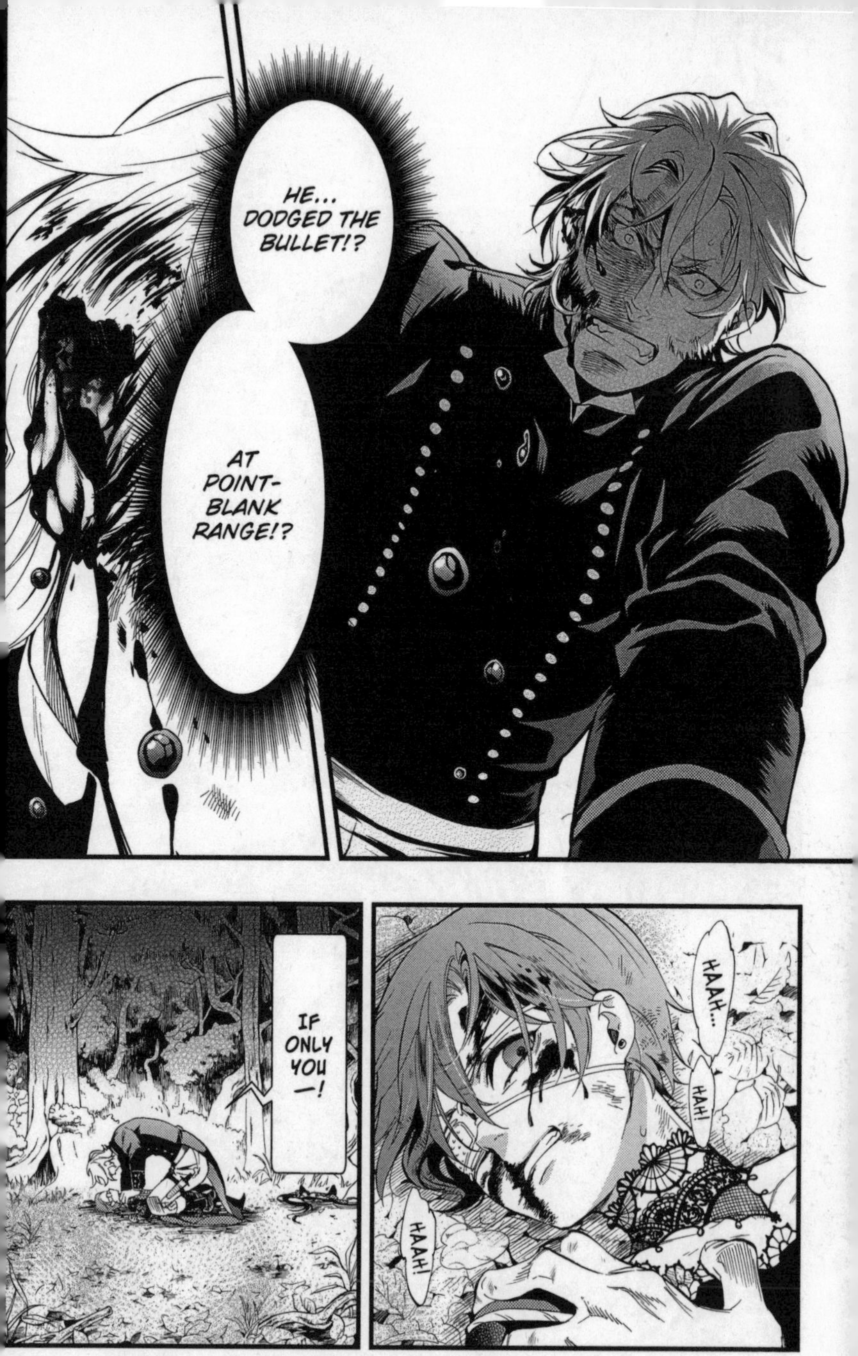
HE... DODGED THE BULLET!?
AT POINT-BLANK RANGE!?
HAAH...
HAH!
HAAH!
IF ONLY YOU—!

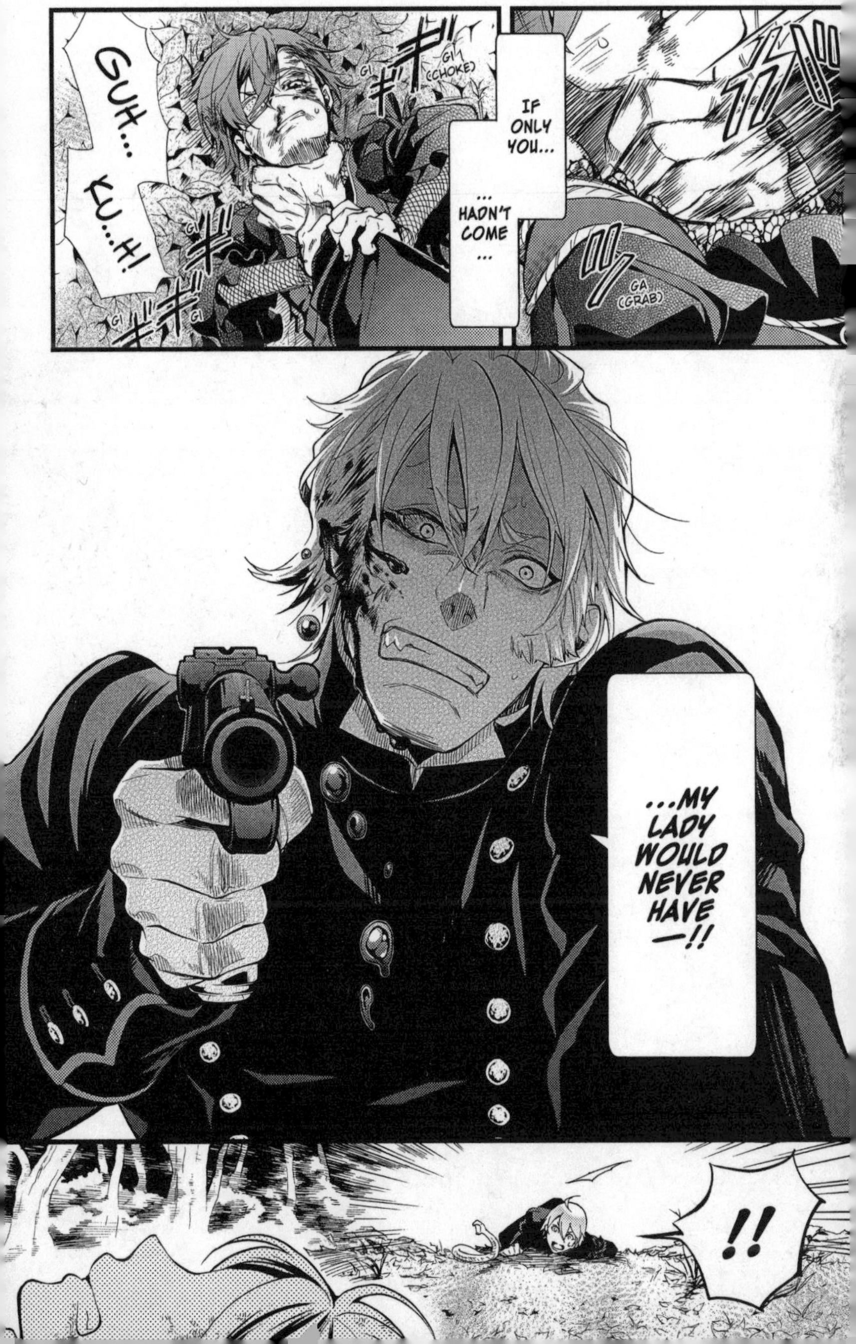
GA (GRAB)
IF ONLY YOU...
...HADN'T COME...
GI GI (CHOKE)
GUH... KU...H!
GI GI
...MY LADY WOULD NEVER HAVE—!!
!!

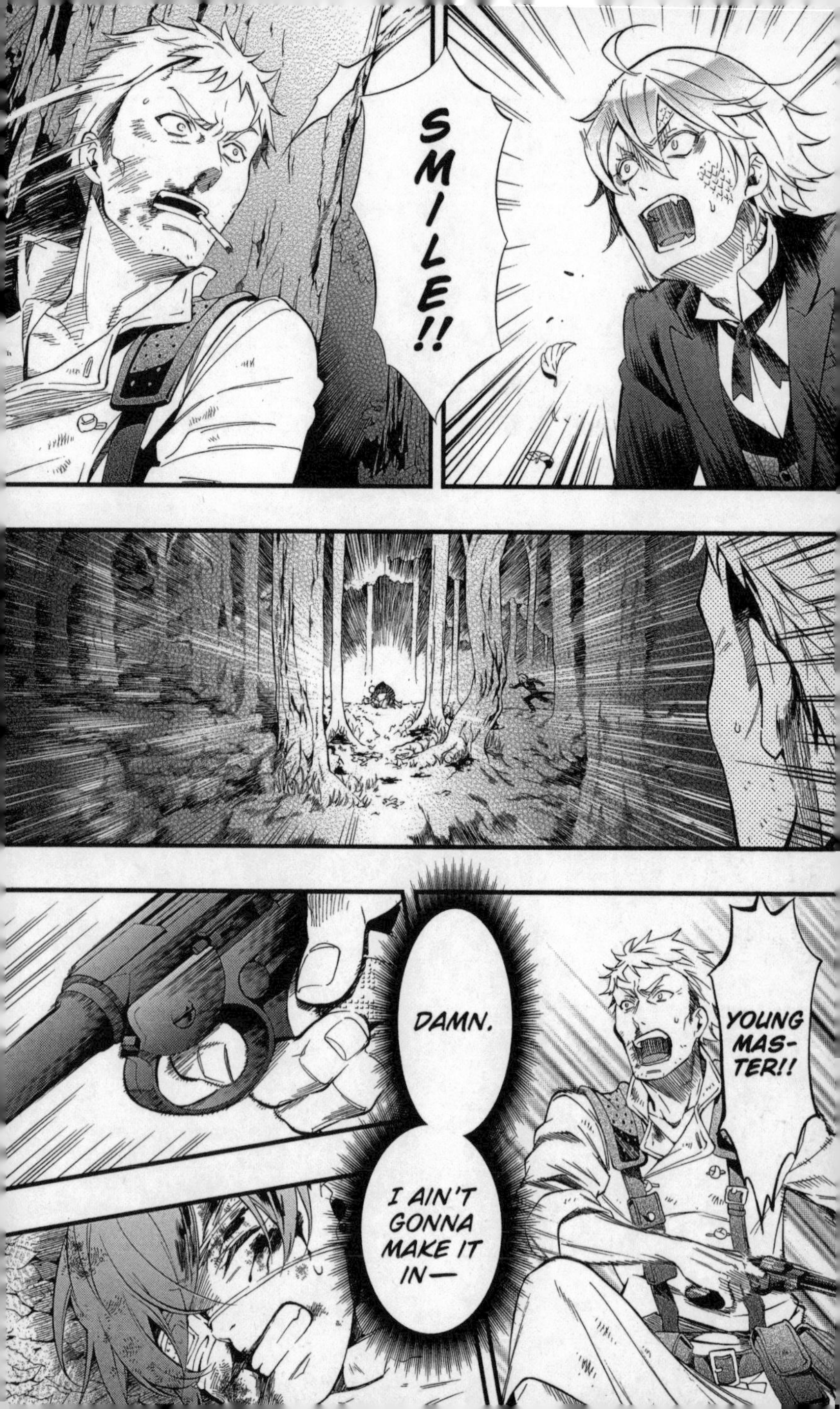
SMILE!!
YOUNG MASTER!!
DAMN.
I AIN'T GONNA MAKE IT IN—

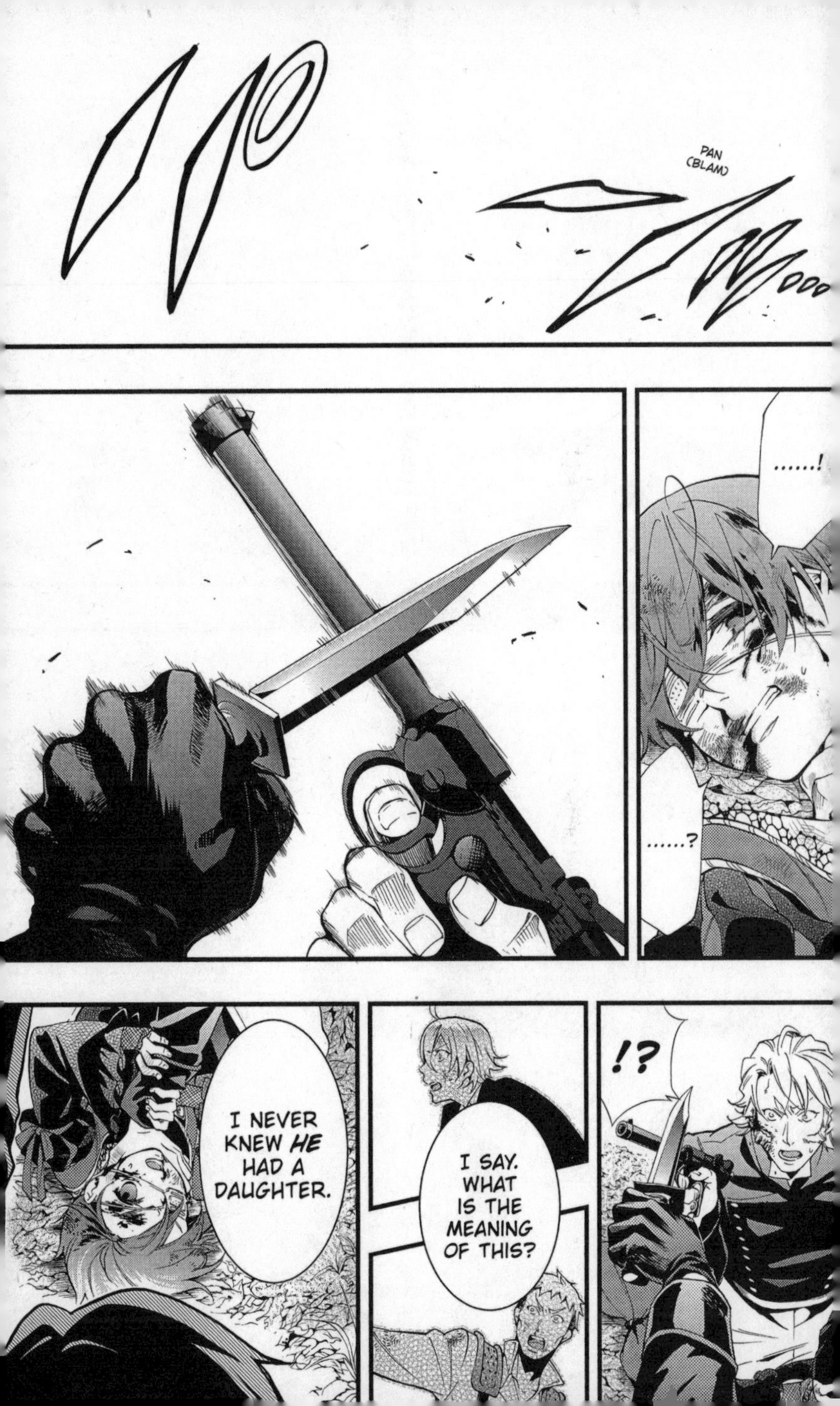
PAN (BLAM)
......!
......?
!?
I SAY. WHAT IS THE MEANING OF THIS?
I NEVER KNEW *HE* HAD A DAUGHTER.

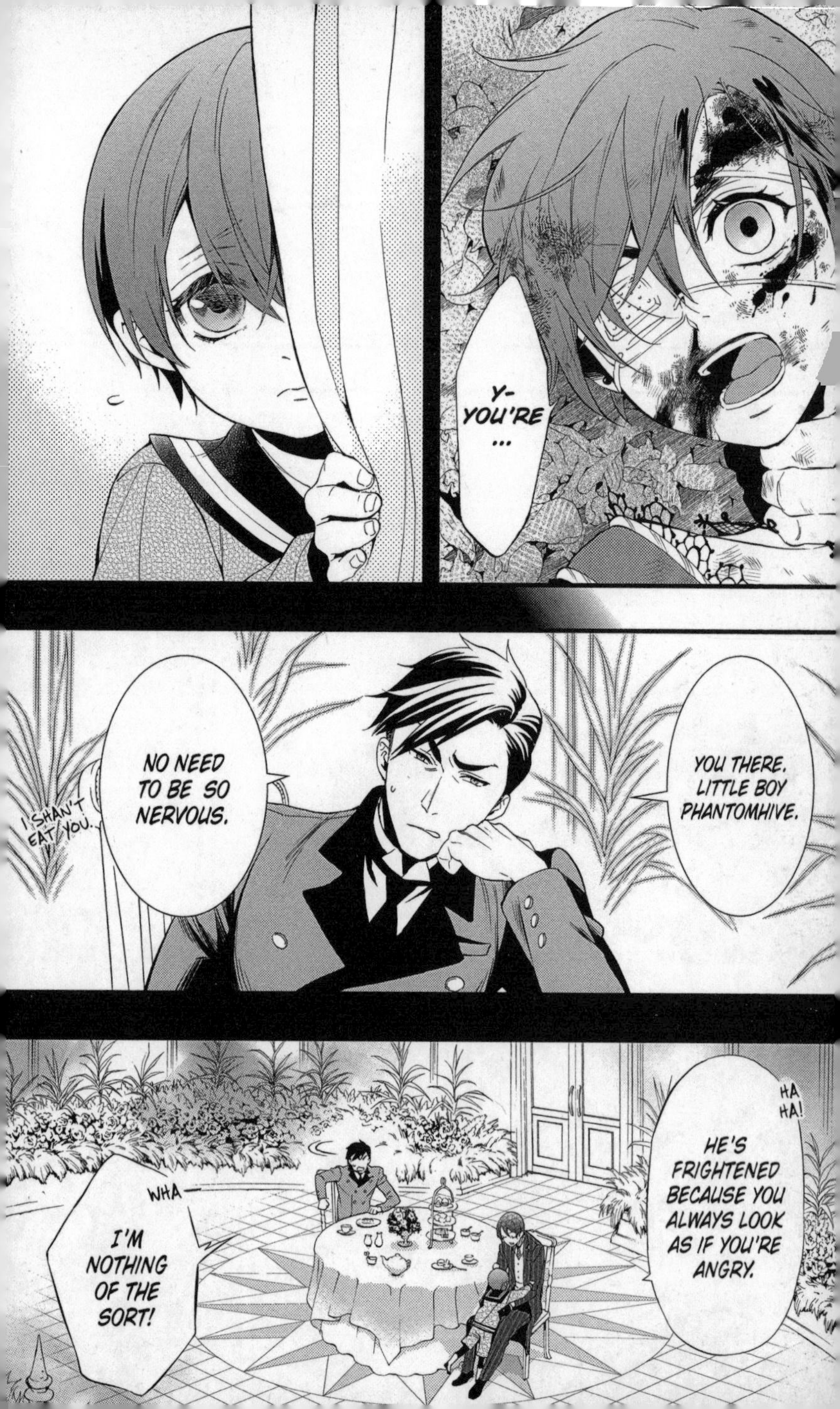

Y-YOU'RE ...
YOU THERE. LITTLE BOY PHANTOMHIVE.
NO NEED TO BE SO NERVOUS.
I SHAN'T EAT YOU.
HA HA!
HE'S FRIGHTENED BECAUSE YOU ALWAYS LOOK AS IF YOU'RE ANGRY.
WHA—
I'M NOTHING OF THE SORT!

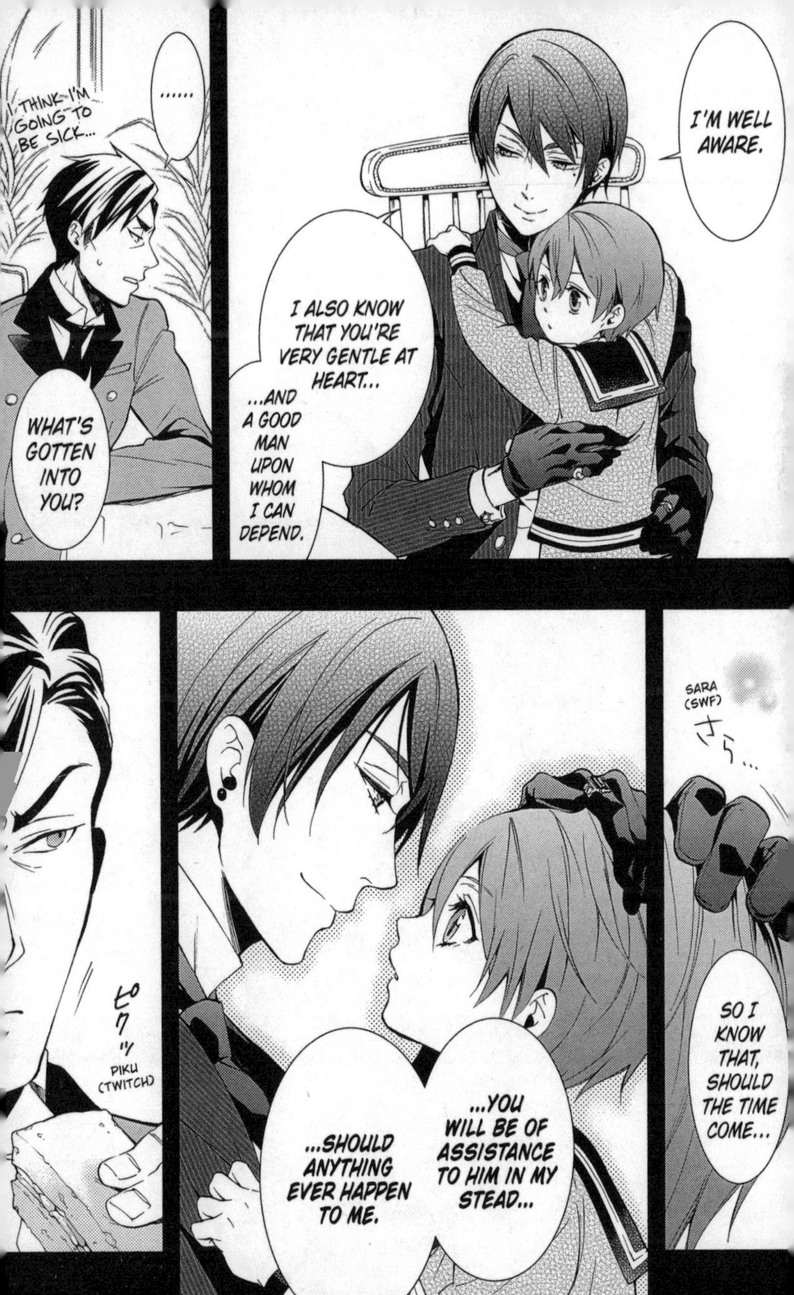
I'M WELL AWARE.
I ALSO KNOW THAT YOU'RE VERY GENTLE AT HEART...
...AND A GOOD MAN UPON WHOM I CAN DEPEND.
......
I THINK I'M GOING TO BE SICK...
WHAT'S GOTTEN INTO YOU?
SARA (SWF)
さら...
SO I KNOW THAT, SHOULD THE TIME COME...
...YOU WILL BE OF ASSISTANCE TO HIM IN MY STEAD...
...SHOULD ANYTHING EVER HAPPEN TO ME.
ピクッ
PIKU (TWITCH)

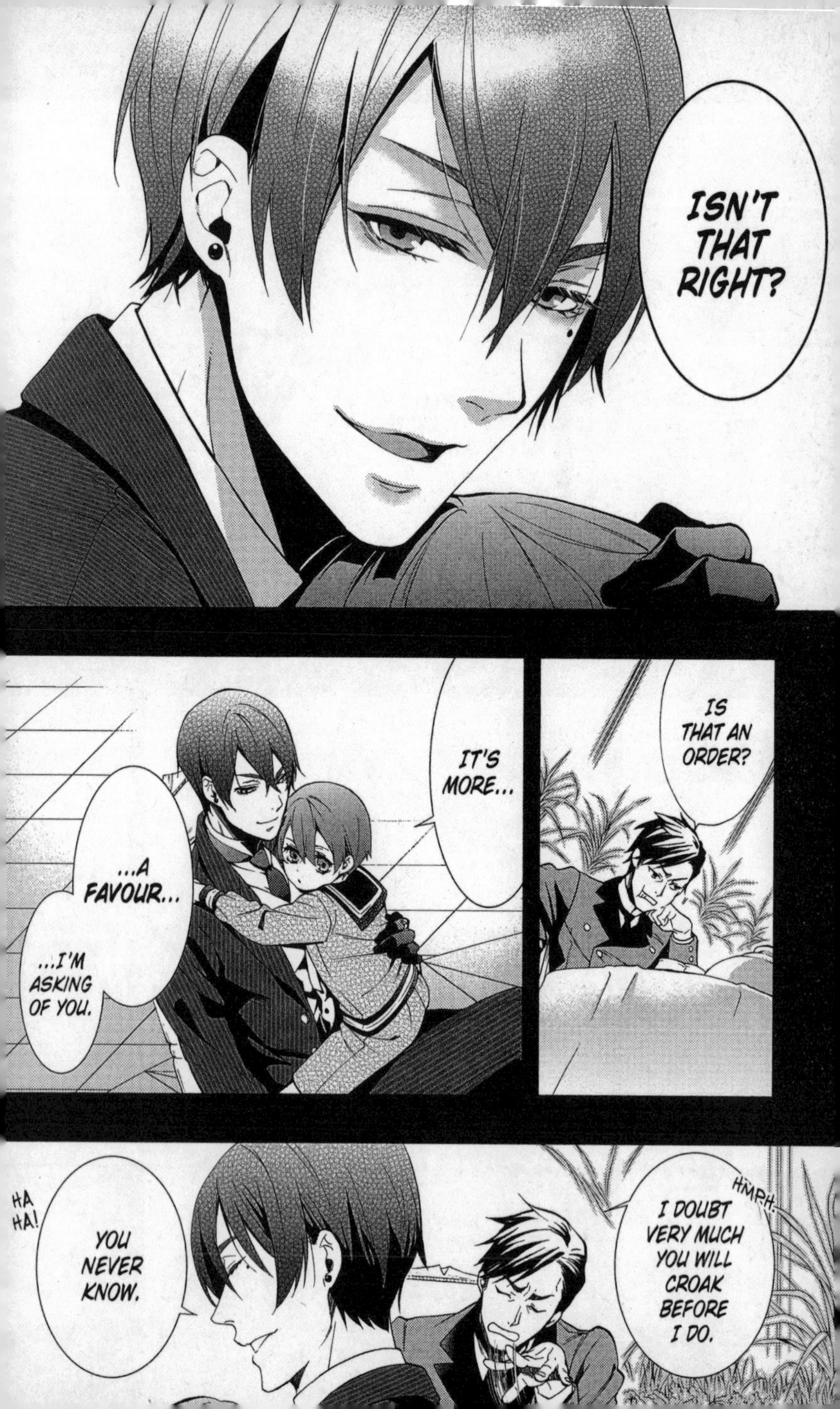
ISN'T THAT RIGHT?
IS THAT AN ORDER?
IT'S MORE...
...A FAVOUR...
...I'M ASKING OF YOU.
HMPH.
I DOUBT VERY MUCH YOU WILL CROAK BEFORE I DO.
YOU NEVER KNOW.
HA HA!

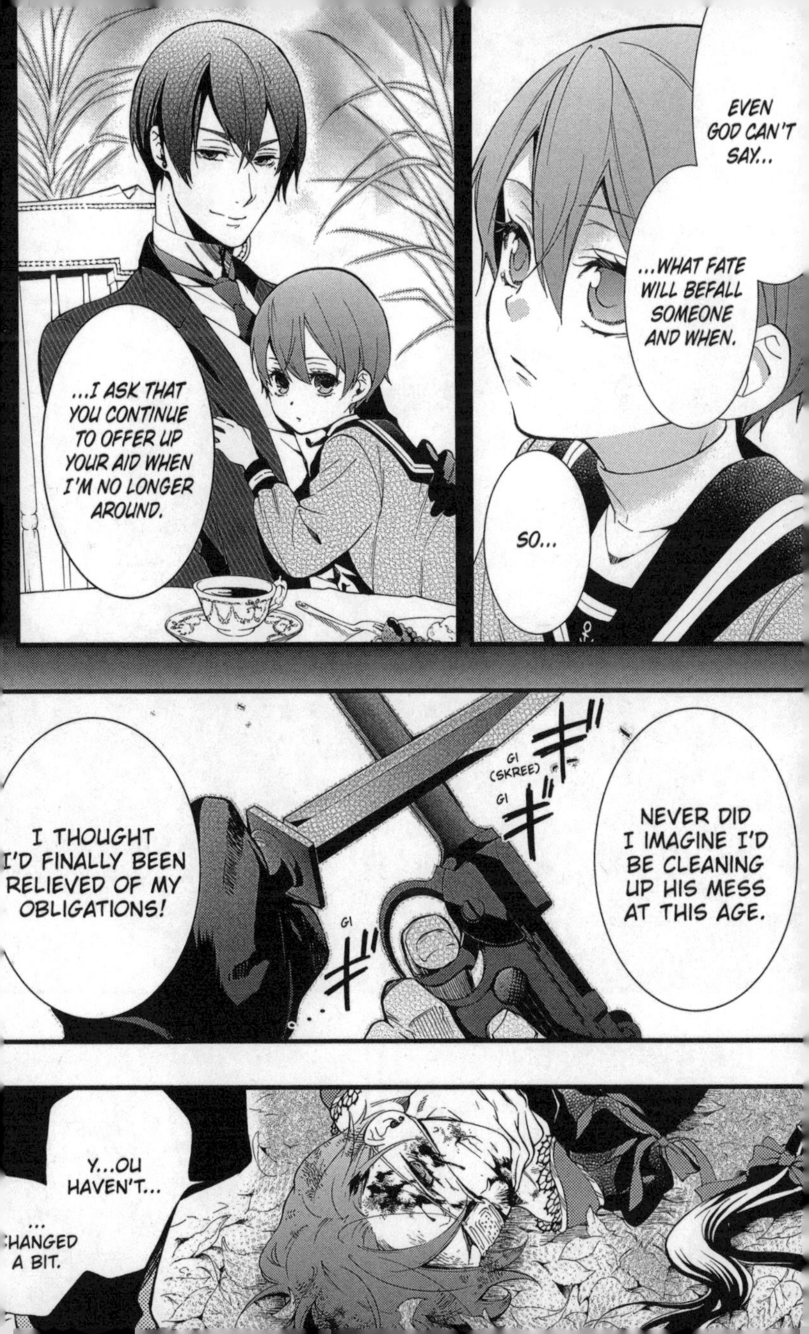
EVEN GOD CAN'T SAY...
...WHAT FATE WILL BEFALL SOMEONE AND WHEN.
SO...
...I ASK THAT YOU CONTINUE TO OFFER UP YOUR AID WHEN I'M NO LONGER AROUND.
NEVER DID I IMAGINE I'D BE CLEANING UP HIS MESS AT THIS AGE.
GI (SKREE)
GI
GI
I THOUGHT I'D FINALLY BEEN RELIEVED OF MY OBLIGATIONS!
Y...OU HAVEN'T...
...CHANGED A BIT.

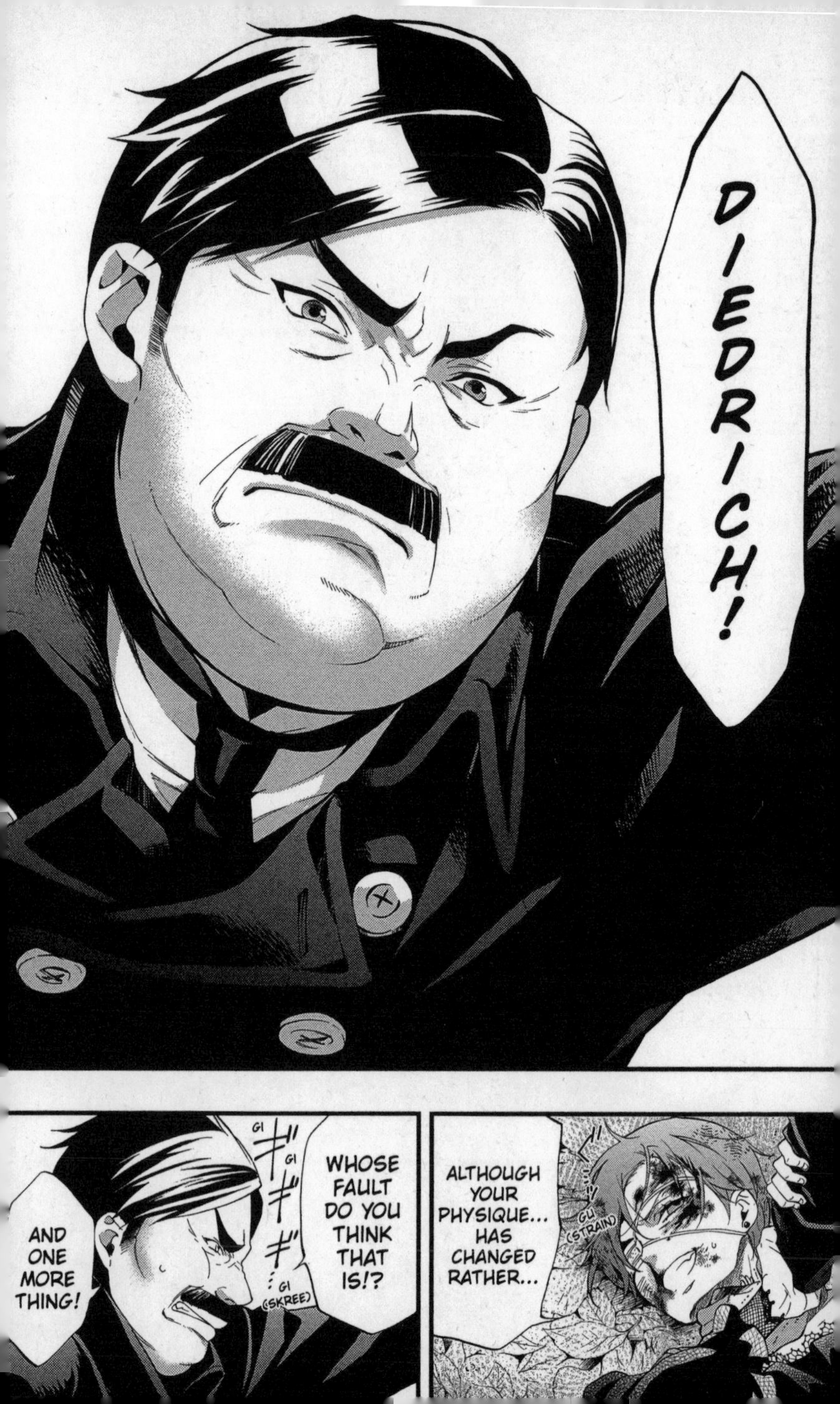
DIEDRICH!
GU (STRAIN)
ALTHOUGH YOUR PHYSIQUE... HAS CHANGED RATHER...
WHOSE FAULT DO YOU THINK THAT IS!?
GI GI GI (SKREE)
AND ONE MORE THING!

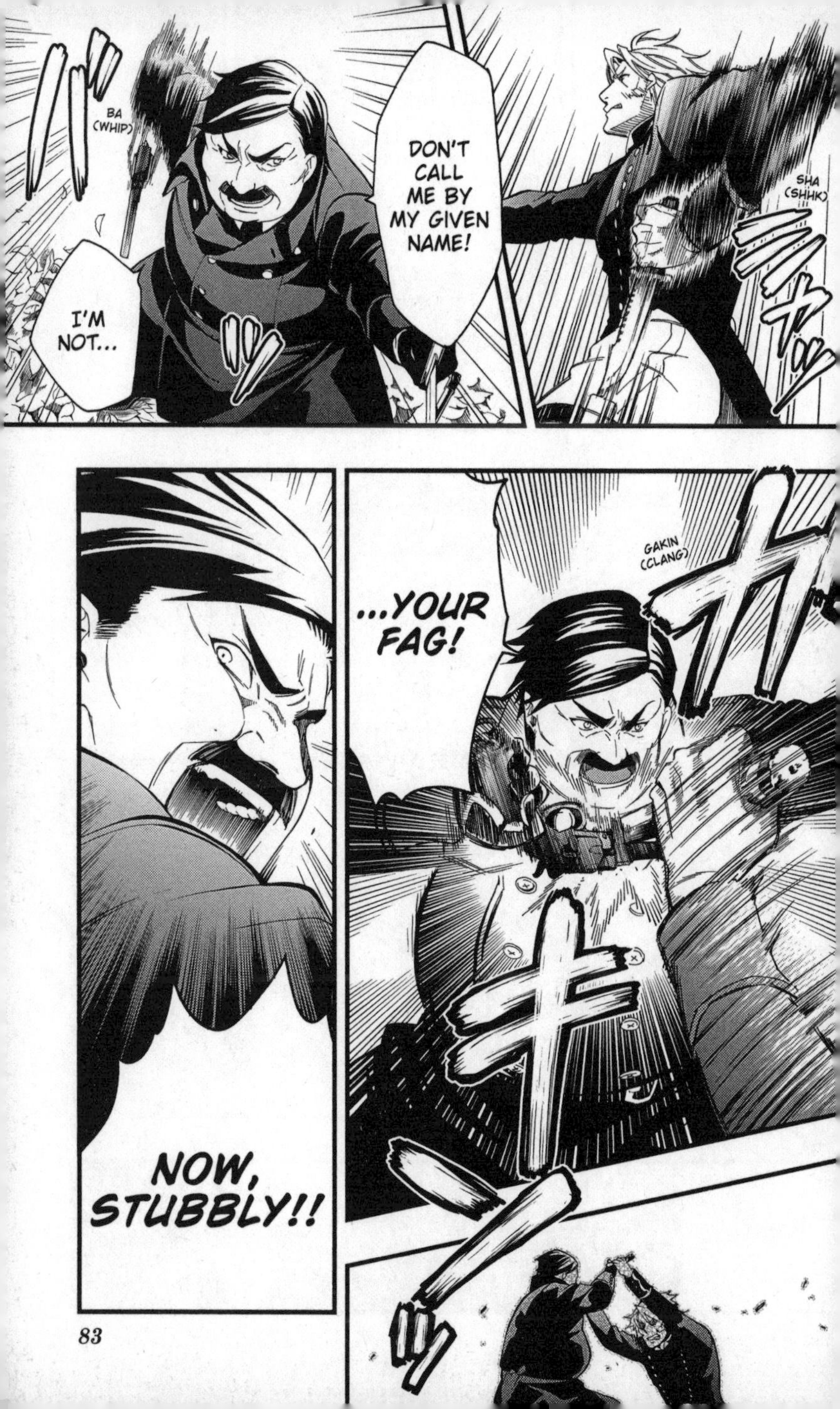
SHA (SHHK)
DON'T CALL ME BY MY GIVEN NAME!
BA (WHIP)
I'M NOT...
GAKIN (CLANG)
...YOUR FAG!
NOW, STUBBLY!!

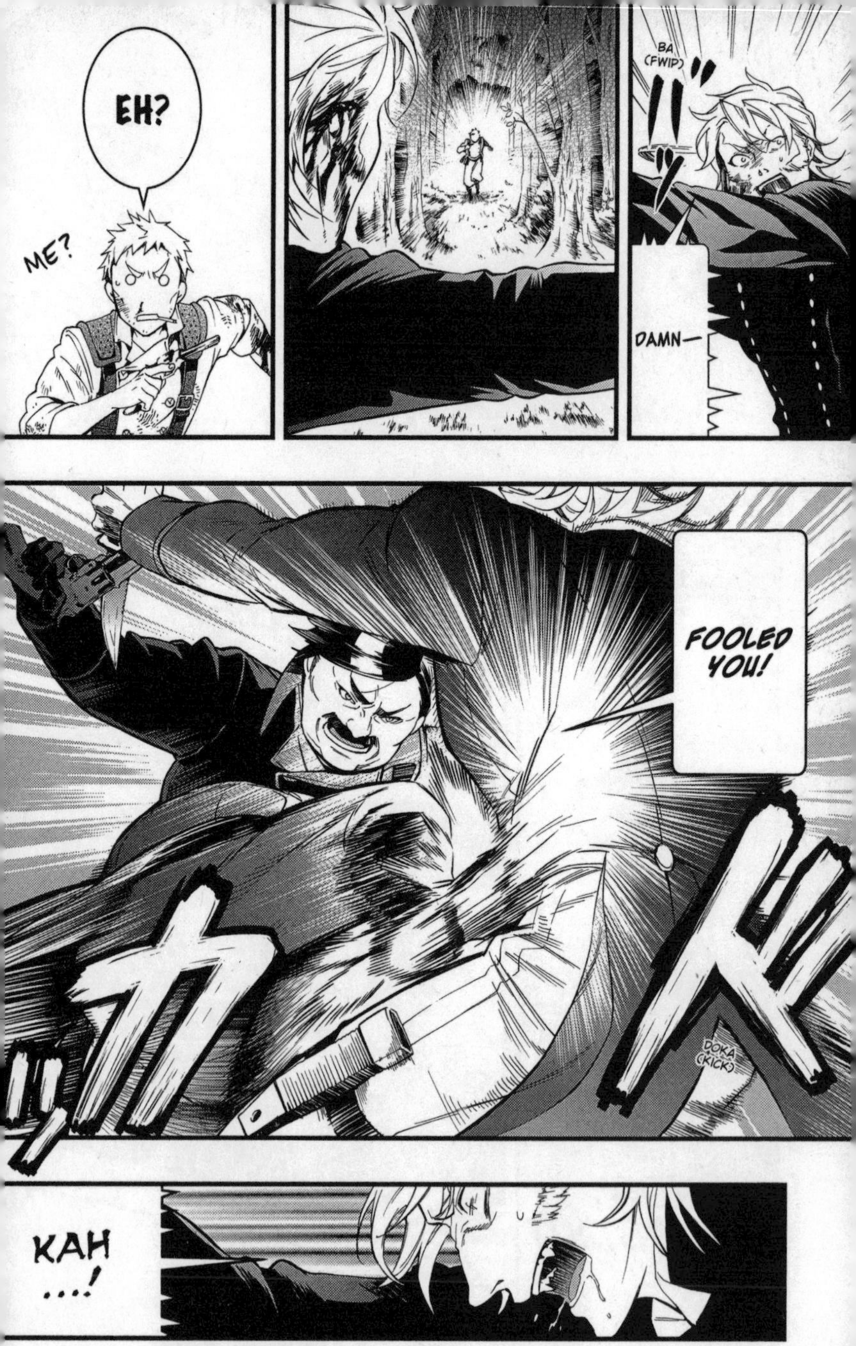
BA (FWIP)
DAMN—
EH?
ME?
FOOLED YOU!
DOKA (KICK)
KAH ...!

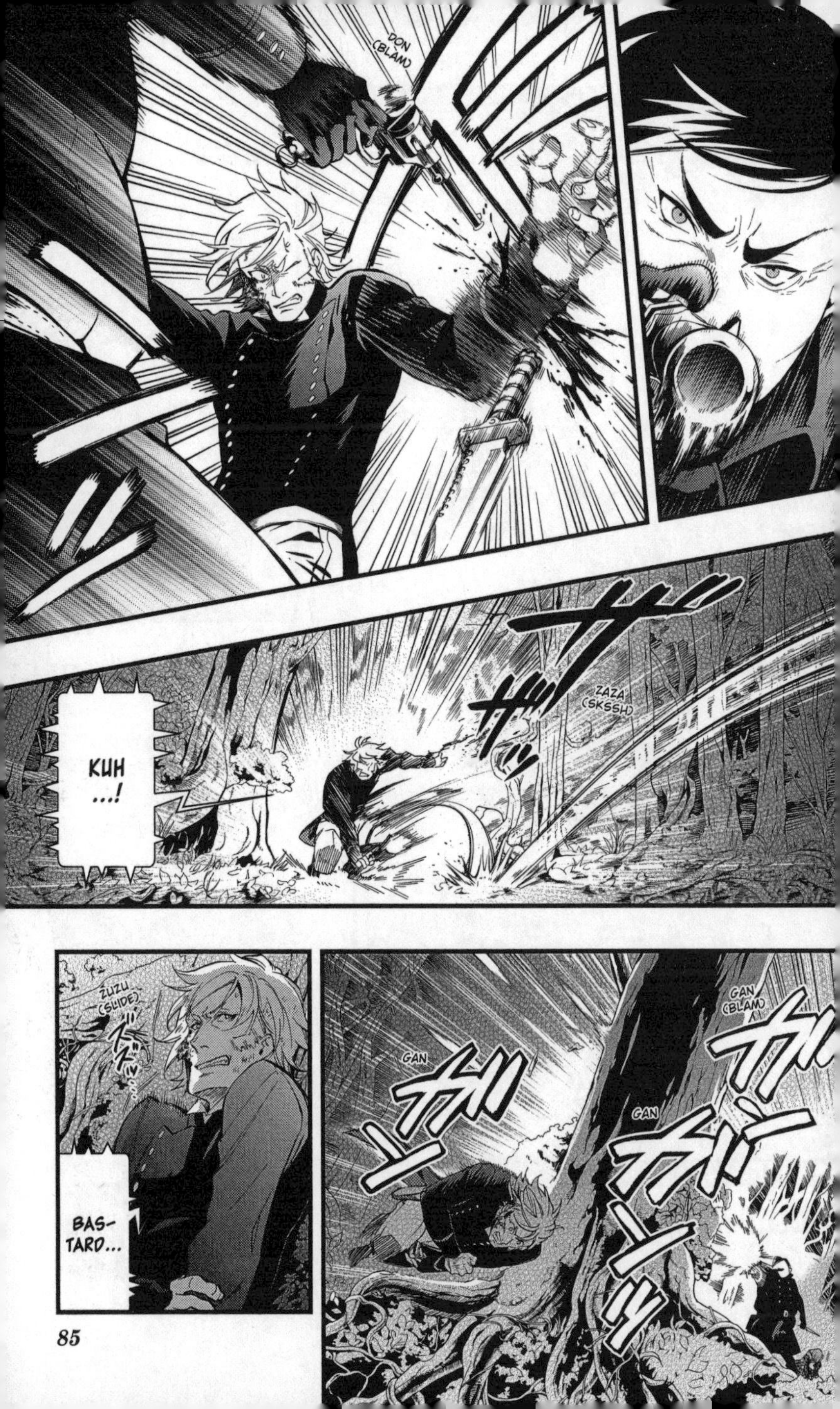
DON (BLAM)
ZAZA (SKSSH)
KUH ...!
GAN (BLAM)
GAN
GAN
ZUZU (SLIDE)
BAS-TARD...

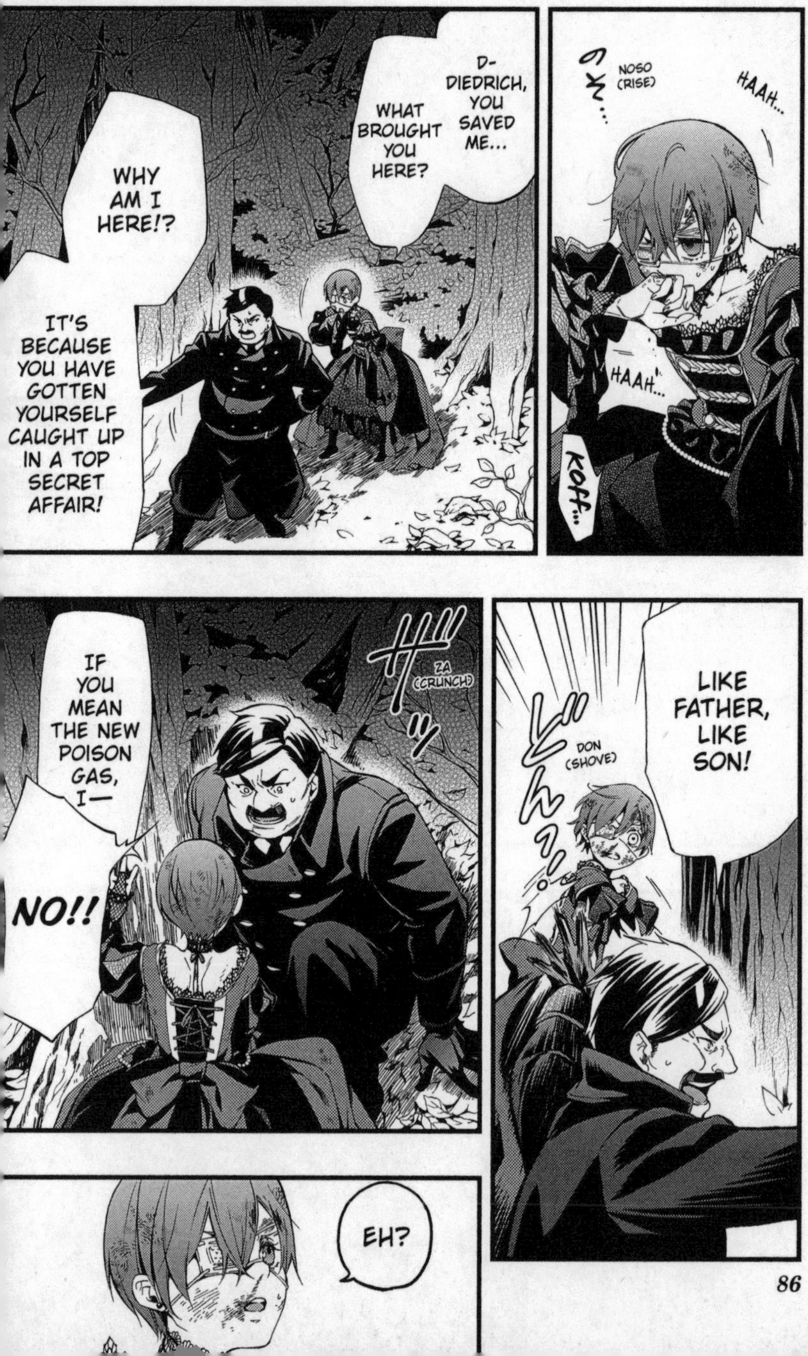
NOSO (RISE)
HAAH...
HAAH...
KOFF...
D-DIEDRICH, YOU SAVED ME...
WHAT BROUGHT YOU HERE?
WHY AM I HERE!?
IT'S BECAUSE YOU HAVE GOTTEN YOURSELF CAUGHT UP IN A TOP SECRET AFFAIR!
LIKE FATHER, LIKE SON!
DON (SHOVE)
ZA (CRUNCH)
IF YOU MEAN THE NEW POISON GAS, I—
NO!!
EH?

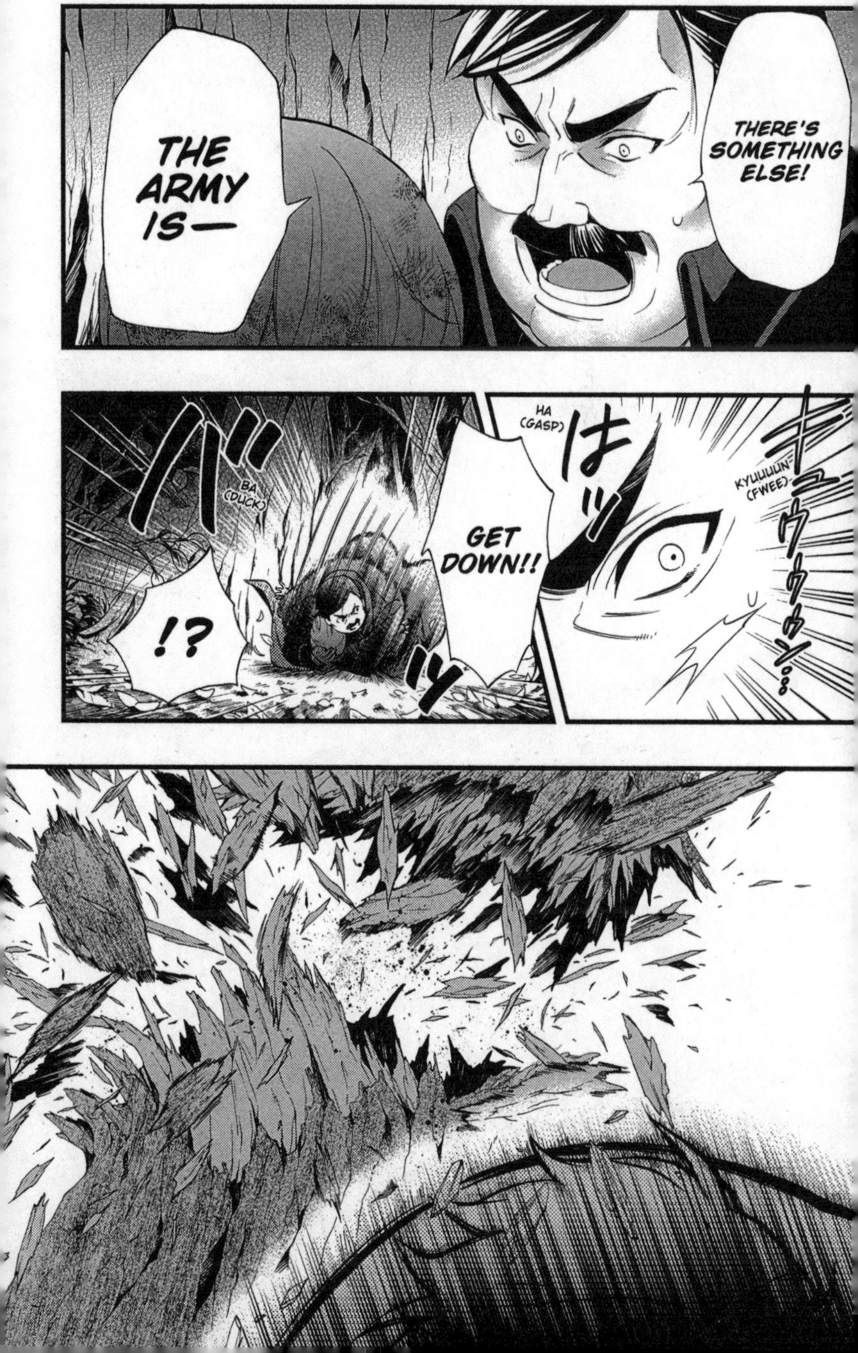
THERE'S SOMETHING ELSE!
THE ARMY IS—
KYUUUUN (FWEE)
HA (GASP)
GET DOWN!!
BA (DUCK)
!?

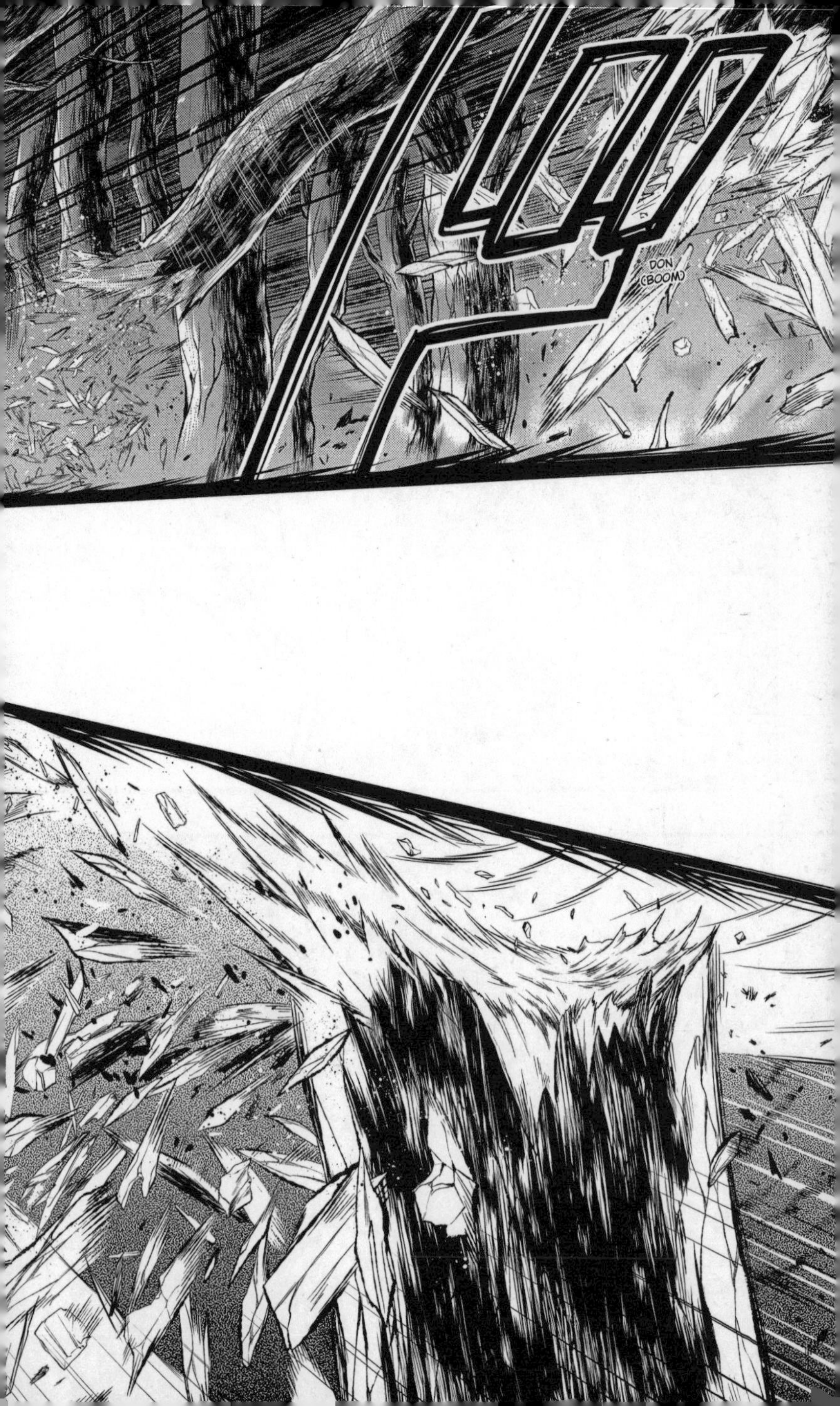
DON
(BOOM)

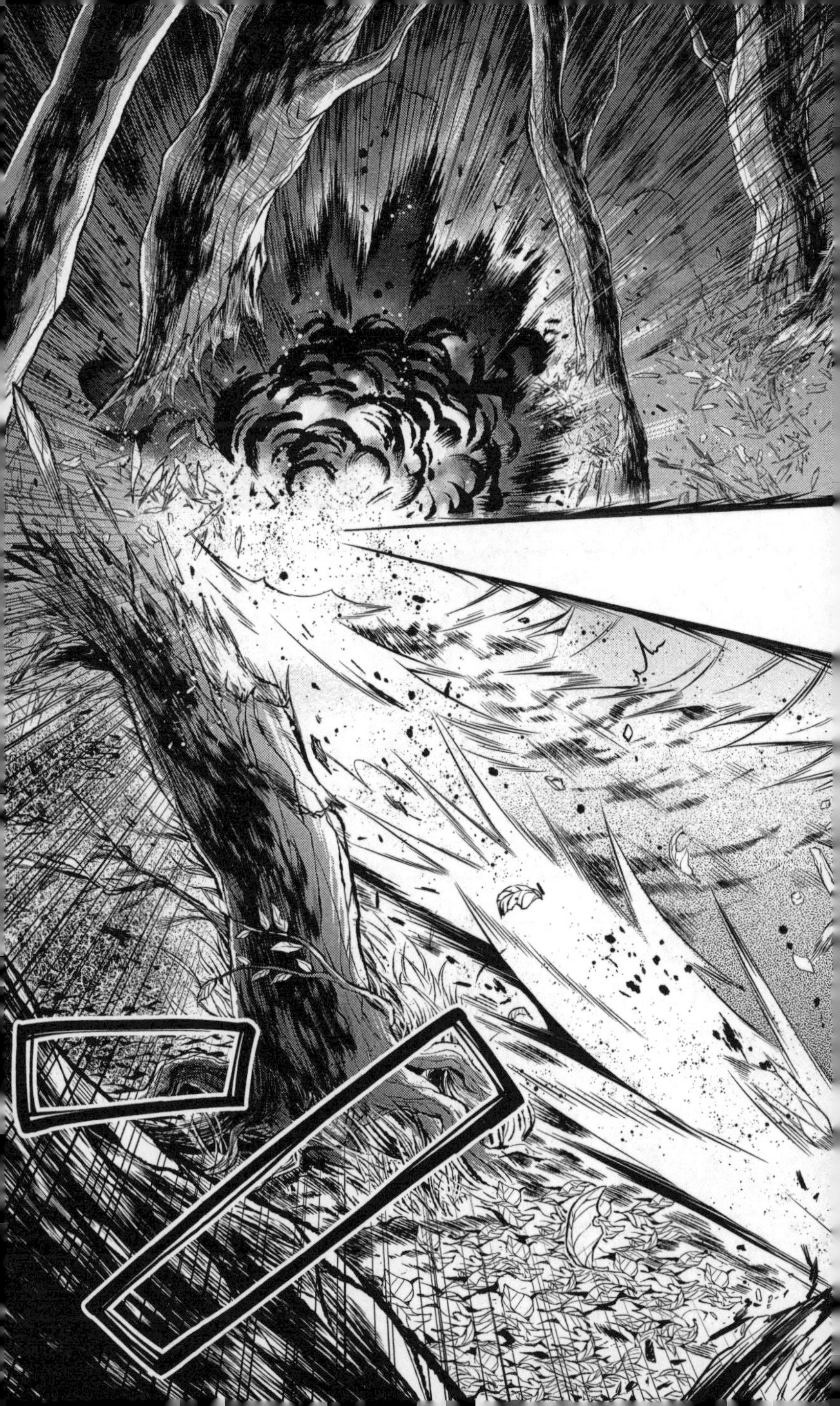

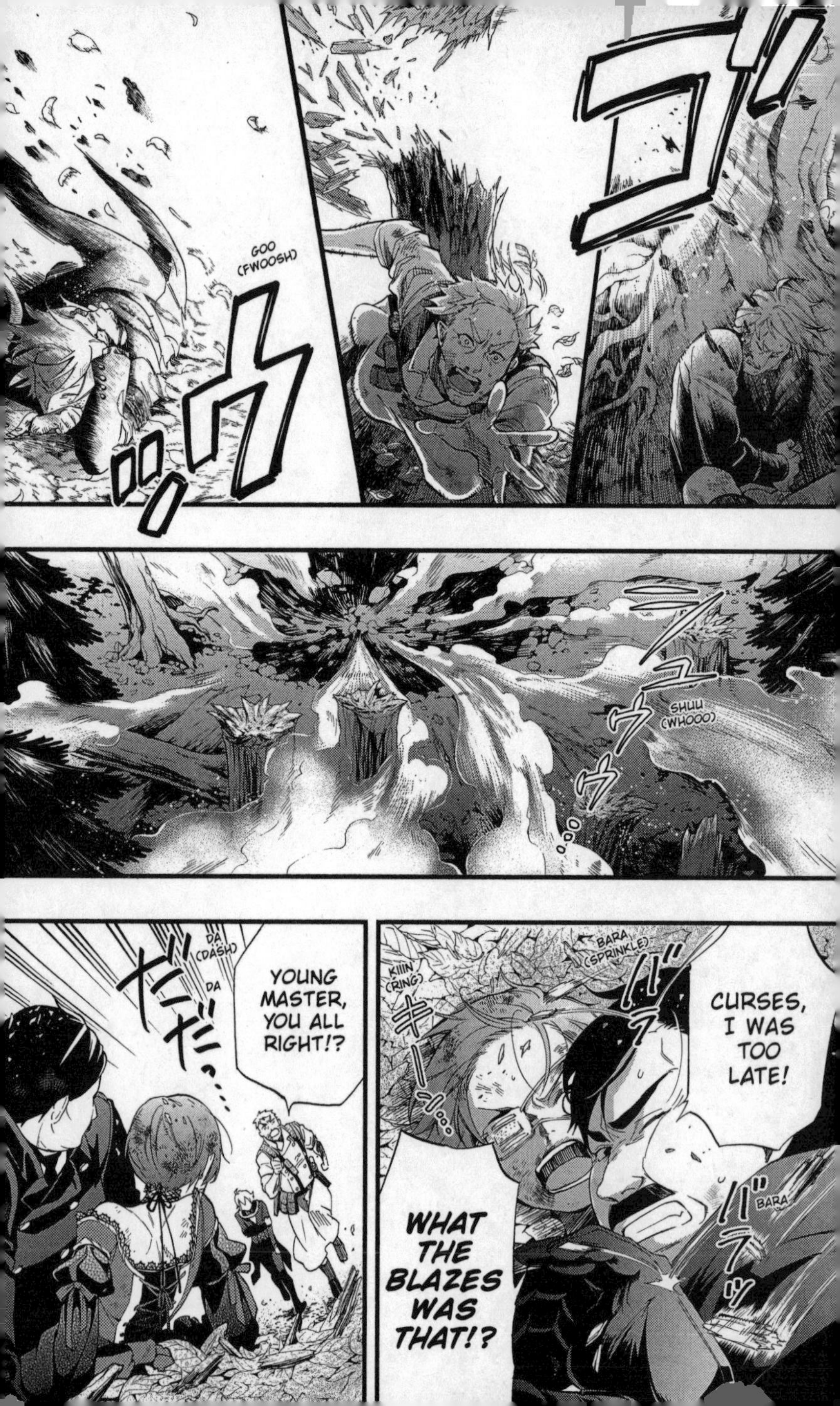
GOO (FWOOSH)
SHUU (WHOOO)
CURSES, I WAS TOO LATE!
BARA (SPRINKLE)
KIIIN (RING)
BARA
WHAT THE BLAZES WAS THAT!?
DA (DASH)
DA
YOUNG MASTER, YOU ALL RIGHT!?

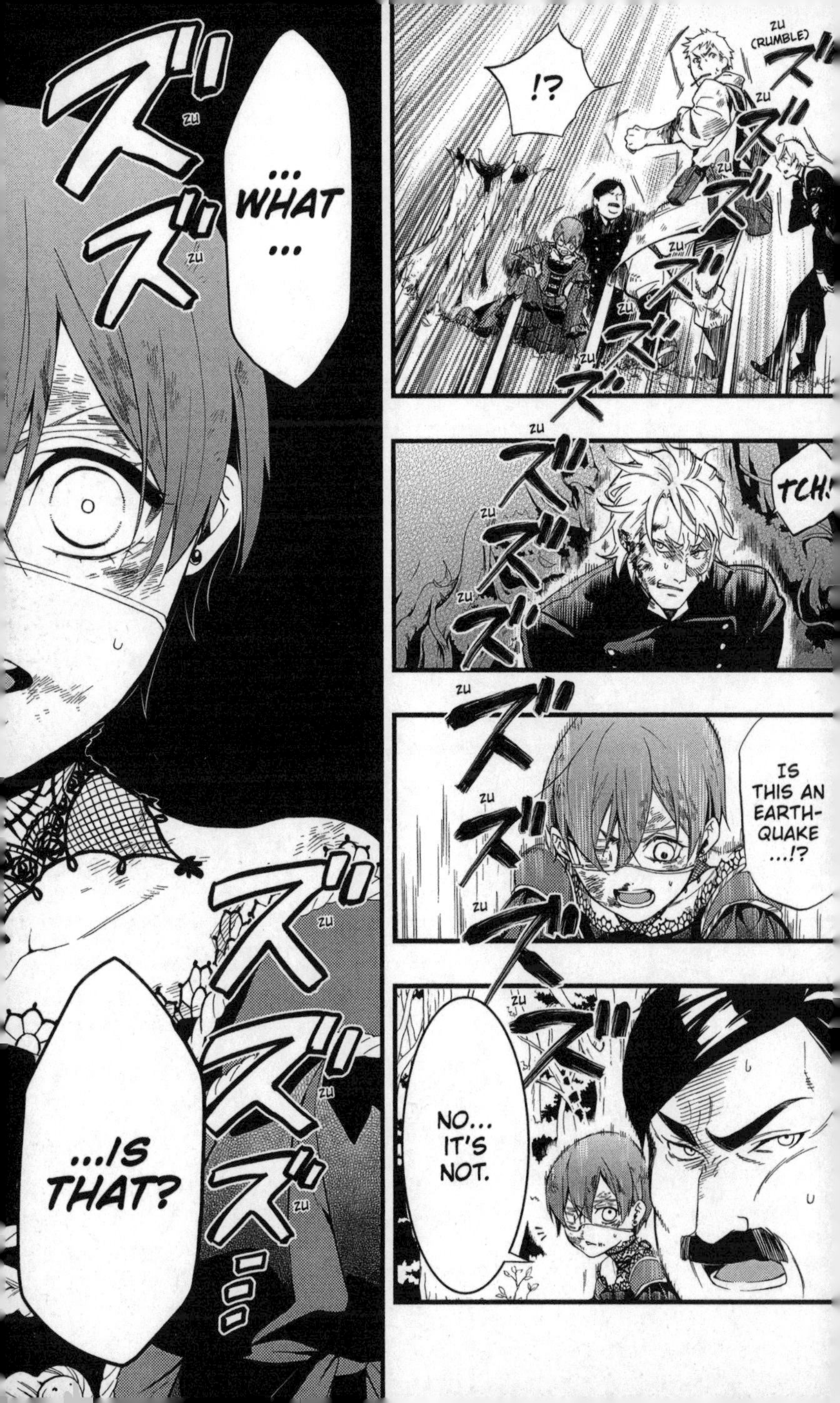
ZU (RUMBLE)
!?
zu
zu
zu
zu
zu
zu
TCH!
zu
zu
zu
IS THIS AN EARTH-QUAKE ...!?
zu
zu
NO... IT'S NOT.
zu
zu
...WHAT...
zu
zu
...IS THAT?
zu

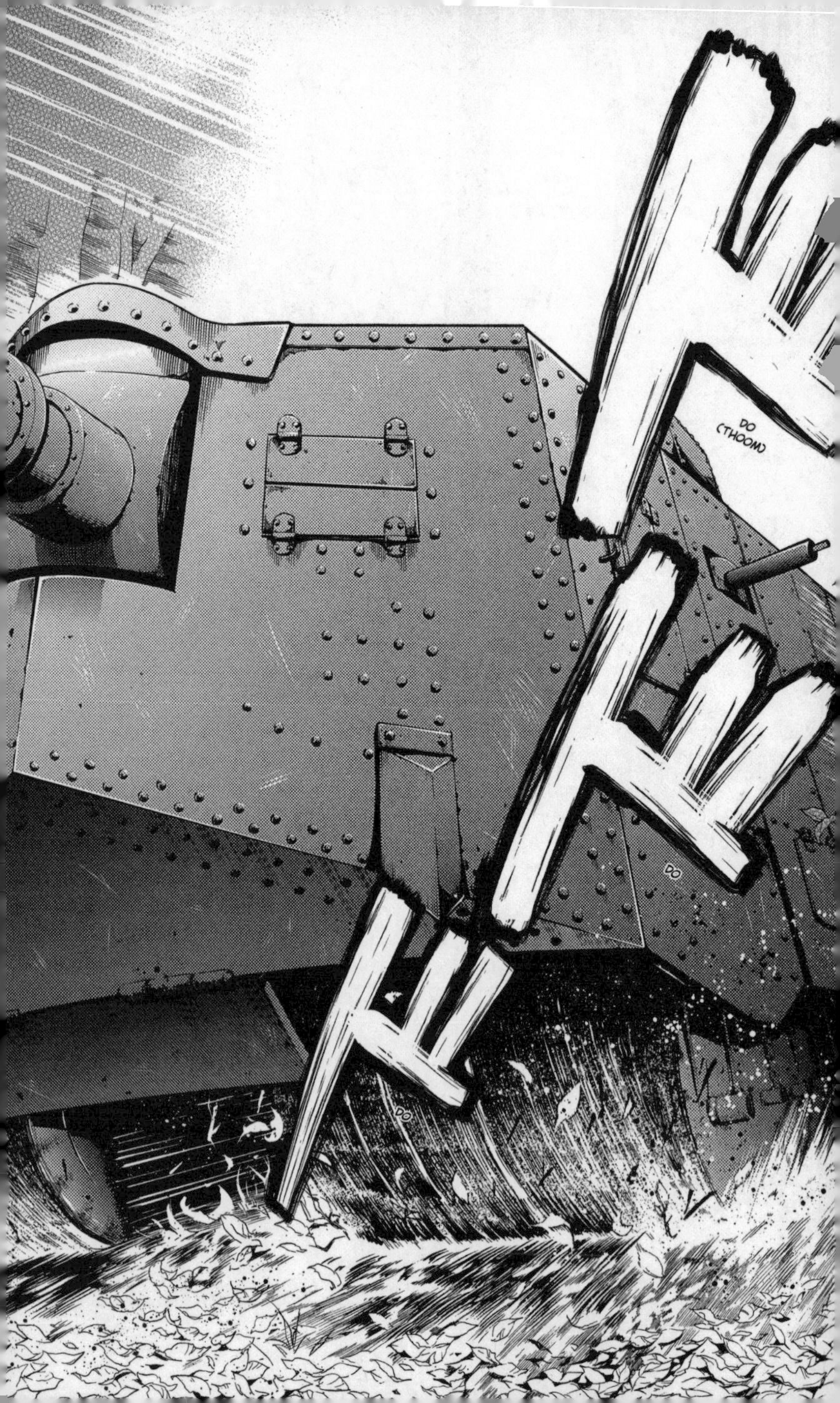
DO
(THOOM)
DO
DO

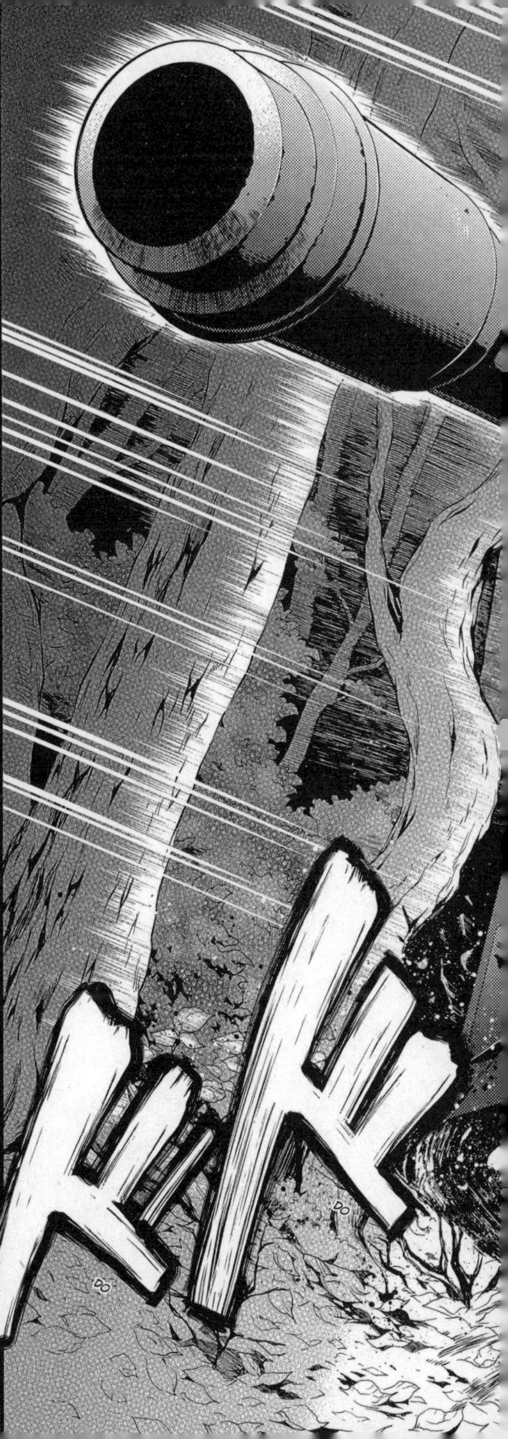
ドド
DO
DO
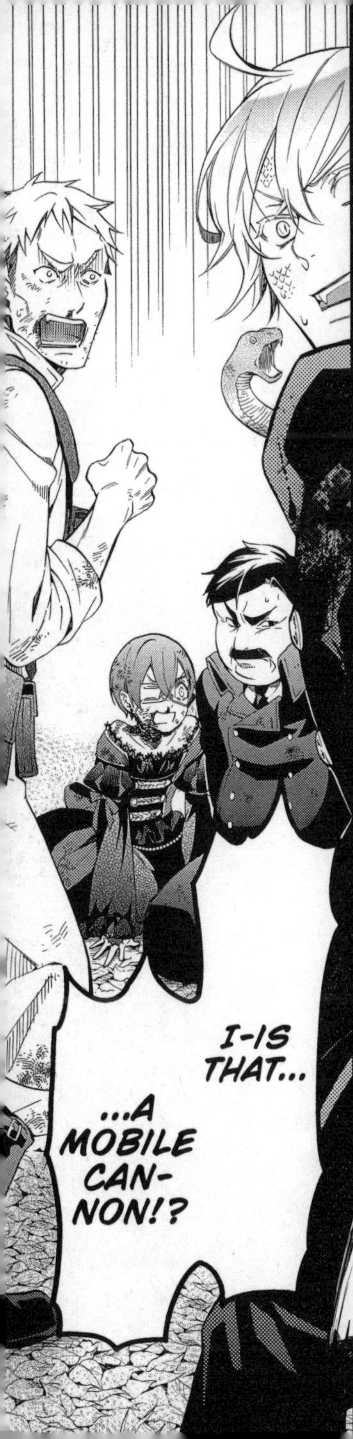
I-IS THAT...
...A MOBILE CAN-NON!?

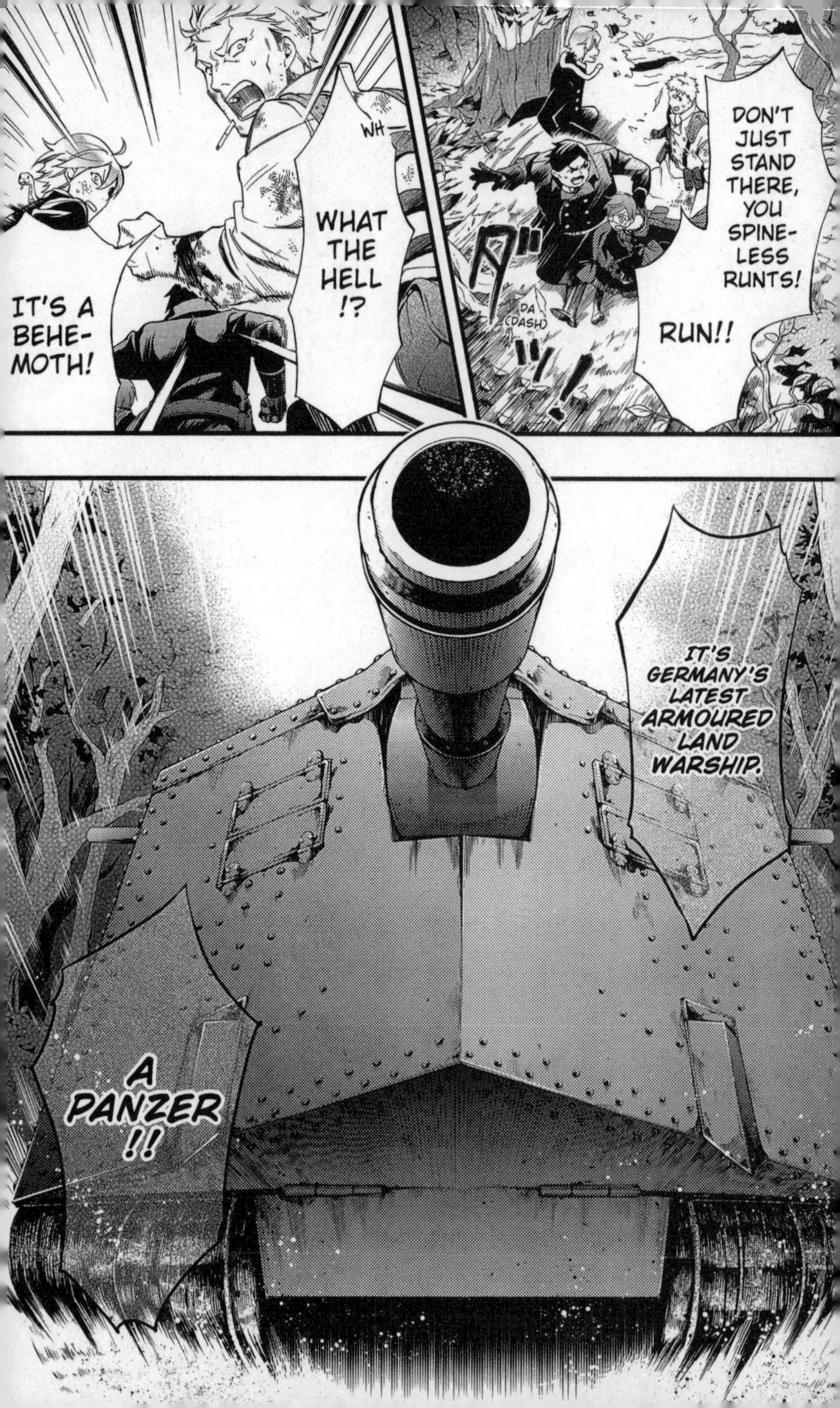
DON'T JUST STAND THERE, YOU SPINE-LESS RUNTS!
RUN!!
DA (DASH)
WH—
WHAT THE HELL!?
IT'S A BEHE-MOTH!
IT'S GERMANY'S LATEST ARMOURED LAND WARSHIP.
A PANZER!!

Black Butler

Chapter 102

At night : The Butler, Exterminating

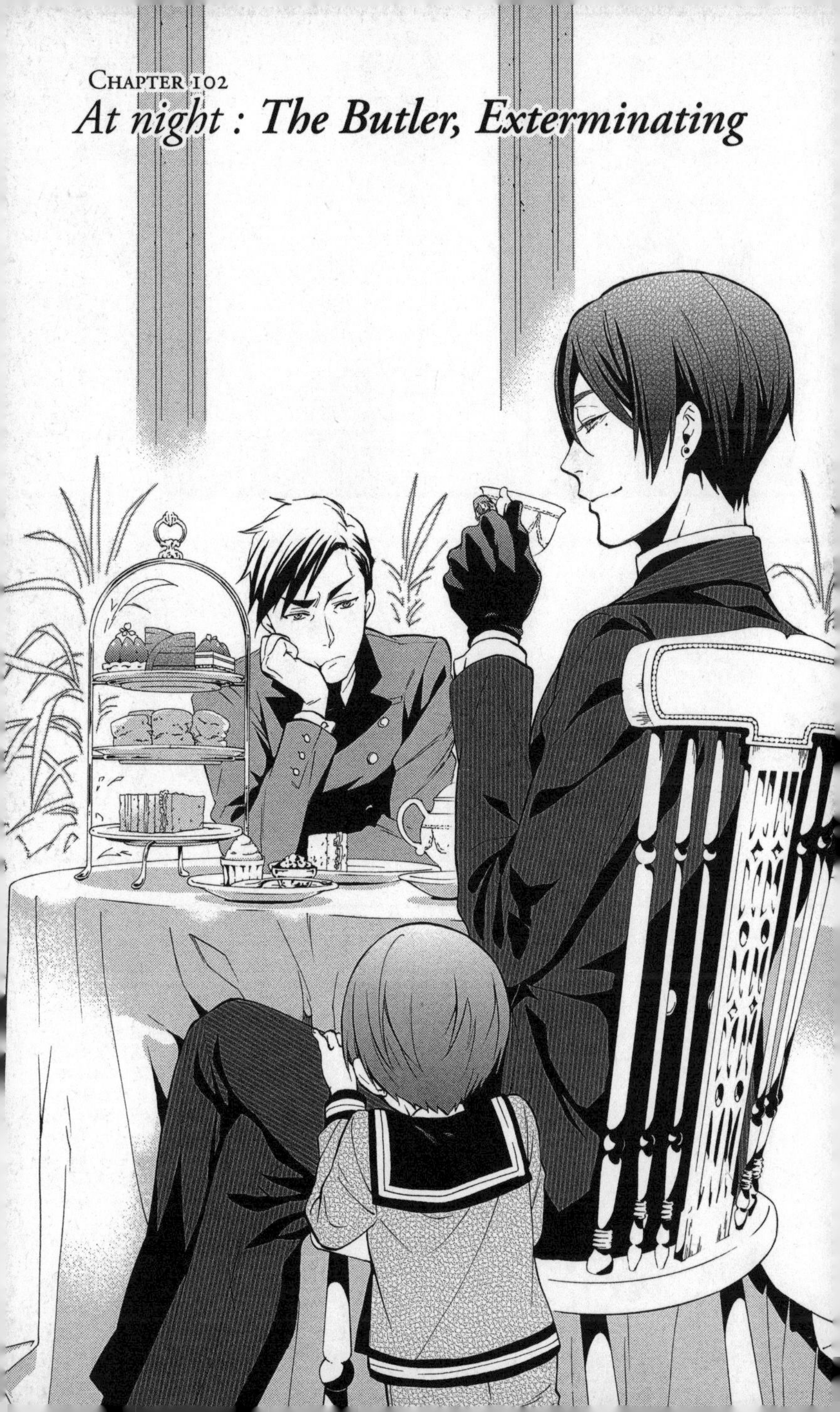

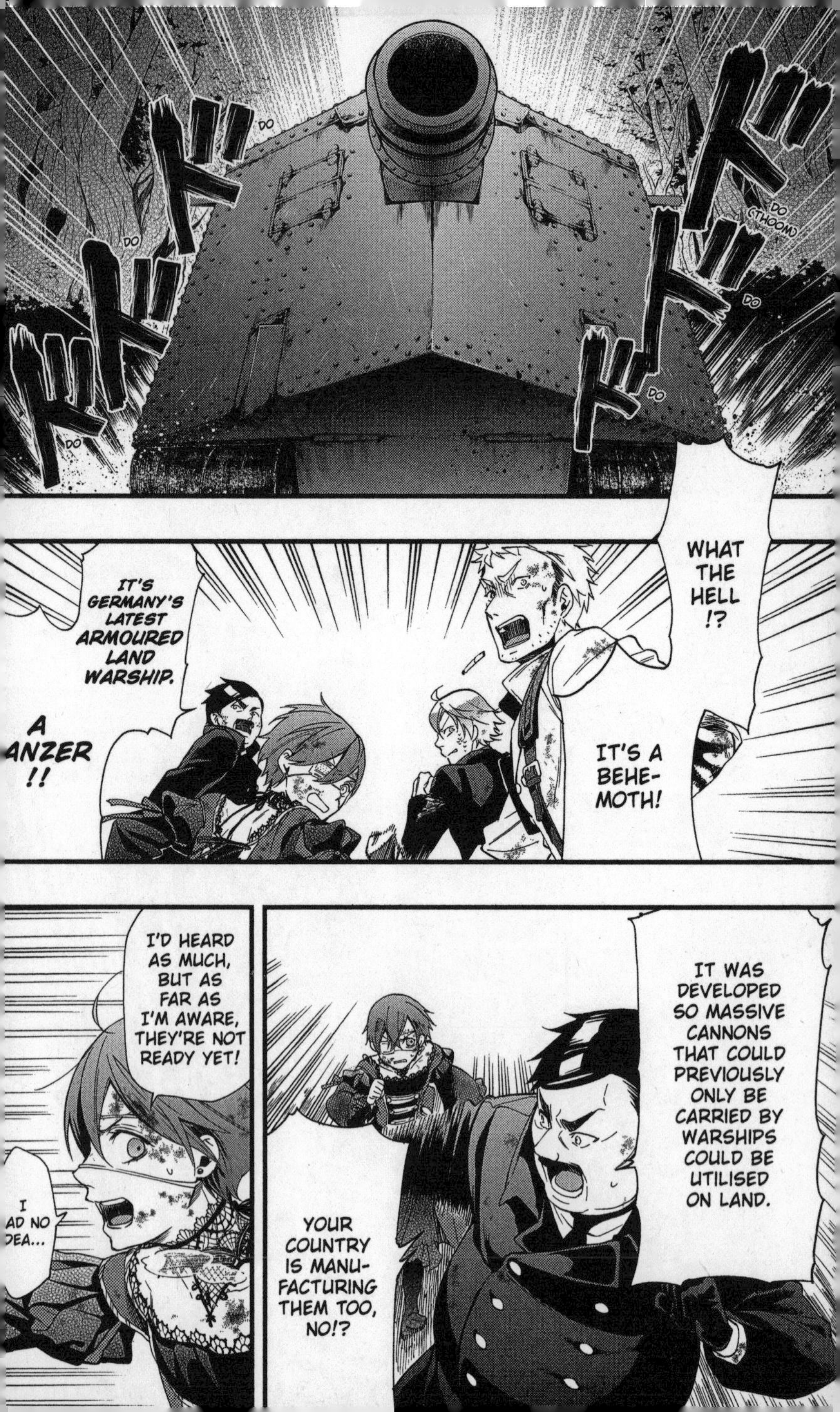
DO (THOOM)
DO
DO
DO
DO
DO
WHAT THE HELL!?
IT'S A BEHE-MOTH!
IT'S GERMANY'S LATEST ARMOURED LAND WARSHIP.
A ANZER!!
IT WAS DEVELOPED SO MASSIVE CANNONS THAT COULD PREVIOUSLY ONLY BE CARRIED BY WARSHIPS COULD BE UTILISED ON LAND.
YOUR COUNTRY IS MANU-FACTURING THEM TOO, NO!?
I'D HEARD AS MUCH, BUT AS FAR AS I'M AWARE, THEY'RE NOT READY YET!
I AD NO DEA...

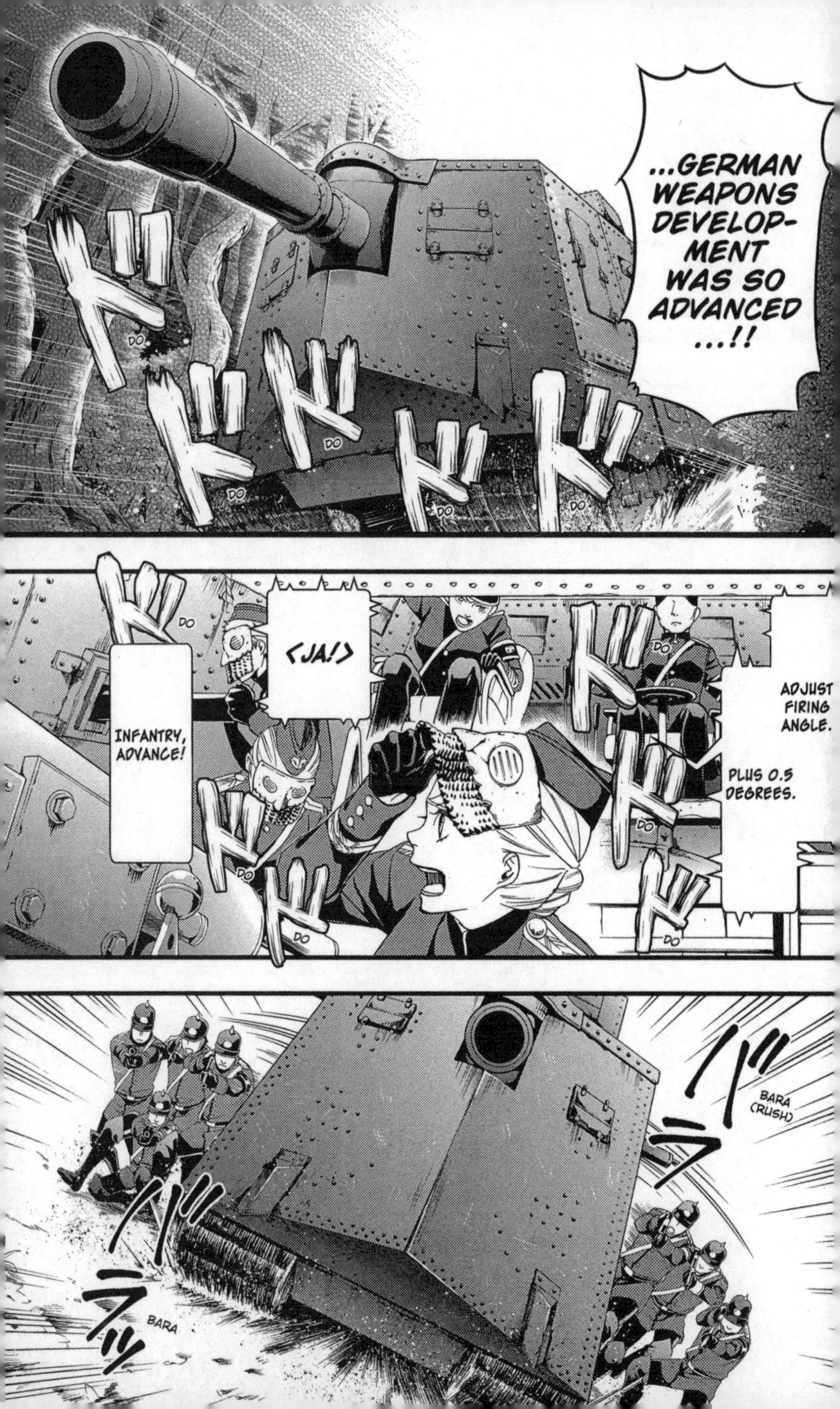

...GERMAN WEAPONS DEVELOPMENT WAS SO ADVANCED...!!
DO
DO
DO
DO
DO
DO
ADJUST FIRING ANGLE.
PLUS 0.5 DEGREES.
DO
DO
DO
<JA!>
INFANTRY, ADVANCE!
DO
DO
DO
BARA (RUSH)
BARA

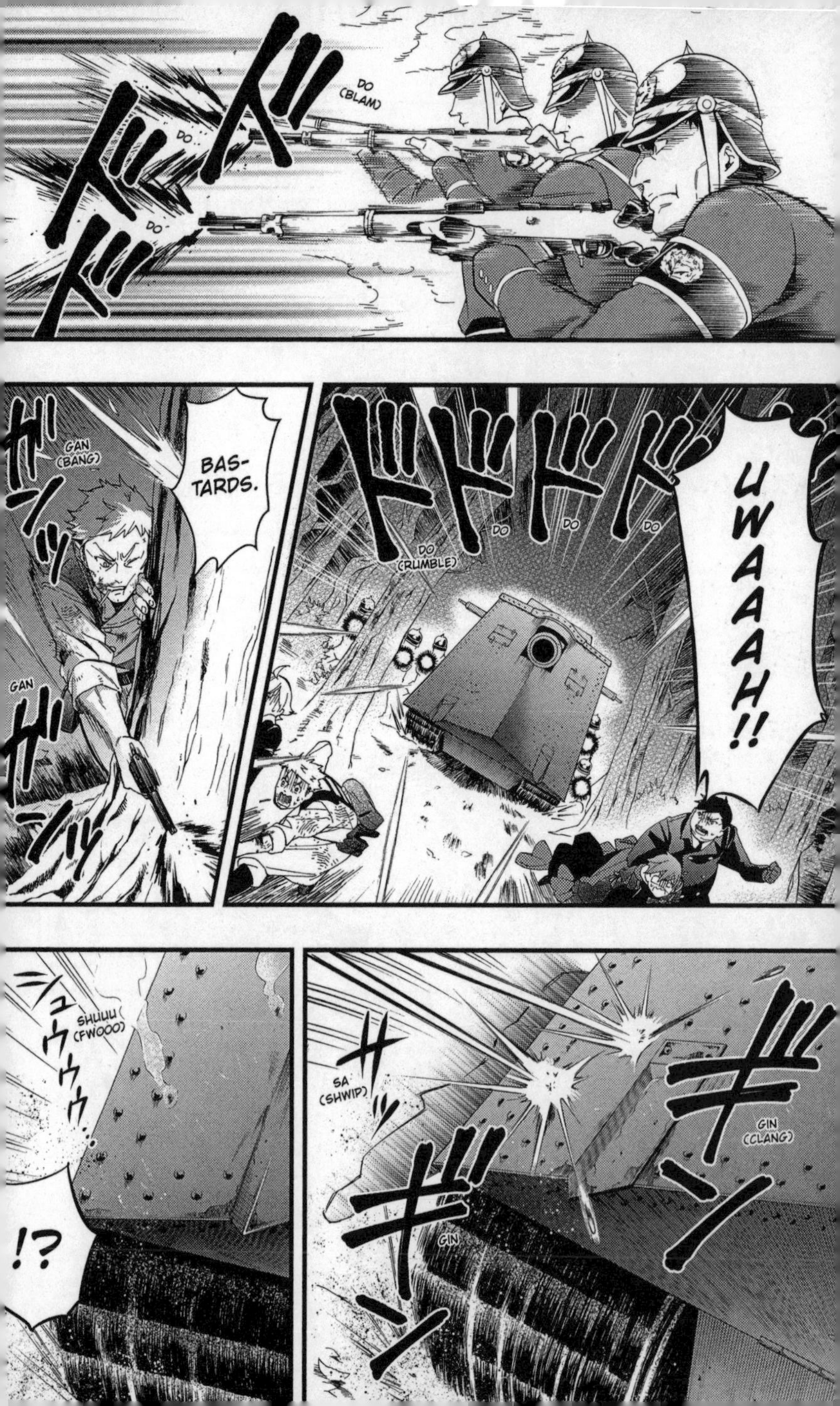

DO
(BLAM)
DO
DO
UWAAAAH!!
DO
DO
DO
DO
(RUMBLE)
GAN
(BANG)
BAS-
TARDS.
GAN
GIN
(CLANG)
SA
(SHWIP)
GIN
SHUUU
(FWOOO)
!?

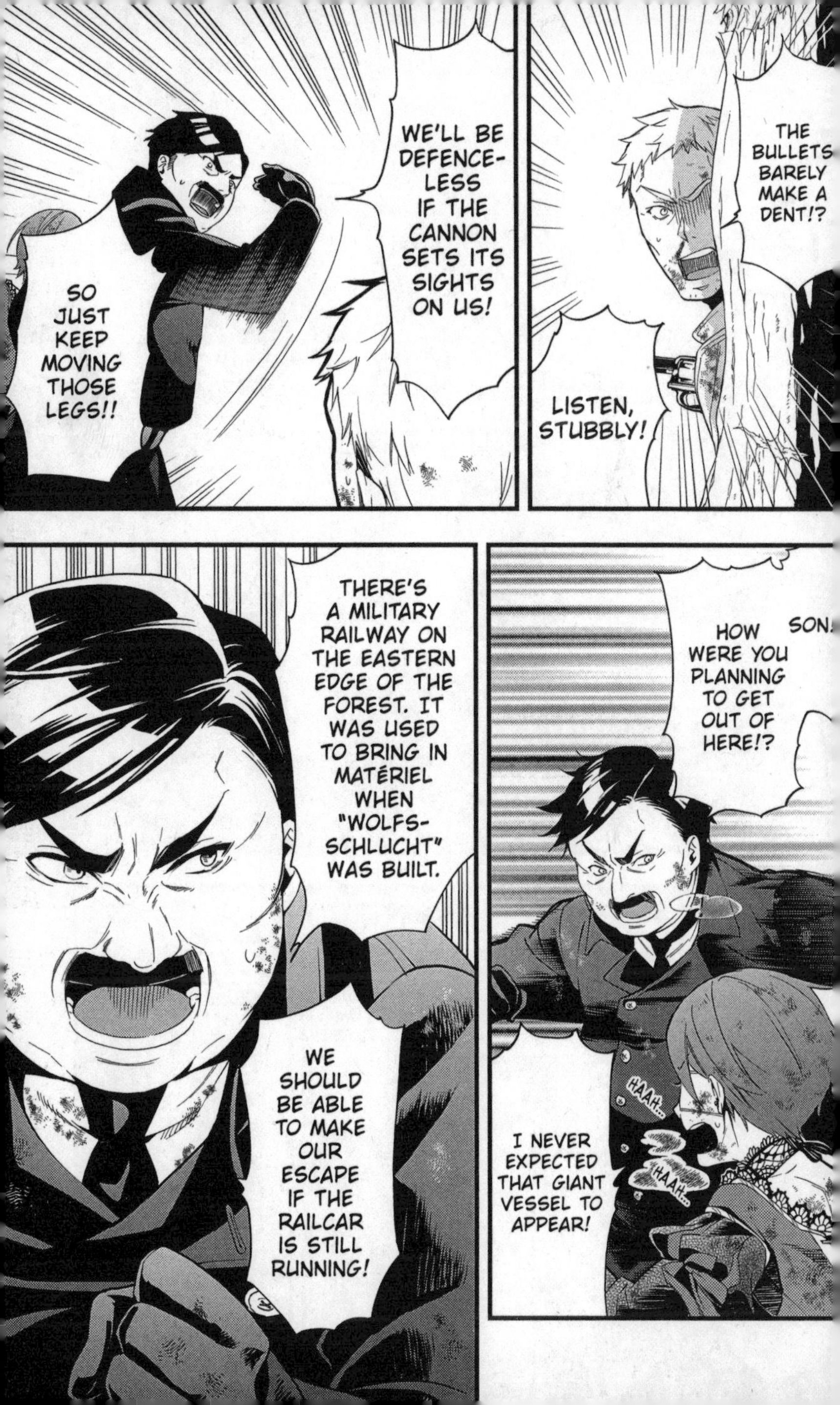
THE BULLETS BARELY MAKE A DENT!?
LISTEN, STUBBLY!
WE'LL BE DEFENCE-LESS IF THE CANNON SETS ITS SIGHTS ON US!
SO JUST KEEP MOVING THOSE LEGS!!
SON.
HOW WERE YOU PLANNING TO GET OUT OF HERE!?
HAAH...
HAAH...
I NEVER EXPECTED THAT GIANT VESSEL TO APPEAR!
THERE'S A MILITARY RAILWAY ON THE EASTERN EDGE OF THE FOREST. IT WAS USED TO BRING IN MATÉRIEL WHEN "WOLFS-SCHLUCHT" WAS BUILT.
WE SHOULD BE ABLE TO MAKE OUR ESCAPE IF THE RAILCAR IS STILL RUNNING!

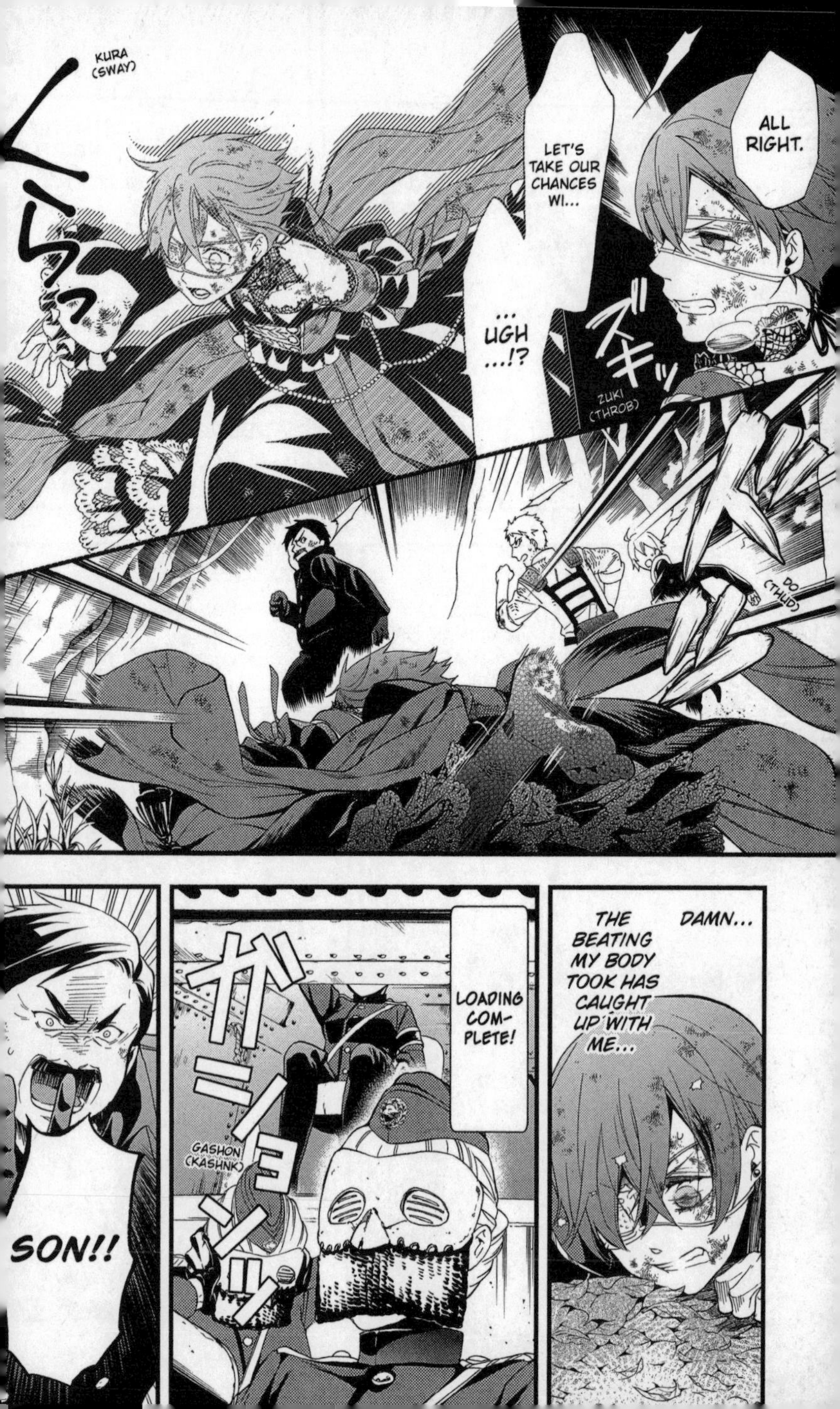
ALL RIGHT.
LET'S TAKE OUR CHANCES WI...
...UGH...!?
ズキッ
ZUKI (THROB)
くらっ
KURA (SWAY)
DO (THUD)
DAMN...
THE BEATING MY BODY TOOK HAS CAUGHT UP WITH ME...
LOADING COM-PLETE!
ガション
GASHON (KASHNK)
SON!!

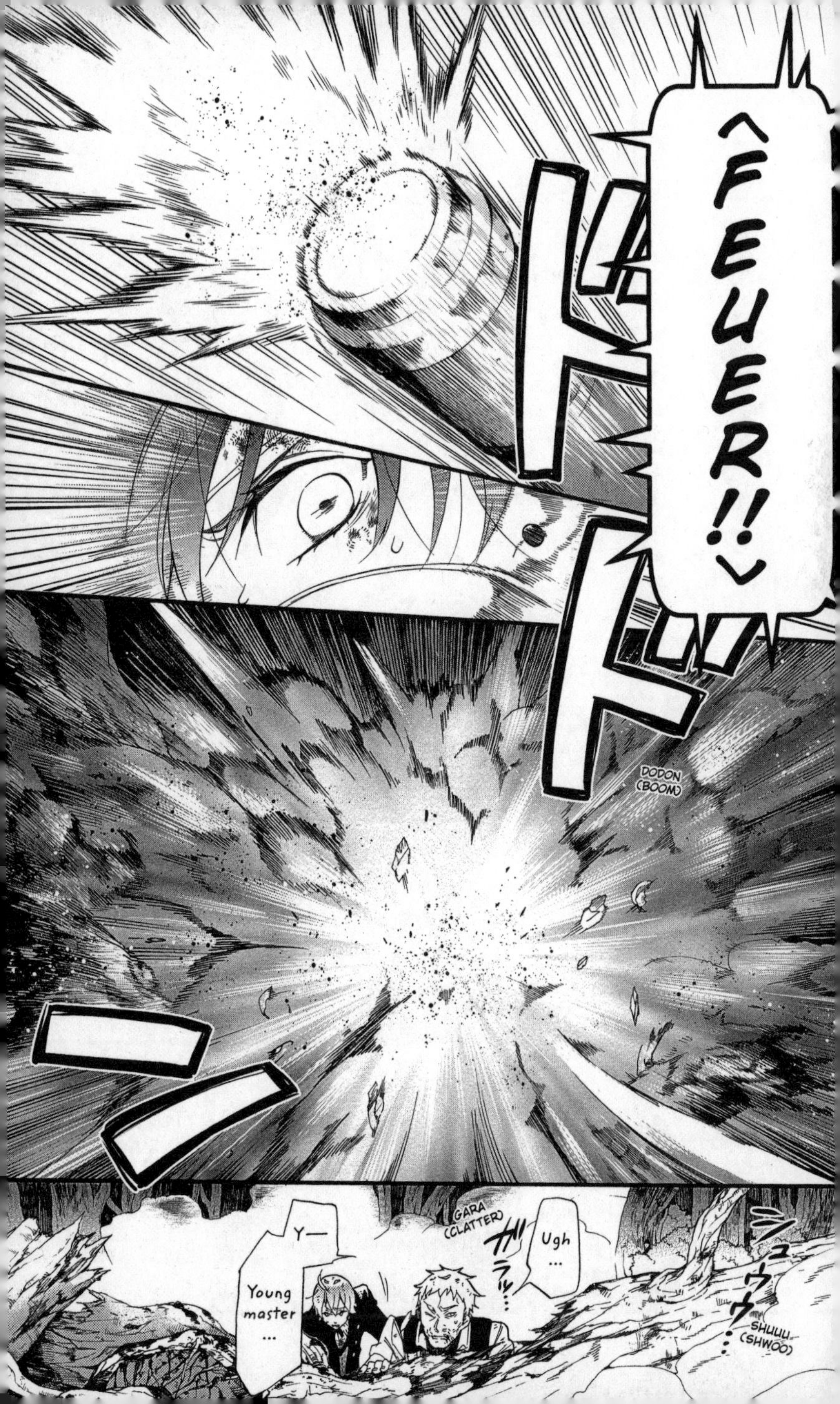
〈FEUER!!〉
DODON (BOOM)
GARA (CLATTER)
Ugh ...
Y—
Young master ...
SHUUU (SHWOO)

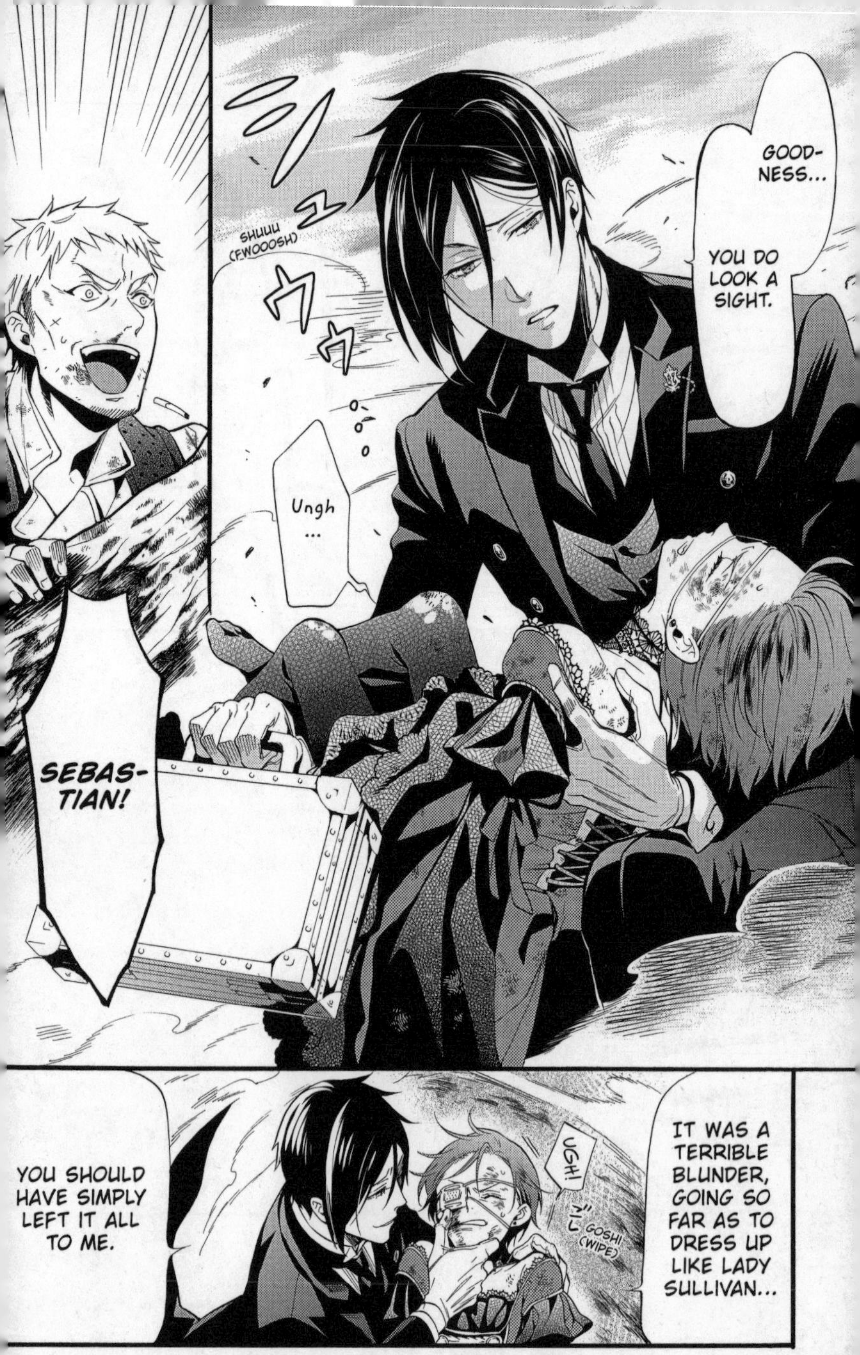
GOOD-NESS...
YOU DO LOOK A SIGHT.
SHUUU (FWOOOSH)
Ungh ...
SEBAS-TIAN!
IT WAS A TERRIBLE BLUNDER, GOING SO FAR AS TO DRESS UP LIKE LADY SULLIVAN...
UGH!
GOSHI (WIPE)
YOU SHOULD HAVE SIMPLY LEFT IT ALL TO ME.

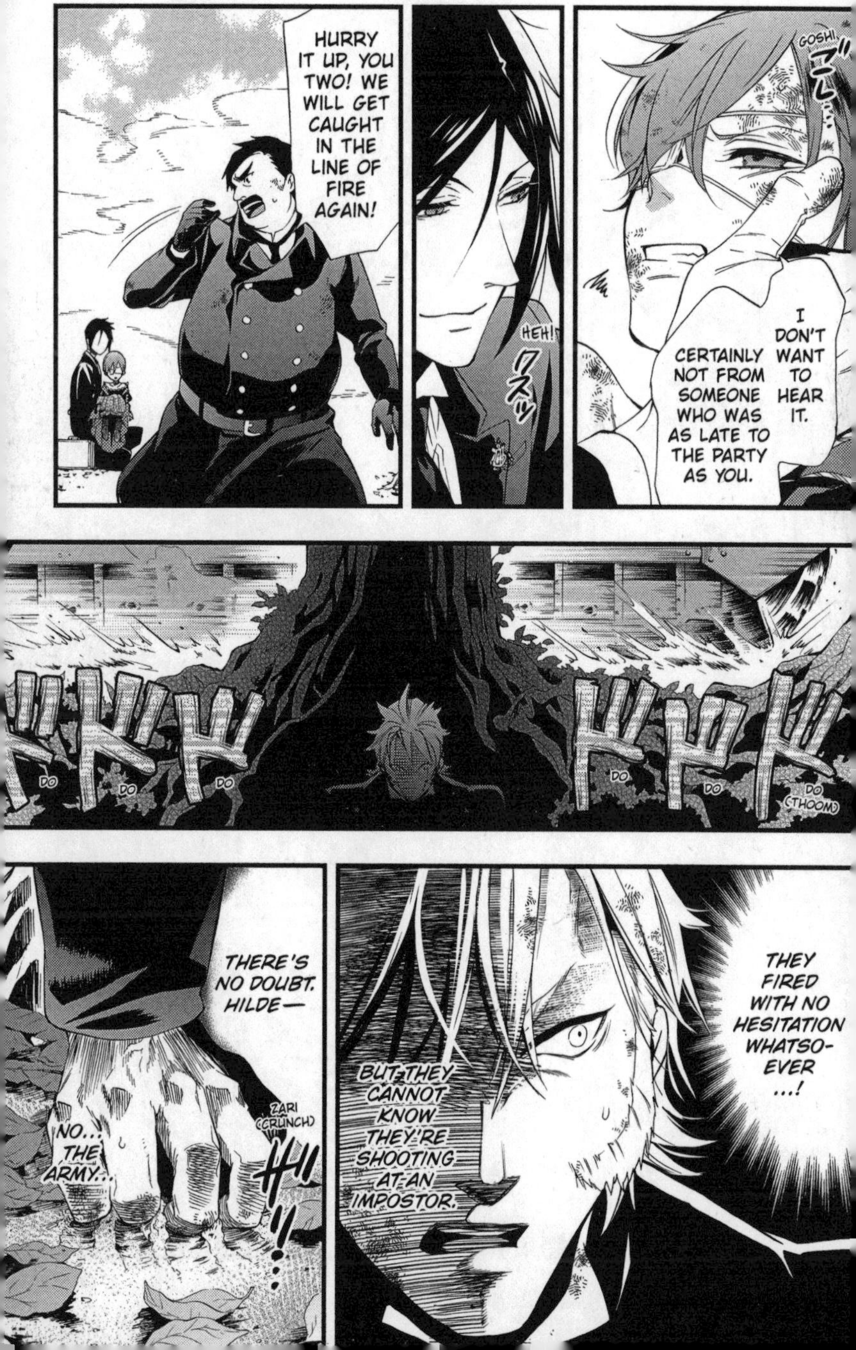
GOSHI
I DON'T WANT TO HEAR IT.
CERTAINLY NOT FROM SOMEONE WHO WAS AS LATE TO THE PARTY AS YOU.
HEH!
HURRY IT UP, YOU TWO! WE WILL GET CAUGHT IN THE LINE OF FIRE AGAIN!
DO
DO
DO (THOOM)
DO
DO
DO
THEY FIRED WITH NO HESITATION WHATSO-EVER ...!
BUT THEY CANNOT KNOW THEY'RE SHOOTING AT AN IMPOSTOR.
THERE'S NO DOUBT. HILDE—
ZARI (CRUNCH)
NO... THE ARMY...

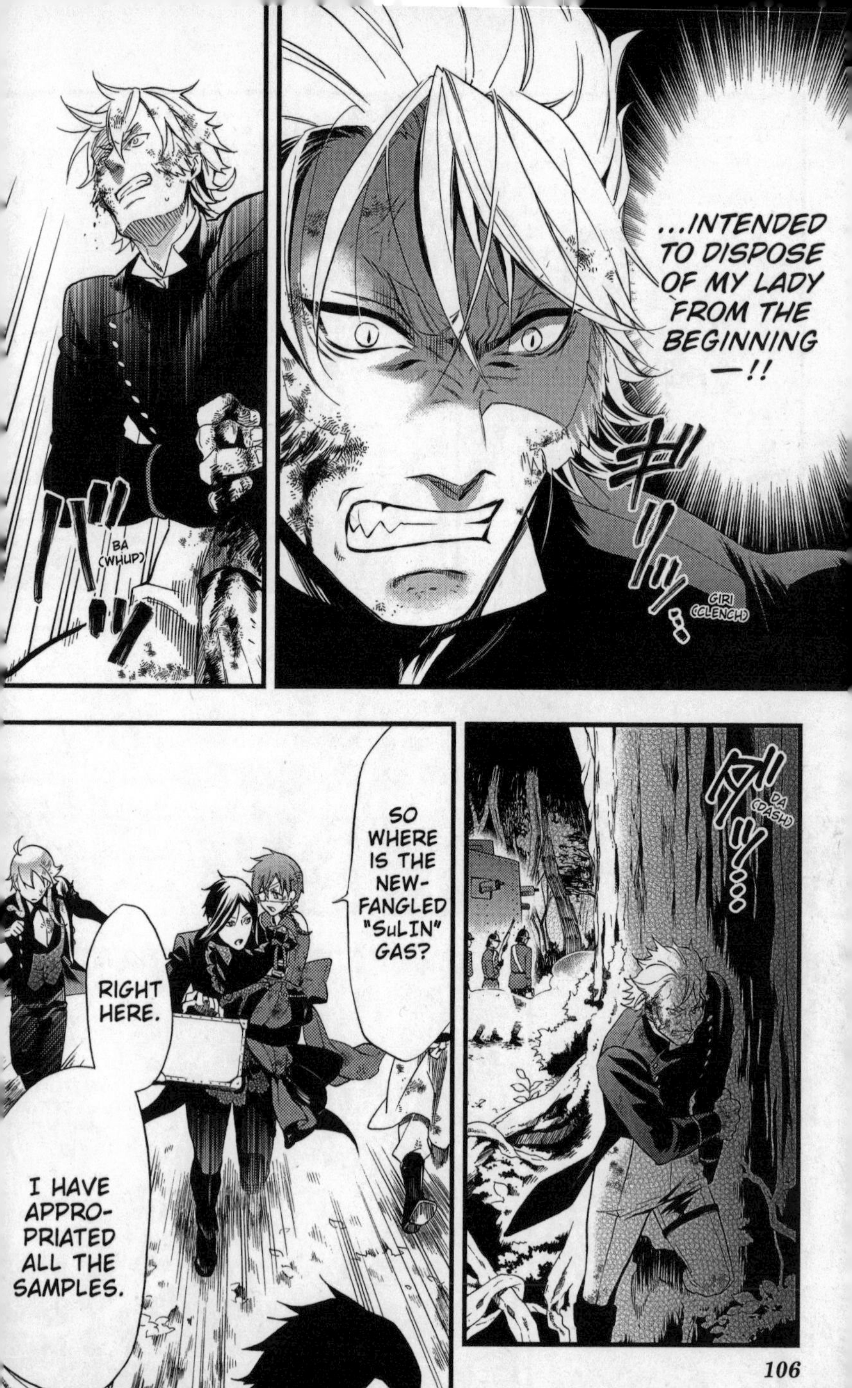
...INTENDED TO DISPOSE OF MY LADY FROM THE BEGINNING—!!
GIRI (CLENCH)
BA (WHUP)
DA (DASH)
SO WHERE IS THE NEW-FANGLED "SuLIN" GAS?
RIGHT HERE.
I HAVE APPRO-PRIATED ALL THE SAMPLES.

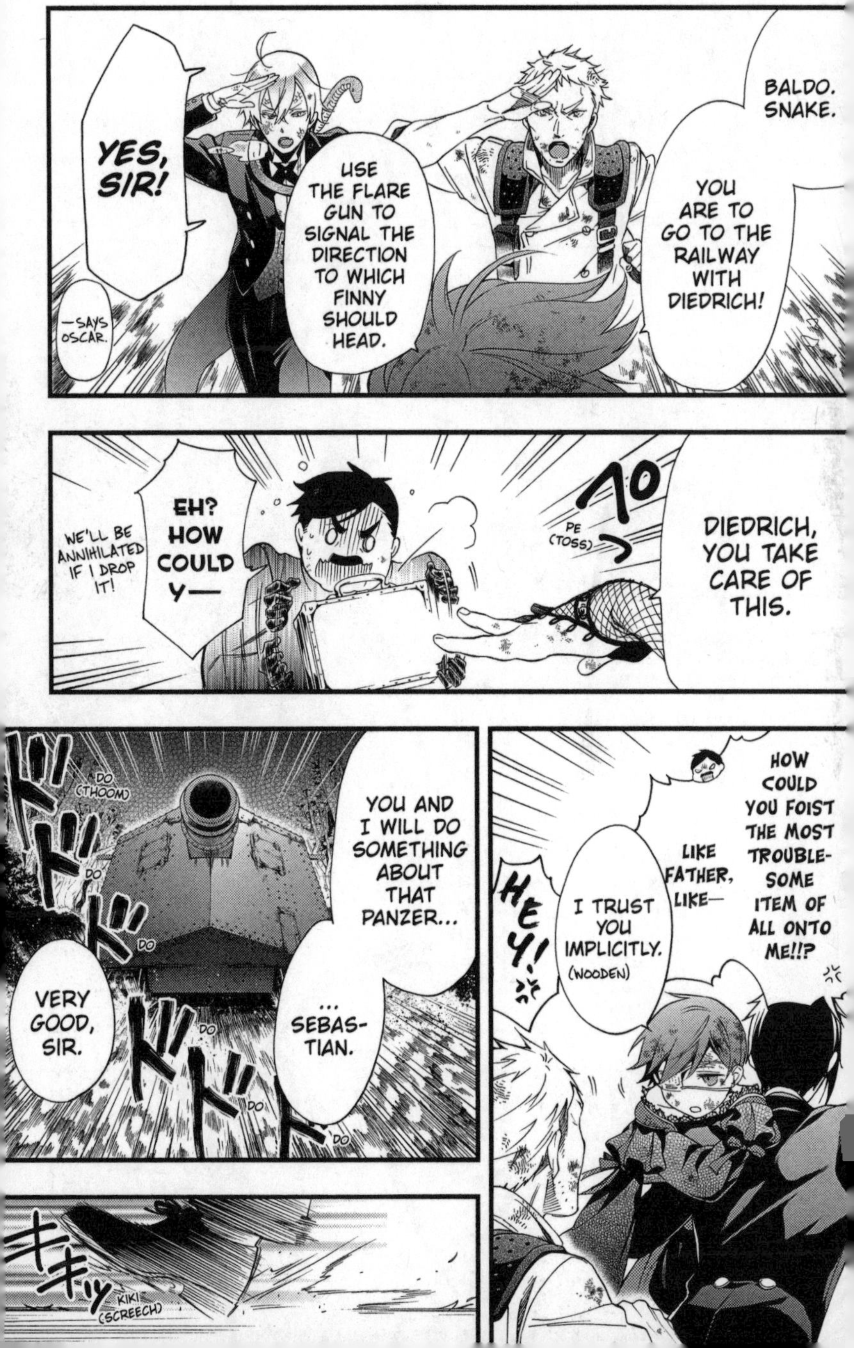
BALDO. SNAKE.
YOU ARE TO GO TO THE RAILWAY WITH DIEDRICH!
USE THE FLARE GUN TO SIGNAL THE DIRECTION TO WHICH FINNY SHOULD HEAD.
YES, SIR!
—SAYS OSCAR.
DIEDRICH, YOU TAKE CARE OF THIS.
PE (TOSS)
EH? HOW COULD Y—
WE'LL BE ANNIHILATED IF I DROP IT!
HOW COULD YOU FOIST THE MOST TROUBLE-SOME ITEM OF ALL ONTO ME!!?
LIKE FATHER, LIKE—
I TRUST YOU IMPLICITLY. (WOODEN)
HEY!
YOU AND I WILL DO SOMETHING ABOUT THAT PANZER...
...SEBAS-TIAN.
DO (THOOM)
DO
DO
VERY GOOD, SIR.
DO
DO
DO
KIKI (SCREECH)

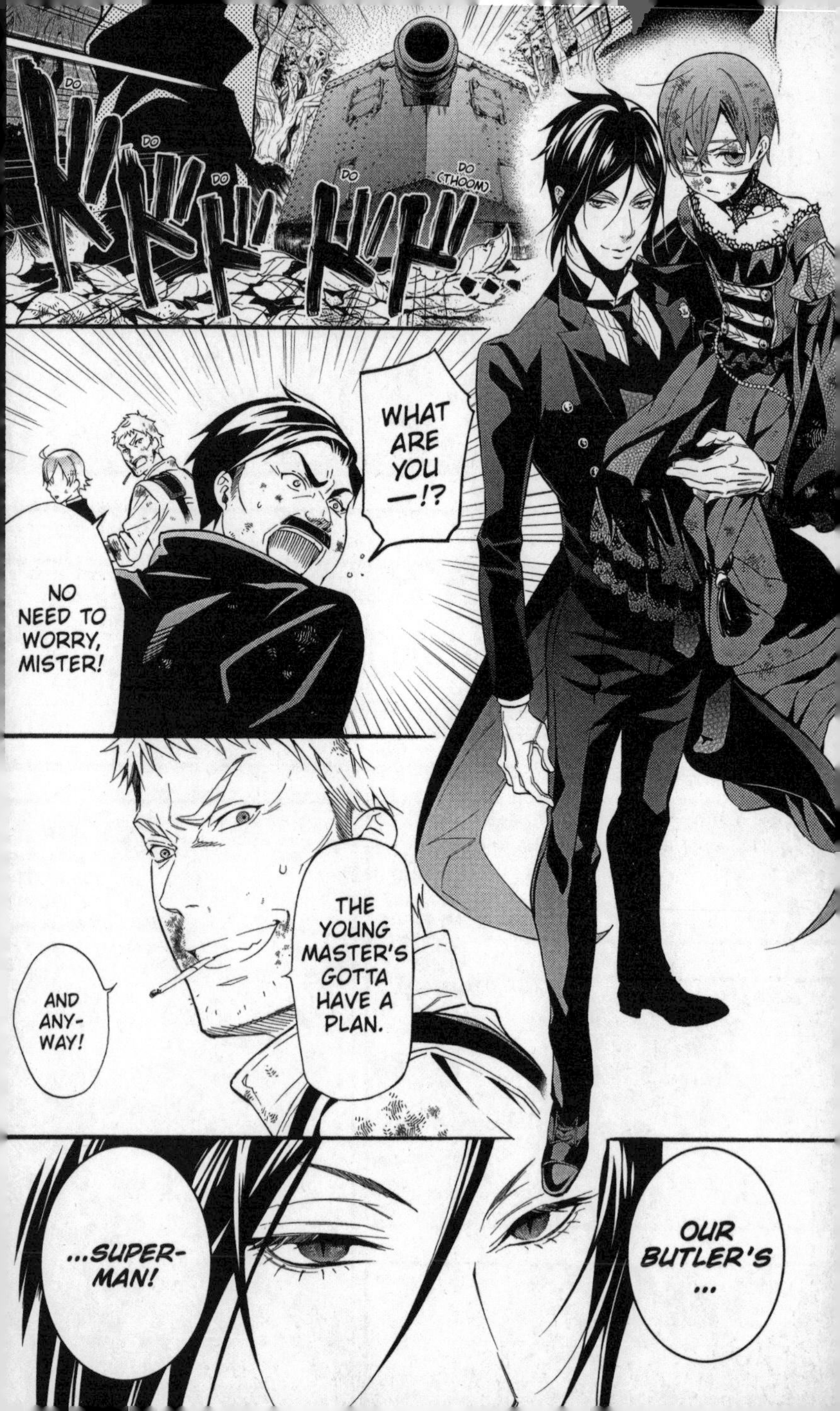
DO (THOOM)
DO
DO
DO
DO
WHAT ARE YOU—!?
NO NEED TO WORRY, MISTER!
THE YOUNG MASTER'S GOTTA HAVE A PLAN.
AND ANY-WAY!
OUR BUTLER'S...
...SUPER-MAN!

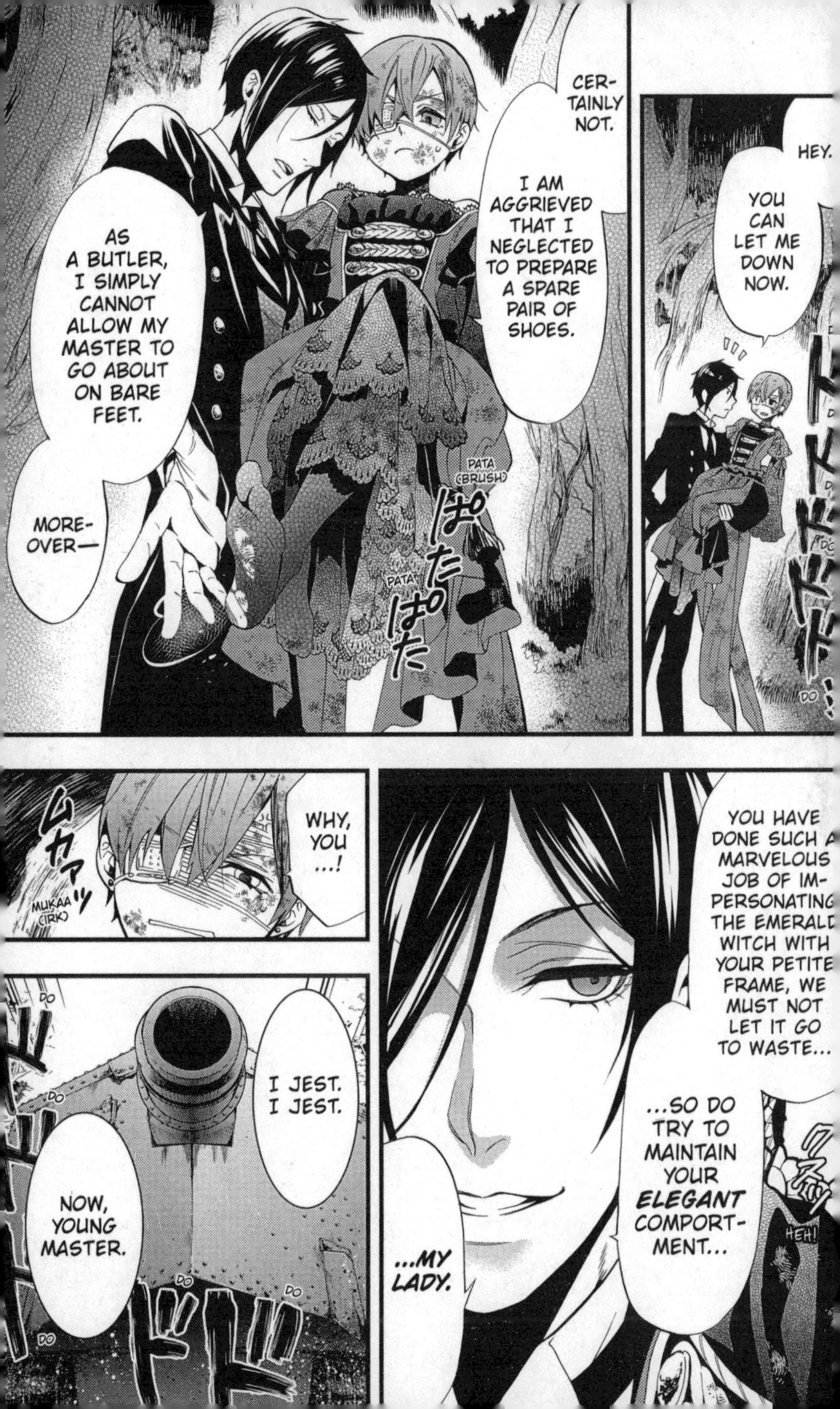
HEY.
YOU CAN LET ME DOWN NOW.
DO
DO
DO
DO
CER-TAINLY NOT.
I AM AGGRIEVED THAT I NEGLECTED TO PREPARE A SPARE PAIR OF SHOES.
AS A BUTLER, I SIMPLY CANNOT ALLOW MY MASTER TO GO ABOUT ON BARE FEET.
MORE-OVER—
PATA (BRUSH)
ぱた
PATA
ぱた
YOU HAVE DONE SUCH A MARVELOUS JOB OF IM-PERSONATING THE EMERALD WITCH WITH YOUR PETITE FRAME, WE MUST NOT LET IT GO TO WASTE...
...SO DO TRY TO MAINTAIN YOUR ***ELEGANT*** COMPORT-MENT...
HEH!
...MY LADY.
WHY, YOU ...!
ムカァッ
MUKAA (IRK)
I JEST. I JEST.
NOW, YOUNG MASTER.
DO
DO
DO
DO
DO

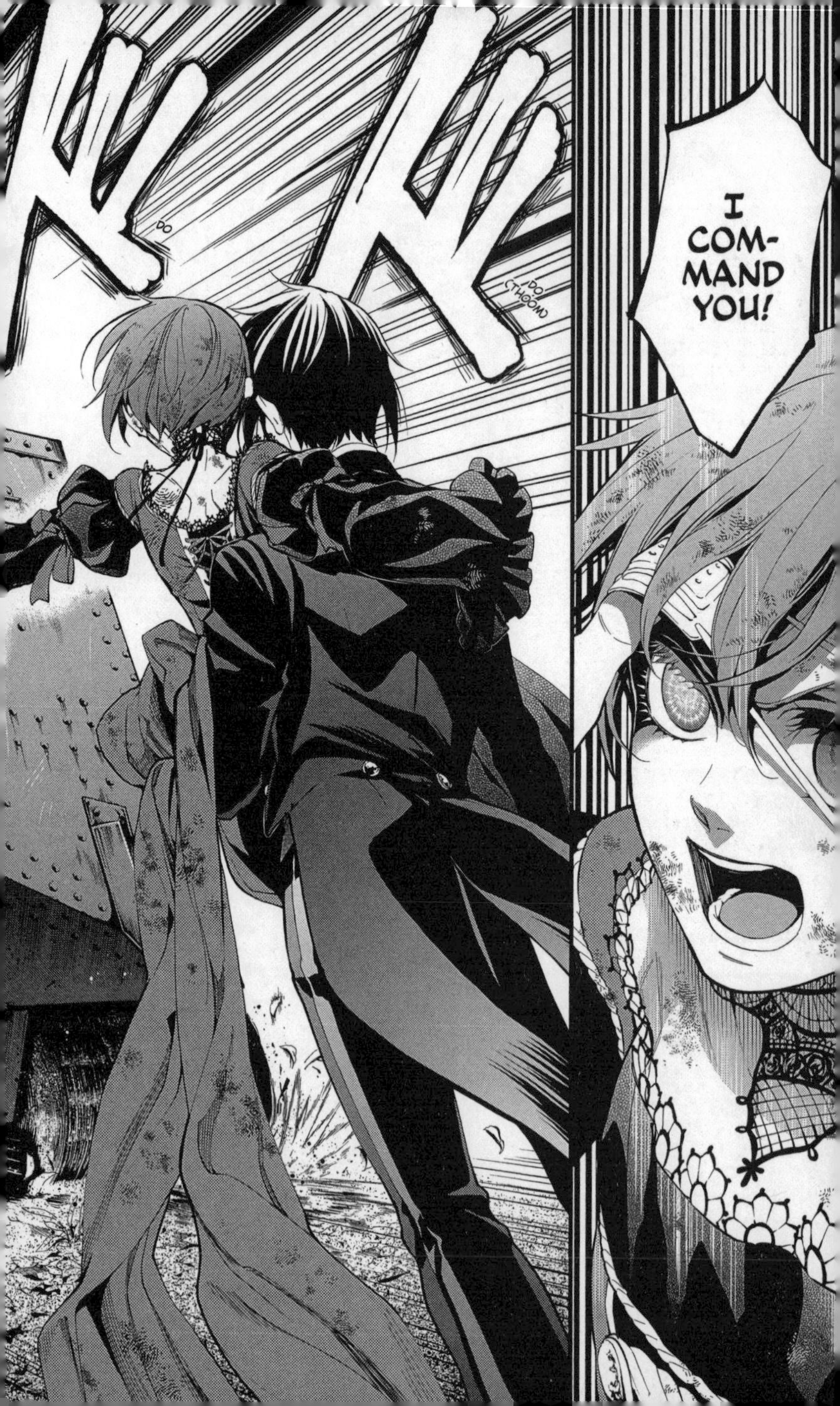
I COMMAND YOU!
DO
DO (THOOM)

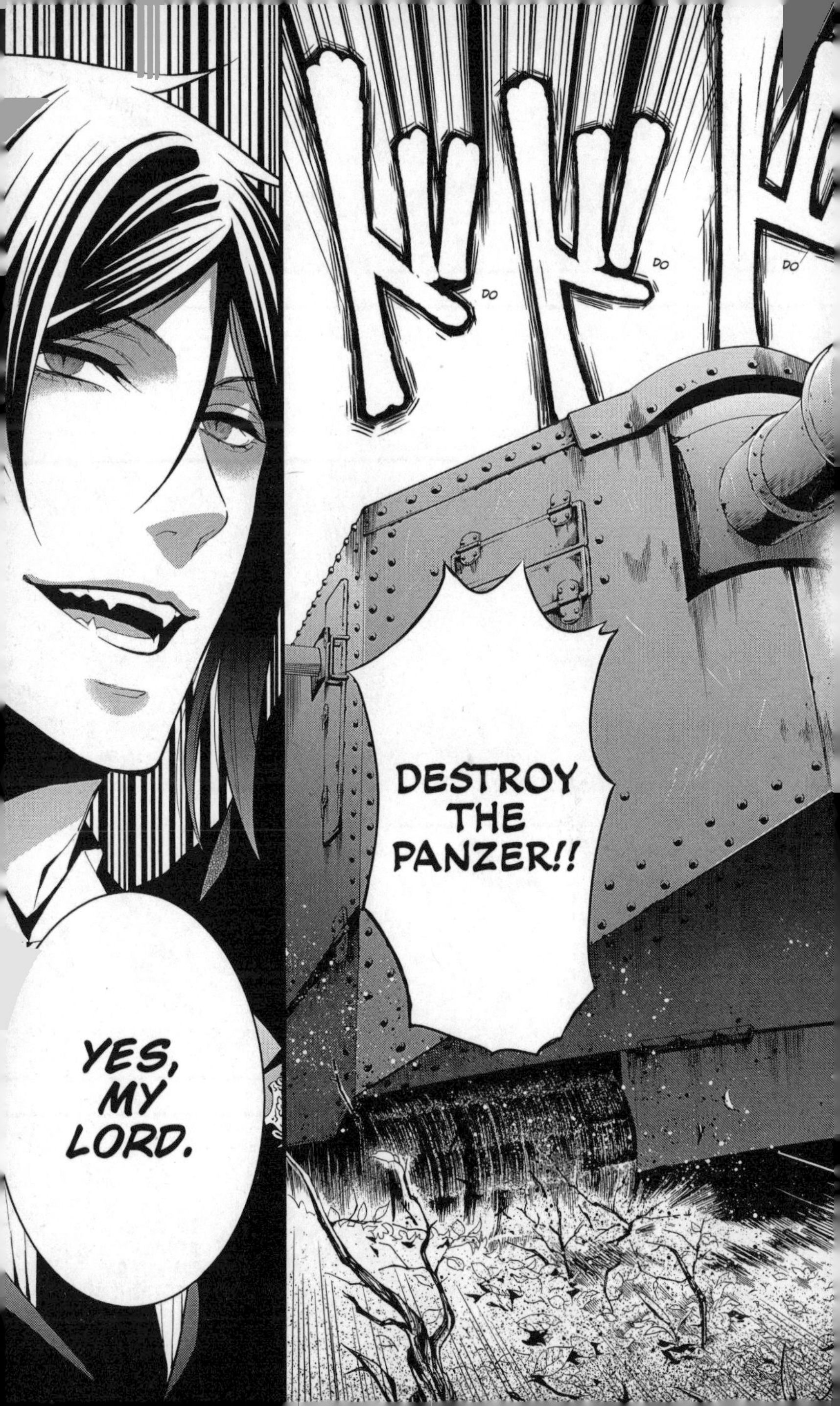
DO
DO
DO
DESTROY THE PANZER!!
YES, MY LORD.

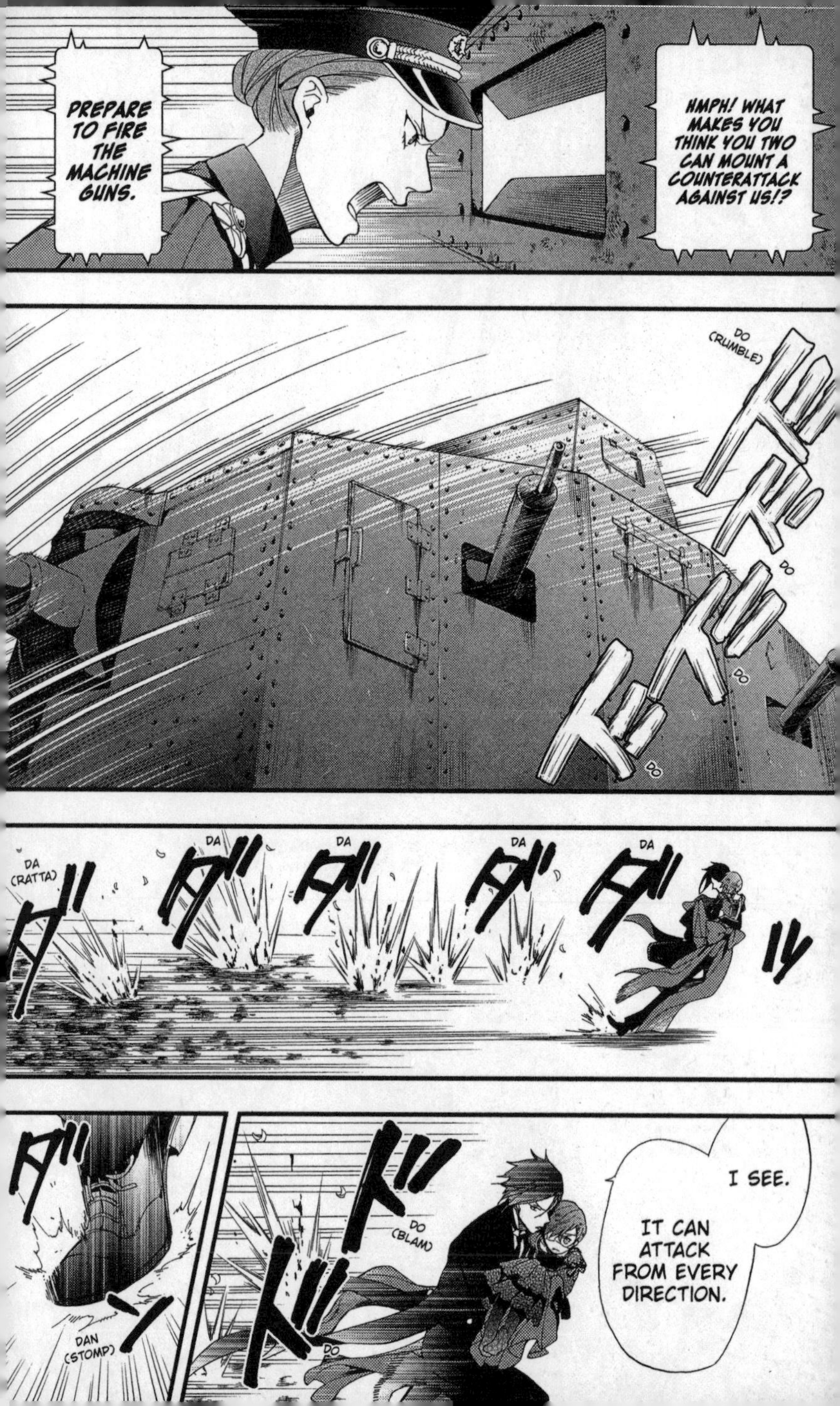
HMPH! WHAT MAKES YOU THINK YOU TWO CAN MOUNT A COUNTERATTACK AGAINST US!?
PREPARE TO FIRE THE MACHINE GUNS.
DO (RUMBLE)
DO
DO
DO
DA
DA
DA
DA
DA (RATTA)
I SEE.
IT CAN ATTACK FROM EVERY DIRECTION.
DO (BLAM)
DO
DAN (STOMP)

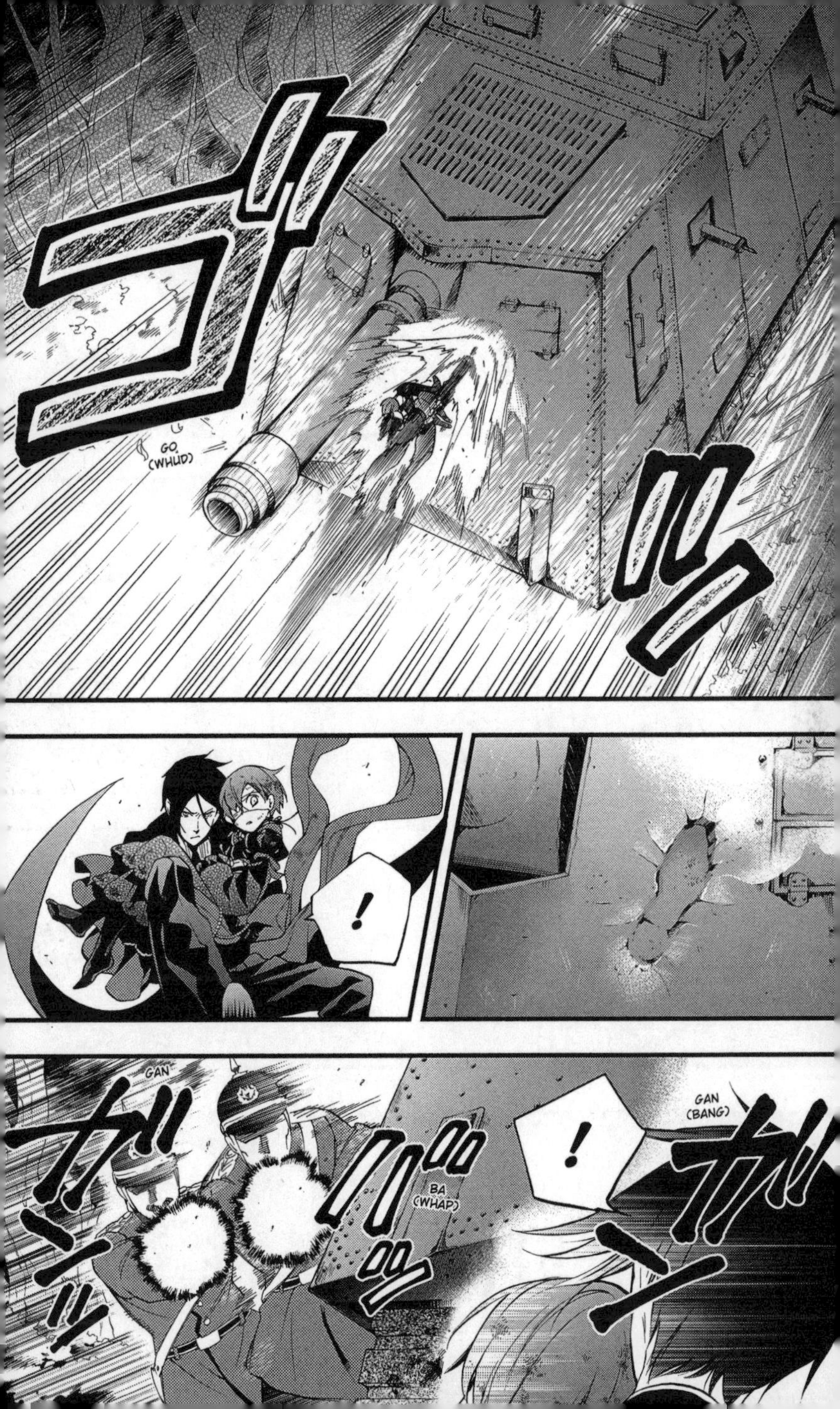
GO
(WHUD)
!
GAN
(BANG)
!
BA
(WHAP)
GAN

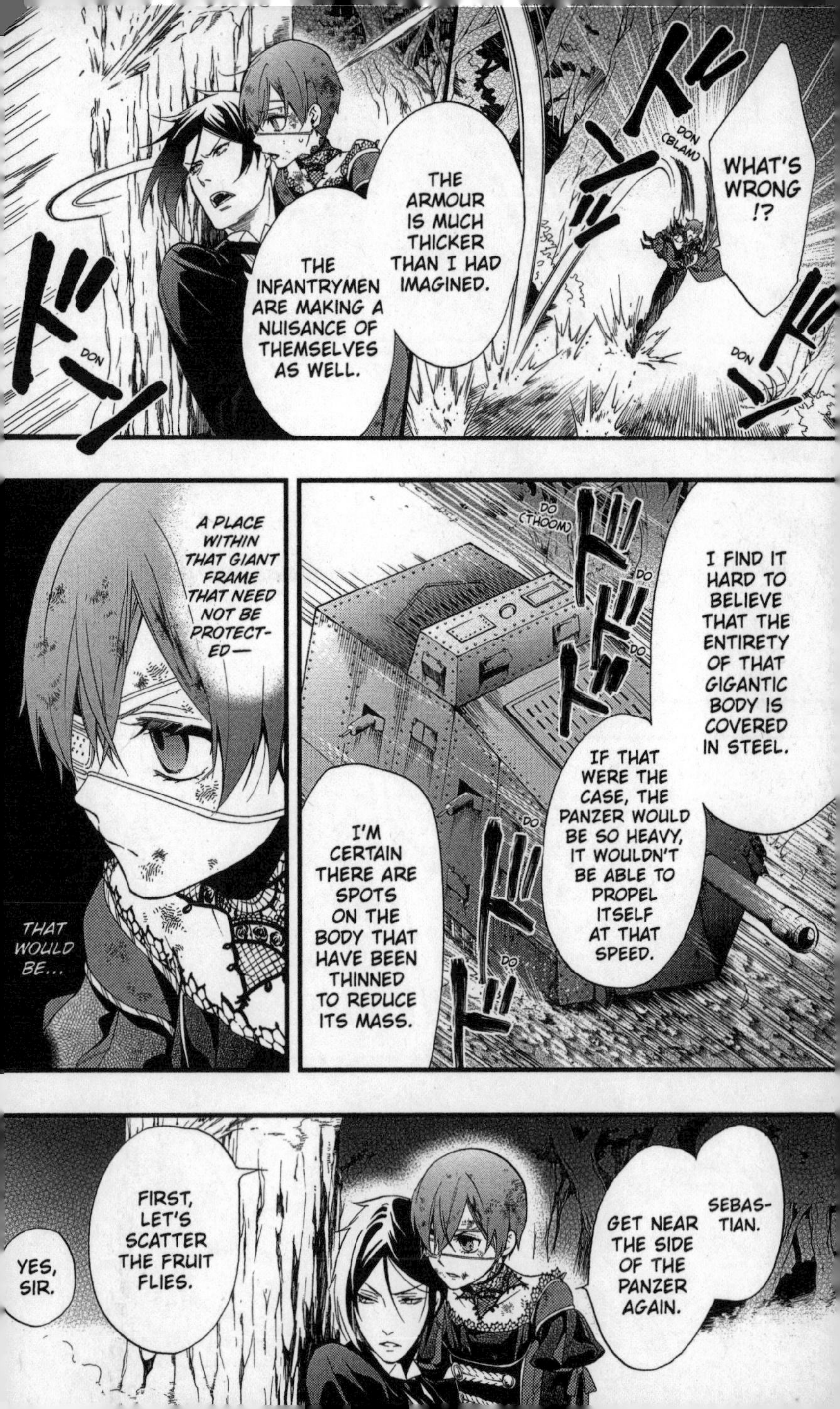
WHAT'S WRONG !?
DON (BLAM)
DON
THE ARMOUR IS MUCH THICKER THAN I HAD IMAGINED.
THE INFANTRYMEN ARE MAKING A NUISANCE OF THEMSELVES AS WELL.
DON
DO (THOOM)
DO
DO
DO
DO
I FIND IT HARD TO BELIEVE THAT THE ENTIRETY OF THAT GIGANTIC BODY IS COVERED IN STEEL.
IF THAT WERE THE CASE, THE PANZER WOULD BE SO HEAVY, IT WOULDN'T BE ABLE TO PROPEL ITSELF AT THAT SPEED.
I'M CERTAIN THERE ARE SPOTS ON THE BODY THAT HAVE BEEN THINNED TO REDUCE ITS MASS.
A PLACE WITHIN THAT GIANT FRAME THAT NEED NOT BE PROTECTED—
THAT WOULD BE...
SEBASTIAN.
GET NEAR THE SIDE OF THE PANZER AGAIN.
FIRST, LET'S SCATTER THE FRUIT FLIES.
YES, SIR.

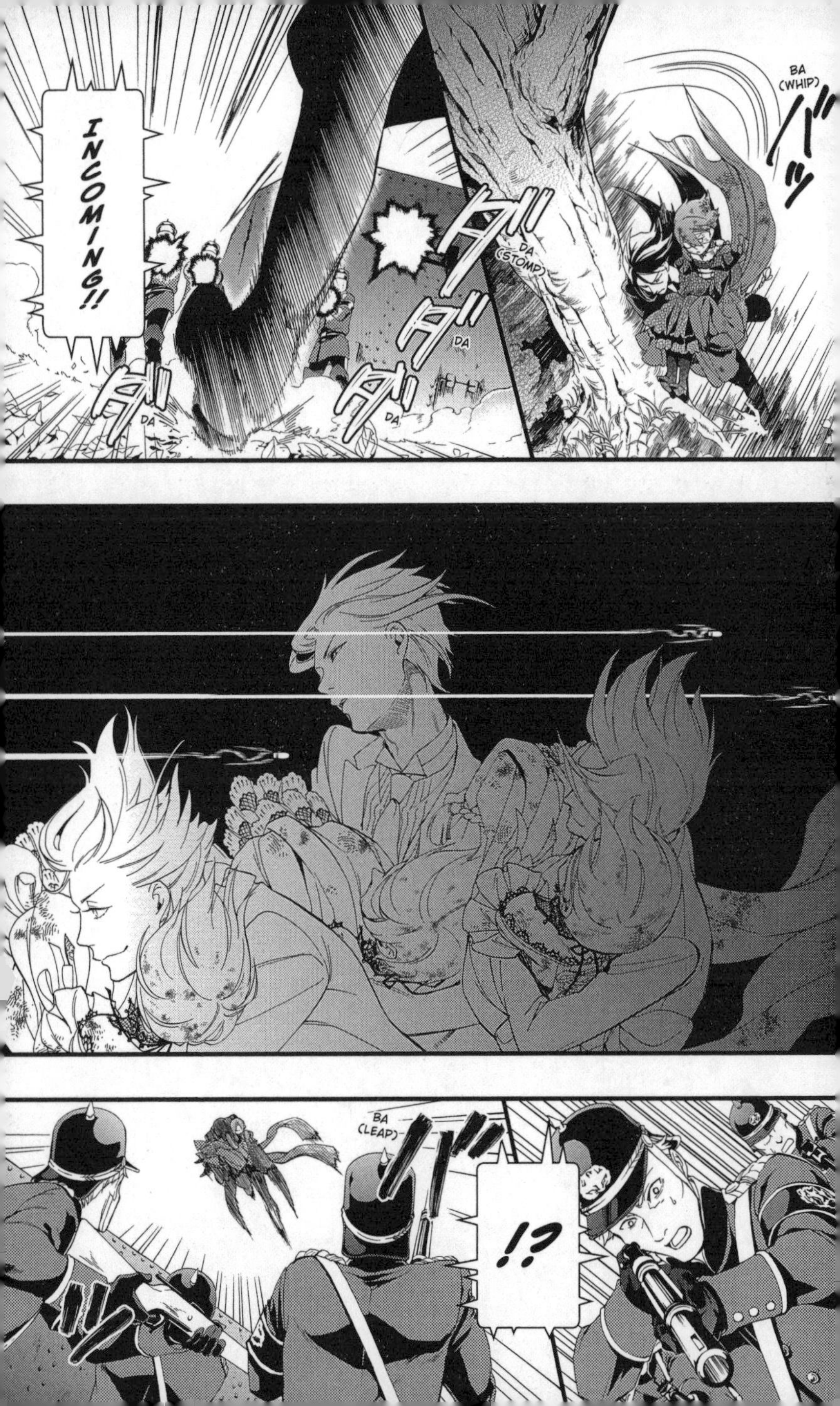
BA (WHIP)
DA (STOMP)
DA
INCOMING!!
DA
DA
BA (LEAP)
!?

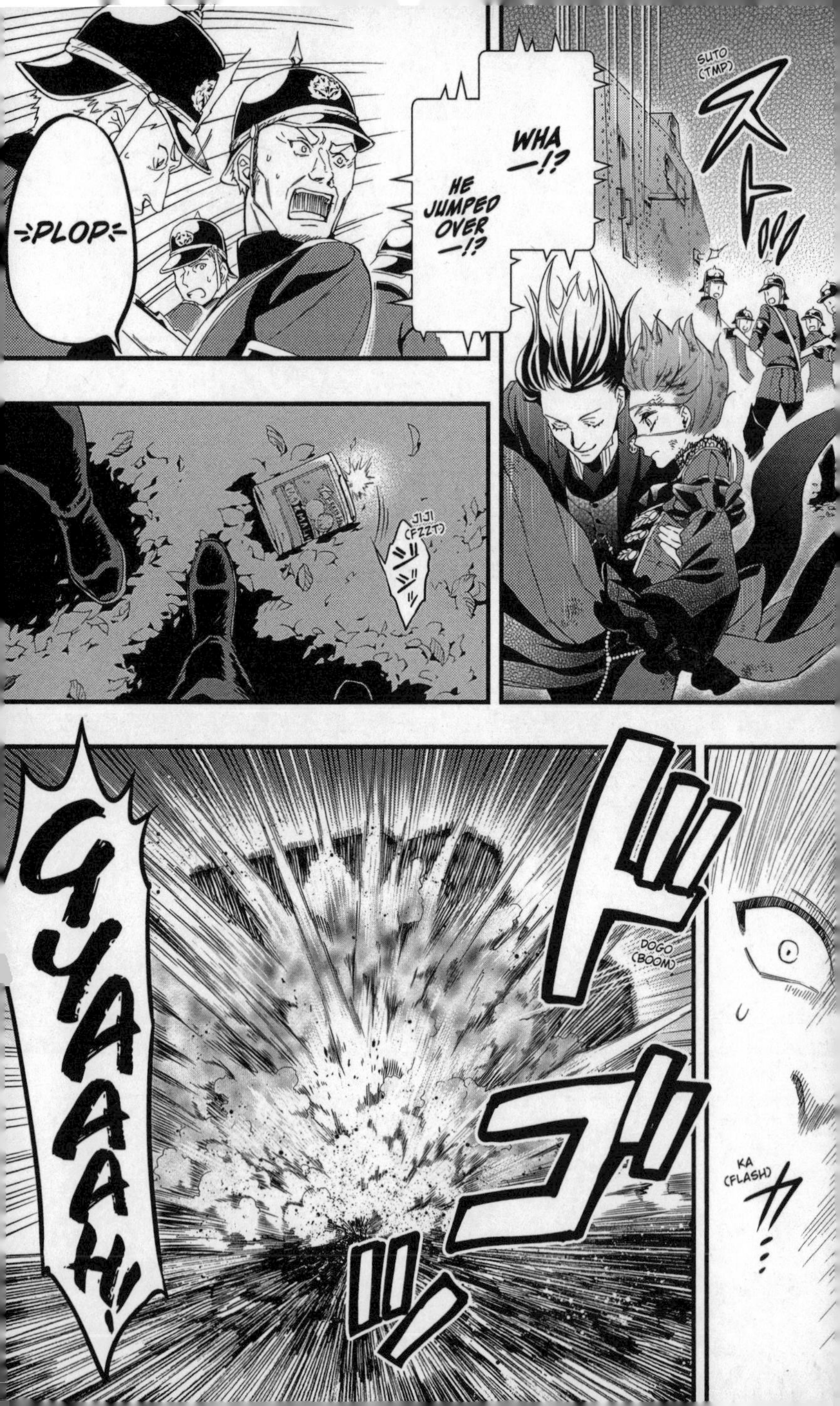
SUTO (TMP)
WHA—!?
HE JUMPED OVER—!?
PLOP
JIJI (FZZT)
KA (FLASH)
DOGO (BOOM)
GYAAAAH!!

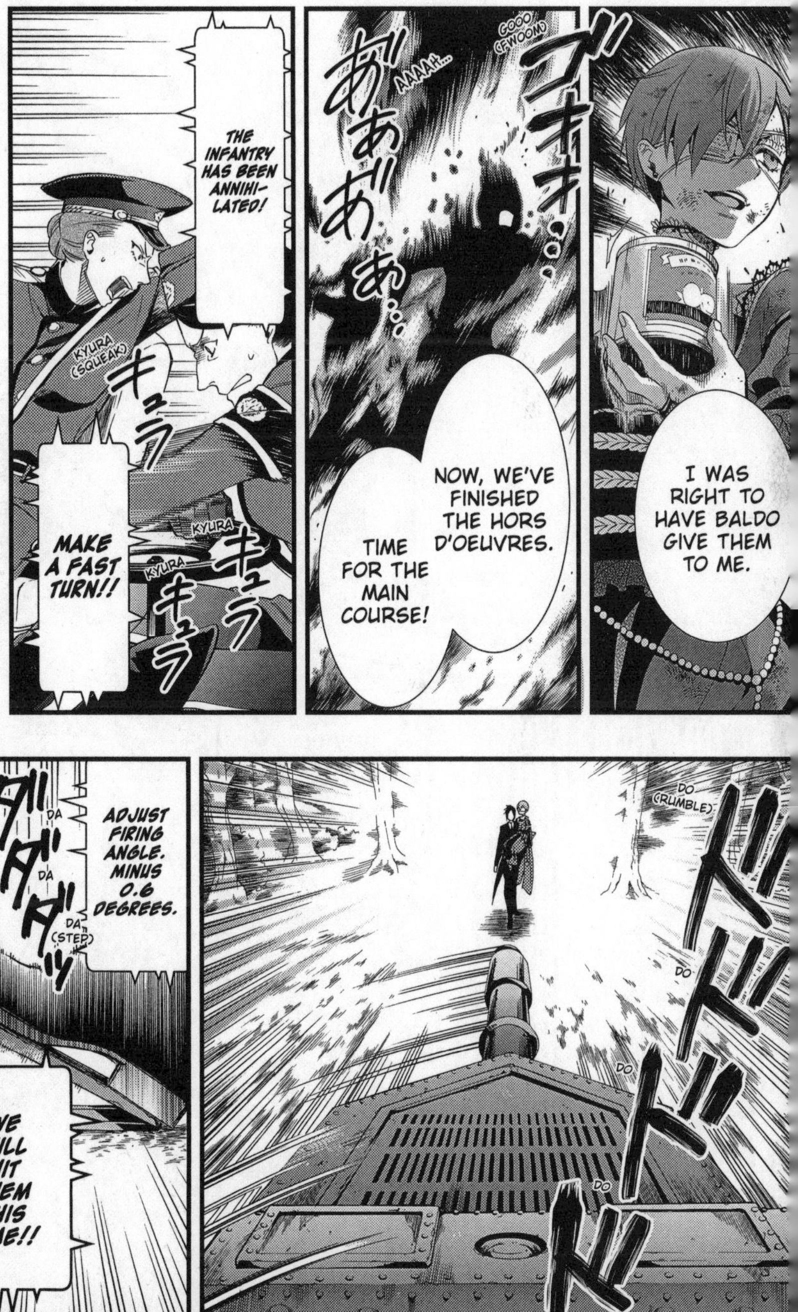
I WAS RIGHT TO HAVE BALDO GIVE THEM TO ME.
GOOO (FWOOM)
AAAAH...
NOW, WE'VE FINISHED THE HORS D'OEUVRES.
TIME FOR THE MAIN COURSE!
THE INFANTRY HAS BEEN ANNIHILATED!
KYURA (SQUEAK)
KYURA
KYURA
MAKE A FAST TURN!!
DO (RUMBLE)
DO
DO
DO
DA
DA
DA (STEP)
ADJUST FIRING ANGLE. MINUS 0.6 DEGREES.
WE WILL HIT THEM THIS TIME!!

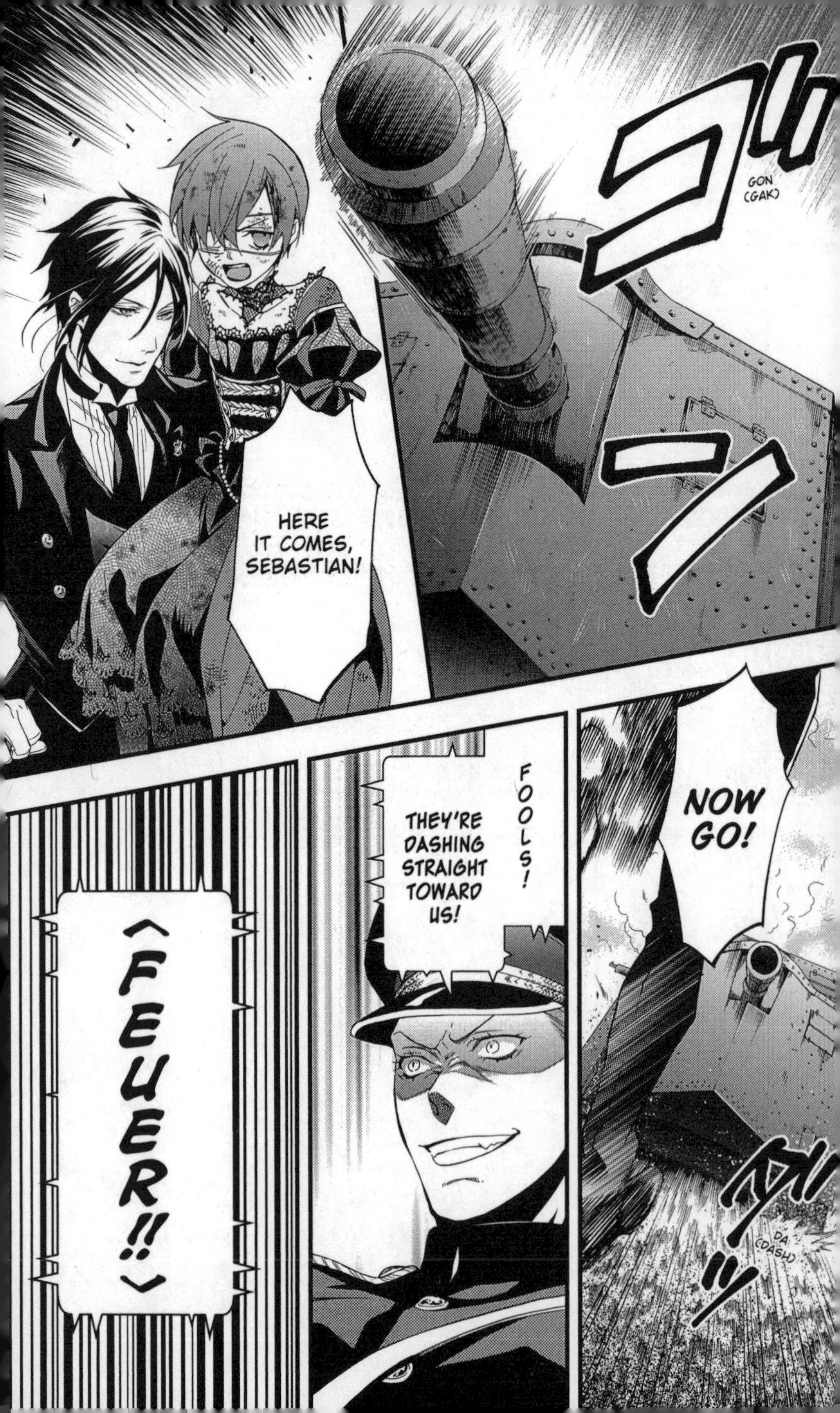
GON (GAK)
HERE IT COMES, SEBASTIAN!
NOW GO!
DA (DASH)
FOOLS!
THEY'RE DASHING STRAIGHT TOWARD US!
〈FEUER!!〉

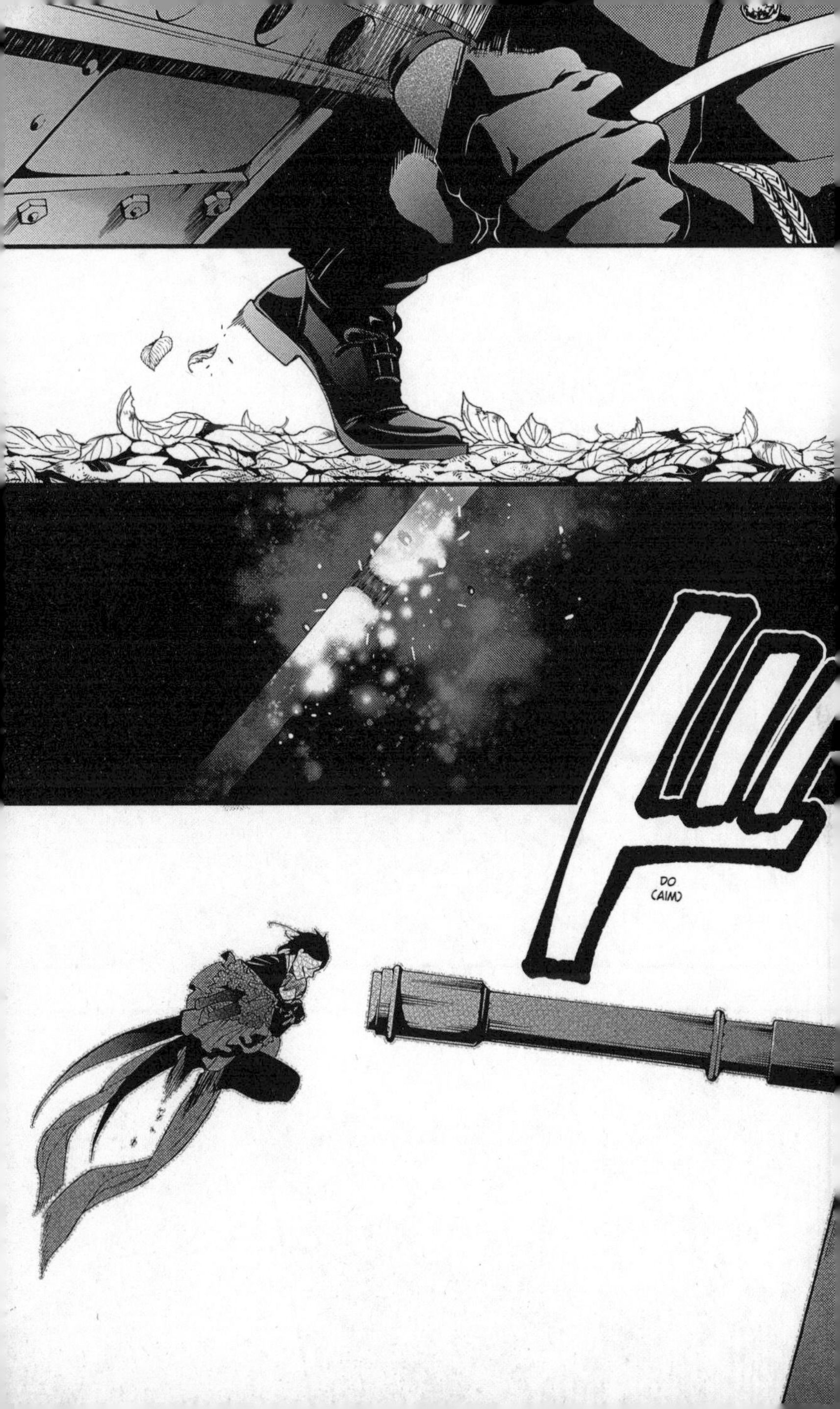
DO
(AIM)

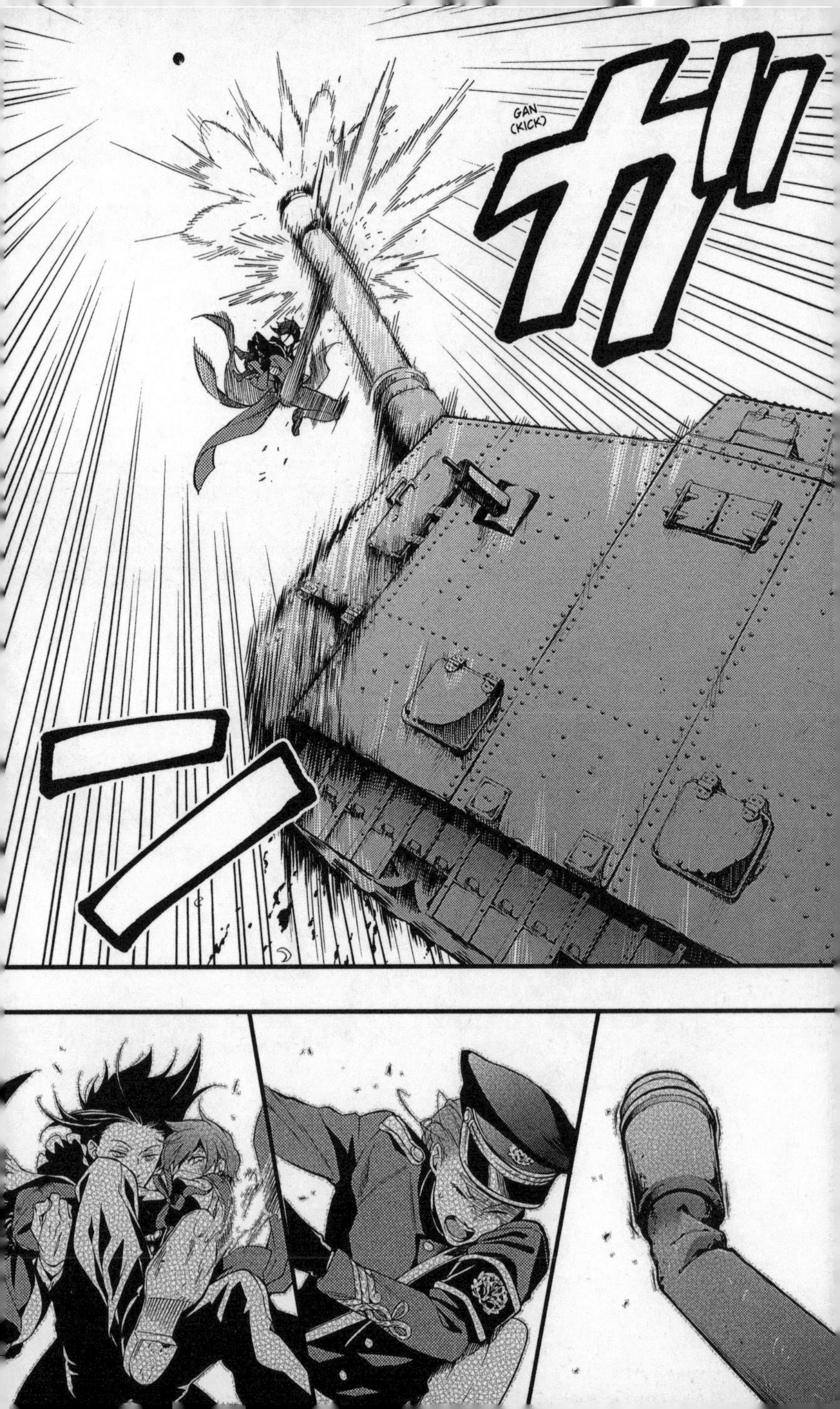
GAN
(KICK)

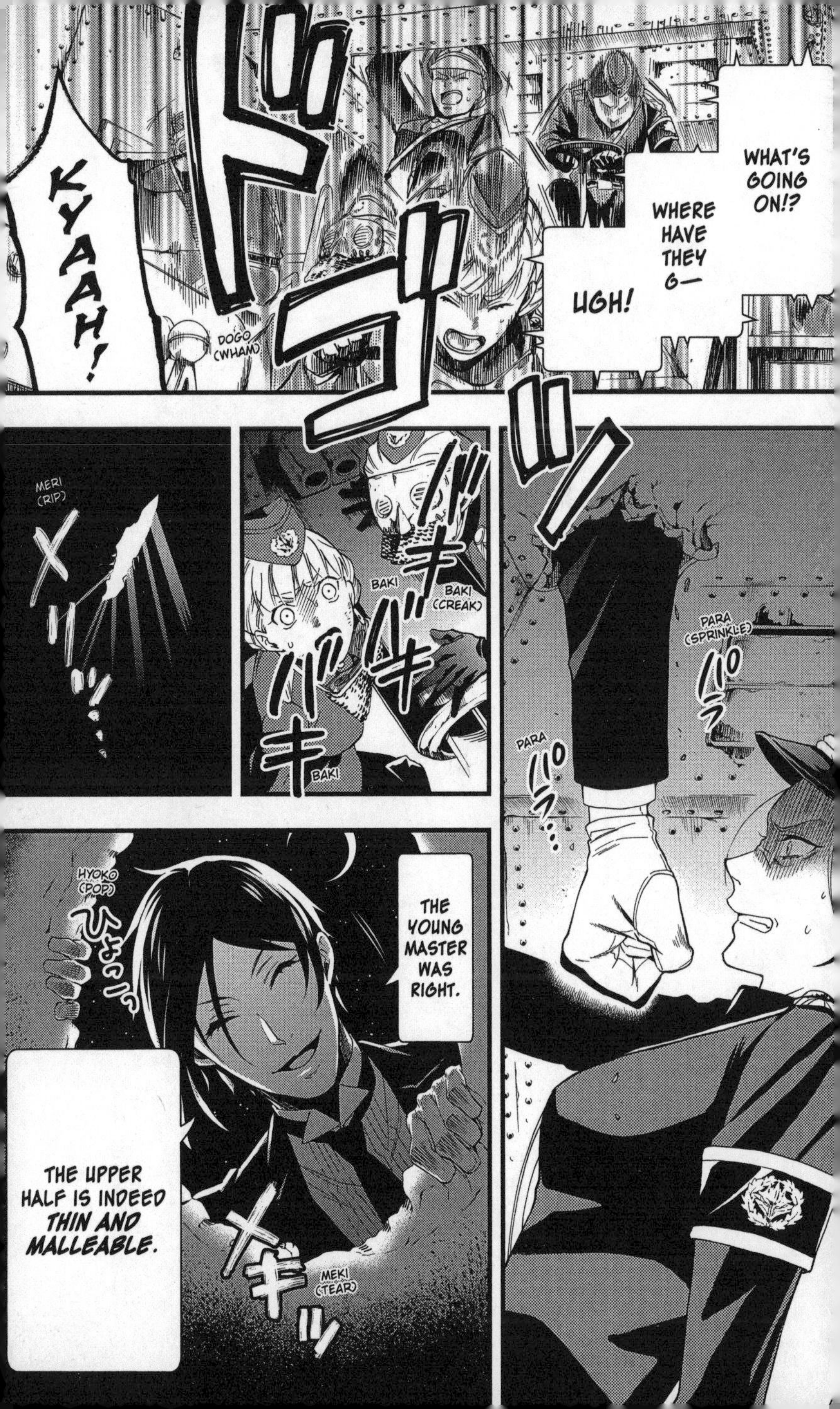

WHAT'S GOING ON!?
WHERE HAVE THEY G—
UGH!
DOGO (WHAM)
KYAAH!
PARA (SPRINKLE)
PARA
BAKI
BAKI (CREAK)
BAKI
MERI (RIP)
THE YOUNG MASTER WAS RIGHT.
HYOKO (POP)
THE UPPER HALF IS INDEED *THIN AND MALLEABLE*.
MEKI (TEAR)

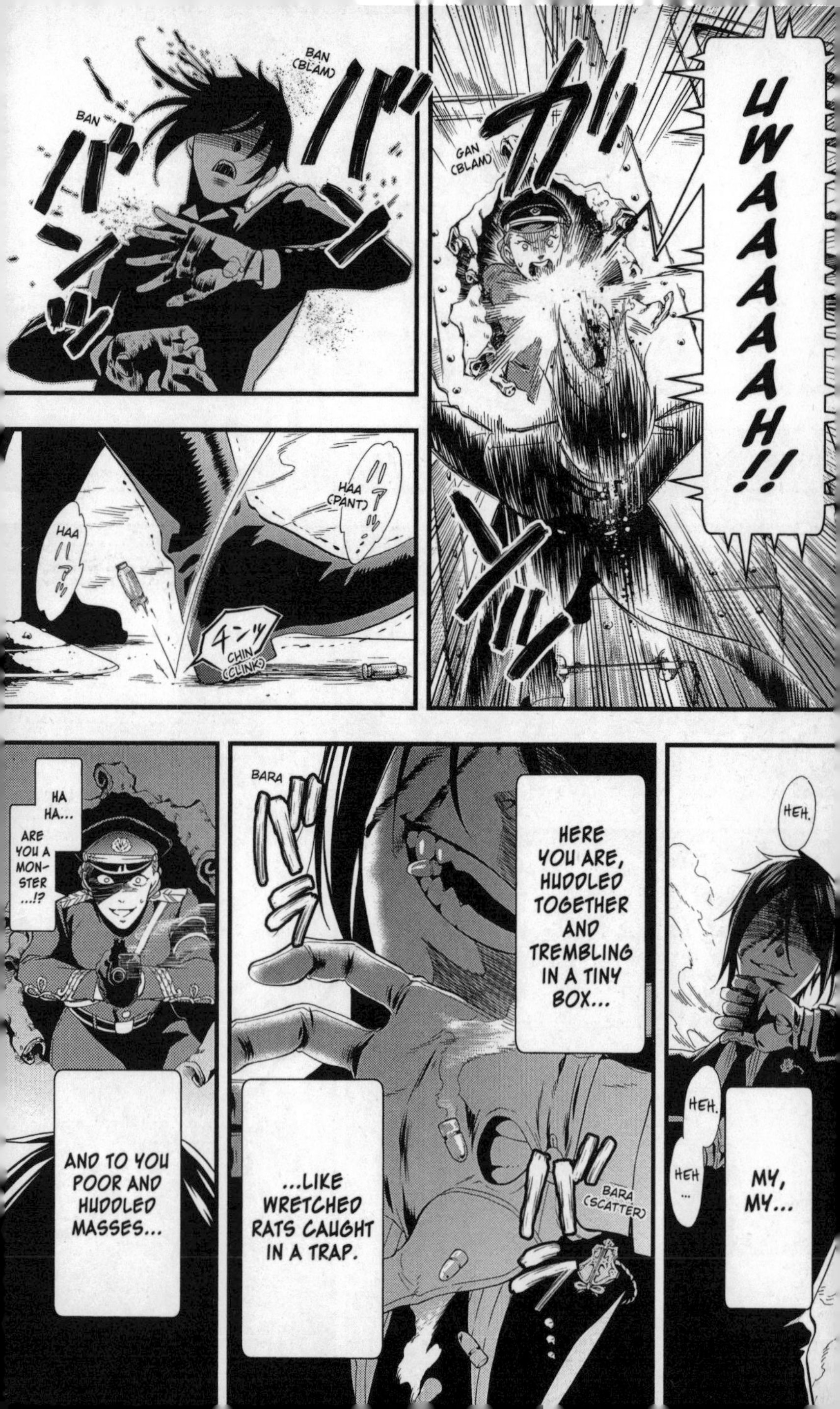
UWAAAAAAH!!
GAN (BLAM)
BAN (BLAM)
BAN
HAA (PANT)
HAA
チンッ
CHIN (CLINK)
HEH.
MY, MY...
HEH.
HEH ...
HERE YOU ARE, HUDDLED TOGETHER AND TREMBLING IN A TINY BOX...
BARA
...LIKE WRETCHED RATS CAUGHT IN A TRAP.
BARA (SCATTER)
HA HA...
ARE YOU A MON-STER ...!?
AND TO YOU POOR AND HUDDLED MASSES...

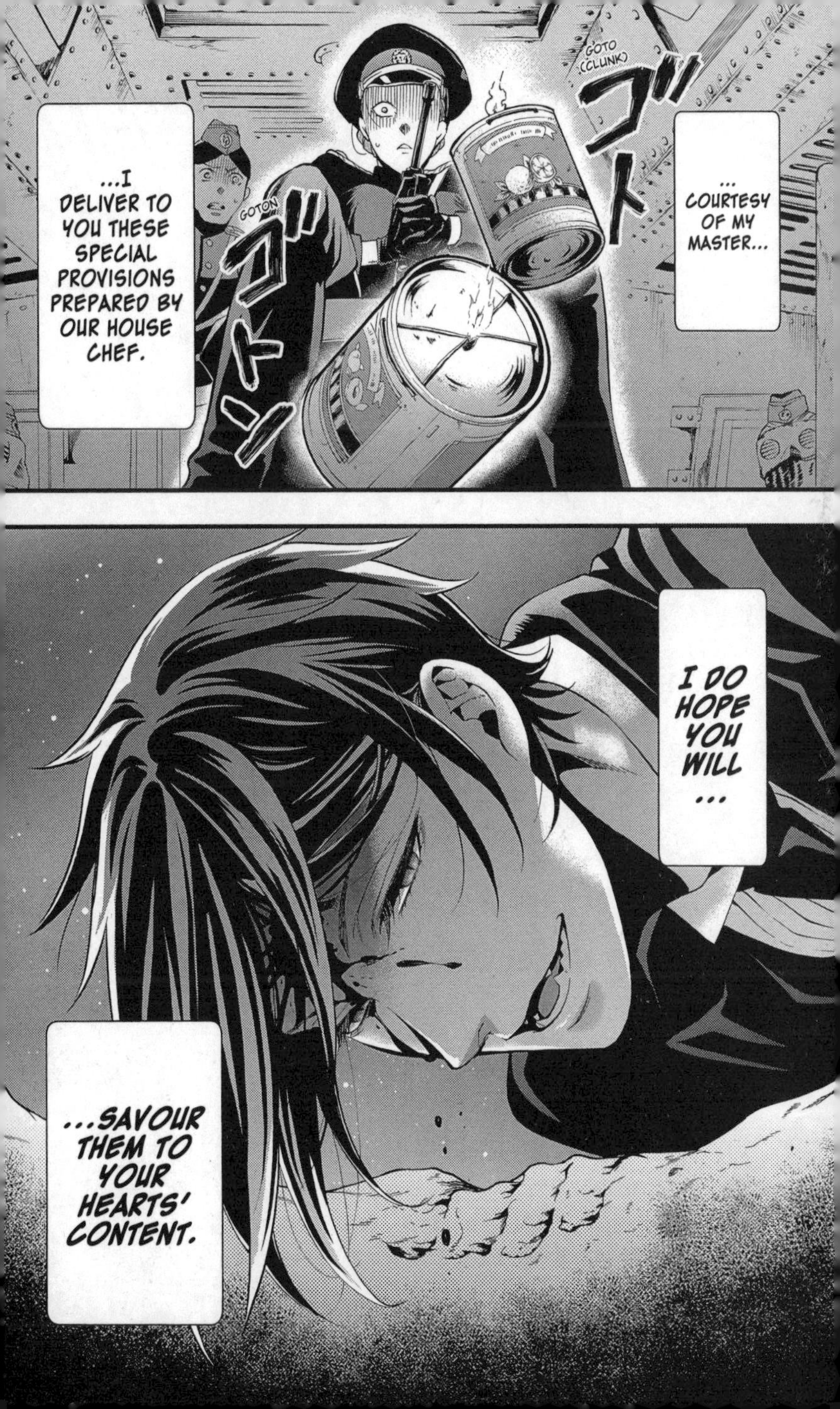
GOTO (CLUNK)
...COURTESY OF MY MASTER...
GOTON
...I DELIVER TO YOU THESE SPECIAL PROVISIONS PREPARED BY OUR HOUSE CHEF.
I DO HOPE YOU WILL...
...SAVOUR THEM TO YOUR HEARTS' CONTENT.

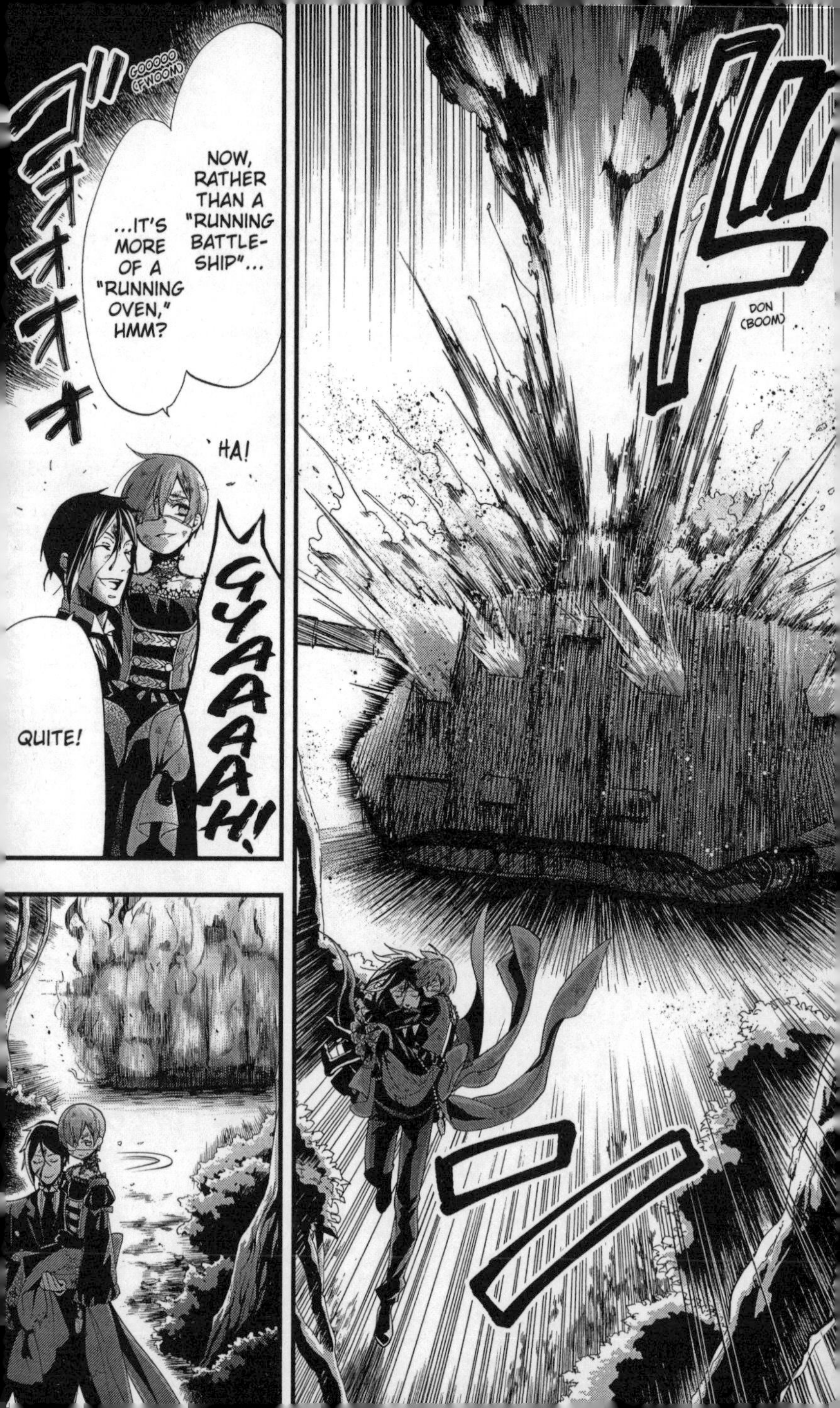
DON (BOOM)
GOOOOO (FWOOM)
NOW, RATHER THAN A "RUNNING BATTLESHIP"...
...IT'S MORE OF A "RUNNING OVEN," HMM?
HA!
GYAAAAAAH!
QUITE!

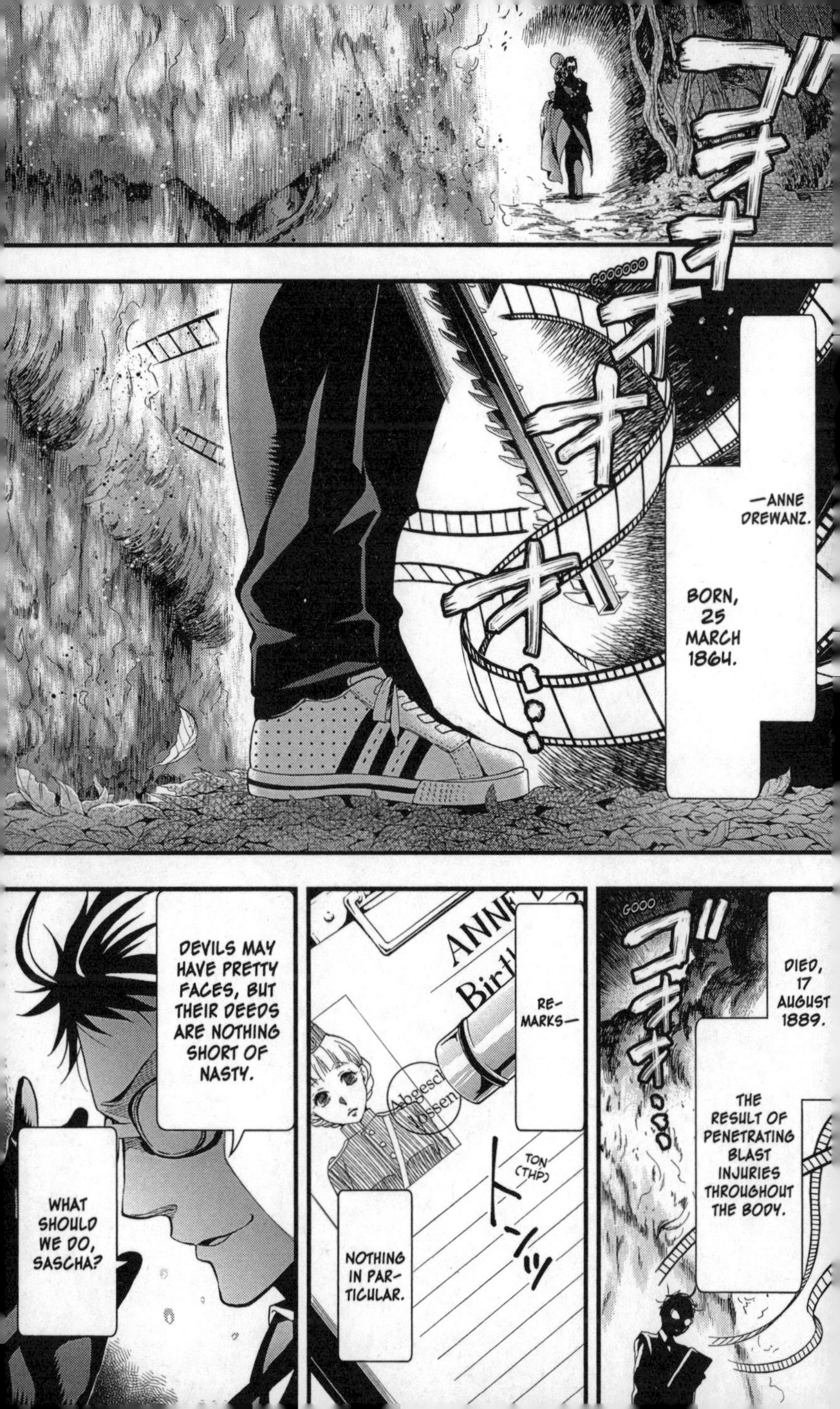
GOOOOOOO
—ANNE DREWANZ.
BORN, 25 MARCH 1864.
GOOO
DIED, 17 AUGUST 1889.
THE RESULT OF PENETRATING BLAST INJURIES THROUGHOUT THE BODY.
ANNE
Birth
Abgeschlossen
RE-MARKS—
TON (THP)
NOTHING IN PAR-TICULAR.
DEVILS MAY HAVE PRETTY FACES, BUT THEIR DEEDS ARE NOTHING SHORT OF NASTY.
WHAT SHOULD WE DO, SASCHA?

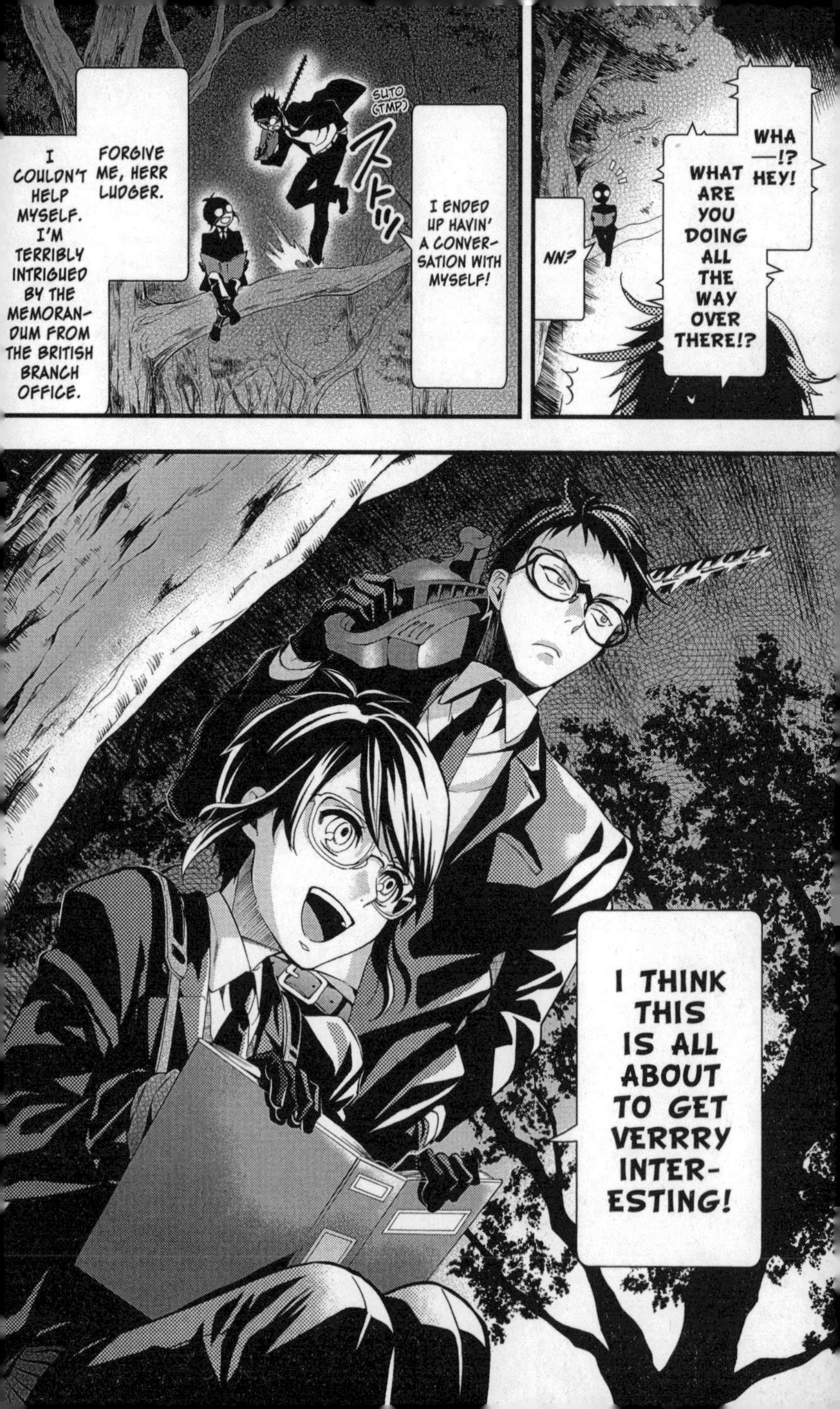
WHA—!? HEY!
WHAT ARE YOU DOING ALL THE WAY OVER THERE!?
NN?
SUTO (TMP)
I ENDED UP HAVIN' A CONVERSATION WITH MYSELF!
FORGIVE ME, HERR LUDGER.
I COULDN'T HELP MYSELF. I'M TERRIBLY INTRIGUED BY THE MEMORANDUM FROM THE BRITISH BRANCH OFFICE.
I THINK THIS IS ALL ABOUT TO GET VERRRY INTERESTING!

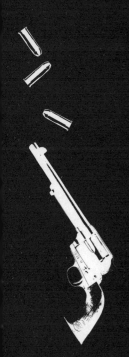

Black Butler

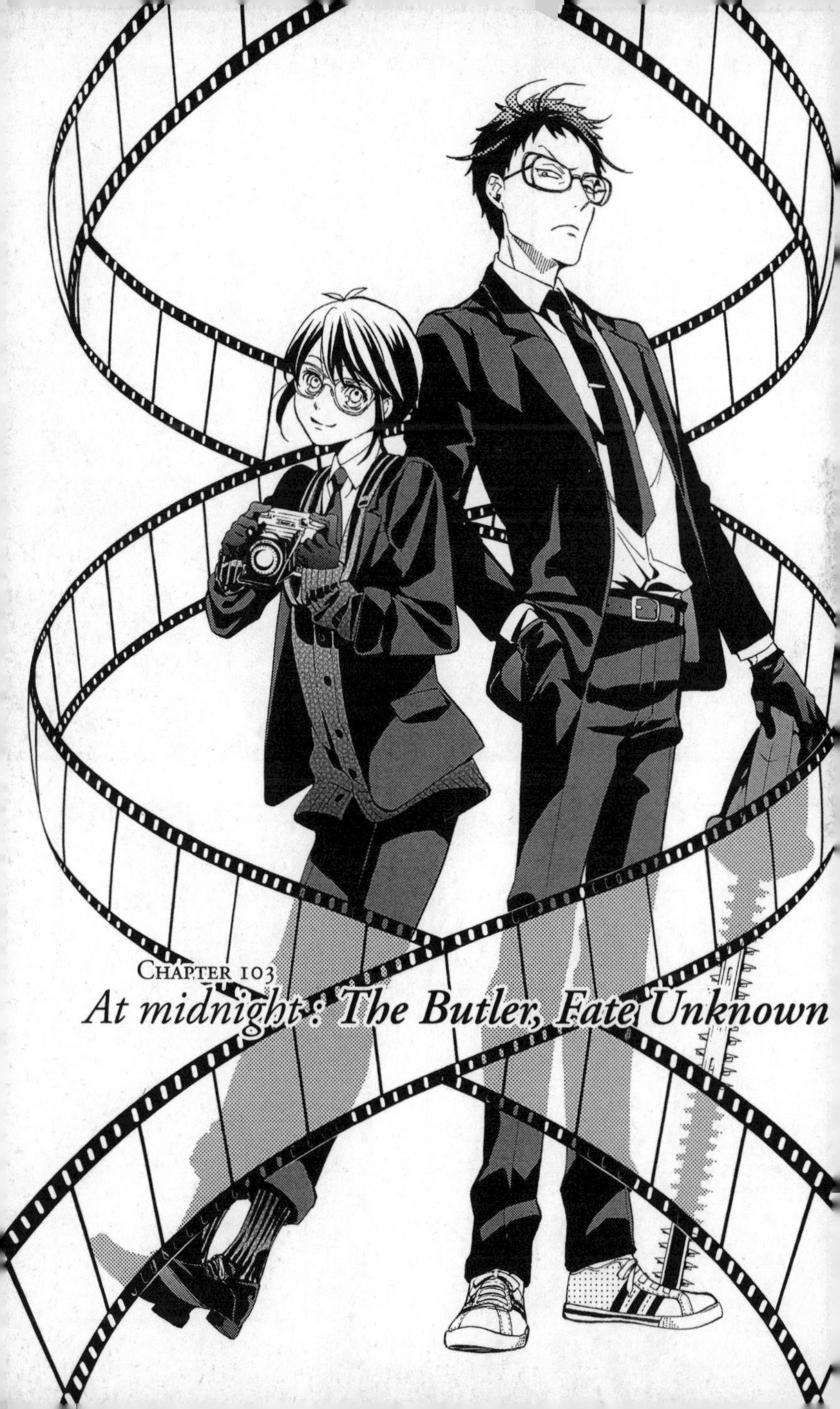
CHAPTER 103
At midnight : The Butler, Fate Unknown

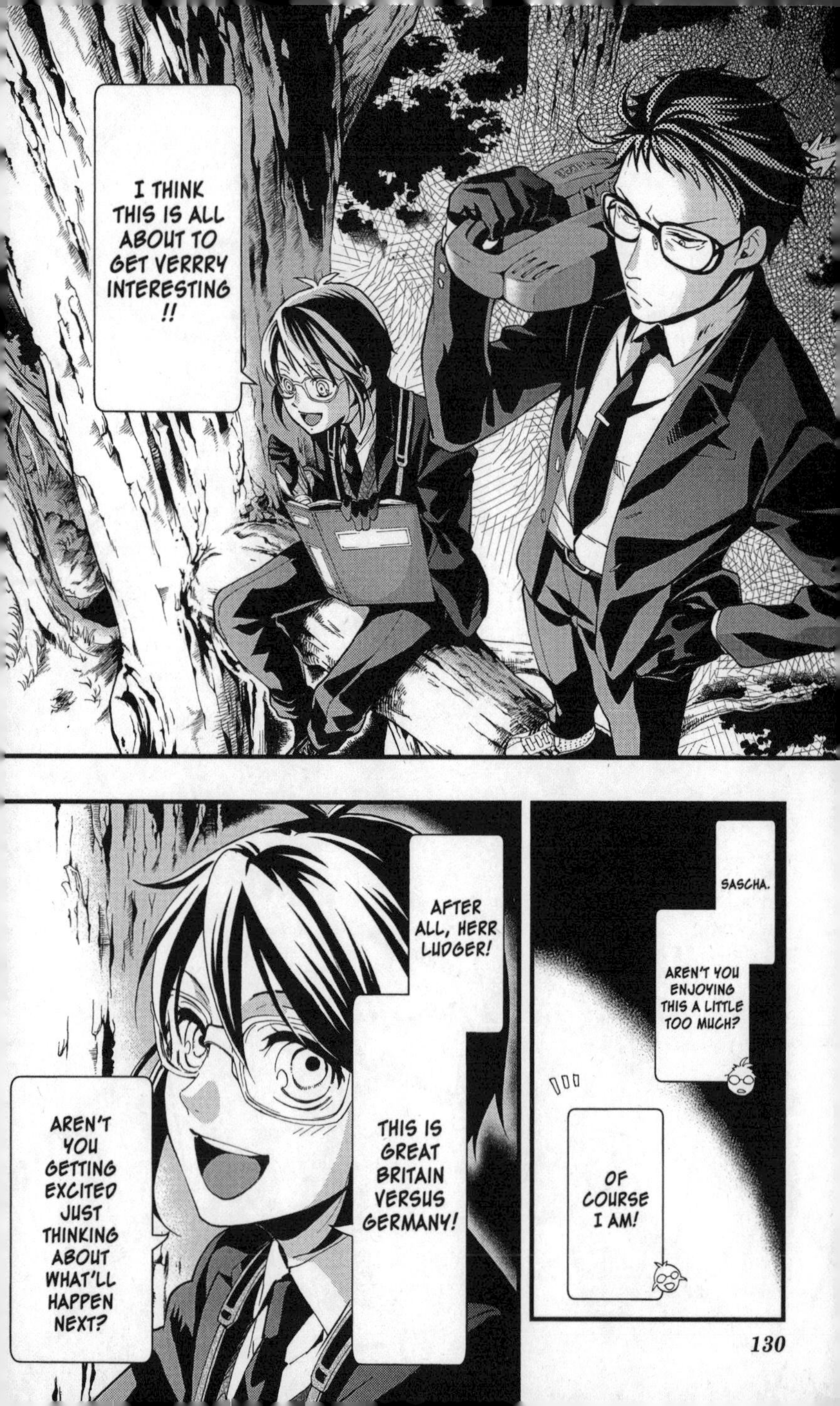

I THINK THIS IS ALL ABOUT TO GET VERRRY INTERESTING!!
AFTER ALL, HERR LUDGER!
THIS IS GREAT BRITAIN VERSUS GERMANY!
AREN'T YOU GETTING EXCITED JUST THINKING ABOUT WHAT'LL HAPPEN NEXT?
SASCHA.
AREN'T YOU ENJOYING THIS A LITTLE TOO MUCH?
OF COURSE I AM!

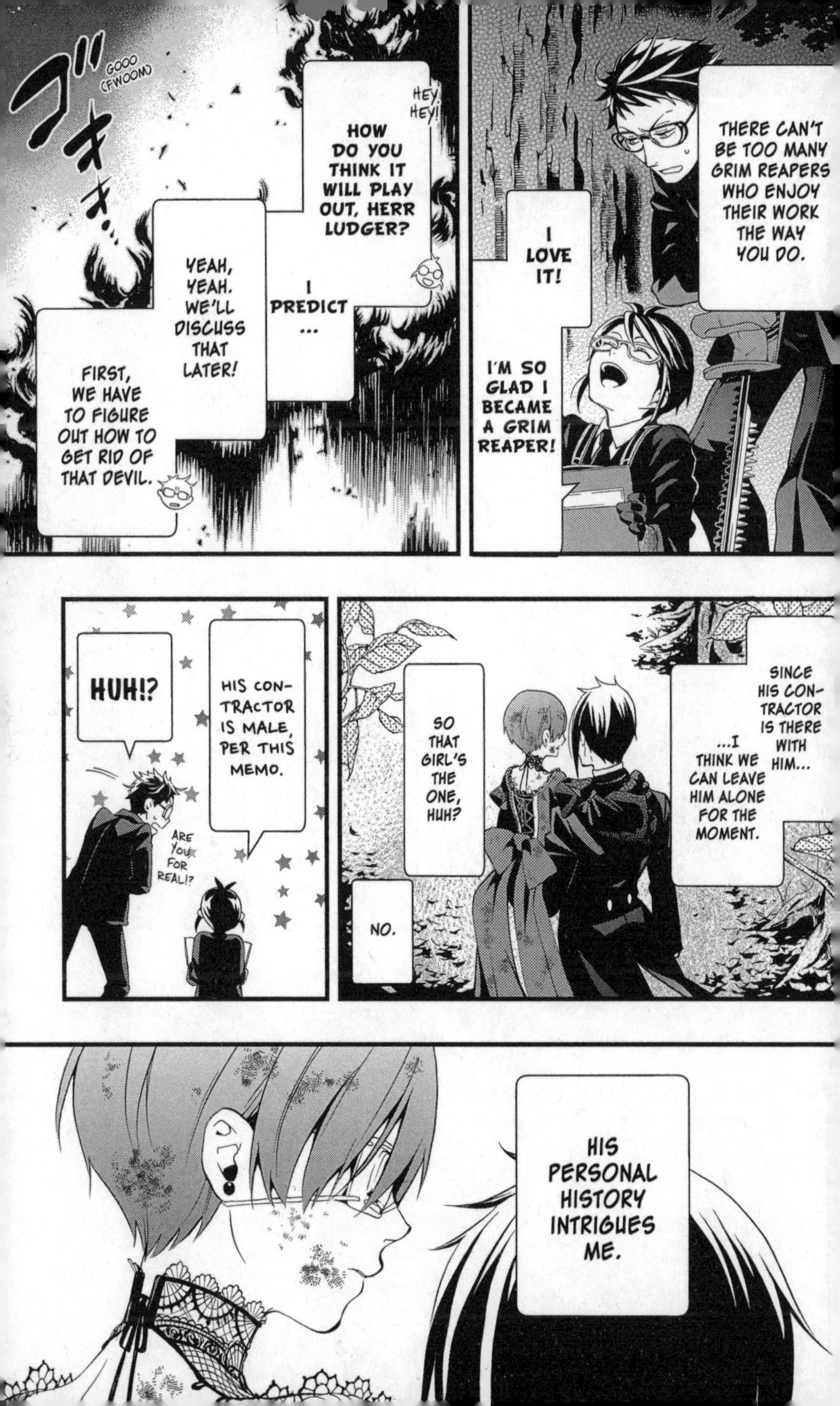
THERE CAN'T BE TOO MANY GRIM REAPERS WHO ENJOY THEIR WORK THE WAY YOU DO.
I LOVE IT!
I'M SO GLAD I BECAME A GRIM REAPER!
GOOO (FWOOM)
HEY HEY!
HOW DO YOU THINK IT WILL PLAY OUT, HERR LUDGER?
I PREDICT...
YEAH, YEAH. WE'LL DISCUSS THAT LATER!
FIRST, WE HAVE TO FIGURE OUT HOW TO GET RID OF THAT DEVIL.
SINCE HIS CONTRACTOR IS THERE WITH HIM...
...I THINK WE CAN LEAVE HIM ALONE FOR THE MOMENT.
SO THAT GIRL'S THE ONE, HUH?
NO.
HIS CONTRACTOR IS MALE, PER THIS MEMO.
HUH!?
ARE YOU FOR REAL!?
HIS PERSONAL HISTORY INTRIGUES ME.

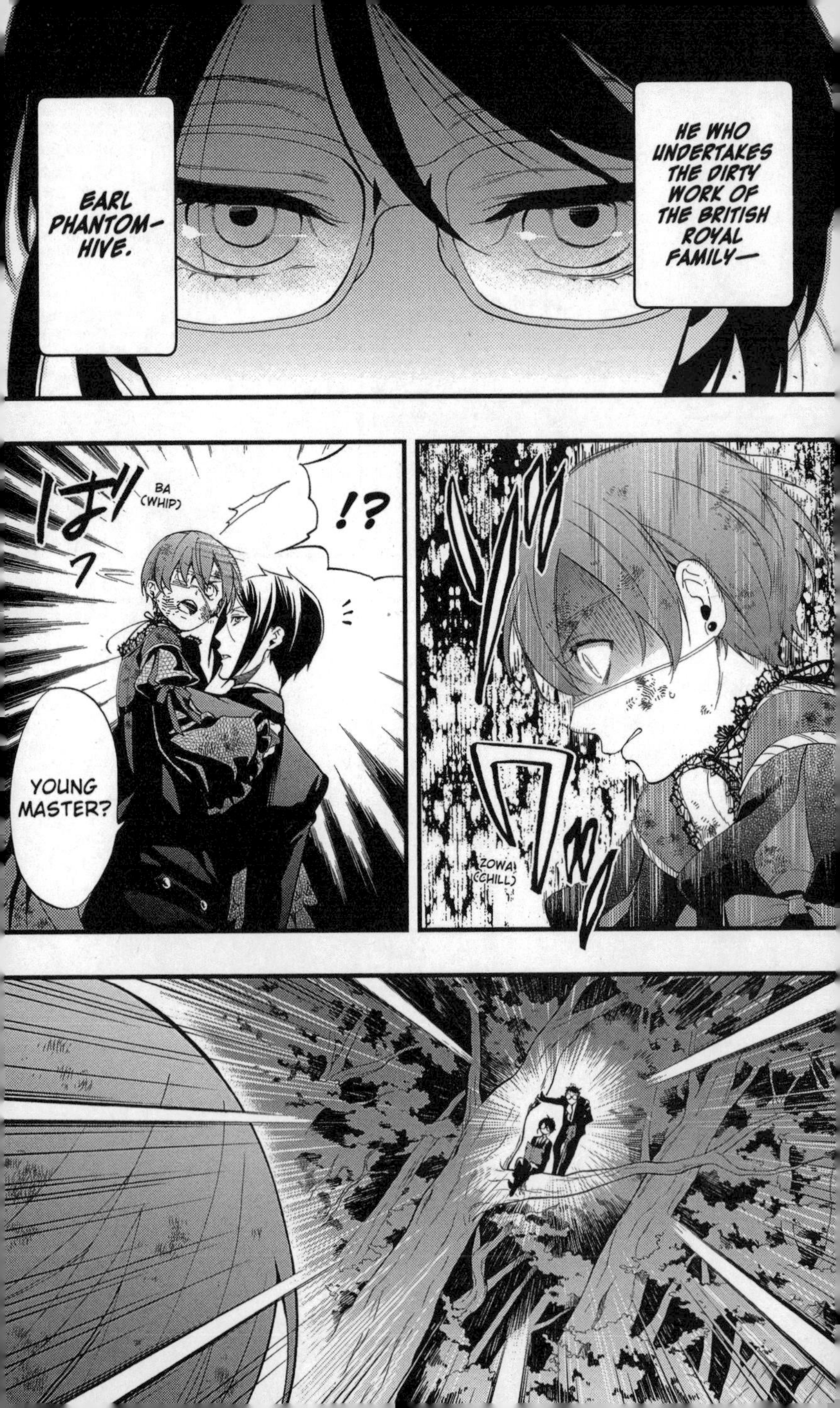
HE WHO UNDERTAKES THE DIRTY WORK OF THE BRITISH ROYAL FAMILY—
EARL PHANTOM-HIVE.
ZOWA (CHILL)
BA (WHIP)
!?
YOUNG MASTER?

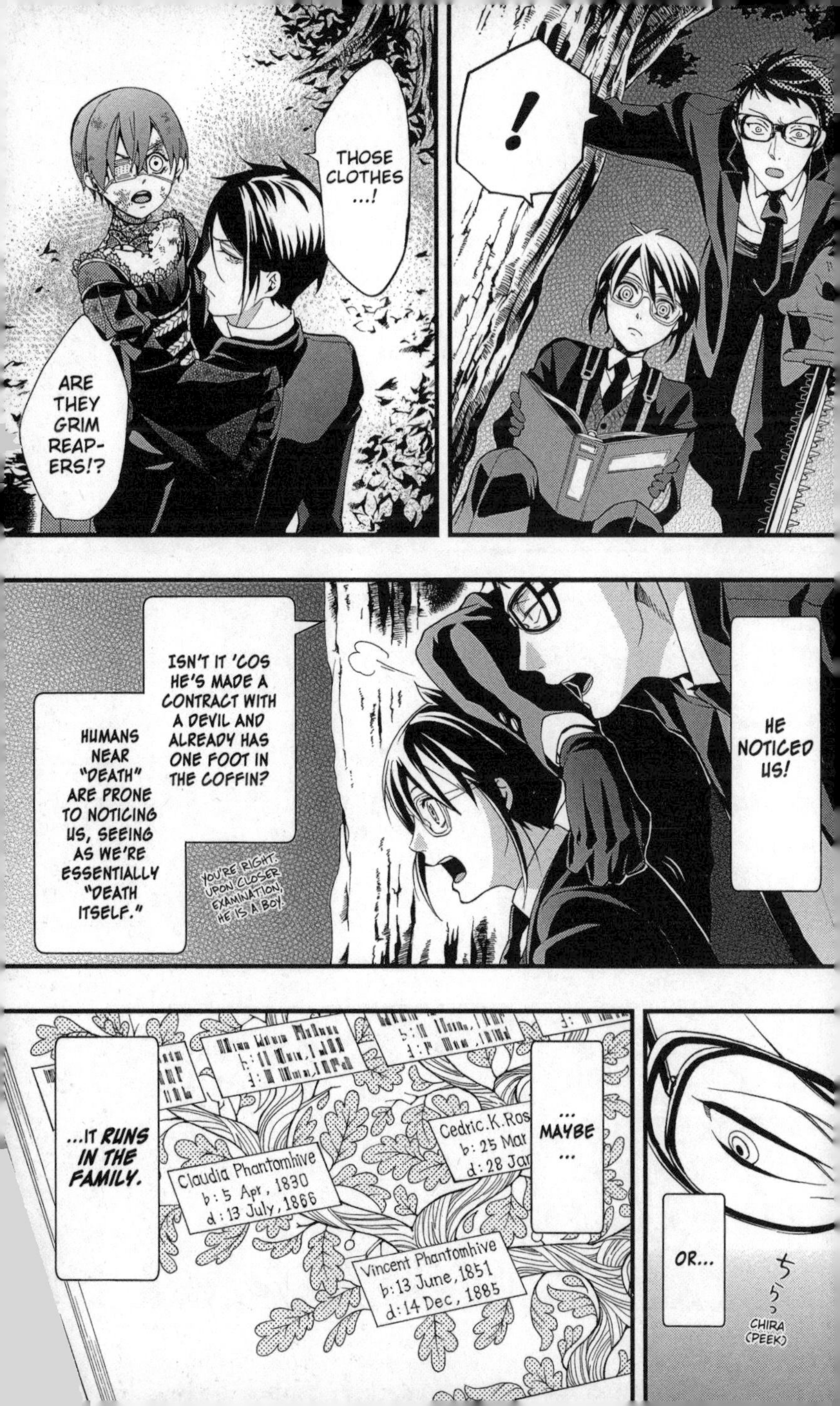
!
THOSE CLOTHES ...!
ARE THEY GRIM REAPERS!?
HE NOTICED US!
ISN'T IT 'COS HE'S MADE A CONTRACT WITH A DEVIL AND ALREADY HAS ONE FOOT IN THE COFFIN?
HUMANS NEAR "DEATH" ARE PRONE TO NOTICING US, SEEING AS WE'RE ESSENTIALLY "DEATH ITSELF."
YOU'RE RIGHT. UPON CLOSER EXAMINATION, HE IS A BOY.
OR...
ちらっ
CHIRA (PEEK)
...MAYBE...
...IT RUNS IN THE FAMILY.
Cedric.K.Ros
b: 25 Mar
d: 28 Jan
Claudia Phantomhive
b: 5 Apr, 1830
d: 13 July, 1866
Vincent Phantomhive
b: 13 June, 1851
d: 14 Dec, 1885

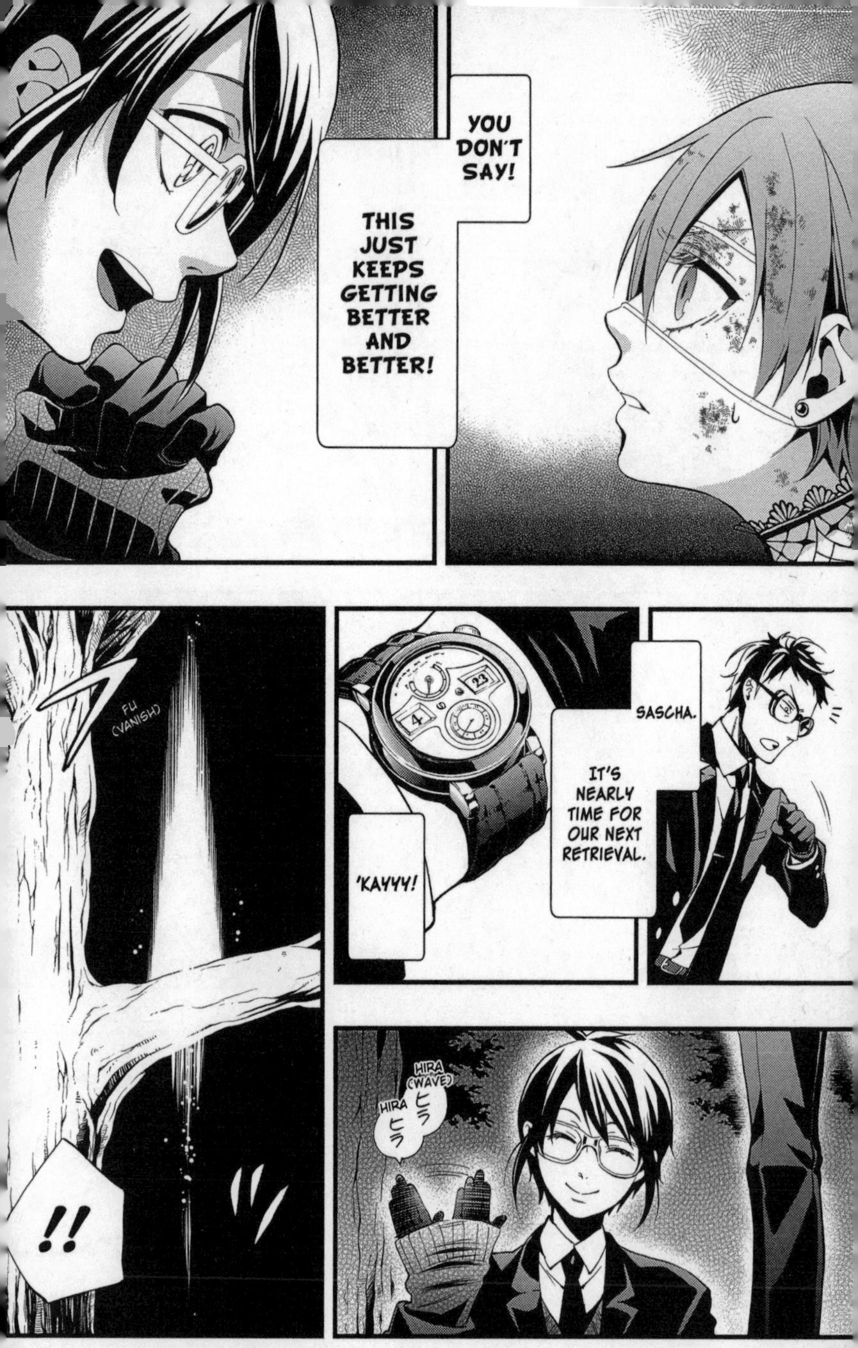
YOU DON'T SAY!
THIS JUST KEEPS GETTING BETTER AND BETTER!
SASCHA.
IT'S NEARLY TIME FOR OUR NEXT RETRIEVAL.
'KAYYY!
HIRA HIRA (WAVE)
ヒラ ヒラ
FU (VANISH)
!!

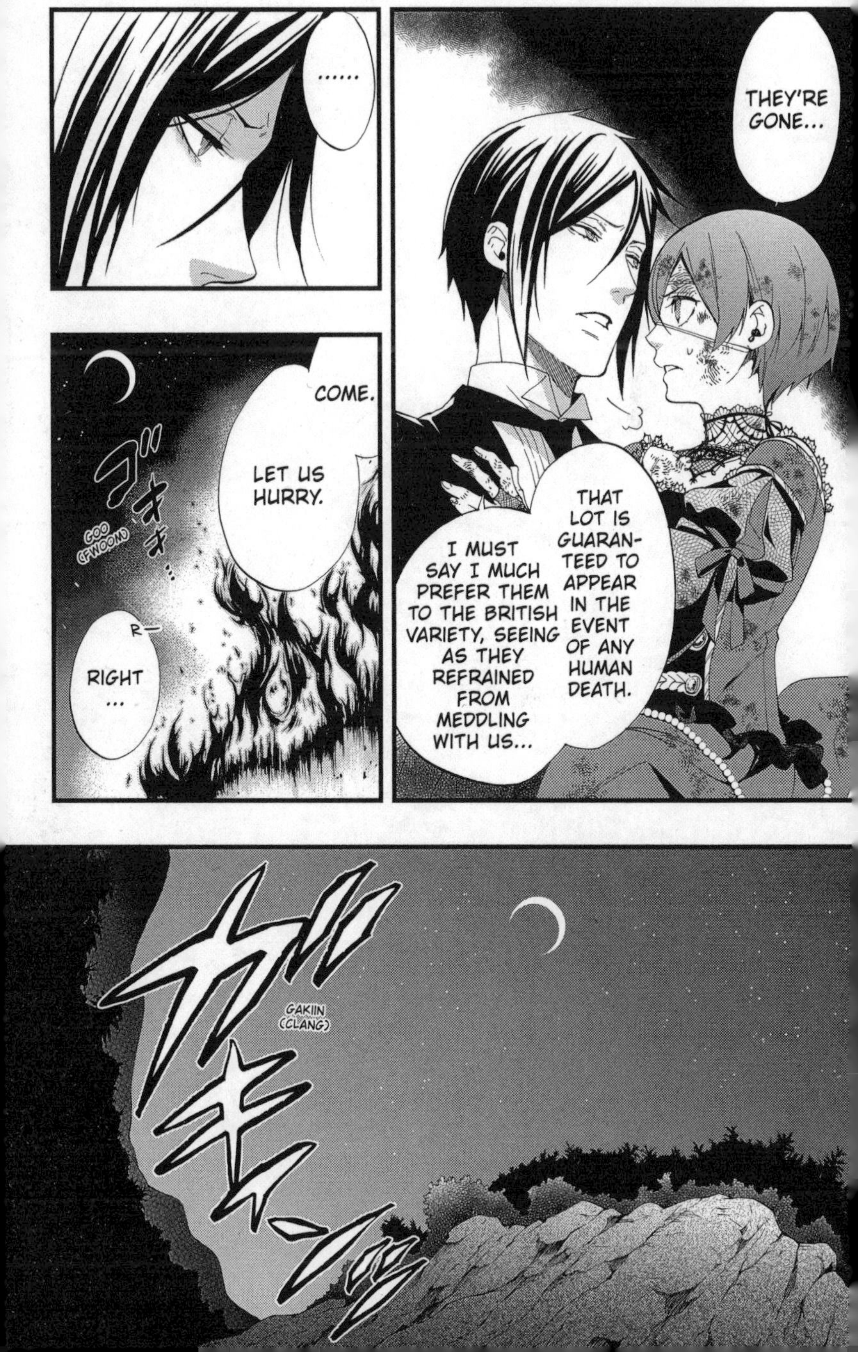
THEY'RE GONE...
THAT LOT IS GUARANTEED TO APPEAR IN THE EVENT OF ANY HUMAN DEATH.
I MUST SAY I MUCH PREFER THEM TO THE BRITISH VARIETY, SEEING AS THEY REFRAINED FROM MEDDLING WITH US...
......
COME.
LET US HURRY.
GOO (FWOOM)
R— RIGHT...
GAKIIN (CLANG)

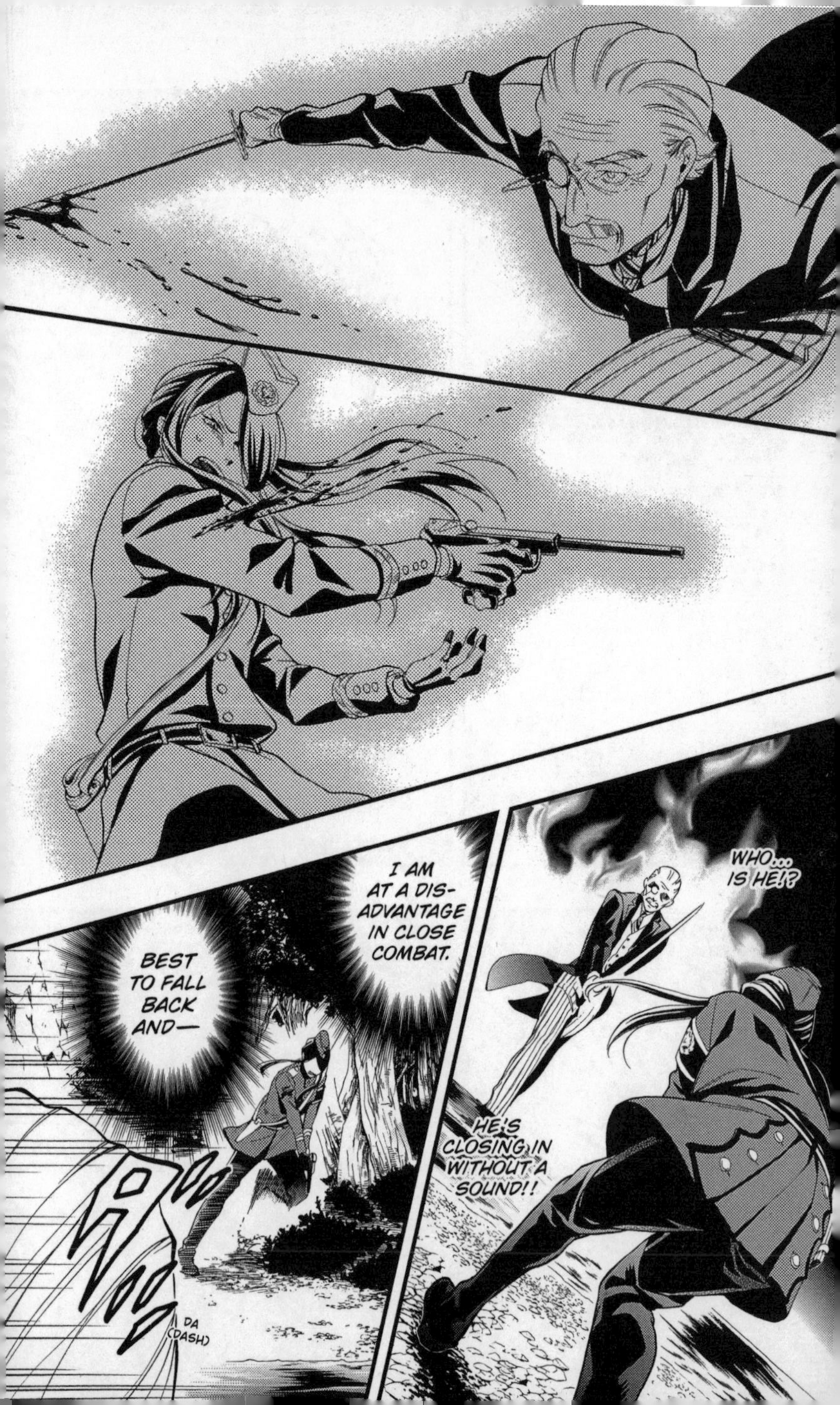
WHO... IS HE!?
HE'S CLOSING IN WITHOUT A SOUND!!
I AM AT A DIS-ADVANTAGE IN CLOSE COMBAT.
BEST TO FALL BACK AND—
DA (DASH)

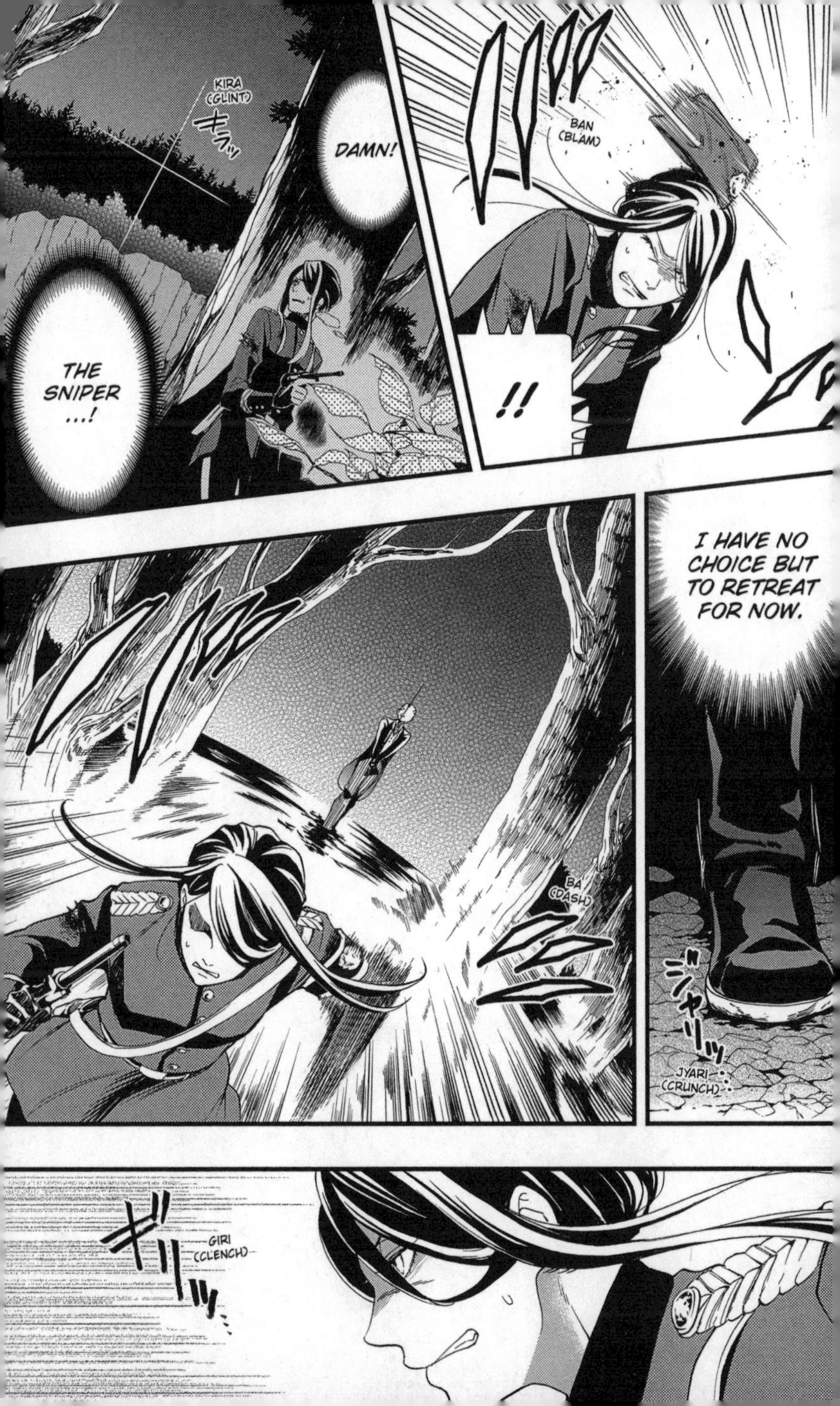
BAN
(BLAM)
!!
DAMN!
KIRA
(GLINT)
ギラッ
THE SNIPER ...!
I HAVE NO CHOICE BUT TO RETREAT FOR NOW.
ジャリッ
JYARI
(CRUNCH)
BA
(DASH)
GIRI
(CLENCH)

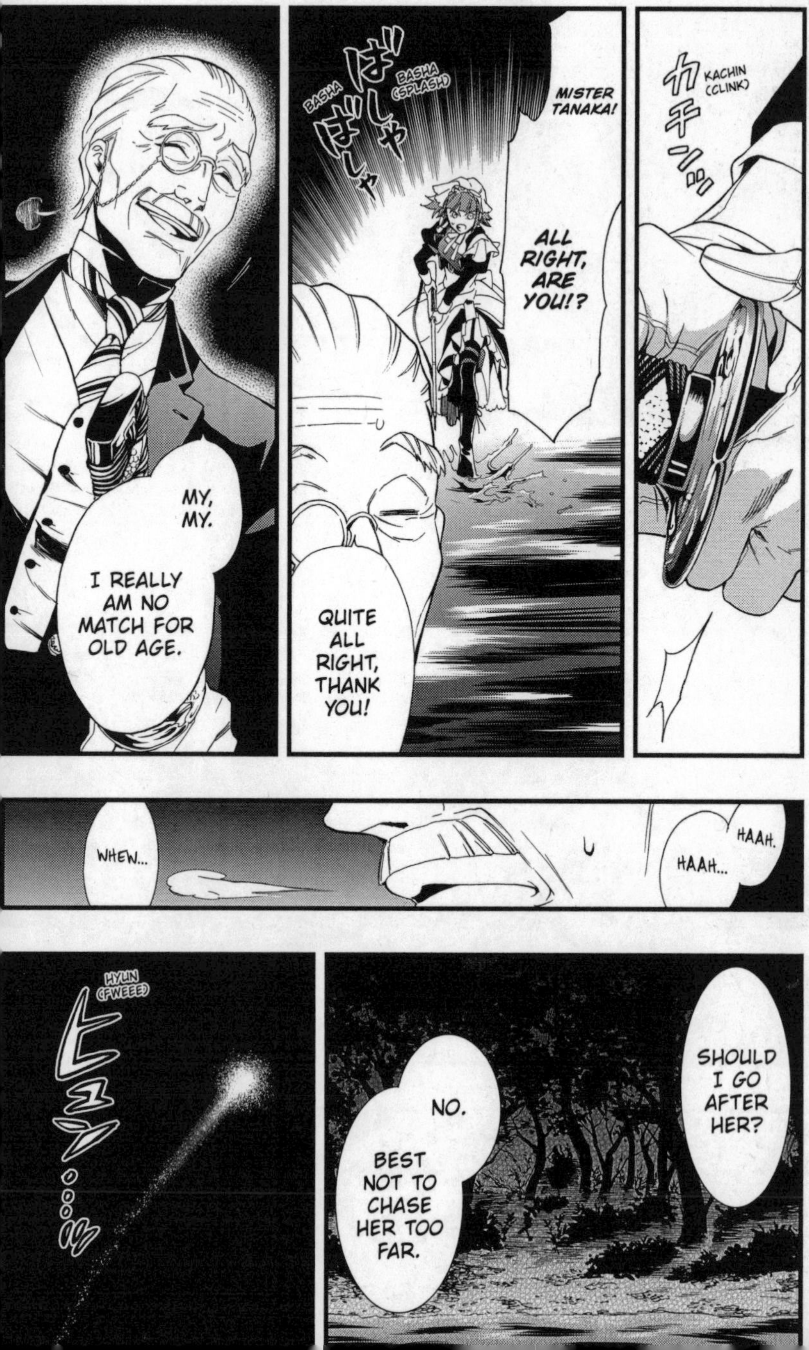
KACHIN (CLINK)
BASHA
BASHA (SPLASH)
MISTER TANAKA!
ALL RIGHT, ARE YOU!?
QUITE ALL RIGHT, THANK YOU!
MY, MY.
I REALLY AM NO MATCH FOR OLD AGE.
HAAH.
HAAH...
WHEW...
SHOULD I GO AFTER HER?
NO.
BEST NOT TO CHASE HER TOO FAR.
HYUN (FWEEE)

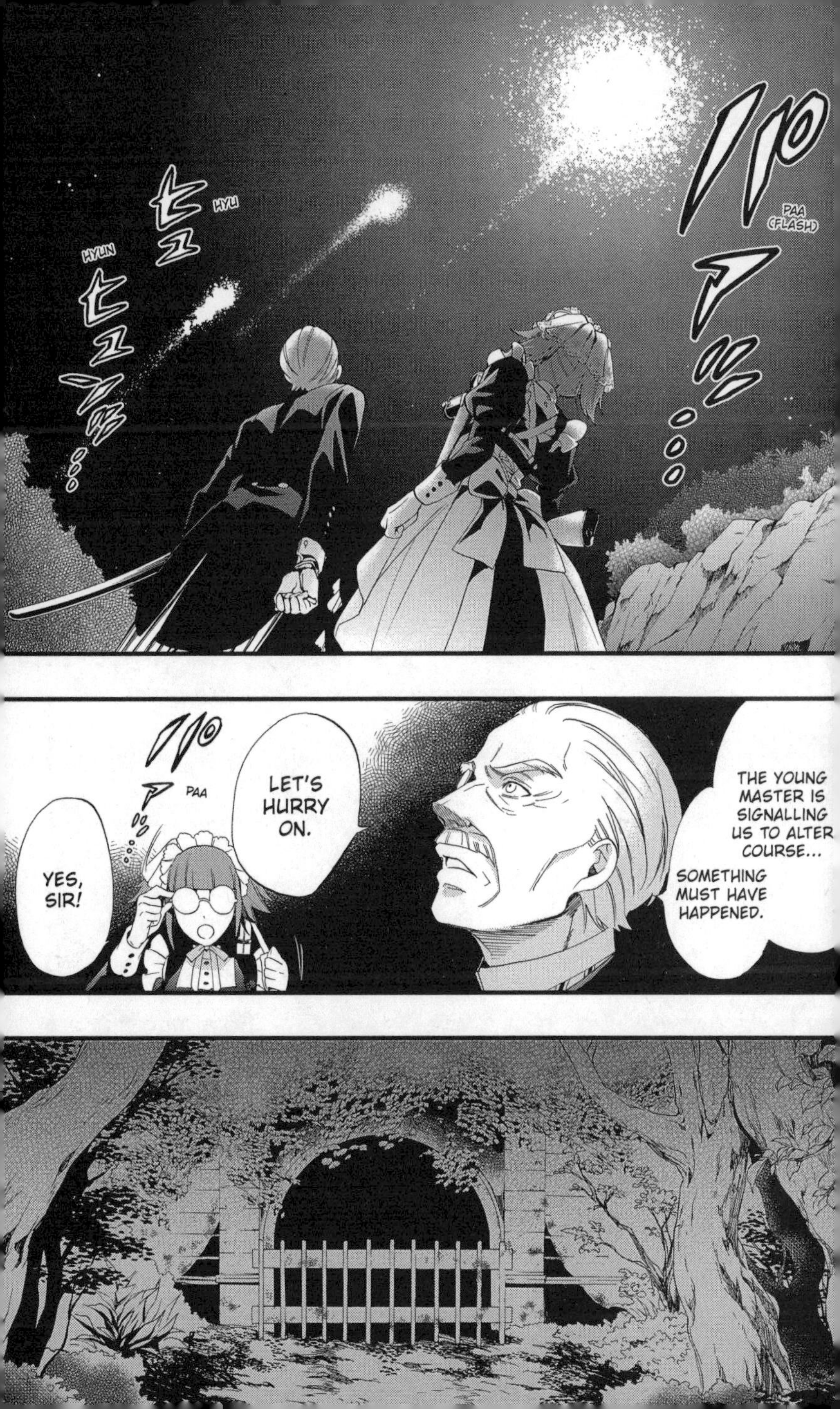
PAA (FLASH)
HYU
HYUN
THE YOUNG MASTER IS SIGNALLING US TO ALTER COURSE...
SOMETHING MUST HAVE HAPPENED.
LET'S HURRY ON.
PAA
YES, SIR!

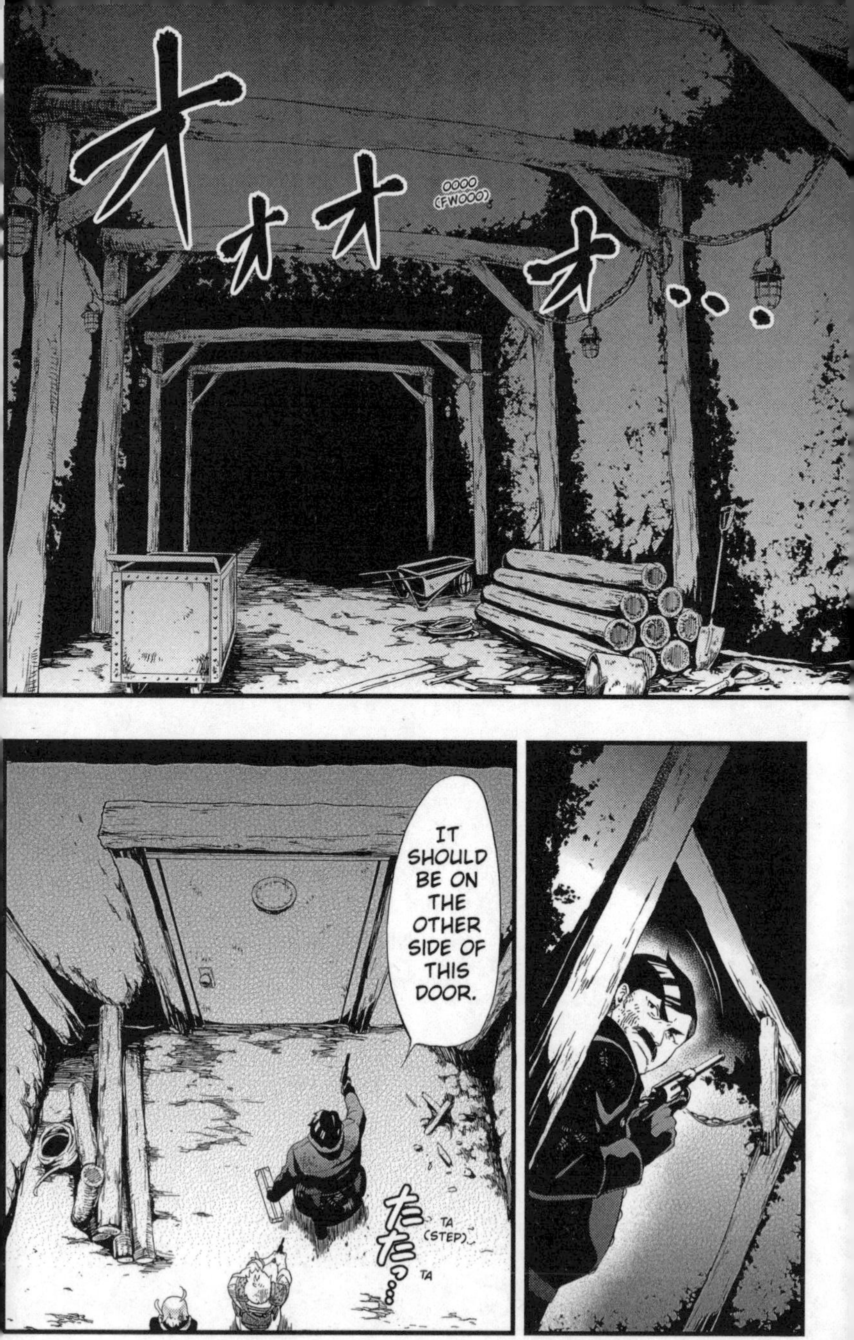
オォォォ...
OOOO (FWOOO)
IT SHOULD BE ON THE OTHER SIDE OF THIS DOOR.
たたっ...
TA (STEP) TA

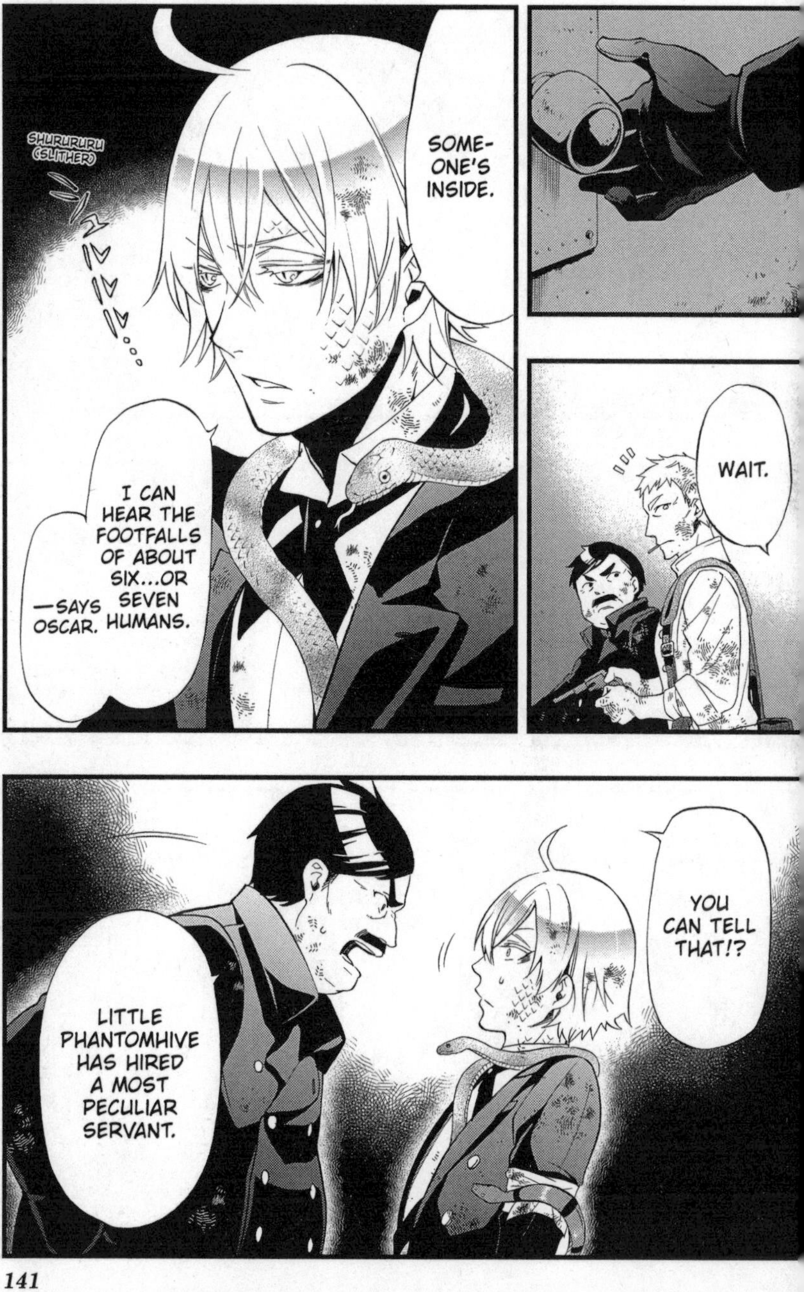
WAIT.
SOME-ONE'S INSIDE.
SHURURURU (SLITHER)
I CAN HEAR THE FOOTFALLS OF ABOUT SIX...OR SEVEN HUMANS.
—SAYS OSCAR.
YOU CAN TELL THAT!?
LITTLE PHANTOMHIVE HAS HIRED A MOST PECULIAR SERVANT.

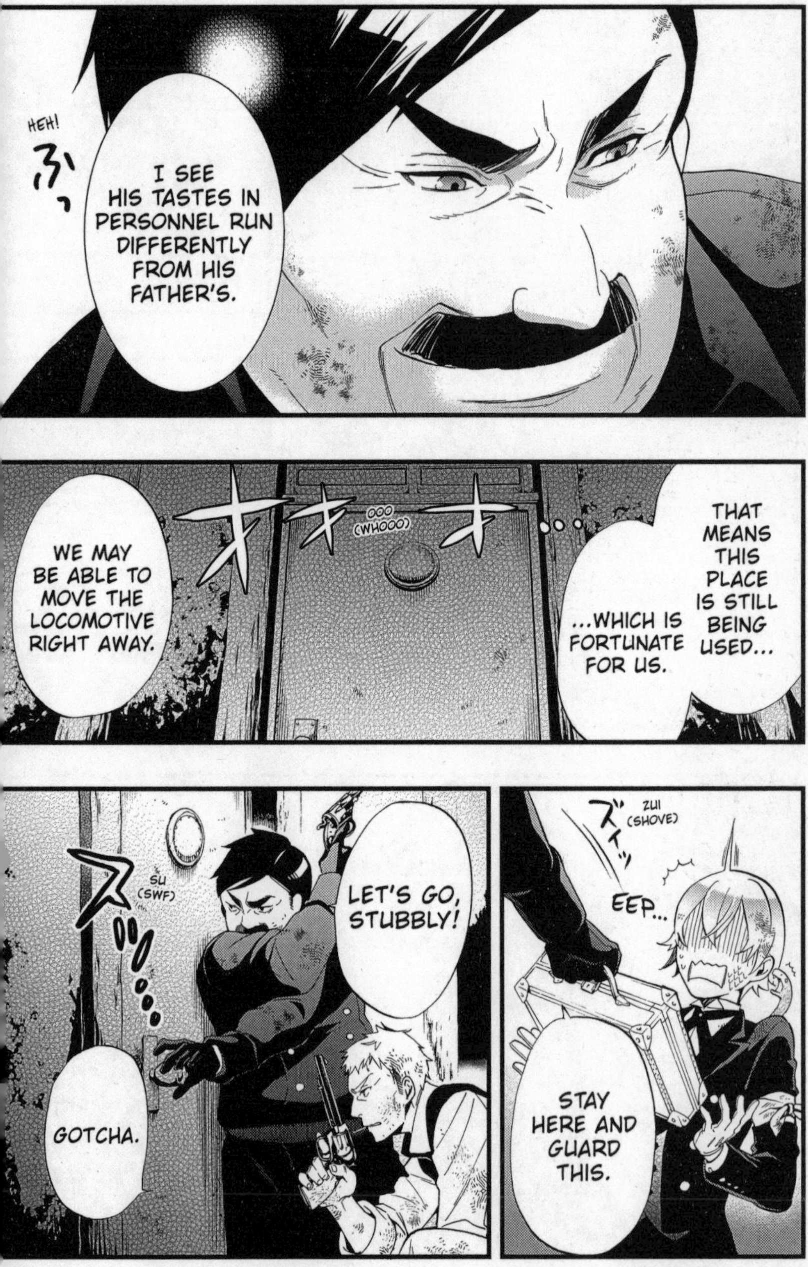
HEH!
ふっ
I SEE HIS TASTES IN PERSONNEL RUN DIFFERENTLY FROM HIS FATHER'S.
THAT MEANS THIS PLACE IS STILL BEING USED...
...WHICH IS FORTUNATE FOR US.
OOO (WHOOO)
WE MAY BE ABLE TO MOVE THE LOCOMOTIVE RIGHT AWAY.
ZUI (SHOVE)
EEP...
STAY HERE AND GUARD THIS.
LET'S GO, STUBBLY!
SU (SWF)
GOTCHA.

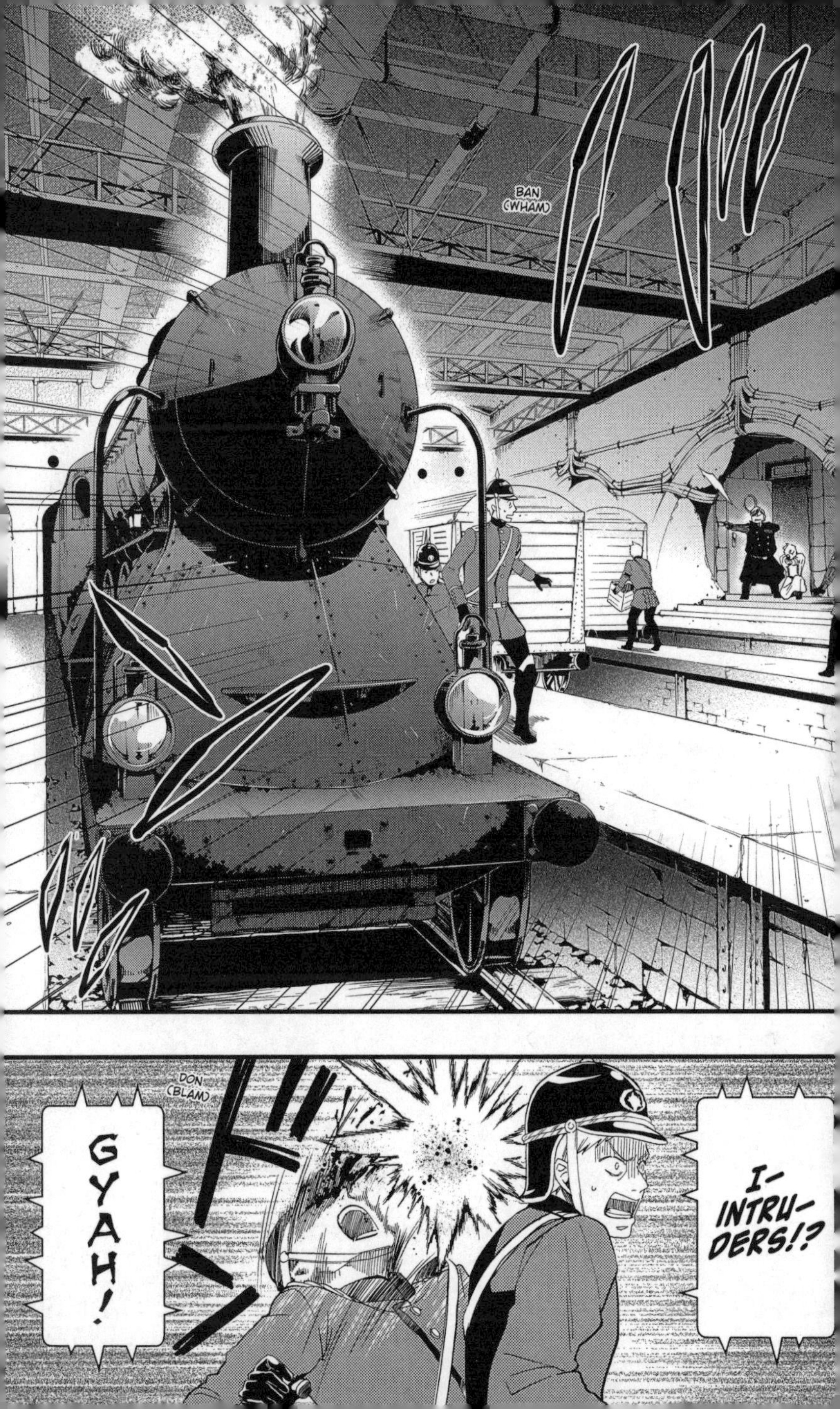
BAN (WHAM)
I-INTRUDERS!?
DON (BLAM)
GYAH!

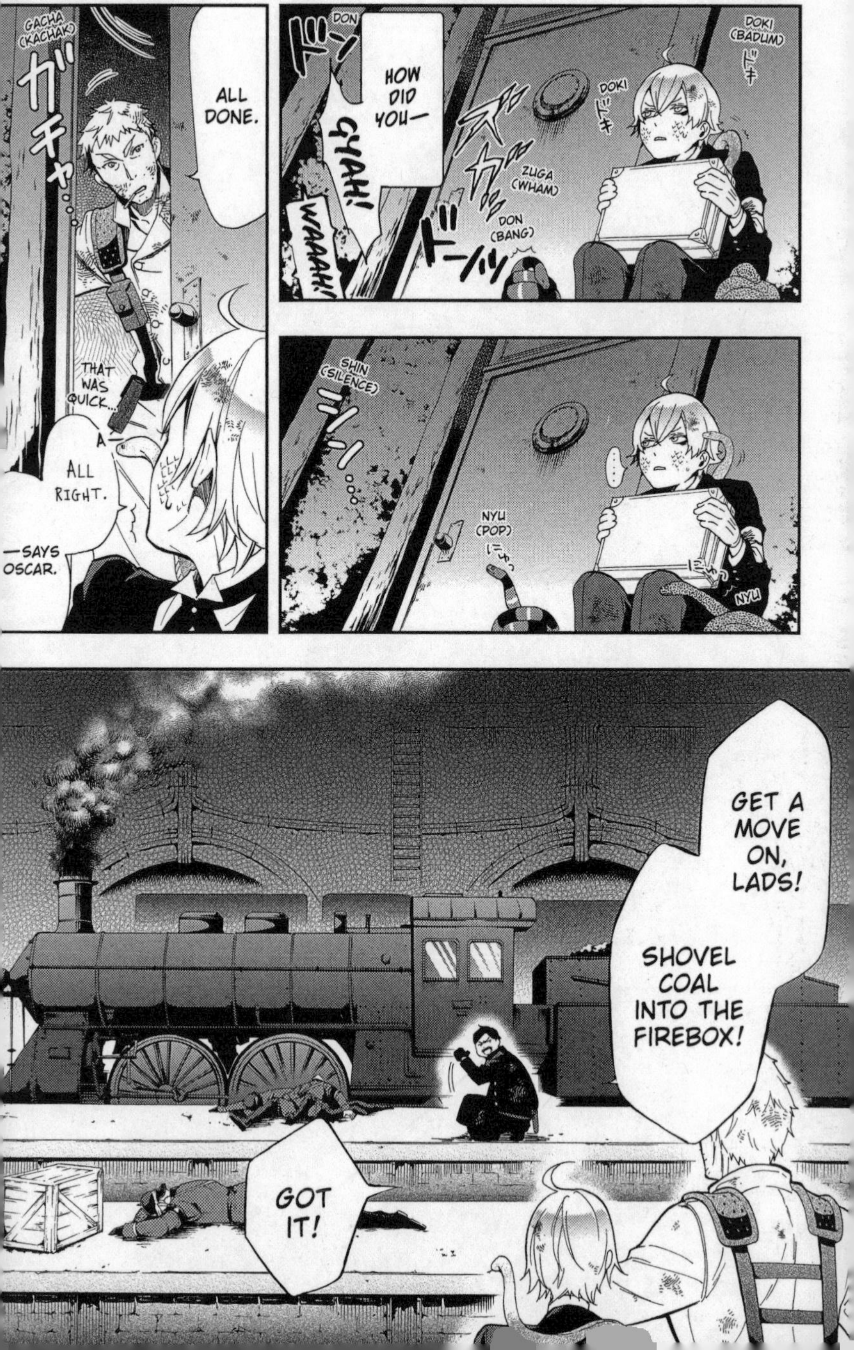
DOKI (BADUM)
DOKI
HOW DID YOU—
DON
ZUGA (WHAM)
GYAH!
DON (BANG)
WAAAAH!
...
NYU
NYU (POP)
SHIN (SILENCE)
ALL DONE.
GACHA (KACHAK)
THAT WAS QUICK...
A— ALL RIGHT.
—SAYS OSCAR.
GET A MOVE ON, LADS!
SHOVEL COAL INTO THE FIREBOX!
GOT IT!

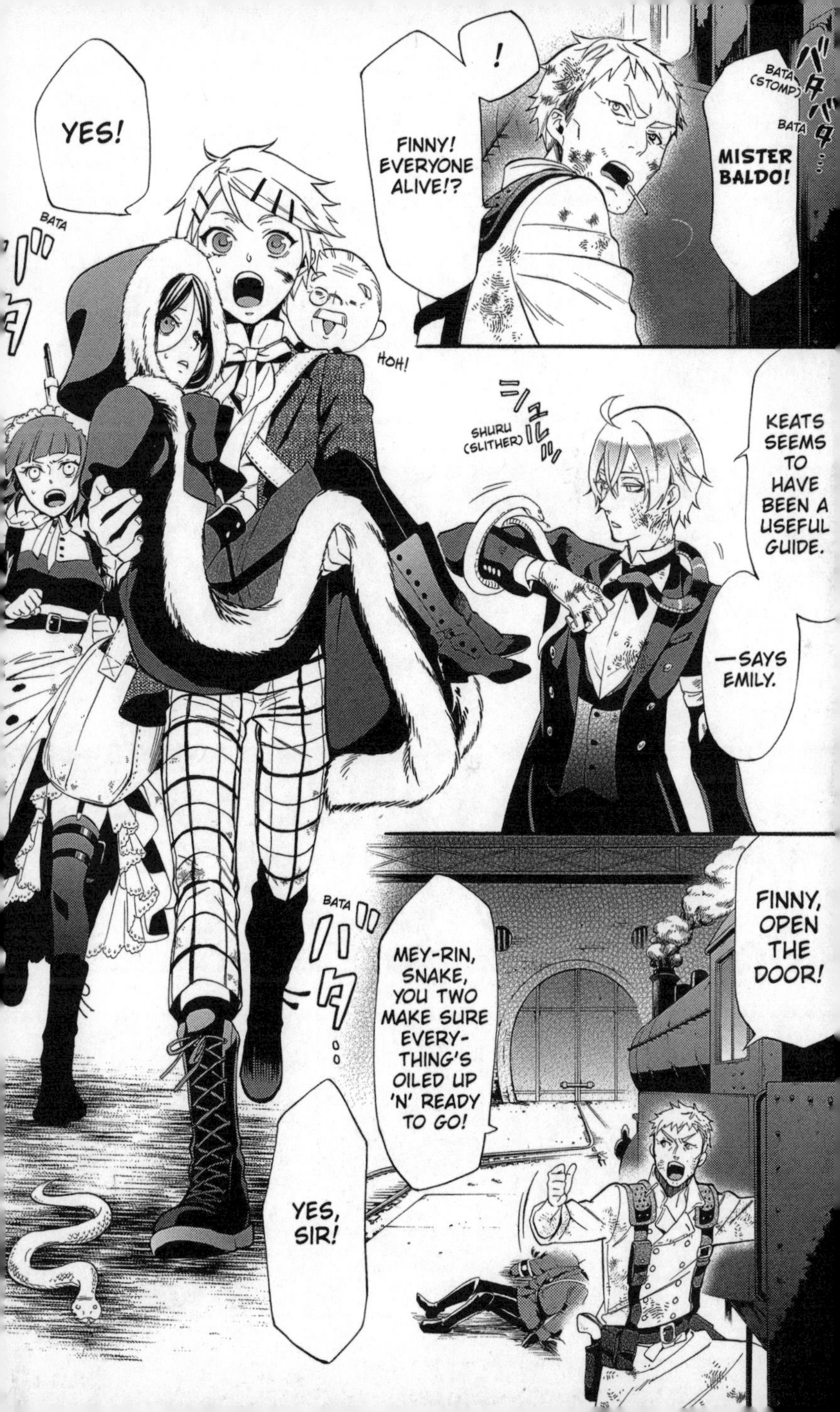
BATA (STOMP)
BATA
MISTER BALDO!
!
FINNY! EVERYONE ALIVE!?
YES!
BATA
HOH!
SHURU (SLITHER)
KEATS SEEMS TO HAVE BEEN A USEFUL GUIDE.
—SAYS EMILY.
FINNY, OPEN THE DOOR!
MEY-RIN, SNAKE, YOU TWO MAKE SURE EVERY-THING'S OILED UP 'N' READY TO GO!
BATA
YES, SIR!

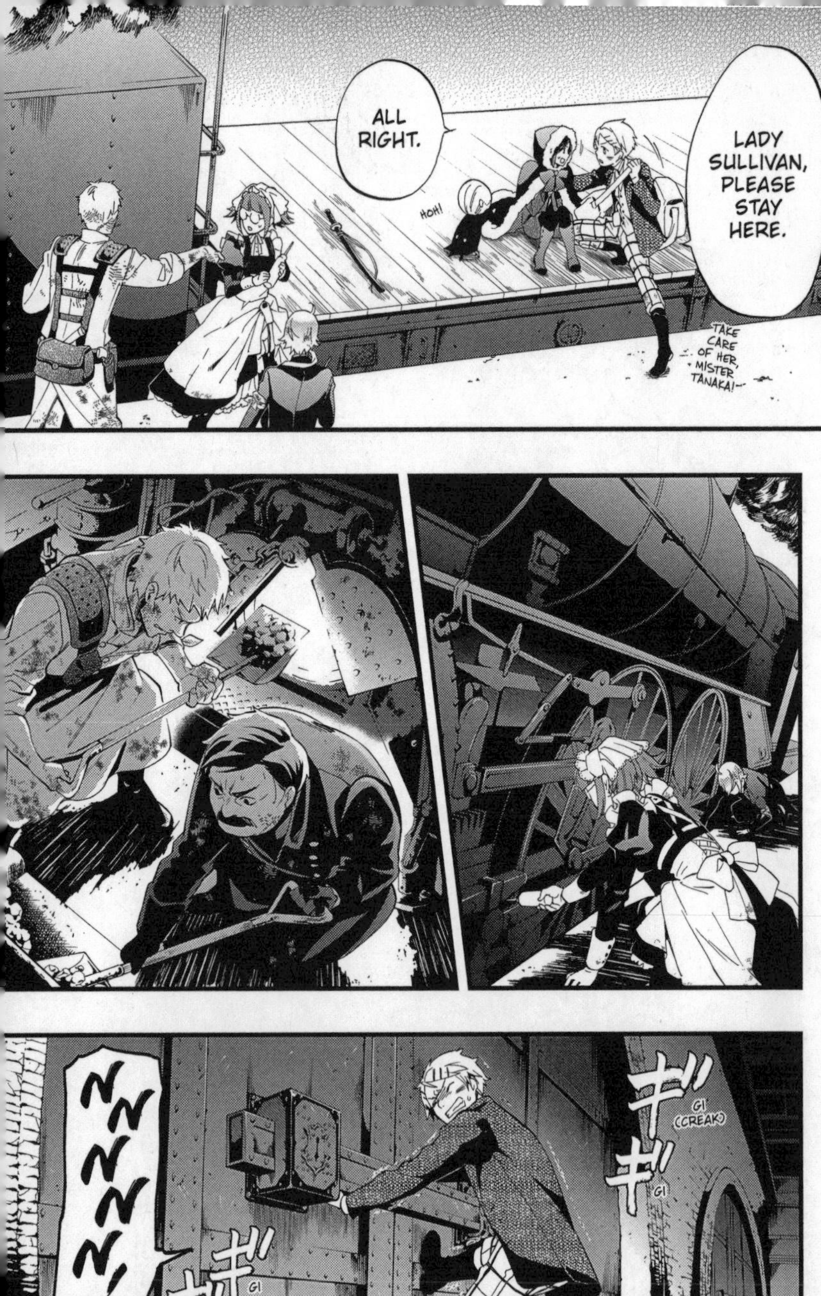
LADY SULLIVAN, PLEASE STAY HERE.
TAKE CARE OF HER, MISTER TANAKA!
ALL RIGHT.
HOH!
ギ GI (CREAK)
ギ GI
NNNNNN!
ギ GI
ギ GI

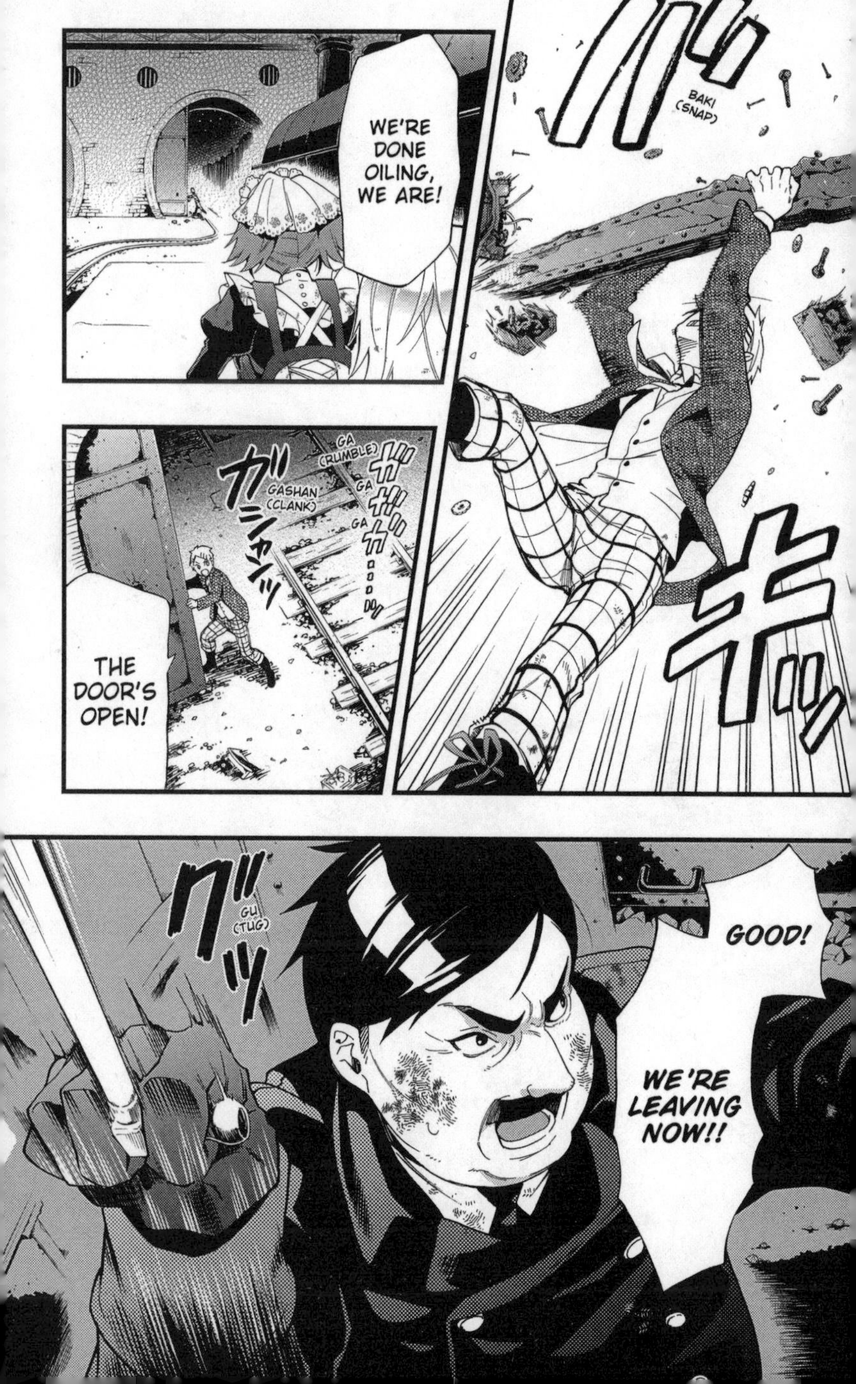
BAKI (SNAP)
WE'RE DONE OILING, WE ARE!
GA (RUMBLE) GA GA
GASHAN (CLANK)
THE DOOR'S OPEN!
GOOD!
WE'RE LEAVING NOW!!
GU (TUG)

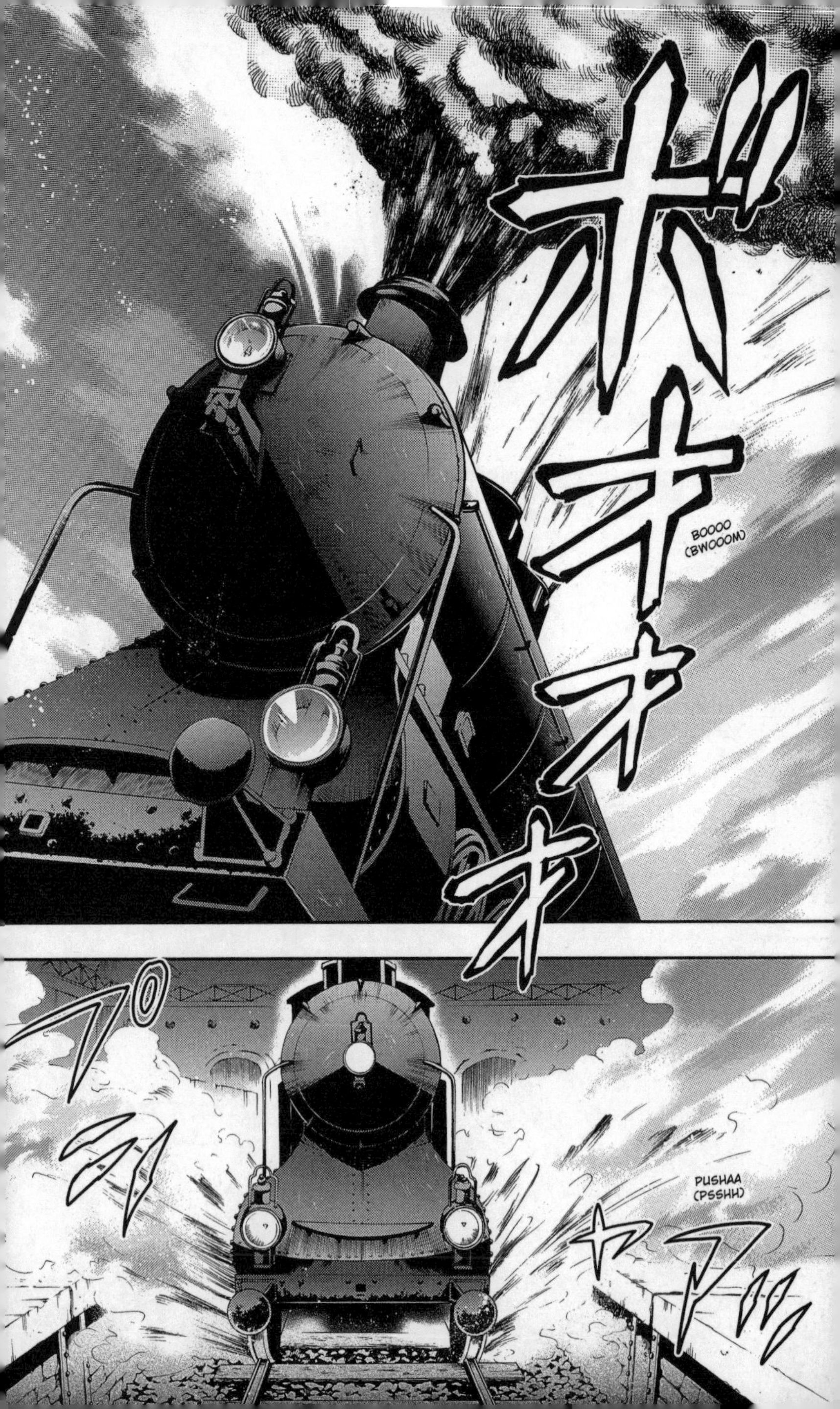
ボオオオ
BOOOO (BWOOOM)
プシャアッ
PUSHAA (PSSHH)

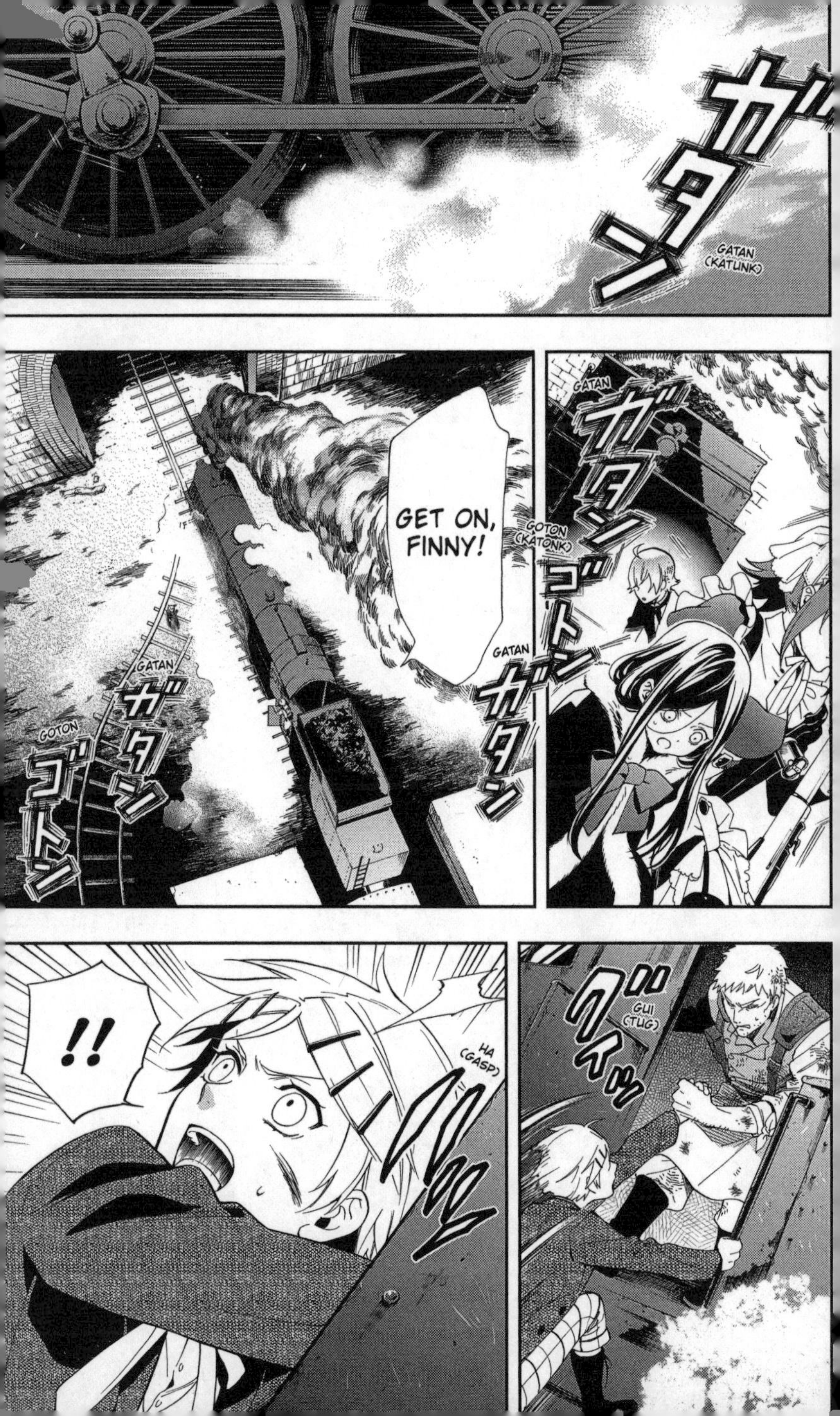
ガタン
GATAN (KATUNK)
GATAN
ガタン
GOTON (KATONK)
ゴトン
GATAN
ガタン
GET ON, FINNY!
GATAN
ガタン
GOTON
ゴトン
GUI (TUG)
!!
HA (GASP)

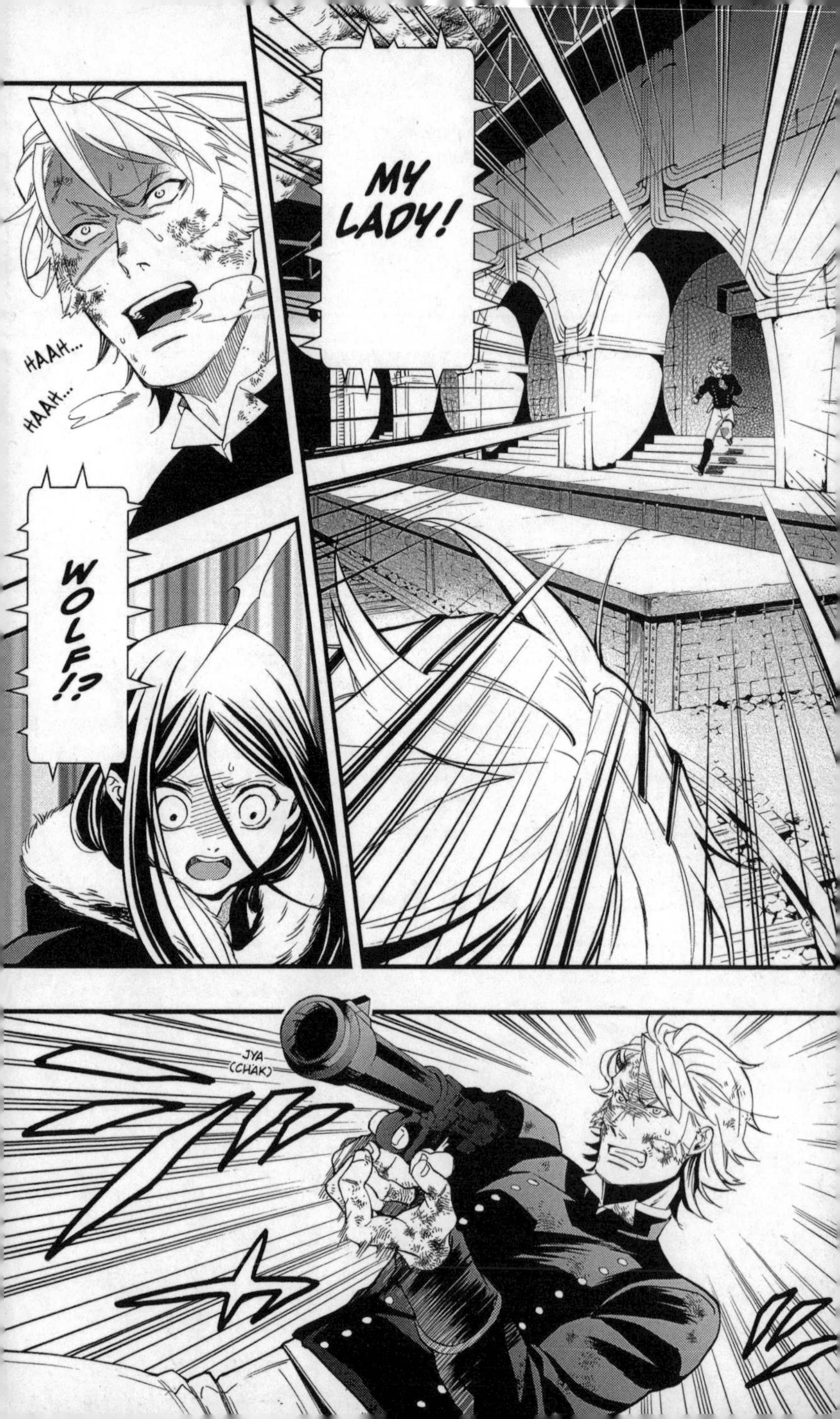
MY LADY!
HAAH... HAAH...
WOLF!?
JYA (CHAK)

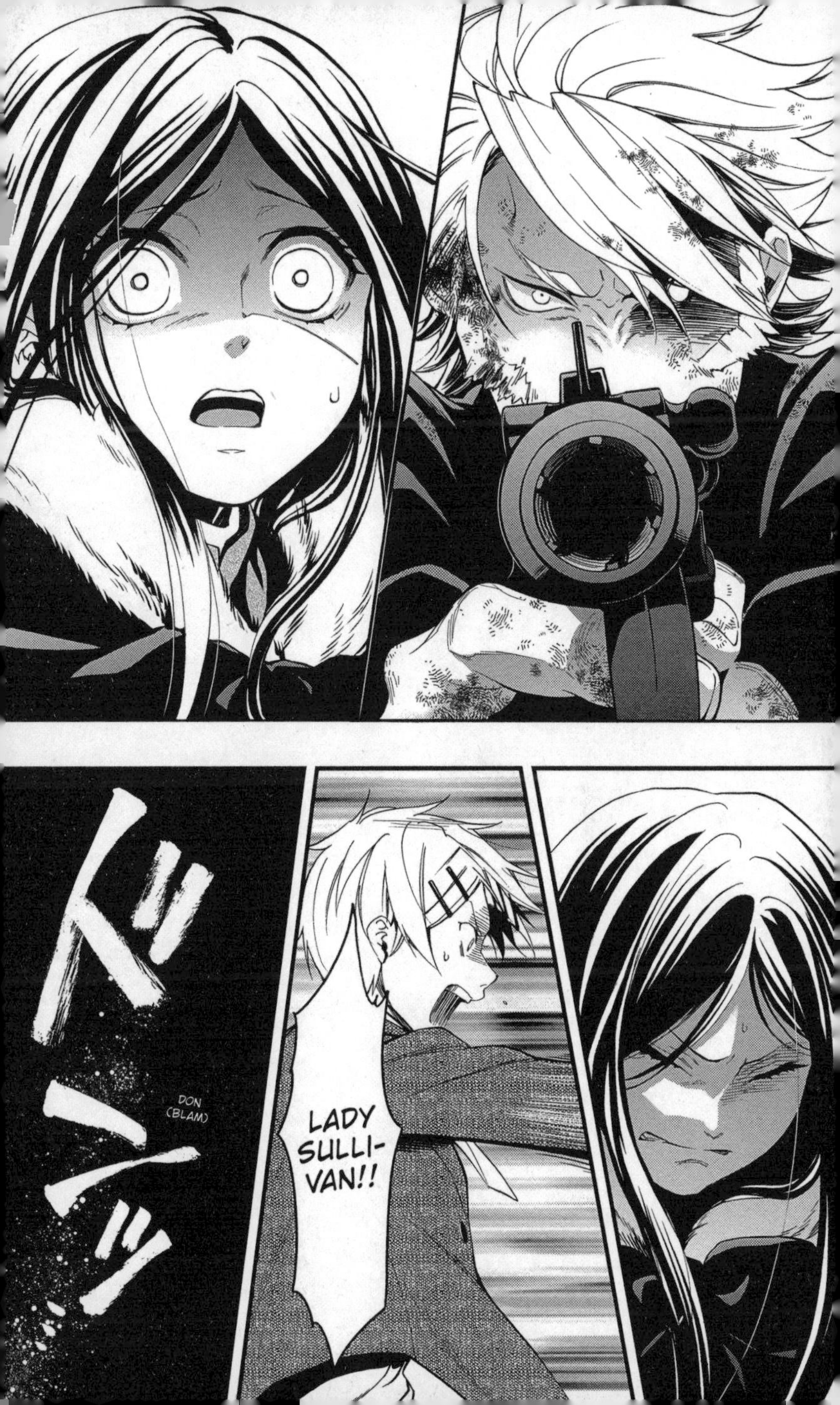
LADY SULLI-VAN!!
DON (BLAM)

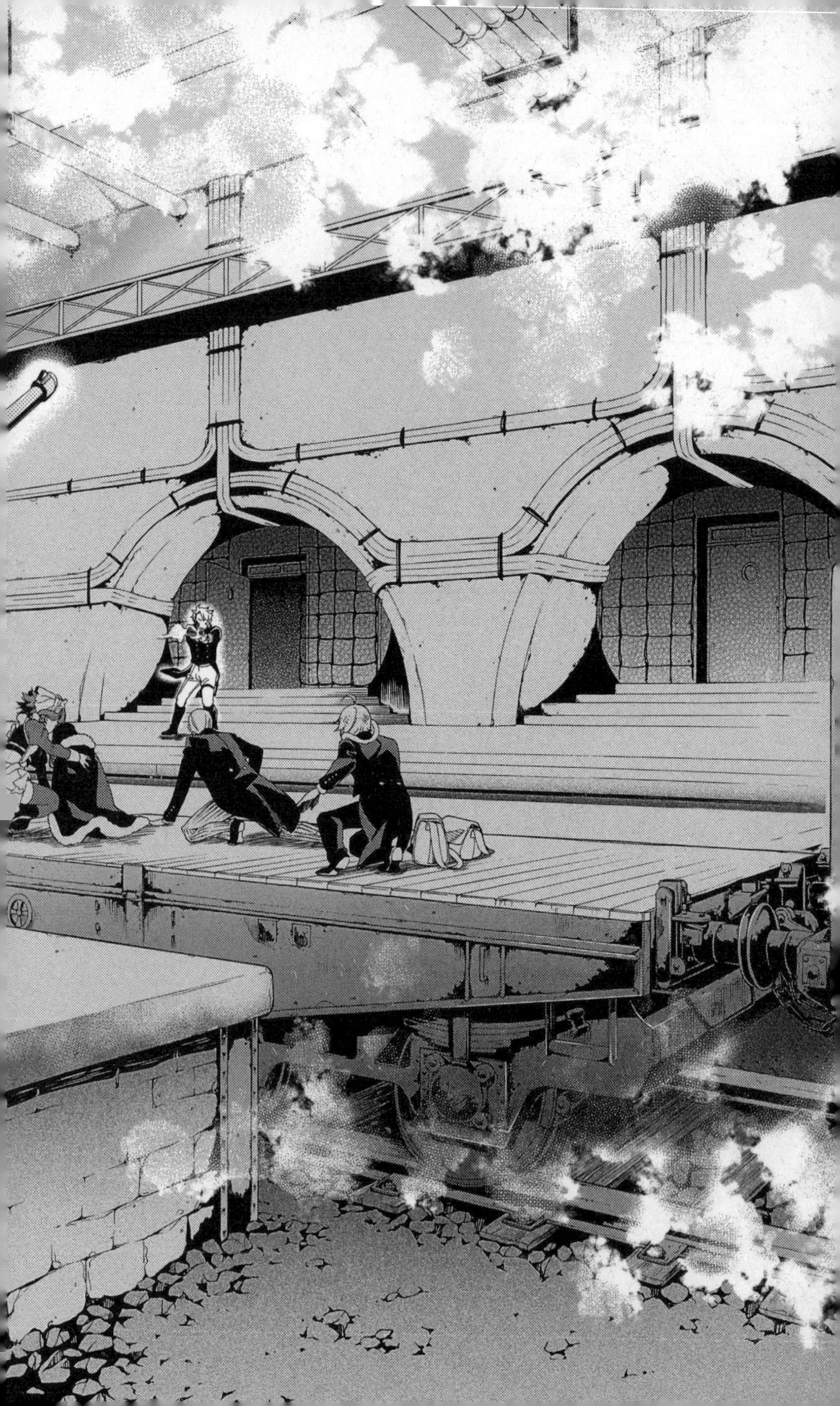

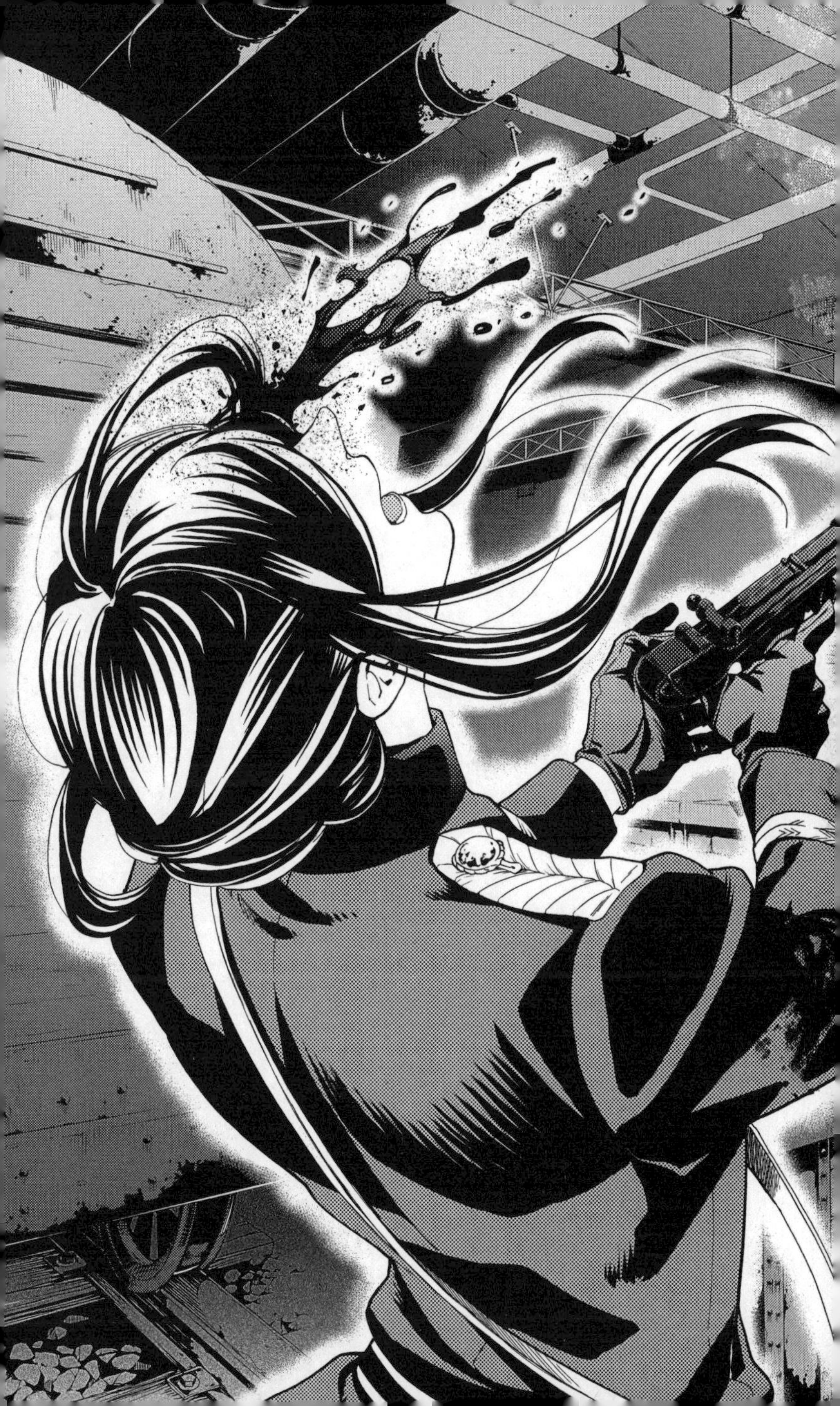

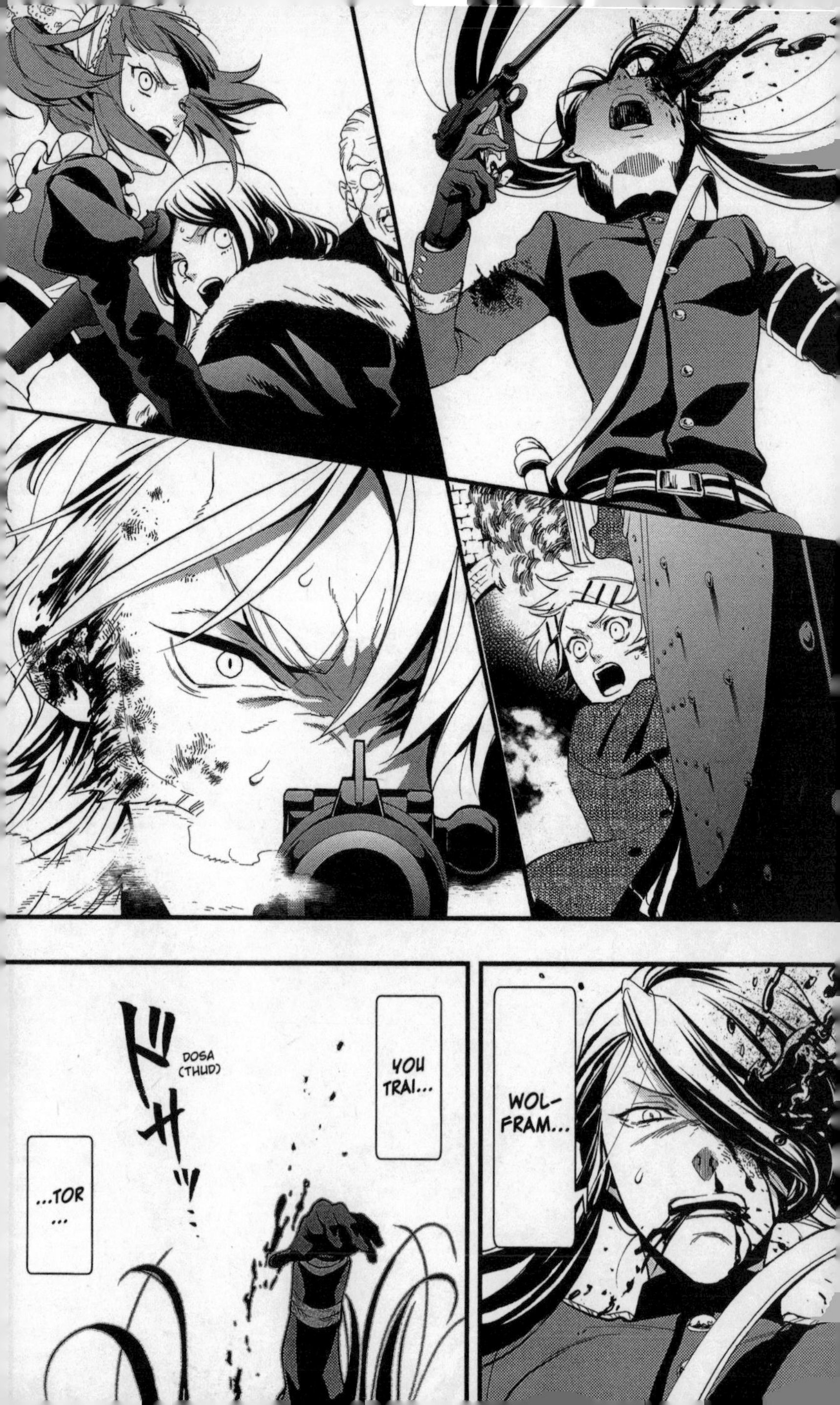
WOL-FRAM...
YOU TRAI...
DOSA (THUD)
...TOR ...

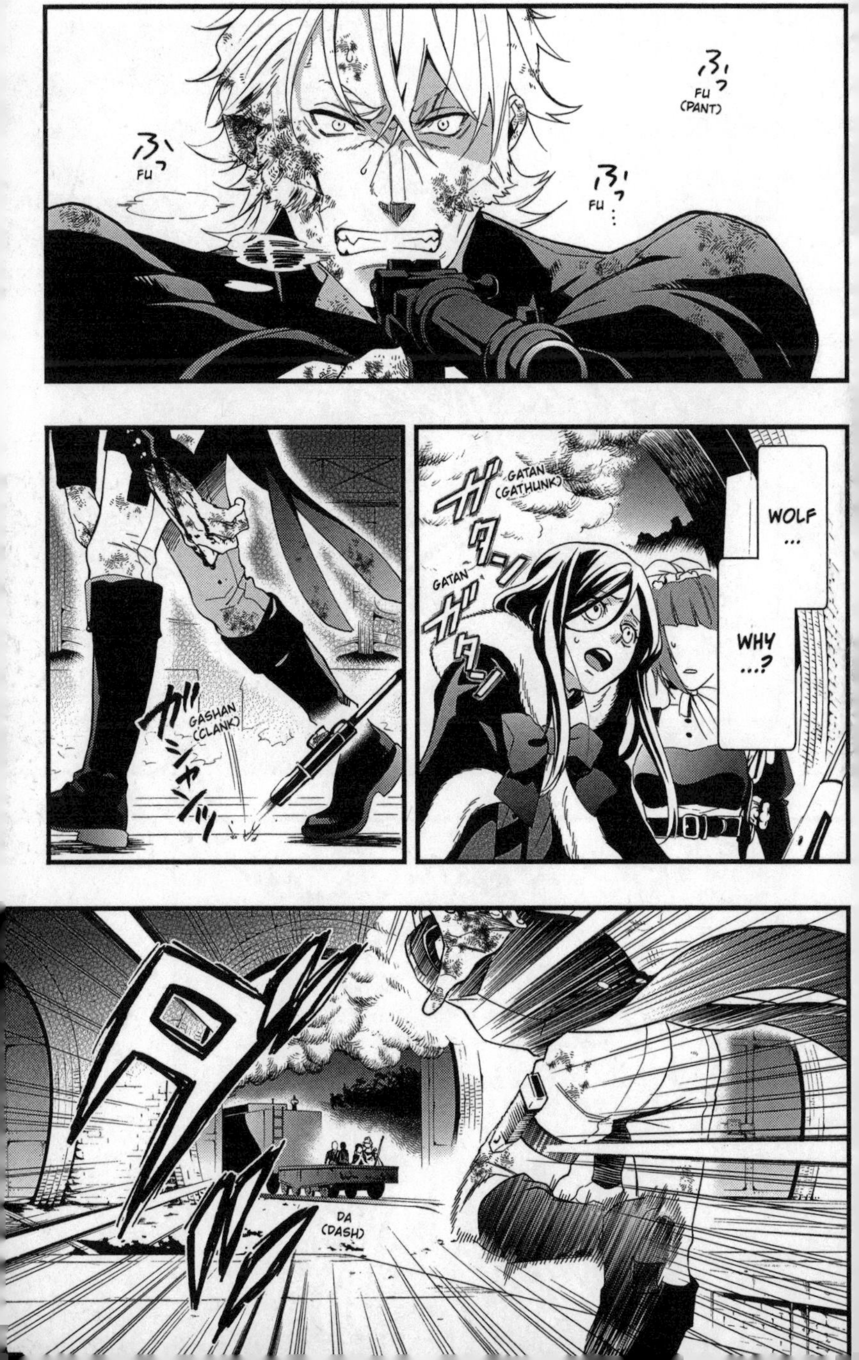
ふっ
FU
(PANT)
ふっ
FU...
ふっ
FU
WOLF...
WHY...?
ガターン
GATAN
(GATHUNK)
ガターン
GATAN
ガシャンッ
GASHAN
(CLANK)
ダッ
DA
(DASH)

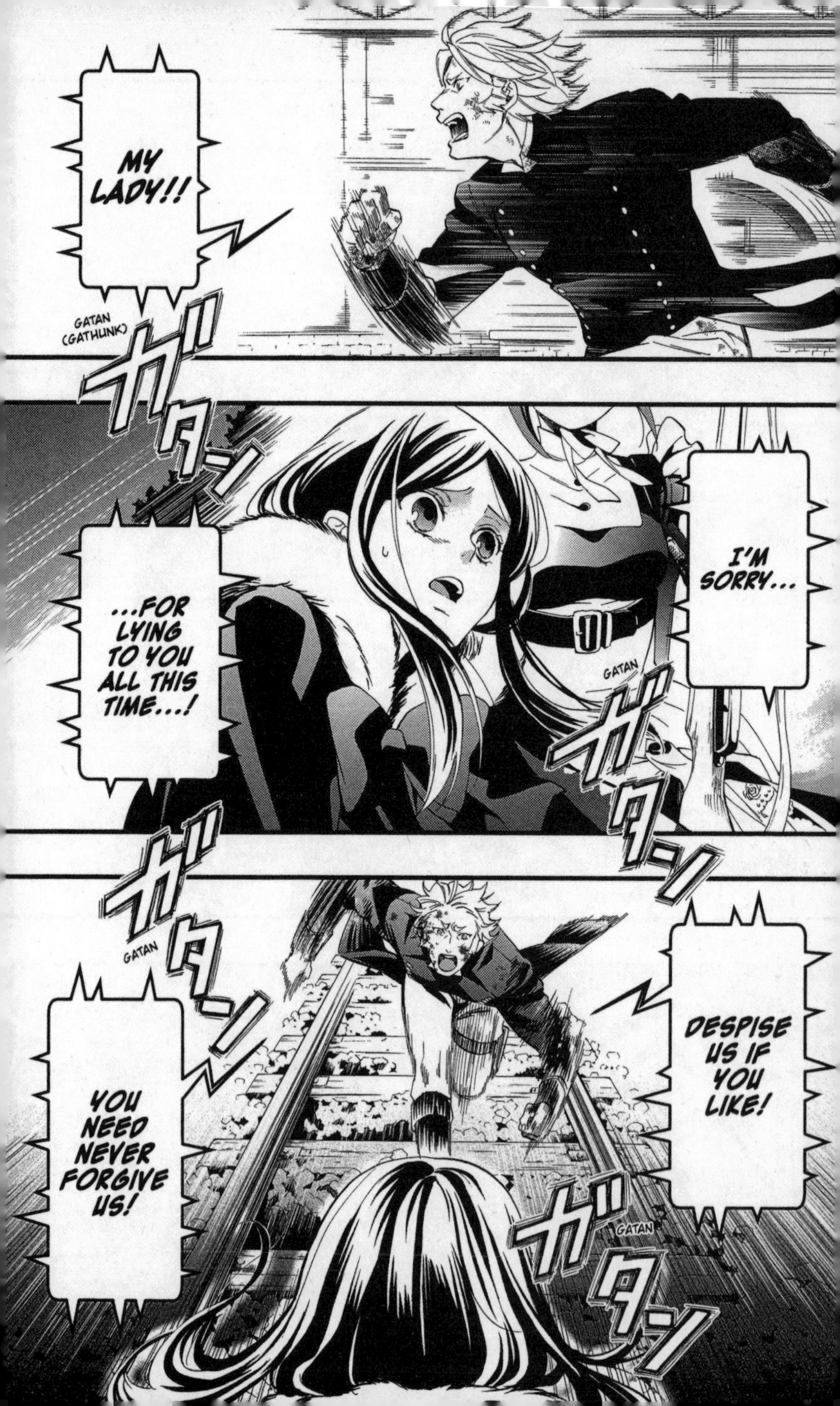
MY LADY!!
GATAN (GATHUNK)
I'M SORRY...
...FOR LYING TO YOU ALL THIS TIME...!
GATAN
DESPISE US IF YOU LIKE!
GATAN
YOU NEED NEVER FORGIVE US!
GATAN

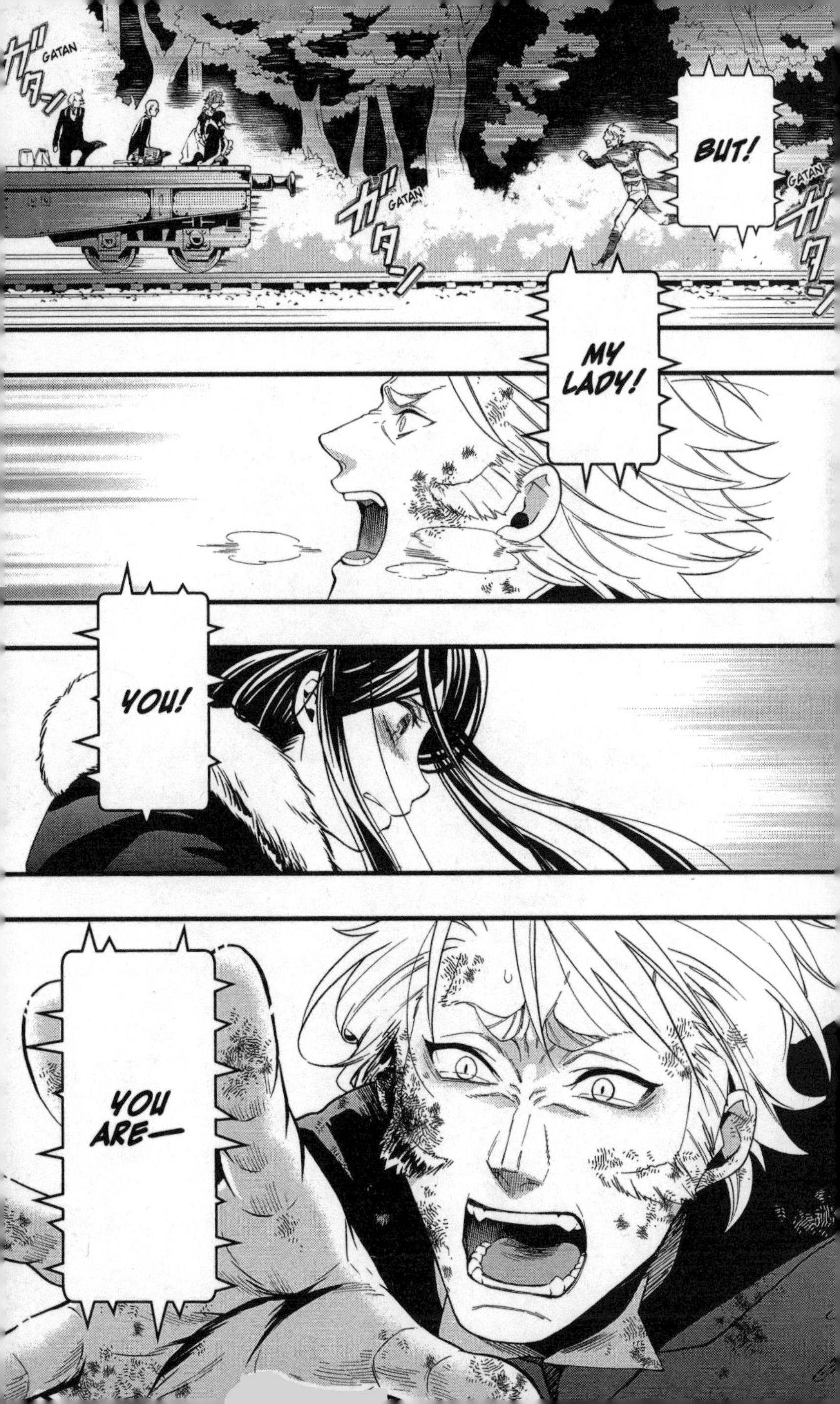
ガタン
GATAN
BUT!
ガタン
GATAN
ガタン
GATAN
MY LADY!
YOU!
YOU ARE—

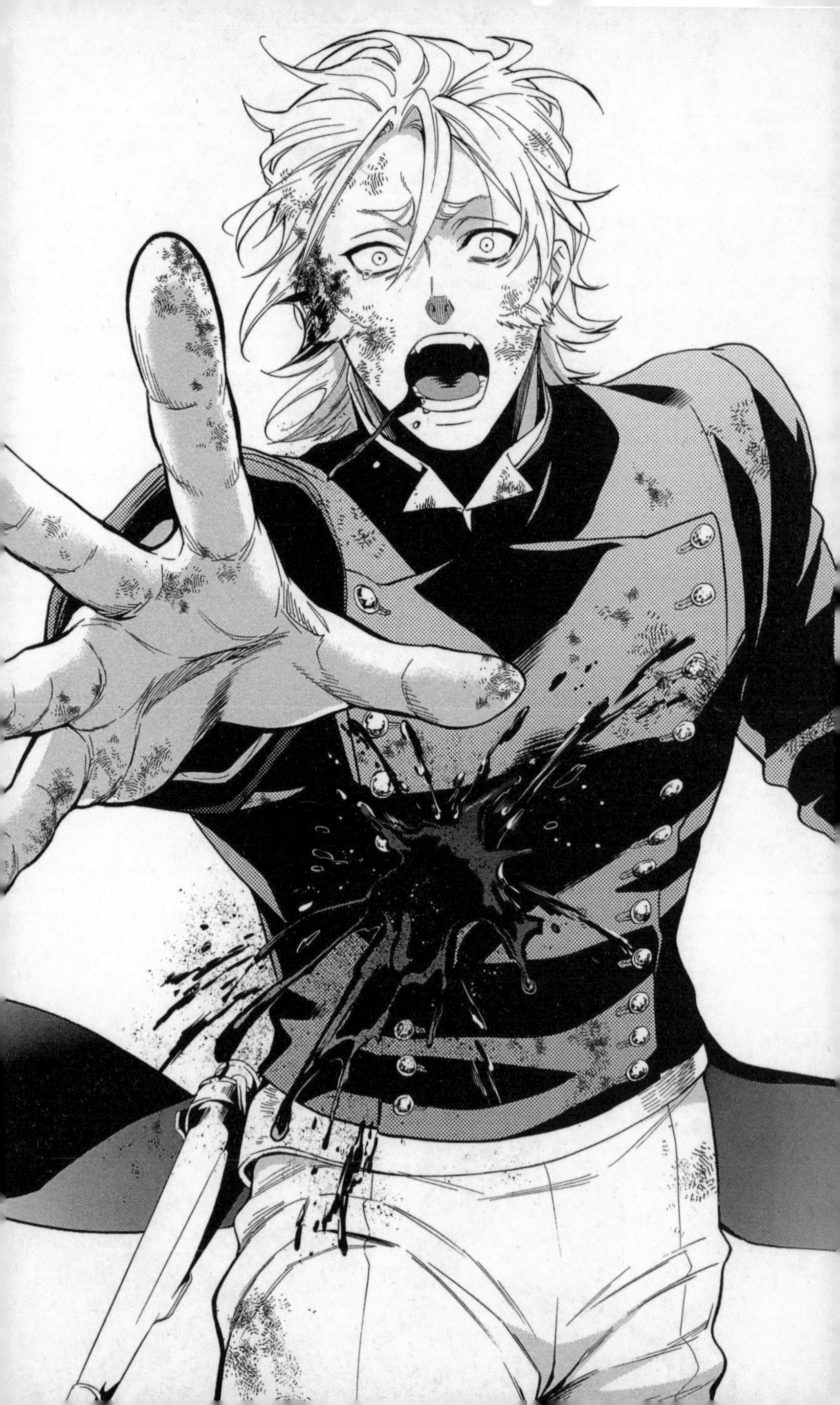

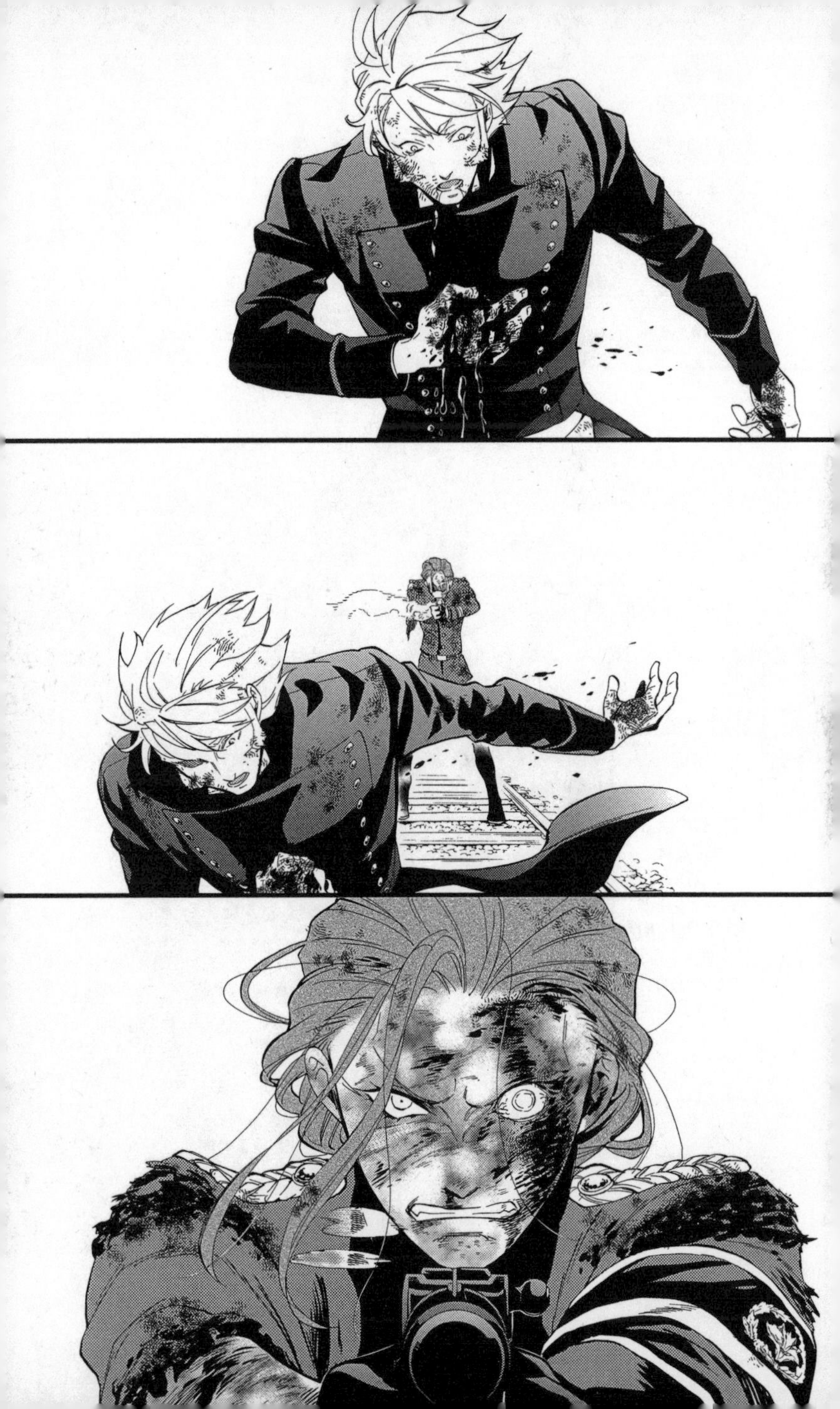

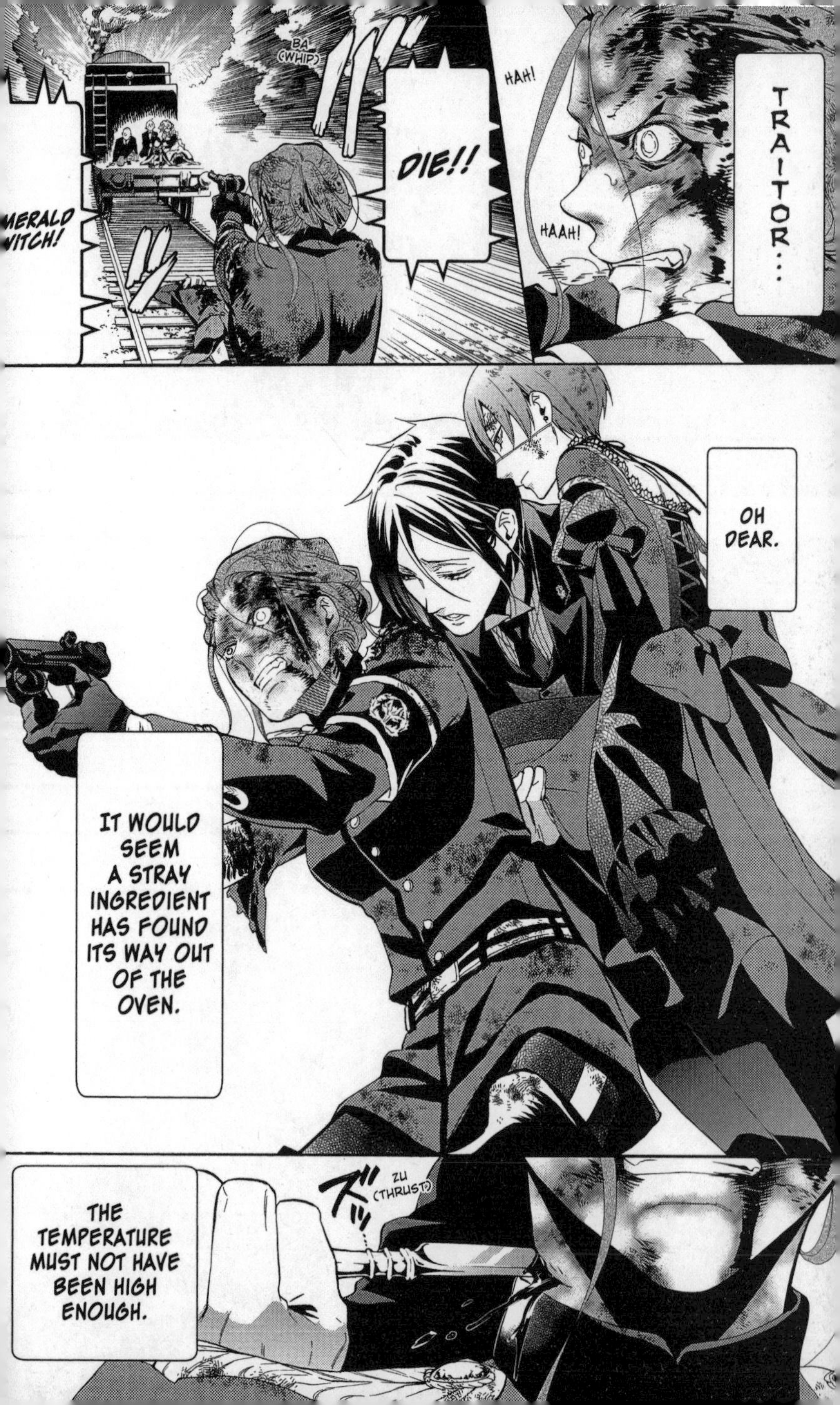
TRAITOR...
HAH!
HAAH!
DIE!!
BA (WHIP)
MERALD WITCH!
OH DEAR.
IT WOULD SEEM A STRAY INGREDIENT HAS FOUND ITS WAY OUT OF THE OVEN.
ZU (THRUST)
THE TEMPERATURE MUST NOT HAVE BEEN HIGH ENOUGH.

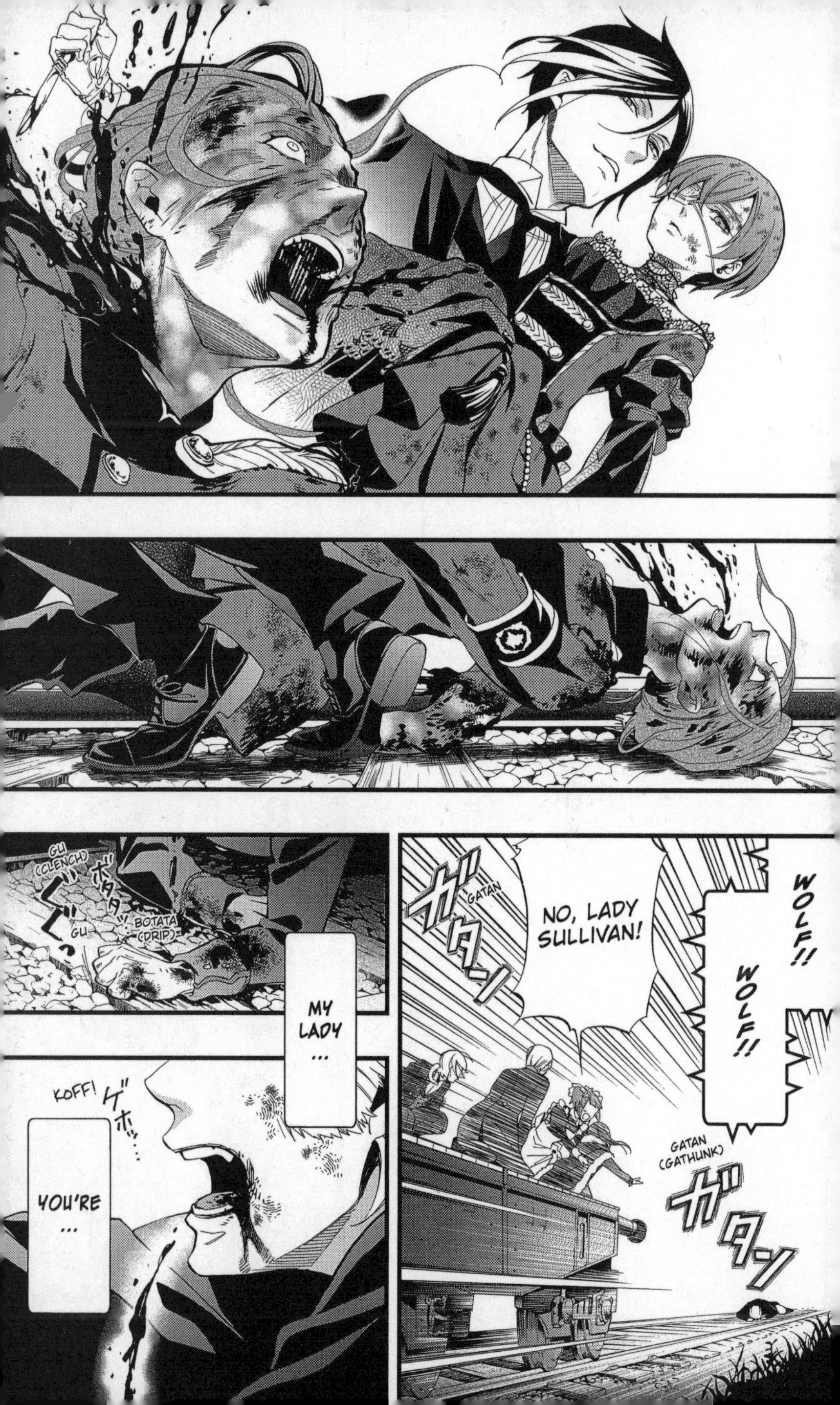

ガタン
GATAN
NO, LADY SULLIVAN!
WOLF!!
WOLF!!
GATAN (GATHUNK)
ガタン
GU (CLENCH)
ボタタ
BOTATA (DRIP)
ぐっ
GU
MY LADY ...
KOFF!
ゲホッ...
YOU'RE ...

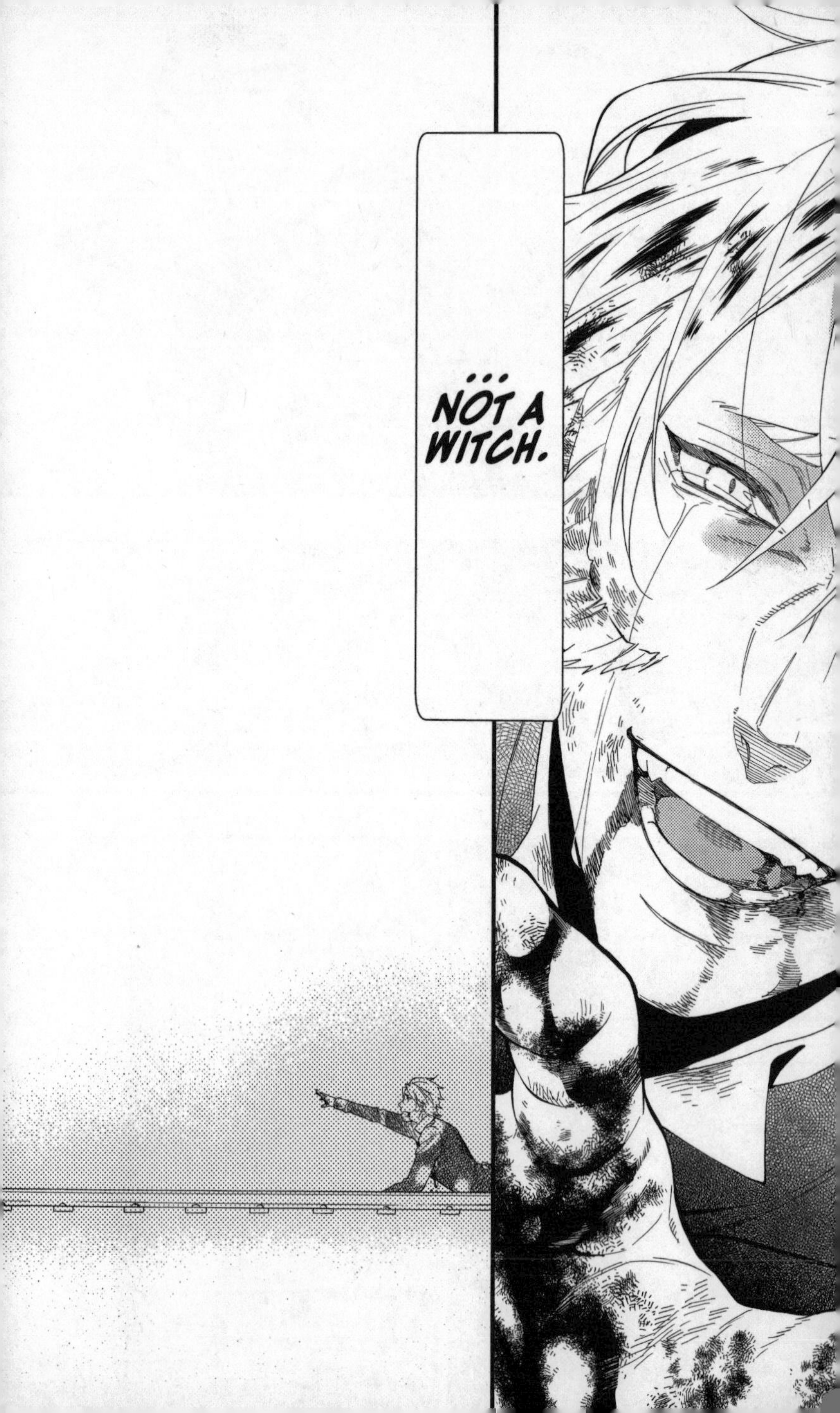
...NOT A WITCH.

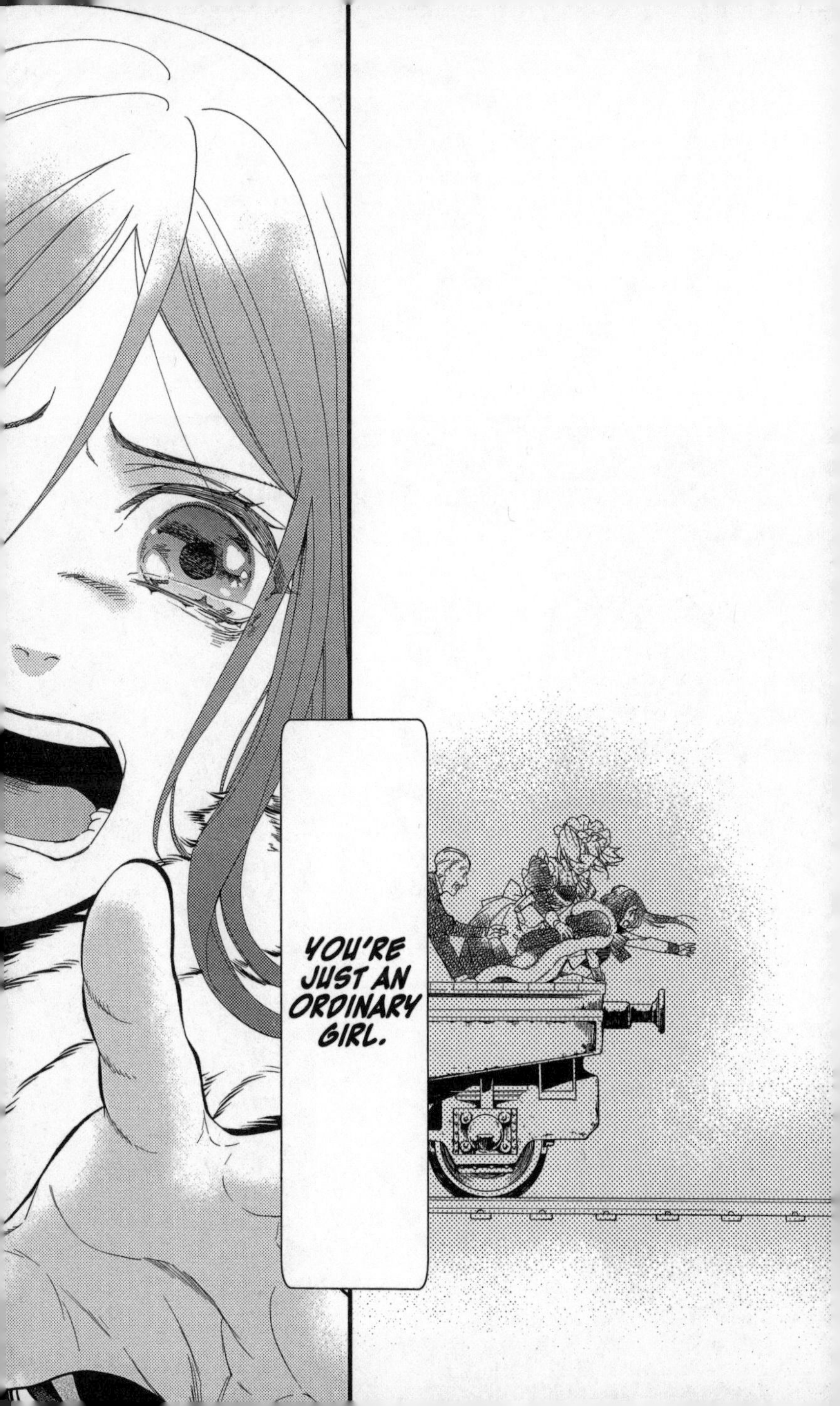
YOU'RE JUST AN ORDINARY GIRL.

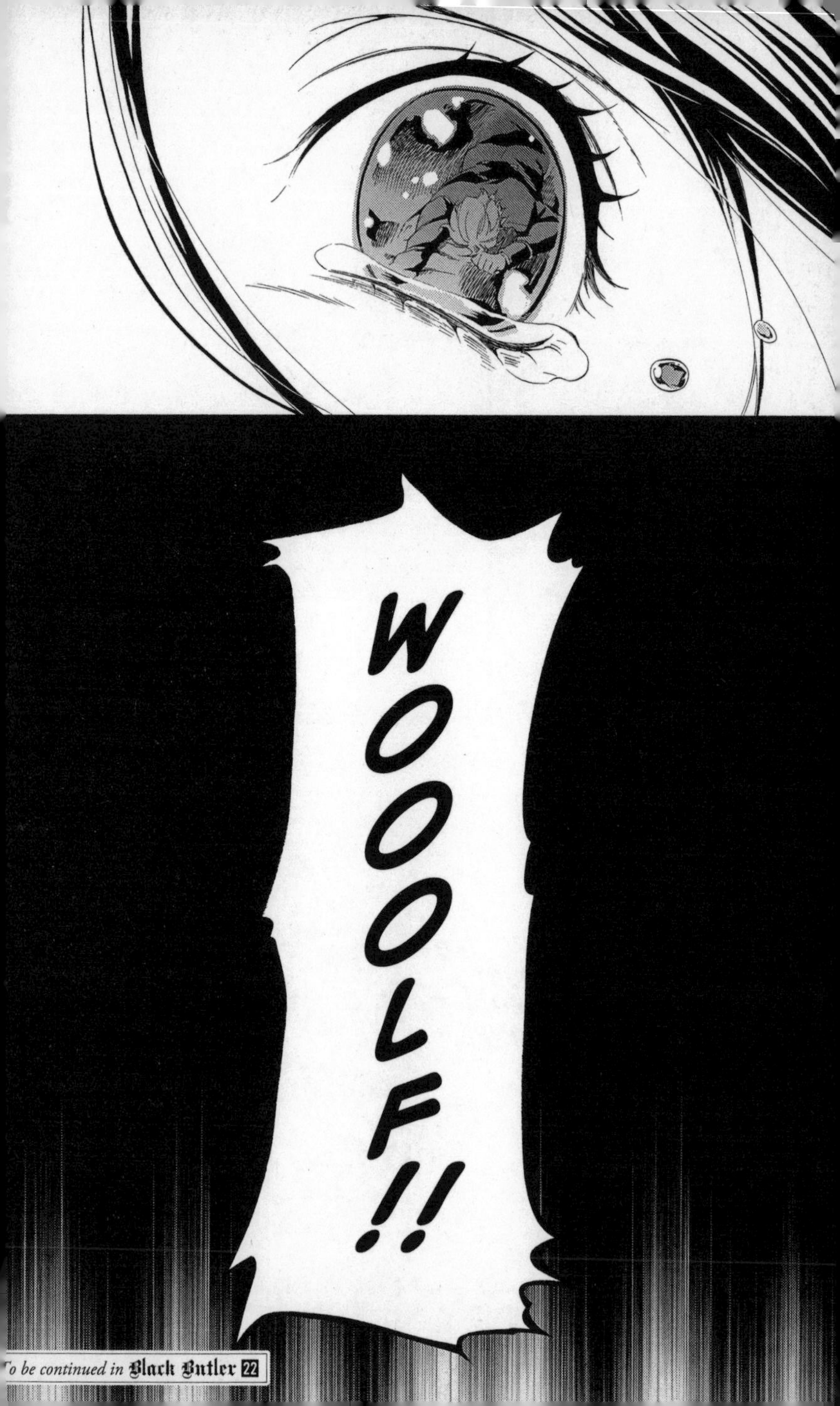
WOOOLF!!

To be continued in Black Butler 22

❖ Black Butler ❖

黒執事

❖

Downstairs

Wakana Haduki
7
Saito Torino
Tsuki Sorano
Chiaki Nagaoka
Asakura
*
Takeshi Kuma
*
Yana Toboso

❖

Adviser

Rico Murakami

*

Special Thanks

Akira Suzuki

and You!

Black Butler

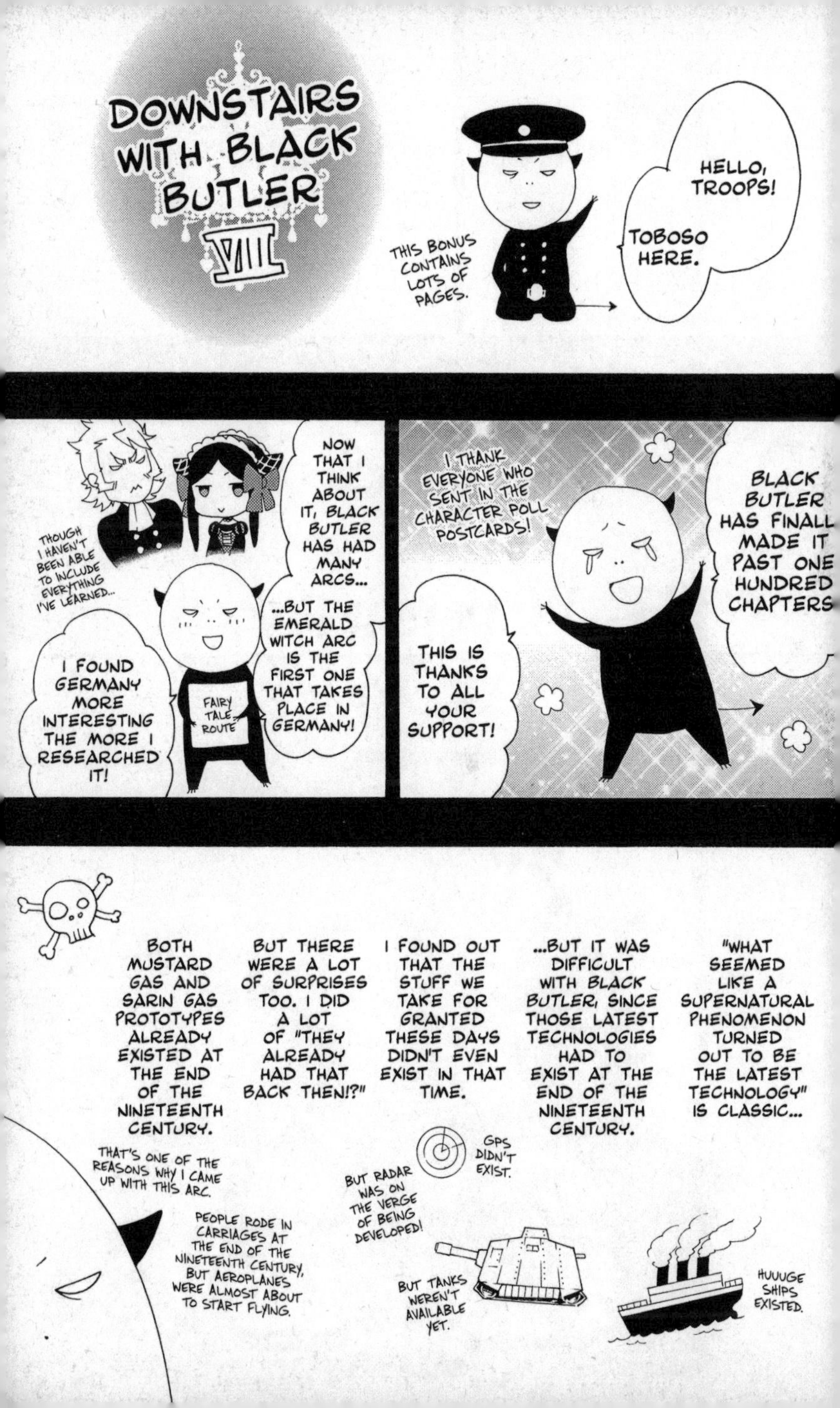
DOWNSTAIRS WITH BLACK BUTLER VIII
HELLO, TROOPS!
TOBOSO HERE.
THIS BONUS CONTAINS LOTS OF PAGES.
BLACK BUTLER HAS FINALL MADE IT PAST ONE HUNDRED CHAPTERS
I THANK EVERYONE WHO SENT IN THE CHARACTER POLL POSTCARDS!
THIS IS THANKS TO ALL YOUR SUPPORT!
NOW THAT I THINK ABOUT IT, BLACK BUTLER HAS HAD MANY ARCS...
...BUT THE EMERALD WITCH ARC IS THE FIRST ONE THAT TAKES PLACE IN GERMANY!
FAIRY TALE ROUTE
THOUGH I HAVEN'T BEEN ABLE TO INCLUDE EVERYTHING I'VE LEARNED...
I FOUND GERMANY MORE INTERESTING THE MORE I RESEARCHED IT!
"WHAT SEEMED LIKE A SUPERNATURAL PHENOMENON TURNED OUT TO BE THE LATEST TECHNOLOGY" IS CLASSIC...
...BUT IT WAS DIFFICULT WITH BLACK BUTLER, SINCE THOSE LATEST TECHNOLOGIES HAD TO EXIST AT THE END OF THE NINETEENTH CENTURY.
I FOUND OUT THAT THE STUFF WE TAKE FOR GRANTED THESE DAYS DIDN'T EVEN EXIST IN THAT TIME.
BUT THERE WERE A LOT OF SURPRISES TOO. I DID A LOT OF "THEY ALREADY HAD THAT BACK THEN!?"
BOTH MUSTARD GAS AND SARIN GAS PROTOTYPES ALREADY EXISTED AT THE END OF THE NINETEENTH CENTURY.
GPS DIDN'T EXIST.
BUT RADAR WAS ON THE VERGE OF BEING DEVELOPED!
THAT'S ONE OF THE REASONS WHY I CAME UP WITH THIS ARC.
HUUUGE SHIPS EXISTED.
BUT TANKS WEREN'T AVAILABLE YET.
PEOPLE RODE IN CARRIAGES AT THE END OF THE NINETEENTH CENTURY, BUT AEROPLANES WERE ALMOST ABOUT TO START FLYING.

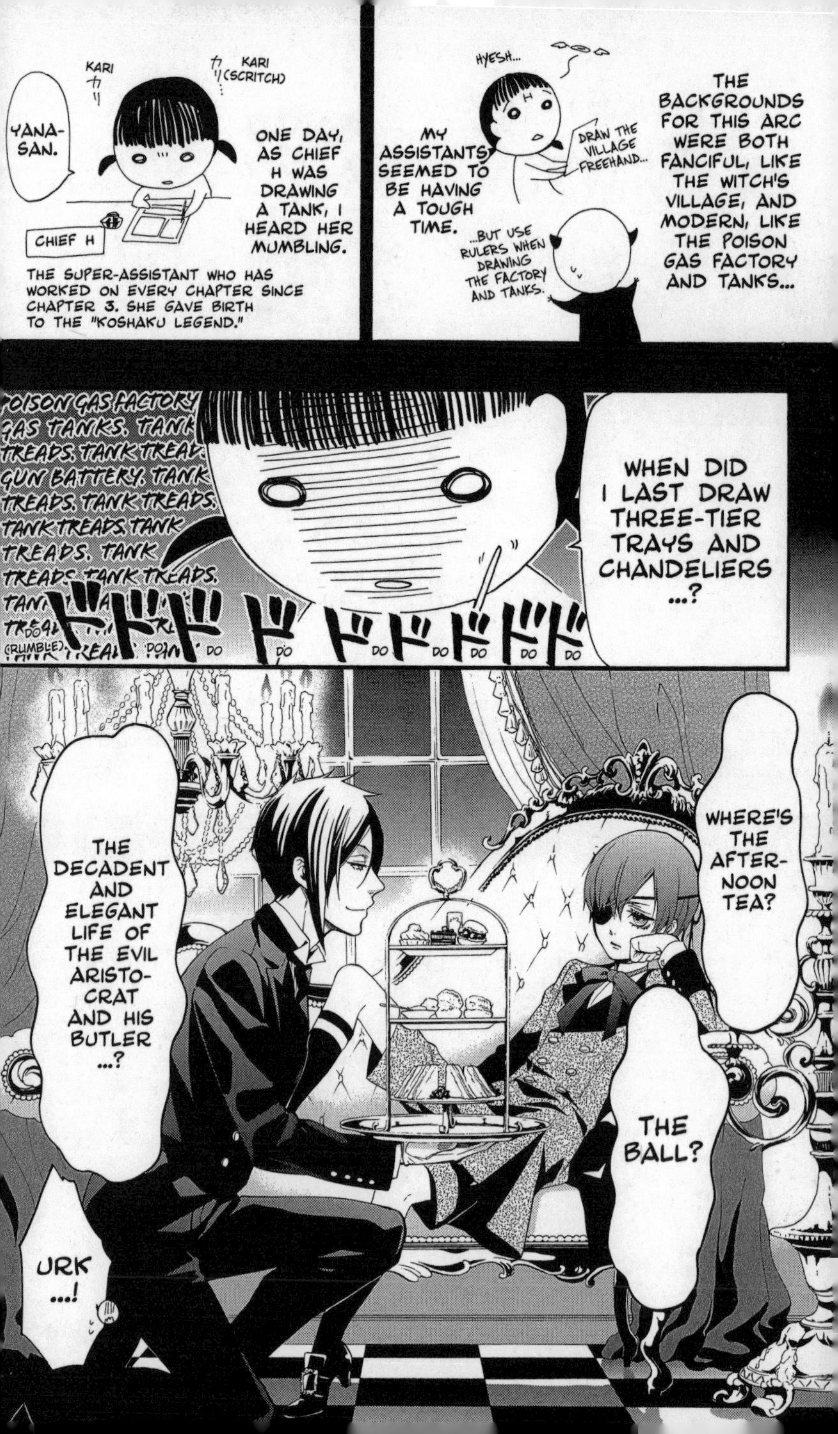
THE BACKGROUNDS FOR THIS ARC WERE BOTH FANCIFUL, LIKE THE WITCH'S VILLAGE, AND MODERN, LIKE THE POISON GAS FACTORY AND TANKS...
HYESH...
MY ASSISTANTS SEEMED TO BE HAVING A TOUGH TIME.
DREW THE VILLAGE FREEHAND...
...BUT USE RULERS WHEN DRAWING THE FACTORY AND TANKS.
カリ KARI (SCRITCH)
カリ KARI
ONE DAY, AS CHIEF H WAS DRAWING A TANK, I HEARD HER MUMBLING.
YANA-SAN.
CHIEF H
THE SUPER-ASSISTANT WHO HAS WORKED ON EVERY CHAPTER SINCE CHAPTER 3. SHE GAVE BIRTH TO THE "KOSHAKU LEGEND."
WHEN DID I LAST DRAW THREE-TIER TRAYS AND CHANDELIERS ...?
POISON GAS FACTORY. GAS TANKS. TANK TREADS. TANK TREADS. GUN BATTERY. TANK TREADS. TANK TREADS. TANK TREADS. TANK TREADS. TANK TREADS. TANK TREADS.
ドドドドドドドドド
DO (RUMBLE) DO DO DO DO DO DO DO DO
WHERE'S THE AFTER-NOON TEA?
THE BALL?
THE DECADENT AND ELEGANT LIFE OF THE EVIL ARISTO-CRAT AND HIS BUTLER ...?
URK ...!

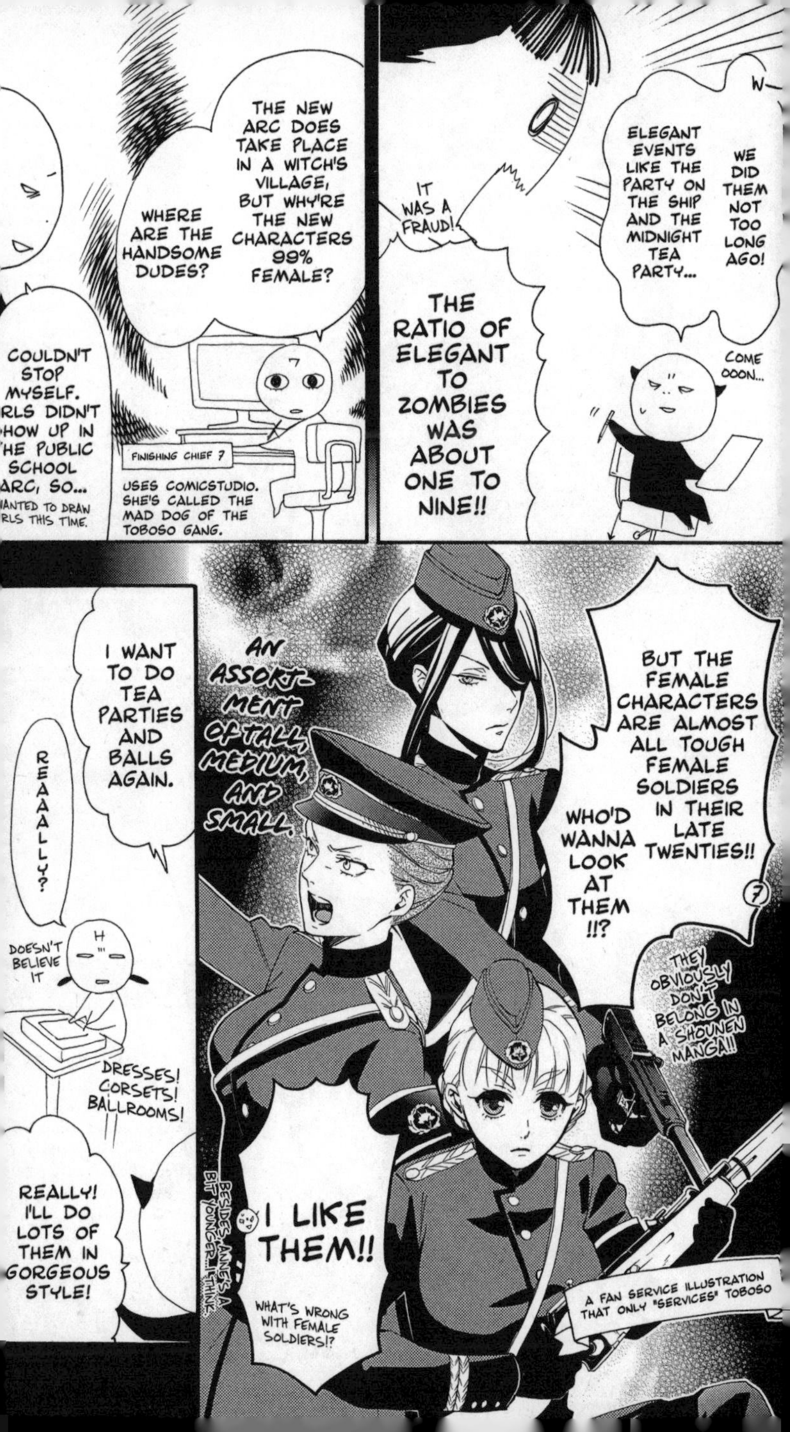
W—
ELEGANT EVENTS LIKE THE PARTY ON THE SHIP AND THE MIDNIGHT TEA PARTY...
WE DID THEM NOT TOO LONG AGO!
IT WAS A FRAUD!
THE RATIO OF ELEGANT TO ZOMBIES WAS ABOUT ONE TO NINE!!
COME OOON...
THE NEW ARC DOES TAKE PLACE IN A WITCH'S VILLAGE, BUT WHY'RE THE NEW CHARACTERS 99% FEMALE?
WHERE ARE THE HANDSOME DUDES?
FINISHING CHIEF 7
USES COMICSTUDIO. SHE'S CALLED THE MAD DOG OF THE TOBOSO GANG.
COULDN'T STOP MYSELF. RLS DIDN'T HOW UP IN HE PUBLIC SCHOOL ARC, SO...
ANTED TO DRAW RLS THIS TIME.
BUT THE FEMALE CHARACTERS ARE ALMOST ALL TOUGH FEMALE SOLDIERS IN THEIR LATE TWENTIES!!
WHO'D WANNA LOOK AT THEM !!?
AN ASSORTMENT OF TALL, MEDIUM, AND SMALL.
THEY OBVIOUSLY DON'T BELONG IN A SHOUNEN MANGA!!
I LIKE THEM!!
BESIDES, ANNE'S A BIT YOUNGER, I THINK.
WHAT'S WRONG WITH FEMALE SOLDIERS!?
A FAN SERVICE ILLUSTRATION THAT ONLY "SERVICES" TOBOSO
I WANT TO DO TEA PARTIES AND BALLS AGAIN.
REAAALLY?
DOESN'T BELIEVE IT
DRESSES! CORSETS! BALLROOMS!
REALLY! I'LL DO LOTS OF THEM IN GORGEOUS STYLE!

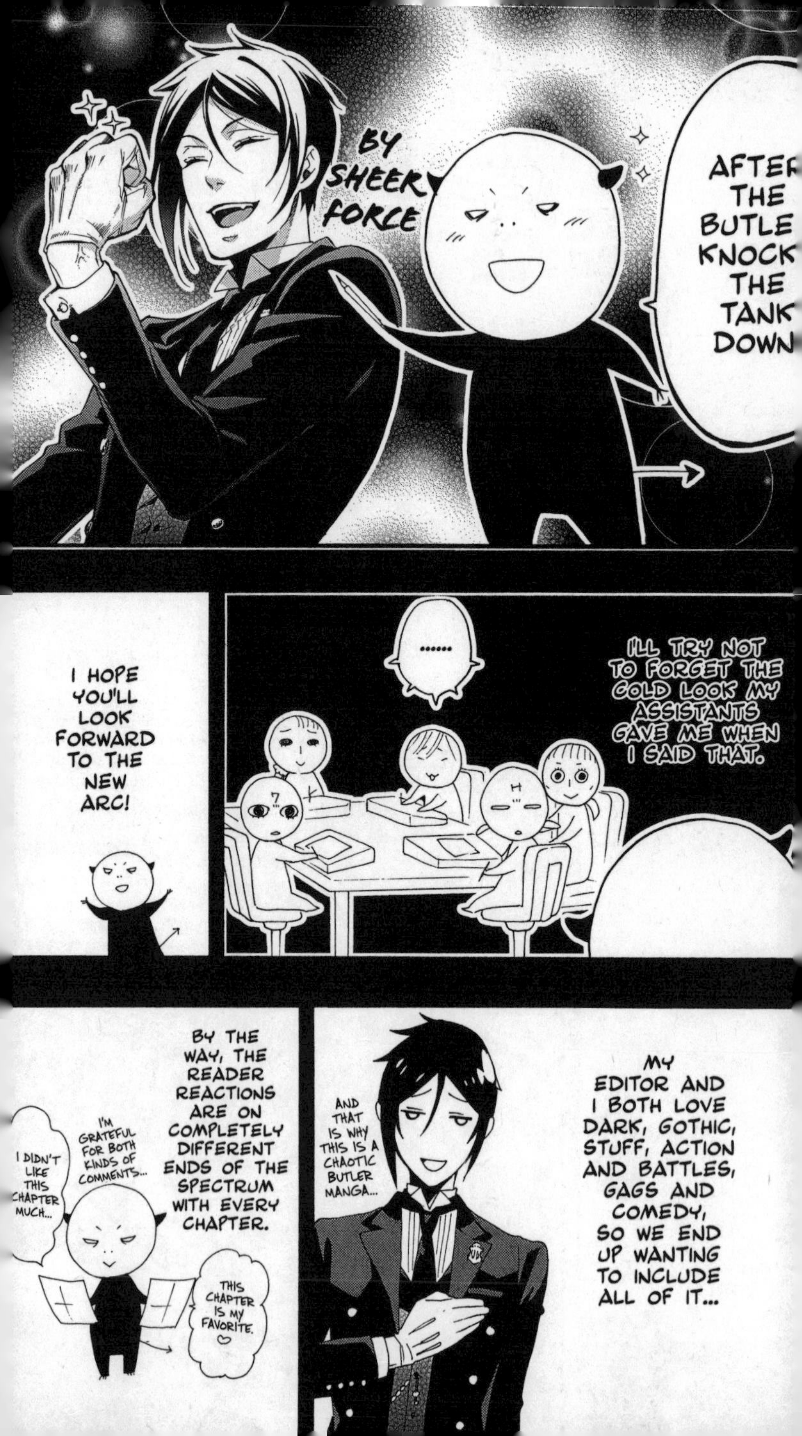

AFTER THE BUTLE KNOCK THE TANK DOWN
BY SHEER FORCE
I'LL TRY NOT TO FORGET THE COLD LOOK MY ASSISTANTS GAVE ME WHEN I SAID THAT.
......
I HOPE YOU'LL LOOK FORWARD TO THE NEW ARC!
MY EDITOR AND I BOTH LOVE DARK, GOTHIC, STUFF, ACTION AND BATTLES, GAGS AND COMEDY, SO WE END UP WANTING TO INCLUDE ALL OF IT...
AND THAT IS WHY THIS IS A CHAOTIC BUTLER MANGA...
BY THE WAY, THE READER REACTIONS ARE ON COMPLETELY DIFFERENT ENDS OF THE SPECTRUM WITH EVERY CHAPTER.
I'M GRATEFUL FOR BOTH KINDS OF COMMENTS...
THIS CHAPTER IS MY FAVORITE.
I DIDN'T LIKE THIS CHAPTER MUCH...

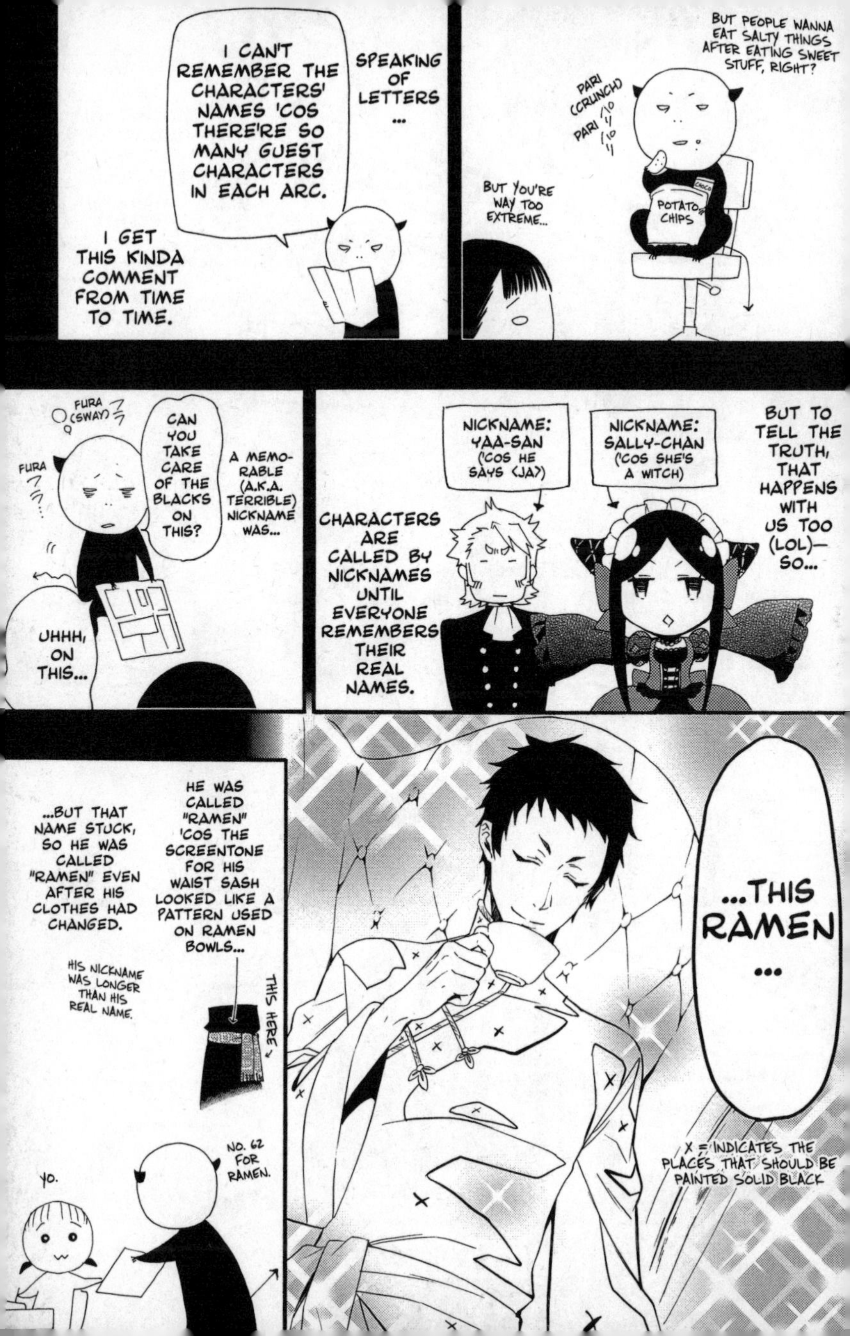
BUT PEOPLE WANNA EAT SALTY THINGS AFTER EATING SWEET STUFF, RIGHT?
PARI (CRUNCH)
PARI
CHOCO
POTATO CHIPS
BUT YOU'RE WAY TOO EXTREME...
SPEAKING OF LETTERS ...
I CAN'T REMEMBER THE CHARACTERS' NAMES 'COS THERE'RE SO MANY GUEST CHARACTERS IN EACH ARC.
I GET THIS KINDA COMMENT FROM TIME TO TIME.
BUT TO TELL THE TRUTH, THAT HAPPENS WITH US TOO (LOL)—SO...
NICKNAME: SALLY-CHAN ('COS SHE'S A WITCH)
NICKNAME: YAA-SAN ('COS HE SAYS <JA>)
CHARACTERS ARE CALLED BY NICKNAMES UNTIL EVERYONE REMEMBERS THEIR REAL NAMES.
A MEMO-RABLE (A.K.A. TERRIBLE) NICKNAME WAS...
CAN YOU TAKE CARE OF THE BLACKS ON THIS?
FURA (SWAY)
FURA
UHHH, ON THIS...
...THIS RAMEN ...
X = INDICATES THE PLACES THAT SHOULD BE PAINTED SOLID BLACK
HE WAS CALLED "RAMEN" 'COS THE SCREENTONE FOR HIS WAIST SASH LOOKED LIKE A PATTERN USED ON RAMEN BOWLS...
...BUT THAT NAME STUCK, SO HE WAS CALLED "RAMEN" EVEN AFTER HIS CLOTHES HAD CHANGED.
THIS HERE
HIS NICKNAME WAS LONGER THAN HIS REAL NAME.
NO. 62 FOR RAMEN.
YO.

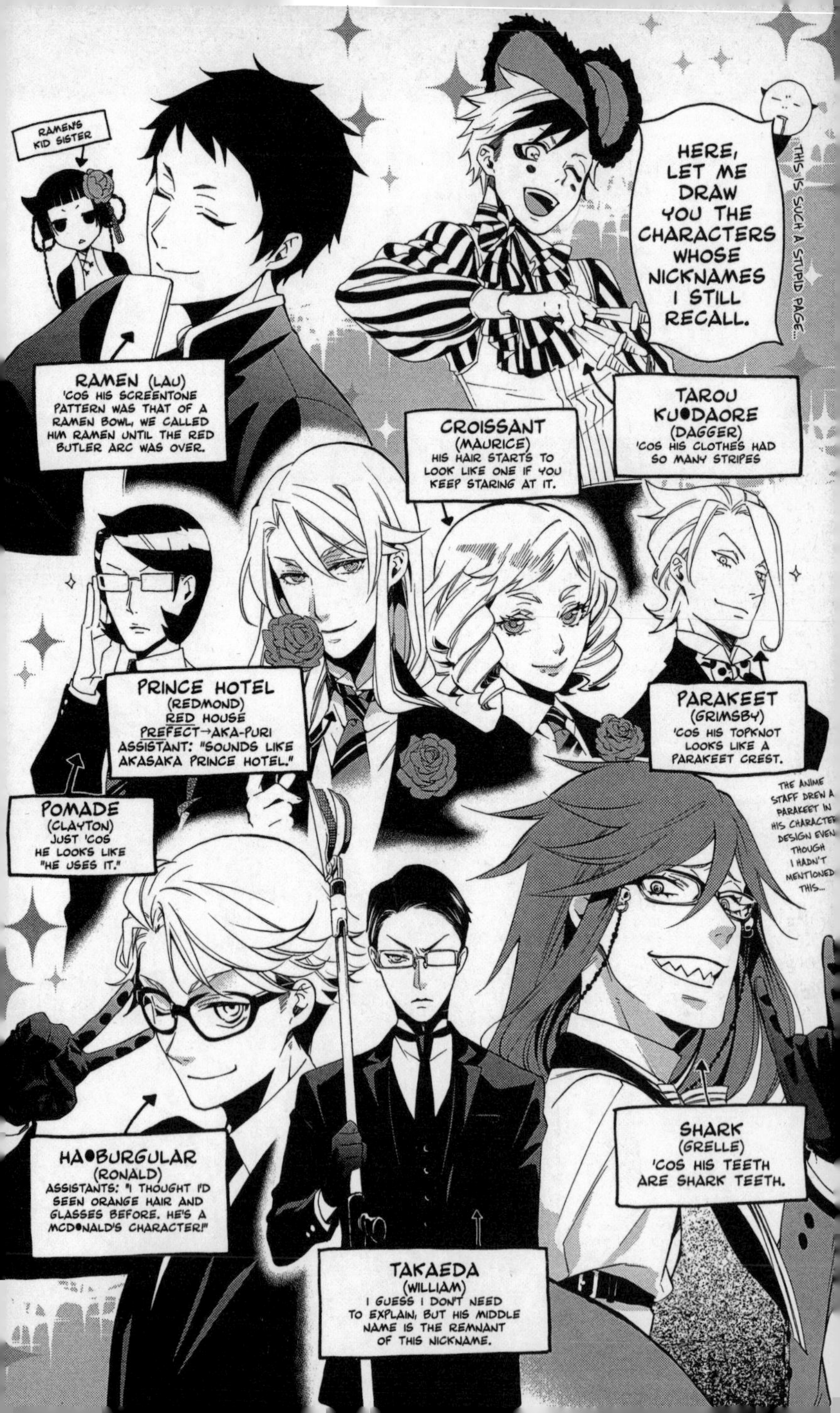

HERE, LET ME DRAW YOU THE CHARACTERS WHOSE NICKNAMES I STILL RECALL.
THIS IS SUCH A STUPID PAGE...
RAMEN'S KID SISTER
TAROU KU●DAORE (DAGGER) 'COS HIS CLOTHES HAD SO MANY STRIPES
CROISSANT (MAURICE) HIS HAIR STARTS TO LOOK LIKE ONE IF YOU KEEP STARING AT IT.
RAMEN (LAU) 'COS HIS SCREENTONE PATTERN WAS THAT OF A RAMEN BOWL, WE CALLED HIM RAMEN UNTIL THE RED BUTLER ARC WAS OVER.
PARAKEET (GRIMSBY) 'COS HIS TOPKNOT LOOKS LIKE A PARAKEET CREST.
THE ANIME STAFF DREW A PARAKEET IN HIS CHARACTER DESIGN EVEN THOUGH I HADN'T MENTIONED THIS...
PRINCE HOTEL (REDMOND) RED HOUSE PREFECT→AKA-PURI ASSISTANT: "SOUNDS LIKE AKASAKA PRINCE HOTEL."
POMADE (CLAYTON) JUST 'COS HE LOOKS LIKE "HE USES IT."
SHARK (GRELLE) 'COS HIS TEETH ARE SHARK TEETH.
TAKAEDA (WILLIAM) I GUESS I DON'T NEED TO EXPLAIN, BUT HIS MIDDLE NAME IS THE REMNANT OF THIS NICKNAME.
HA●BURGULAR (RONALD) ASSISTANTS: "I THOUGHT I'D SEEN ORANGE HAIR AND GLASSES BEFORE. HE'S A MCDONALD'S CHARACTER!"

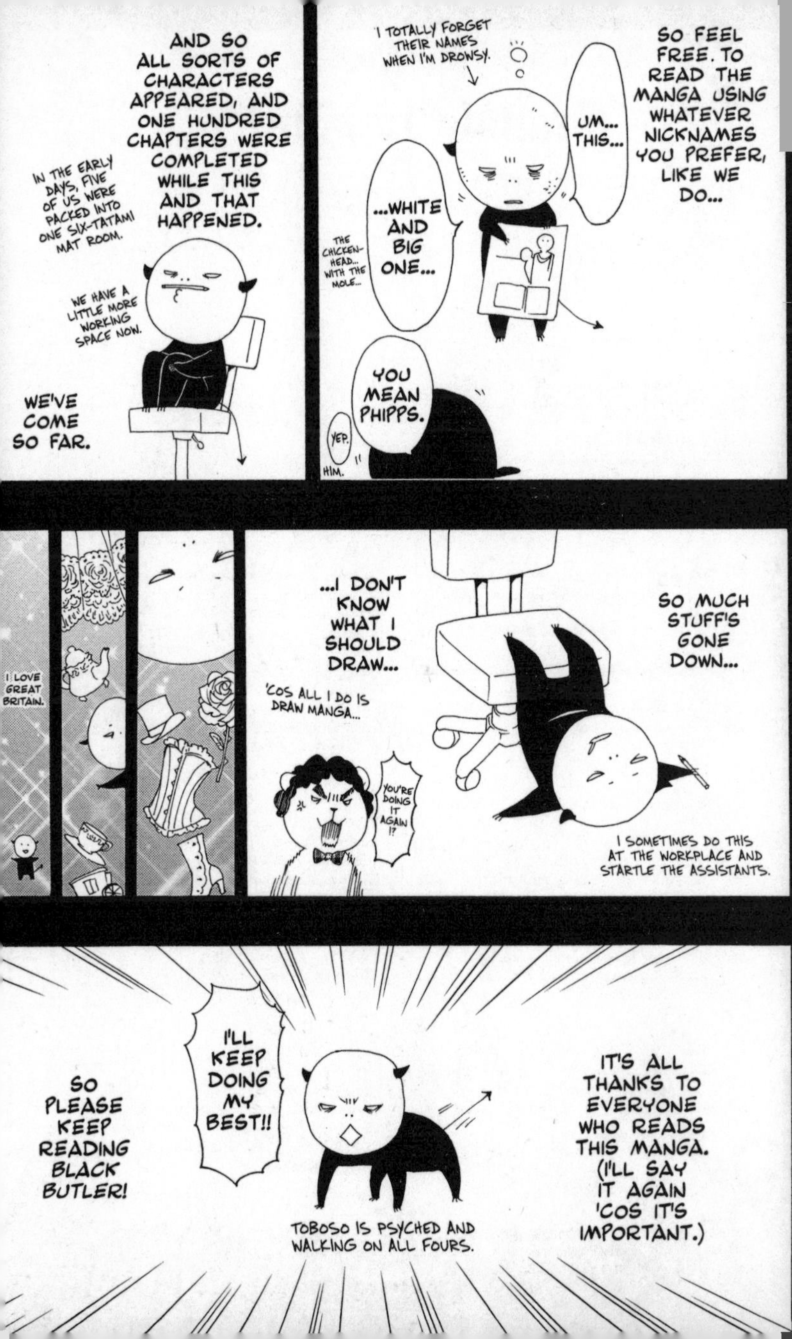
SO FEEL FREE. TO READ THE MANGA USING WHATEVER NICKNAMES YOU PREFER, LIKE WE DO...
I TOTALLY FORGET THEIR NAMES WHEN I'M DROWSY.
UM... THIS...
...WHITE AND BIG ONE...
THE CHICKEN-HEAD... WITH THE MOLE...
YOU MEAN PHIPPS.
YEP.
HIM.
AND SO ALL SORTS OF CHARACTERS APPEARED, AND ONE HUNDRED CHAPTERS WERE COMPLETED WHILE THIS AND THAT HAPPENED.
IN THE EARLY DAYS, FIVE OF US WERE PACKED INTO ONE SIX-TATAMI MAT ROOM.
WE HAVE A LITTLE MORE WORKING SPACE NOW.
WE'VE COME SO FAR.
SO MUCH STUFF'S GONE DOWN...
...I DON'T KNOW WHAT I SHOULD DRAW...
'COS ALL I DO IS DRAW MANGA...
YOU'RE DOING IT AGAIN!?
I SOMETIMES DO THIS AT THE WORKPLACE AND STARTLE THE ASSISTANTS.
I LOVE GREAT BRITAIN.
IT'S ALL THANKS TO EVERYONE WHO READS THIS MANGA. (I'LL SAY IT AGAIN 'COS IT'S IMPORTANT.)
I'LL KEEP DOING MY BEST!!
TOBOSO IS PSYCHED AND WALKING ON ALL FOURS.
SO PLEASE KEEP READING BLACK BUTLER!

Translation Notes

Inside Front and Back Covers

Showa era
The period in Japanese history marked by the rule of Emperor Hirohito. His lengthy reign ran from 1926 to 1989 and so included World War II and its aftermath.

Evacuation
During the last years of World War II, the Japanese government evacuated grade schoolers from urban areas to the countryside in order to avoid wartime destruction as a result of the anticipated bombing of major cities by American forces.

Page 27
Kommandant, kommando
The former is German for "commanding officer," while the latter refers to a military unit led by one such officer.

Page 40
Jam tin grenade
This improvised explosive, like those used by Baldo, was first used in World War I trench warfare by the British army and its allies. It is said that the soldiers resorted to this type of bomb when their supplies of grenades were exhausted. The jam tin grenades were often made from containers of jam or condensed milk left over from the soldiers' rations.

Page 52
Zwölf
This word is German for "twelve."

Page 52
Fionn mac Cumhaill
This legendary Irish hero was head of the Fianna, an independent band of fierce warriors. The exploits of the Fianna under Fionn's leadership were recorded in the Fenian Cycle, a collection of tales and poems of Irish myth. The Old Irish word *finn/fionn*, from which Finnian is derived, means "white" or "fair."

Page 94
Panzer
This is the German word for "armour." It is also the term for German tanks used in armoured warfare during World War II.

Page 101
Matériel
This French loan word refers to supplies and other equipment used by military personnel.

Page 103
Feuer
The German word for "fire."

Page 117
Foot pedals
The tanks used by Germany in World War II used foot pedals to slew, or turn, the gun turrets (where the guns are attached).

Page 125
Abgeschlossen
The German word for "complete."

Page 144
Firebox
To move a steam locomotive, fuel, usually coal, is burned in the train's firebox. The resultant heat from burning causes the water in the boiler to boil, creating the steam needed to propel the vehicle.

Page 145
Oiling up the train
Baldo asks Mey-Rin and Snake to lubricate the parts of the train because not doing so causes galling, or adhesive wear, to the cylinders of the locomotive.

Page 168
***Koshaku* legend**
"Viscount" is *shishaku* in Japanese, but the first character in the word is the kanji for "child" and can be read as *ko*, hence Toboso's assistant reading it as *koshaku*.

Page 172
Character nicknames
Tarou Ku●daore (Dagger) is a reference to Tarou Kuidaore, a symbol of Osaka. This mascot character of a now-closed restaurant sports a bright, red-and-white striped costume while beating a drum. Prince Hotel (Redmond) is a reference to the former Akasaka Prince Hotel, which, like Redmond, was known by the nickname "Aka-Puri" (*aka* means "red" in Japanese). Finally, Takaeda (William) in Japanese means "high branches."

Yana Toboso

AUTHOR'S NOTE

This series has made it past one hundred chapters! We couldn't have done it without your support. Thank you!

I feel I should be grateful every day for being fortunate enough to work on this series without illness or injury. I don't know how much longer *Black Butler* will continue, but I'd like to devote myself even more so the manga can keep making people happy.

And so this is Volume 21!

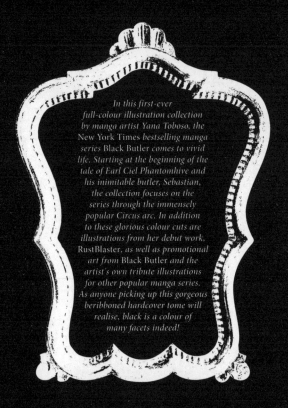

In this first-ever full-colour illustration collection by manga artist Yana Toboso, the New York Times bestselling manga series Black Butler comes to vivid life. Starting at the beginning of the tale of Earl Ciel Phantomhive and his inimitable butler, Sebastian, the collection focuses on the series through the immensely popular Circus arc. In addition to these glorious colour cuts are illustrations from her debut work, RustBlaster, as well as promotional art from Black Butler and the artist's own tribute illustrations for other popular manga series. As anyone picking up this gorgeous beribboned hardcover tome will realise, black is a colour of many facets indeed!

YANA TOBOSO

Black Butler

ARTWORKS

1

Yana Toboso's first art book—

On sale now!

BLACK BUTLER ㉑

YANA TOBOSO

Translation: Tomo Kimura • Lettering: Alexis Eckerman

This book is a work of fiction. Names, characters, places, and incidents are the product of the author's imagination or are used fictitiously. Any resemblance to actual events, locales, or persons, living or dead, is coincidental.

KUROSHITSUJI Vol. 21 © 2015 Yana Toboso / SQUARE ENIX CO., LTD. First published in Japan in 2015 by SQUARE ENIX CO., LTD. English translation rights arranged with SQUARE ENIX CO., LTD. and Hachette Book Group through Tuttle-Mori Agency, Inc.

Translation © 2015 by SQUARE ENIX CO., LTD.

All rights reserved. In accordance with the U.S. Copyright Act of 1976, the scanning, uploading, and electronic sharing of any part of this book without the permission of the publisher is unlawful piracy and theft of the author's intellectual property. If you would like to use material from the book (other than for review purposes), prior written permission must be obtained by contacting the publisher at permissions@hbgusa.com. Thank you for your support of the author's rights.

Yen Press
Hachette Book Group
1290 Avenue of the Americas, New York, NY 10104

www.HachetteBookGroup.com
www.YenPress.com

Yen Press is an imprint of Hachette Book Group, Inc. The Yen Press name and logo are trademarks of Hachette Book Group, Inc.

The publisher is not responsible for websites (or their content) that are not owned by the publisher.

First Yen Press Edition: November 2015

ISBN: 978-0-316-35209-3

10 9 8 7 6 5 4 3 2 1

BVG

Printed in the United States of America

DISCARD